E–Banking and Emerging Multidisciplinary Processes:
Social, Economical and Organizational Models

Mohammad Ali Sarlak
Payam Noor University, Iran

Asghar Abolhasani Hastiani
Payam Noor University, Iran

BUSINESS SCIENCE REFERENCE

Hershey · New York

Director of Editorial Content:	Kristin Klinger
Director of Book Publications:	Julia Mosemann
Acquisitions Editor:	Lindsay Johnston
Development Editor:	Christine Bufton
Publishing Assistant:	Milan Vracarich Jr.
Typesetter:	Casey Conapitski
Production Editor:	Jamie Snavely
Cover Design:	Lisa Tosheff

Published in the United States of America by
Business Science Reference (an imprint of IGI Global)
701 E. Chocolate Avenue
Hershey PA 17033
Tel: 717-533-8845
Fax: 717-533-8661
E-mail: cust@igi-global.com
Web site: http://www.igi-global.com/reference

Library of Congress Cataloging-in-Publication Data

E-banking and emerging multidisciplinary processes: social, economical and organizational models / Mohammad Ali Sarlak and Asghar Abolhasani Hastiani, editors.
      p. cm.
   Includes bibliographical references and index.   Summary: "This book advances the knowledge and practice of all facets of electronic banking and develops a comprehensive framework of e-banking by taking a multidisciplinary approach to understanding its implications on traditional banks, businesses and economies"--Provided by publisher. ISBN 978-1-61520-635-3 (hardcover) -- ISBN 978-1-61520-636-0 (ebook) 1. Internet banking. 2. Banks and banking--Automation. I. Sarlak, Mohammad Ali, 1970- II. Hastiani, Asghar Abolhasani, 1966- III. Title. HG1708.7.E13 2010
   332.1'702854678--dc22

British Cataloguing in Publication Data
A Cataloguing in Publication record for this book is available from the British Library.

All work contributed to this book is new, previously-unpublished material. The views expressed in this book are those of the authors, but not necessarily of the publisher.

Table of Contents

Section 3
The Models

Section 4
The Technologies

Detailed Table of Contents

Section 1
The Evolution

Chapter 1

The traditional mode of delivering products and services by banks to the consumers is through a single distribution channel and that is physical bank branches. Financial services industry is metamorphosing due to the advent of Internet, rapid technological evolutions, deregulation, globalization, as well as the impact of changing competitive and regulatory forces. In order to cope with the quick changes in the business scenario, banks started to rely on distribution channels as an alternative strategy for differentiation and gaining further competitive advantage. The abovementioned paved way for the development of the e-banking phenomena. This chapter attempts to provide a comprehensive explanation of what e-banking is, the evolution of e-banking, existing trends of e-banking in developed, developing, and newly industrialized nations, future directions for further possible research, and concluding remarks. The content provided in this chapter would be useful for existing and potential banks to better understand the global e-banking trends and thus aid in the effective formulation of channel management strategies and reap the benefits out of it.

Chapter 2

There are many proposals offer anonymous and non-repudiation e-payment protocols. But they have the drawbacks that the anonymity can be misused by fraudulent to perform a perfect crimes. Currently, the hot research concentrates on the accepting of e-payment protocols where the anonymity of the coins is cancelable via a trusted authority in the case of criminal entities. In the chapter, we suggest an efficient protocol for e-payment scheme that offers a good level of security with appreciate to its efficiency. The proposed protocol prevents the blind office and the bank from impersonate an entity, so that the entity could not repudiate it when the entity misused a coin. Another benefit is that it is constructed from efficient cryptography schemes so that its security can simply be analyzed. The strength of this scheme is in its easiness. So, we claim that the suggested protocol is more efficient than the existing schemes, since it allows to both a blind office and a bank to impersonate an entity to find and to spend a coin without to be noticed. It might cause a repudiation difficulty where the entity can repudiate his bad activities by proposing that both the bank and the blind office acted inaccurately. Other relevant issues related to the new protocol will be discussed in the section of the security of the scheme.

Section 2
The Strategies

Chapter 3

Electronic Banking as a Strategy for Customer Service Improvement in the
Asma Mobarek, Stockholm Business School, Sweden

The objective of the chapter is to present a brief review of e-banking services especially in the developing economies, highlighting the major challenges of e-banking in the developing economies with a guideline or recommendations to address those challenges. Technology has introduced new ways of delivering banking to the customer. Developed countries (DC) customers of the e-banking services are fully aware of the services but the customers in the developing economies are still lag behind. It is clearly seen that delivery channels are lacking in meeting the demands of the customer by not making them aware of e-banking and using obsolete or not too up-to-date technology. I would thus conclude that banks in the developing countries should drown themselves in all the intricacies regarding e-banking to determine ways that will affect the customers in and use it to their maximum benefit. The other issue is that there are very few or no banking facilities in the rural areas and furthermore, access to the Internet is close to impossible in these areas therefore awareness and utilization of these services is very little or none at all. At last but not the least is that banks must adapt to the electronics age. Consumers demand it. Economics drives it. Banks must exploit it.

Chapter 4

Factors Influencing KM Strategic Alignment in the Banking Sector: The Case of Persian
Jafleh Hassan Al-Ammary, University of Bahrain, Bahrain

In today's business environment, knowledge is increasingly recognized as the most important and valuable asset in organizations and a key differentiating factor in business. Therefore, many organizations are positioning themselves strategically based on their tangible and intangible internal resources, and their capabilities rather than on their products and services. However, in order to an organization to be successful in the exploitation of knowledge assets to drive competitive advantages, a holistic approach that spans Knowledge Management (KM), business strategy, and organizational and human factors should be used. The aim of this study is to investigate the effect of some factor on KM Strategic Alignment between KM and business strategy in the banking sector at Persian Gulf Countries. The results have indicated factors such as knowledge sharing, trust, openness to change, IT infrastructure and skills, and existence of CKO are strongly correlated to the strategic alignment between KM and business strategy. Thus, managers in the Persian Gulf banking sectors should adopt new rules using flexible organizational culture, reforming and redesigning their organizational structure, and incorporating an advanced information technology in their operations for competitive advantage.

Chapter 5

Internet banking strategy can be generally very challenging, but more challenging in an economic environment infested with high degree of corruption, insecurity, bad governance, poverty, and financial system instability. Due to its global nature, Internet banking, under such situation, is threatened by the easiness at which off-line crimes are transmitted into online businesses, and the difficulty in building trusts and confidence in online business relationships. Using the Nigerian case, this chapter aims at establishing some theoretical link between offline country image and Internet banking reputation. The chapter summarizes the structural and regulatory challenges in the Nigerian banking system. It represents and relates the country's socioeconomic conditions with its Internet business reputation, and lays down past regulatory and global efforts to control the menace of the Nigerian version of Internet frauds. The last two sections of the chapter, respectively, suggest some future research direction and conclude the chapter.

Section 3
The Models

Internet is not simply one more distribution channel among the multi-channel strategies used by the financial industry; it is fostering new "e-Business Models" such as Internet-primary banks. However, in spite of its strong development potential, this type of bank has often achieved a weak breakthrough onto this market and shows modest financial results. The goal of this chapter is to study the "e-Business Model" of Internet-primary banks and to determine if it can perform better than the "Business Model" of a traditional bank.

Chapter 7

Nowadays, e-banking plays an important role in e-society and human life. Imagine an e-society without e-banking is not possible. The e-banking is considered as an enabler factor to e-business, e-commerce, e-government, and other e-initiatives. Despite the pivotal role of e-banking in our lives, yet a comprehensive conceptual model of electronic banking success factors has not been provided by the researchers. The present chapter is trying to provide a comprehensive conceptual model by categorizing factors affecting implementation of electronic banking. In this regard, the factors affecting implementation of electronic banking was classified based on Co-structural factors, Content factors, and Context factors. We called this conceptual model as the Tri-Category (3C) Model. The questionnaire used for gathering data. The results showed that there is a positive relationship between successful implementation of e-banking and attention to Co-structural, Content, and Contextual factors. At the end of chapter, several recommendations have been offered to implementing successful e-banking.

Section 4
The Technologies

Chapter 8

This chapter introduces Banking Technology as a confluence of several disparate disciplines such as Finance (including risk management), Information Technology, Computer Science, Communication Technology and Marketing Science. It presents the evolution of banking, the tremendous influence of information and communication technologies on banking and its products, the quintessential role played by computer science in fulfilling banks' marketing objective of servicing customers better at a less cost and thereby reap more profits. It also highlights the use of advanced statistics and computer science to measure, mitigate, and manage various risks associated with banks' business with its customers and other banks. The growing influence of customer relationship management and data mining in tackling various marketing related problems and fraud detection problems in banking industry is well documented. Of particular significance is the set of latest trends this chapter presents in terms of biometric ATMs, RFID enabled bank notes, Antiphishing techniques that make Internet banking secure, and the applications of Web 2.0 in banking. The chapter concludes by predicting that the Banking Technology discipline is all set for rapid growth in future.

Chapter 9

Nowadays, the banks are using new technologies to provide better services to customers. One of these new technologies is RFID. In this chapter, first a brief introduction presented about RFID technology and its components. Then, some applications of RFID in banking sector such as RFID applications in the cheques between banks, reducing the manual operation, customer relationship management, tracking and tracing, money transferring system, countering counterfeiting, contactless smart cards, people identification, phone banking, establishing security, checking purpose, and so on are explained. Finally, some of the barriers to technology acceptance by the customers and some methods to data protection and increasing security in RFID systems are described.

Chapter 10

The emergence of e-banking has created a significant transformation towards the services provided by the banks. E-banking provides alternatives for faster delivery of banking services to a wider scope of customers, hence creating a major impact towards e-society. Nowadays, e-banking has gained increasing popularity in delivering online services for e-society. However, prior to the implementation of e-banking, several factors and best practices must be identified to ensure a more efficient execution of e-banking services towards the development of e-society. E-banking factors are found to have a significant effect on the success of e-societies.

Preface

There is a general consensus that the innovative utilization of Internet and other information and communication technologies in the banking sector has resulted in emergence of e-banking phenomenon. E-banking has been known as the most important field in the e-society. So the formation of economical and social processes in e-society such as e-commerce, e-business, e-government, e-services, e-collaboration and so on, depends on getting access to certain bases of e-banking. From theoretical perspective, e-banking is not a single, stand-alone discipline, but a confluence of several disparate fields such as finance, information technology, communication technology, computer science and marketing science. According to recent evolutions in E-banking world, it's time for all researchers and practitioners to provide both a theoretical and practical approaches to e-banking phenomenon. So a scholarly publication in this field is of a great importance and it will expand the field of research.

The main objective of this book is to provide an opportunity to researchers and practitioners to advance the knowledge and practice of all facets of electronic banking. Emerging e-banking theories, technologies, strategies, and challenges are emphasized to stimulate and disseminate cutting edge information into research, business, and banking communities in a timely fashion. The secondary objective of this publication is to develop a comprehensive framework of e-banking by taking a multidisciplinary approach to understanding its implications on traditional banks, businesses and economies.

ORGANIZATION OF THE BOOK

The book contains ten chapters written by professional researchers coming from the field of academic and industry. The chapters have been organized into four interrelated sections.

Section 1: The E-Banking Evolution

The chapters in this section make an overview of the e-banking evolution.

Chapter 1. The chapter titled *"Global E-Banking Trends: Evolution, Challenges and Opportunities"* authored by Adapa attempts to provide a comprehensive explanation of what e-banking is, the evolution of e-banking, existing trends of e-banking in developed, developing and newly industrialized nations, future directions for further possible research and concluding remarks. The content provided in this chapter would be useful for existing and potential banks to better understand the global e-banking trends and thus aid in the effective formulation of channel management strategies and reap the benefits out of it.

Chapter 2. The chapter titled *"Improving E-Society through E-Banking"* authored by Shanmugam and Supramaniam. According to the authors, nowadays, e-banking have gained increasing popularity in delivering online services for e-society. However, prior to the implementation of e-banking, several factors and best practices must be identified to ensure a more efficient execution of e-banking services towards the development of e-society. E-banking factors are found to have a significant effect on the success of e-society. This chapter has focused on factors which could determine the development of e-society through e-banking.

Section 2: The E-Banking Strategies

Chapters introduce strategies appropriate to increasing the effectiveness of the operation of e-banking.

Chapter 3: The chapter titled *"Electronic Banking as a Strategy for Customer Service Improvement in The Developing Economy"* authored by Mobarek and attempts to present a brief review of E-banking services as a strategic tool especially in the developing economies.

Chapter 4: The chapter titled *"Factors Influencing KM Strategic Alignment in The Banking Sector: The Case of Persian Gulf Countries"* authored by Al-Ammary and tries to investigate the effect of some factors on KM Strategic Alignment between KM and business strategy in the banking sector at Persian Gulf Countries.

Chapter 5: The chapter titled *"Internet Banking Strategy in a Highly Volatile Business Environment: The Nigerian Case"* authored by Ezeoha. This chapter summarizes the structural and regulatory challenges in the Nigerian banking system. It represents and relates the country's socioeconomic conditions with its Internet business reputation; and lays down past regulatory and global efforts to control the menace of the Nigerian version of Internet frauds.

Section 3: The E-Banking Models

Two chapters in this section deal with conceptual models of Internet Banking.

Chapter 6: The chapter titled *"Business Model of Internet Banks"* authored by Sahut and attempts to study the "e-Business Model" of Internet-primary banks and to determine if it can perform better than the "Business Model" of a traditional bank.

Chapter 7: The chapter titled *"Toward a Conceptual Framework for Recognition and Analysis of Effective Factors in Successful Implementation of Electronic Banking"* authored by Hosseini and Ghorbani. This chapter examines the factors that can speed up the successful implementation of electronic banking innovations in the Iran's country.

Section 4: The E-Banking Technologies

The Modern Banking Technologies and Anonymous and Non-Repudiation E-Payment Protocols are introduced in this section.

Chapter 8: The chapter titled *"Introduction to Modern Banking Technology and Management"* authored by Ravi. This chapter introduces Banking Technology as a confluence of several disparate disciplines such as Finance (including risk management), Information technology, Computer Science, Communication technology and marketing science.

Chapter 9: The chapter titled *"Application of RFID Technology in Banking Sector"* authored by Ghorbani, Forozandeh and Aliahmadi attempts to study the Applications of RFID Technology in Banking Sector.

Chapter 10: The chapter titled *"Anonymous and Non-Repudiation E-Payment Protocol"* authored by Aboud. In this chapter the author suggest an efficient protocol for e-payment scheme that offers a good level of security with appreciate to its efficiency. The proposed protocol prevents the blind office and the bank from impersonate an entity, so that the entity could not repudiate it when the entity misused a coin.

The editors hope that book will be a useful summary of current studies on the e-banking evolution, strategies, models and technologies.

Mohammad Ali Sarlak
Asghar Aholhasani Hastiani
Editors

Section 1
The Evolution

Chapter 1
Global E-Banking Trends:
Evolution, Challenges and Opportunities

Sujana Adapa
University of New England, Australia

ABSTRACT

The traditional mode of delivering products and services by banks to the consumers' is through a single distribution channel and that is physical bank branches. Financial services industry is metamorphosing due to the advent of internet, rapid technological evolutions, deregulation, globalization as well as the impact of changing competitive and regulatory forces. In order to cope with the quick changes in the business scenario, banks started to rely on distribution channels as an alternative strategy for differentiation and gaining further competitive advantage. The abovementioned paved way for the development of the ebanking phenomena. This chapter attempts to provide a comprehensive explanation of what ebanking is, the evolution of ebanking, existing trends of ebanking in developed, developing and newly industrialized nations, future directions for further possible research and concluding remarks. The content provided in this chapter would be useful for existing and potential banks to better understand the global ebanking trends and thus aid in the effective formulation of channel management strategies and reap the benefits out of it.

INTRODUCTION

Considering the traditional methods, banks delivered their products and services to their prospective customers through only physical bank branches. However, the scenario of the financial services industry is changed with the advent of the internet, rapid technological evolutions, globalization and financial deregulations, liberalization and consolidation of the financial markets (Jeevan, 2000; Mia *et al.,* 2007). Many businesses are forced to change their traditional modes of operation and banks indeed are no exception to the abovementioned. As a result, financial services industry became much more competitive (Thornton & White, 2001). Banks realised that

DOI: 10.4018/978-1-61520-635-3.ch001

relying exclusively on the traditional modes of competition such as on price factors is difficult and in order to increase the revenue and market share, banks started looking at various options. It is evident that the largest expenses incurred by banks are maintenance of branch network associated with human resources in the form of overhead costs. Banks started to realize non-price factors such as distribution as an alternative strategy for differentiation, gaining competitive advantage and cost cutting (Daniel, 1999).

Rapid technological advancements coupled with the expansion of the global economy in the past two decades paved way for the transformation of the banking system role from traditional trade financing to mobilizing and channeling financial resources more effectively. In an intensifying competitive environment, superior distribution strategies concerned with how to communicate with and deliver products to the customer effectively provides a competitive advantage to the banking institutions in the market place (Kerem *et al.*, 2005). Customers are also demanding greater convenience and accessibility as reflected in longer branch opening hours and an increase in the choice of delivery mechanisms. Therefore, many banks globally have started to take initiatives to set in place more cost-effective alternative service delivery systems (Shih & Fang, 2004).

And the trend has been the proliferation of service delivery channels through which consumers can interact with the banks. Therefore modern banks provide their consumers with increased channel choice, reach out consumers through many routes. As such, ATMs, telephone, internet and wireless channels are now available to the consumers to perform their banking transactions in addition to the traditional branch banking. Banks cannot go back in the future by reducing the number of channels as consumers have become somewhat accustomed to and indeed are utilizing a broad range of options (Durkin, 2004).

Therefore the present chapter attempts to address the objectives such as:

- To understand what ebanking is.
- To look at the evolution of ebanking as a phenomena.
- To analyze the existing global ebanking trends in various countries.
- To identify the opportunities and challenges associated with ebanking.
- To suggest future research directions and recommendations.

BACKGROUND

There is no consensus among the researchers in defining what is called ebanking to date. Ebanking is often used as a supplement for internet banking. Thus, from the previous studies varied definitions of ebanking are in use.

What is E-Banking?

Often E-banking is defined as web based banking (Hertzum *et al.*, 2004). Deployment of retail or wholesale banking services over the internet is often referred as ebanking which involves individual and corporate clients, and includes bank transfers, payments and settlements, documentary collections and credits, corporate and household lending, card businesses and some others (UNCTAD, 2002). Other researchers related ebanking to type of products and services through which bank customers request information and carryout most of their retail banking activities through computer, television or mobile phone (Mols, 1998; Sathye, 1999; Daniel, 1999). Ebanking is described as an electronic connection between bank and customers in order to prepare, manage and control financial transactions (Burr, 1996). Since the thorough analysis of the secondary data depicts that internet banking globally shows a phenomenal uptake, the main focus in the present study is internet banking. The rest of the chapter deals with the evolution of ebanking, global trends of ebanking, opportunities and challenges associated with the ebanking, future directions and concluding remarks.

E-Banking Evolution

Modern scenario projects that ebanking is shaping the financial services industry. Henceforth, it is imperative to understand comprehensively the evolution of e-banking. A brief history and trend analysis of the evolution of ebanking industry globally using document analysis reveals the major barriers, impediments and boosters for the rapid transition of the banking sector and uptake of ebanking. Document analysis is the systematic analysis of a particular topic, using documents such as newspapers, annual reports, employment records, published and unpublished articles, industry and consultancy reports, ongoing academic working papers, government white paper reports and white papers (Neuman, 1997).

In a broader perspective, electronic banking is defined as the provision of banking services via means other than traditional physical branches (Liao *et al.,* 1999). Electronic banking offers its financial services to its prospective customers through various forms such as:

1. Automated Teller Machines (ATM)
2. Telephone Banking
3. Home Banking
4. Internet Banking
5. Mobile Banking

In order to gain competitive advantage and eliminate the costs associated with the traditional bank branches, one of the key objectives of electronic banking is to offer higher interest rates and lower service charges on their savings accounts (Talmor, 1995). The different forms of the electronic banking are discussed in detail subsequently.

Automated Teller Machines (ATM)

The first form of electronic banking was the ATM (Kass, 1994). An ATM is a computerized telecommunications device that provides the customer of a financial institution with access to financial transactions in a public space without the need for a bank teller. On most modern ATM's, the customer is identified by inserting a plastic ATM card with a magnetic strip or a plastic smart card with a chip, that contains a unique card number and some security information, such as an expiration date. Security is provided in form of entering a Personal Identification Number (PIN) by the customer (Ghose, 1987). By using an ATM, customers can access their bank accounts and perform transactions such as cash withdrawals and balance inquiry. ATM's are known by various casual terms including automated banking machine, money machine, cash machine, hole-in-the-wall, cash point or bancomat (in Europe and Russia).

Telephone Banking

Telephone banking is a service provided by a financial institution which allows its customers to perform transactions over the telephone. Most of the telephone banking uses an automated phone answering system with phone keypad response or voice recognition capability. To guarantee security, the customers must initially authenticate through a numeral or verbal password or through security questions asked by a representative. With the obvious exception of cash withdrawals and deposits, telephone banking offers all the virtual features that are accessed with the use of an ATM such as balance inquiry, check latest transactions, bill payments, order statements, check foreign exchange rate, activate cards, change passwords and funds transfer between customer accounts (Al-Ashban & Burney, 2001).

Home Banking

Telephone banking paved the way for the development of home banking services. Home banking is defined as conducting the transactions and accessing bank account information via personal computers. Often home banking is referred to as electronic banking. In order to perform home banking, a personal computer, a modem and a telephone line are required. In addition, specific banking application software needs to be installed to perform various banking functions (Liao *et al.*, 1999).

Internet Banking

The advent of the internet has a significant impact on the banking service that is traditionally offered by the branches to the customers. Internet banking often referred to as 'online banking' can be defined as performing financial transactions over the internet through a bank's website (Shao, 2007). The objective of internet banking is to provide financial services to the customers 24 hours a day, 365 days a year from locations with internet accessibility. Banks expect advantages such as reducing operating costs, wide customer reach, promote business diversification, and retain market share (Carlson, 2001, Centeno, 2003).

Mobile Banking

Mobile banking refers to provision and availment of banking and financial services with the help of mobile telecommunication devices. The scope of offered services may include facilities to conduct bank and stock market transactions, to administer accounts and to access customized information (Gurau, 2002). Mobile banking today is most often performed via SMS (Short Message Service) or the mobile internet. Mobile banking presents an opportunity for banks to retain their existing, technology-savvy customer base by offering value-added, innovative services and thus

attracting potential customers. Mobile banking provides account information (access to loan and card statements, alerts on accounts activity), Payments and transfers (domestic and international funds transfer, mobile recharging, commercial payment processing), investments (portfolio management services, personalized alerts on security prices, real time stock quotes), support (ATM location, exchange of data messages and email, cheque book requests) and content services (loyalty related offers, location based services).

GLOBAL E-BANKING TRENDS

Rapid technological advancements coupled with the expansion of the global economy in the past two decades paved way for the transformation of the banking system role from traditional trade financing to mobilizing and channeling financial resources more effectively. In an intensifying competitive environment, superior distribution strategies concerned with how to communicate with and deliver products to the customer effectively provides a competitive advantage to the banking institutions in the market place. Thus, in effect distribution may provide the basis for differentiation rather than the core service itself (Howcroft *et al.*, 2002). Therefore, many banks globally have started to take initiatives to set in place more cost-effective alternative service delivery systems in the form of internet and mobile banking. It has been estimated that the average cost of service delivery at a typical bank ranges from 285 to 350 basis points per dollar of deposits which is far higher than that for non-bank competitors (Barrett, 1997). For example, considering the cost per transaction of a customer to check account balance costs $10.00 using a branch, $3.00 using a telephone and a live representative, $0.40 using an automated telephone system and just a few cents using the internet (Barrett, 1997). An overview of the various technological developments in the banking sector reveals that internet and mobile banking are the recent electronic banking service delivery channels. The following sections briefly describe the internet and mobile banking evolution in global context.

Technological Evolution of E-Banking Services in the USA

It is evident from the existing literature that the average consumer has accepted the electronic banking services with phenomenal intensity particularly with regard to the service delivery channel ATM (Centeno, 2003). ATMs globally are well adopted by the consumers and in many countries the adoption trend is above the critical mass. The world is now a home to 1.65 million ATM's and is expected to grow by 1.7 million by 2009. USA and other parts of the Western world were the first to experience ATM proliferation with the trend subsequently spreading to other developing countries. It has been reported that in USA individuals prefer ATM usage and in Canada 75% of the consumers prefer banking through ATM (Finextra, 2005c). ATM users based on the discriminant analysis were classified as users and non-users in Canada based on five predictors such as education, social orientation, convenience, familiarity with other technology and attitude towards ATM technology (Marshall & Heslop, 1988). The trend is changing with tele-banking gaining much greater acceptance and a 16% increase in usage of tele-banking has been reported by Datamonitor (Aladwani, 2001). According to a survey conducted by Dove Associates for US Banker, 15.5% of transactions were conducted by the customers in USA through telephone (Milligan, 1997). However, with the advent of internet and mobile banking, the usage of telephone banking reduced to 20% in 2004 from 26% in 2001 in USA. Convenience is the main attraction for 79% of consumers to use internet banking services and 71% of consumers use for time saving (Fox, 2002). Also it has been reported that 30% of the consumers use internet

banking for cost savings and 52% to have better control over their finances (CRM Today, 2003a). Though different market research analysts estimated the increase in internet banking adoption by consumers in USA, the current status depicts an alternate situation (Tedeschi, 2005). Low internet diffusion rate has been attributed to consumer's attitude towards internet banking adoption as well as their perception regarding the benefits offered by internet banking (Carlson, 2001). It has also been reported that cross-selling issues concern the customers regarding banks performance and making it difficult for the customers to access key information regarding internet banking products and services on the bank's websites (Finextra, 2005b). Contrastingly, another report indicates that 44% of the internet users performed internet banking in 2004 in USA, which is an increase of 47% from 2002. The usage is more prominent among young people and in broadband user's category (e Marketer, 2004).

The major barriers to the internet banking adoption were identified as the availability of alternative service delivery channels in Canada (Finextra, 2005c). Consumers in Canada often presume that internet banking is not for everyone and 59% of the consumers visit bank branches to carry out transactions which remain unchanged since 2003 (Finextra, 2005c). Mobile banking is growing rapidly in all concerns of the world, often in different ways, for varying reasons and using a broad range of mobile technologies. In the USA there has been a flurry of activity recently as mobile operators, technology providers and retail banks compete to launch mobile banking services to consumers (Kolodinsky *et al.*, 2004). Citibank is making a downloadable mobile banking application available to its customers, while Wells Fargo is experimenting with different technology approaches through a series of consumer pilots. AT&T Cingular has recently announced a generic federated rich mobile banking offering to the major retail banks in the USA (Nathan, 1999). Structure and performance characteristics of the banks were analyzed by estimating the number of banks offering internet services in USA (Legris *et al.,* 2003). There exists a significant shift to electronic payments by consumers and businesses in USA (Furst *et al.,* 1998). A survey of the websites of various banks in USA reveals that the websites were of basic or intermediary level (Diniz, 1998). National banks offering internet services in US accounted to 90% of national banking system assets and 84% of small deposit accounts (Furst *et al.,* 2000). Internet only banks substantially under perform the established banks at first and the gaps systematically diminish over time as new banks grow older and larger in USA (DeYoung & Rice, 2001a). A comparative study of internet and non-internet banks in USA revealed that institutions with internet banking outperformed non-internet banks in profitability (Furst *et al.,* 2002).

Technological Evolution of E-Banking Services in Europe

UK, Spain, France, Germany and Italy account for a massive 77% of the installed base. Greatest growth is being led by Turkey, the Netherlands and Greece as well as from the countries in the Eastern European region. In Western Europe, on-premise ATM market is increasingly mature, and growth opportunities for off-premise are still available. At the end of 2006, Western Europe has just fewer than 350,000 ATM's (Source: Retail Banking Research). On an average an ATM in Western Europe alone completes 2888 cash withdrawals per month. Many studies about adoption of service delivery systems with reference to ATM usage have been conducted worldwide. A number of those studies have investigated the profiles of ATM users and non-users, demographic differences and the importance of perceptual factors as predictors of ATM usage. Filotto *et al.,* (1997) investigated the demographic characteristics of ATM users and non-users on Italian bank customers and identified that the public has been largely reluctant to adopt innovative service delivery mechanism in

spite of higher adoption rates among the young consumers. One of the most commonly discussed stories in relation to telephone banking is the UK bank-First Direct (Devlin, 1995). First Direct was launched in 1989 as a tele-banking service provider and at the end of 1998; it had 1.2 million account holders (Management Today, 1998). According to the European Central Bank, although all major banks offer internet banking services, the level of services and its quality differ according to the country and the banks (Centeno, 2003). Even in countries such as Finland and Sweden where internet penetration is more than 50%, consumers tend to prefer branch banking and around 60% of the consumers are reluctant to make online banking transactions (Bughin, 2001). Further, disparities in adoption of internet banking also exist among several countries in Europe.

First electronic banking services were introduced in Estonia in 1996. Electronic banking applications gained a quick momentum in Estonia due to high internet penetration and speed in the internet access (Emor, 2002). In Estonia, 18-25% of population are using internet banking services, whereas Italian bank almost had no online consumers by early 2000 and banks in Malta launched internet banking only in 2002 (Centeno, 2003). The percentage of internet usage was 43% in 2002 and Estonia recorded the highest internet penetration rate in comparison with the other East European countries (Kerem *et al.,* 2003). Scandinavian banks are best performing due to push and pull effects than Irish and French banks (Bughin, 2001). Existence of a strong correlation between internet diffusion and cost of service access, confidence in the security of the system, privacy and trust on banks hindered the adoption of internet banking (Gurau, 2002). Similarly, access to ATM, use of cashless payments and value of cash in circulation to gross domestic products (GDP) also influence the rate of internet banking adoption, but the results are either mixed or inconclusive in prior studies (Centeno, 2003). Western European consumers are expected to consolidate their lead in terms of number of internet banking customers, which would go past 60 million. Pure internet banking would be unlikely to succeed in Europe since high level of technology investment and high consumer acquisition cost would hinder economic viability and it has been revealed that the success of internet banking would be more promising by integrating with other traditional channels (Centeno, 2003). In UK, HSBC's subsidiary First Direct introduced SMS services in 1999 and has since adopted the Montise service, A third party provider, Montise enables, the download of a mobile application that enables consumers to review their balances, view recent transactions and top-up their mobile phone account. Montise is technically available to all UK banks.

Technological Evolution of E-Banking Services in Africa

In South Africa, internet banking is relatively new with only four banks providing internet banking services in 2002 with slow progress (Singh, 2002). About 92% consumers depend on ATMs mainly and the frequency of internet banking ranges from 12% daily to 59% monthly. 69% of the consumers were identified as non-users and the main reason for non-adoption pertains to unsafe transactions, cost and unawareness of the benefits and products and services offered through internet banking. Also about 33% of the consumers were found to be ignorant of internet banking (Singh, 2002). In short internet banking is significantly a new phenomenon in African countries with a very low diffusion rate. And the current situation with regard to mobile banking could not be further analyzed due to lack of information and the limited amount of published reports (Varma, 2001).

Technological Evolution of E-Banking Services in Middle East

In Middle East it has been reported that more number of customers prefers using ATM's (Al-Ashban

and Burney, 2001). Electronic banking system such as ATM has been perceived by consumers as the convenient transition in the banking sector and 50% of the transactions conducted outside bank branches and 74% of the total Australian population currently use ATM (Jesse, 1996). Customers increasingly tend to use tele-banking as their experience grows with the system and education and income play a vital role in usage as well as adoption of tele-banking by customers in Saudi-Arabia (Al-Ashban & Burney, 2001). Only 19% of the banks have full transactional capability in their current services in Middle East (Guru *et al.*, 2003). It has been reported that Islamic banks can no longer ignore the importance of internet banking as 20% of their customers are willing to switch to other financial institution if their current bank fails to offer financial services over the internet (Guru *et al.*, 2003). According to the Economic Intelligence Unit report, 14% of the region's internet users are currently registered to internet banking services. Three leading countries in the Middle East with internet banking adoption are Bahrain with 17%, the United Arab Emirates with 21% and Kuwait with 29% (Roth, 2001). Significant disparity is evident in Gulf countries with regard to internet adoption and no banks in Iran, Palestine and Yemen offer sufficient online transaction facilities (Awamleh *et al.*, 2003). In Saudi Arabia, use of internet banking is a marginal activity with about 73% of the banks having their own websites, out of which 25% sites are offering full services over the internet. Very few banks offered internet banking services in Oman and Jordan, though the banks maintained an informational website with basic interactive capability (Awamleh *et al.*, 2003).

Technological Evolution of E-Banking Services in Asia

In Asia, Japan, South Korea and Hong Kong reported the presence of more ATM's per person. However, the ATM networks currently operating in Japan are not compatible with global networks (Pyun *et al.*, 2002). In India 89% of the population prefer to conduct transactions using ATM and the concentration of the ATM's is in urban areas (Mishra, 2001). Income was the most important variable that influences the frequency of ATM usage in Hong Kong (Steyen & Chan, 2003). Telephone banking is gaining its momentum in India particularly by its acceptance by many firms (India Infoline, 2000). Home Banking failed to gain acceptance in Hong Kong (Liao *et al.*, 1999). Results indicate that over half a million users visited an online banking site in Hong Kong from their home computers initially and with the advent of internet banking the number of home banking consumers drastically reduced (Steyen & Chan, 2003).

The growth of online banking consumers is by 63% across South Korea, Hong Kong, Singapore, China and Taiwan. The total internet banking population for this region has increased by 4 million in one year time. South Korea has the largest number of internet banking users followed by China and Taiwan. More affluent and educated people tend to shift towards internet banking adoption and banks in the near future; will be challenged to remain focused to service online customers (Guru *et al.*, 2003). The level of awareness on internet banking is lacking among non-users in Malaysia (Suganthi et al., 2001). Preference to human interface, trust and security affect the diffusion of internet banking services in Malaysia (Suganthi & Balachandran, 2001). 51.6% of commercial banks and 48% of public sector banks provide internet banking services in India (Rao & Prathima, 2003). Foreign and private sector banks offer a wide rage of services over the internet. Japan Net is the first virtual bank in Japan without a physical branch in 2000. In 2001 Sony bank, a second online bank was started by Sony an electronic giant (Pyun *et al.*, 2002). Japan has been a world leader when it comes to mobile payments. Consumers also readily access banking services through the dominant mobile technology

in Japan iMode (a browser-based user experience) (Mia *et al.*, 2007). Mobile phone usage in India and China is exploding with nearly 200,000 connections every day. ICICI India's second largest bank provides its customers with a broad range of SMS transactions including bill payments, branch finder and bill view, in addition to balance enquiries and recent transactions (Straeel, 1995).

Technological Evolution of E-Banking Services in Australia and New Zealand

The Market Intelligence Strategy Centre (MISC) reported over 7.2 million customer's accessed 27 millions accounts online (Sathye, 1999). Among users, women in particular are becoming increasingly attracted to internet banking services and baby boomers are considered to be the fastest growing segment. Banks are considering active user's growth and increase in the number of online transactions are the factors that determine the performance of online banking channel rather than the number of new registrations. Highest interest rate in online savings account motivated users to perform internet banking transactions and also driving the major banks in offering similar products. Consumers' in New Zealand are accustomed to use safe and secure electronic information and money transfer systems (Chung & Paynter, 2002). Consumers in New Zealand are reluctant to online purchases compared to USA and Europe (Straeel, 1995). Although internet penetration and usage has reached to a significant level, still use of internet banking services is the lowest amongst all the banking facilities in New Zealand (Chung & Paynter, 2002). BPAY in Australia allows customers to perform phone banking since 1997 (Beatty, 1998). In Australia, Bank of Queensland and Credit Union Australia have deployed a comprehensive set of SMS banking services, In New Zealand; retail banks have taken the lead. All New Zealand, retail banks now offer mobile banking services, and two of the major banks, ANZ and

National Bank have made richer mobile banking and payment services to customers via mobile Java applets (Luarn & Lin, 2004).

ISSUES, CONTROVERSIES, PROBLEMS

There are several benefits associated with the introduction of ebanking. Benefits might vary depending upon various perspectives. From the banks perspective, provision of ebanking service delivery channel to consumers would enhance their opportunity to maximize their profits. The chief goal of many businesses in monetary terms is associated with profit maximization (Nathan, 1999). More over, from the banks' point of view, proliferation of the ebanking service delivery channels is an essential requisite not only in terms of cost saving by reducing the human interaction, improving competitiveness by way of differentiation and retaining existing customer base as well as attracting potential consumers. Banks throughout the world face an increasingly tough challenge of boosting their revenues while controlling their costs (Durkin, 2004). Therefore the common trend followed by many banks globally is streamlining their branch networks and redirecting their consumers to alternative service delivery channels and encouraging consumers to adopt self service technologies. Thus, banks are reducing the costs incurred in maintaining the branch staff (Pyun *et al.,* 2002). Also, banks often build better brand image by way of responding to the rapid market changes and would therefore be perceived as leaders in adoption of innovative technologies.

From the consumers' point of view, automation of banking services by introducing ebanking service delivery channels provides 24 hours accessibility, reduced costs in accessing and using of banking products and services, proper cash management, reduced time demands, increased comfort as well as quick and continuous access to the information (Aladwani, 2001). Existing studies report that consumers by way of utilizing ebanking channels can manage funds in a better manner. Majority of the consumers are happy with the speed and convenience associated with the ebanking (Gurau, 2002). Ebanking eliminates uncertainties by standardizing services and reduces the prevalent heterogeneity that might commonly exist between bank staff and consumers.

From the economic perspective, some studies indicate that using ebanking facilities increases the overall savings in the economy by 0.93% of the gross domestic product in Estonia (Aarma & Vensel, 2001). Unlike the US, there has been no acceleration in the trend rate of labor productivity in Finland, though the growth of output in Finnish market sector has increased from 0.3% in early 1990s to 0.7% in late 1990s due to the use of information and communication technologies (Pohjola, 2002). Thus extant studies indicate a significant contribution to the economy with regard to the introduction of ebanking.

Associated with the opportunities mentioned earlier there are concerns and challenges exerted by the banks as well as the consumers' with regard to the uptake and use of ebanking. Banks initially promoted their core capabilities through the internet such as products and services with some advice. Due to the relative newness of the technology associated with ebanking, banks as well as consumers are often concerned about the security of internet access to clients accounts (Stamoulis, 2000). Several studies indicate that the acceptance of ebanking by consumers' is affected by perceived security (Dourish & Redmiles, 2002). Several banks in order to maintain their competitive advantage mimic new channel approaches quickly as product differentiation is very difficult for banks (Nemzow, 1999). As many countries have deregulated their banking sector, government policies no longer form an entry barrier to banks competitors and technology know-how also provides only low protection to existing banks (Mia *et al.,* 2007). Typical attributes of an oligopoly market such as risk avoidance and undifferentiated customer service made the banking sector susceptible to encroachment by software giants, thus attempting to replace banks as intermediaries (Kalakota and Frei, 1998). Moreover, the threat of substitutes to banking in terms of competition from non-banking, financial and micro credit sector is increasing rapidly (Mia *et al.*, 2007). The competition is fierce in the banking and financial sector environment as every entrant is participating to some extent of ebanking which raises the issues of security, privacy and risk (Constantine, 2000).

SOLUTIONS AND RECOMMENDATIONS

E-banking success depends on the rate of internet penetration in a country. Since the developed nations have good infrastructure and more per capita income possession of a computer as well as internet is not a problem for many consumers. However, with regard to the developing nation's poor infrastructure in conjunction with low levels of internet penetration is a serious problem. Internet service providers and banks should provide certain incentives and subsidize the surfing cost. It would be beneficial for the consumers' if free training sessions and mock demonstrations about the use of internet and ebanking are provided by the banks and service providers. Multiple access facilities combining telephone, internet, mobile and ATM would likely motivate more number of consumers' to adopt and use ebanking. Provision of proper authentication facilities and assurance by the banks to maintain consumers' identity and confidentiality would essentially initiate the uptake of e-banking by many. Government intervention is essential and appropriate particularly in developing countries. Government should work in conjunction with the banks to improve the infrastructure facilities as well as regulate and supervise the economic policies periodically. Often intervention of the government would create positive attitudes among the consumers' who

might be motivated to use ebanking. Aggressive marketing programs play a critical role in taking the ebanking to large number of consumers. Marketing communications is an effective tool and banks should properly utilize the appropriate marketing techniques to reach the large mass of consumers. Marketing communications should also devise a specific plan that strategically incorporates ebanking service delivery channel promotion. Personal online help should be provided continuously which would substantially eliminate the consumers' fear associated with the ebanking and often encourages them to use complex products and services provided by the banks.

FUTURE RESEARCH DIRECTIONS

Despite the phenomenal uptake of ebanking in many nations, existing literature stresses that not all the consumers' are willing to perform their banking transactions electronically. Even to date in the developed nations also, ebanking usage by consumers' is related to basic banking facilities such as balance inquiries, monitoring savings and current account facilities and viewing summaries of their report transactions. High end banking products and services involving personal loans, foreign exchange, mortgage, car loans etc., are not utilized by the consumers through ebanking service delivery channel. The reason behind this could be related to the perceived personalization aspect by the consumers. When dealing with comprehensive decisions involving large monetary transactions consumers are comfortable with the reassurance of face to face interactions provided by the bank staff. Incorporating personal help through ebanking service delivery channels could minimize the apprehensions of the consumers associated with the security aspects and thus enhance their adoption of ebanking as well as utilizing complex banking services and product facilities. Thus consumers often tend to manage their potential uncertainty through personal interaction.

Furthermore, there exist minimal studies focusing on the adoption of ebanking by consumers in Africa, Middle East and Asian countries. Therefore future research should incorporate exploring the key antecedents and inhibitors of ebanking adoption in those countries.

CONCLUSION

From the abovementioned discussion it is evident that the new generation of the electronic banking transactions created a bundle of opportunities as well as challenges to the existing banks, financial institutions and consumers. It is visible from the extant documentary analysis that almost all the major banks irrespective of the level of country's advancement have rapidly introduced innovative ebanking technologies. However, the rate of ebanking adoption by consumers in developed nations comparatively took more time as consistent with the technology apprehension and ambiguity exerted by the innovative technologies on consumers. Thus, it is clear that in newly industrialized nations, electronic banking is gaining its momentum as the banks operating globally have declared ebanking as one of the core strategies for future development. There exists a potential scope to gear on the opportunities related to the electronic banking channels with a particular emphasis on the developing nations. Banks should work in conjunction with the government to improve the security, safety and privacy issues and maintaining the confidentiality of their prospective consumers would enhance the uptake of ebanking in developing nations. Moreover, the success or failure of ebanking in a country largely depends on several dimensions such as consumers' trust in a particular bank, service quality offered by the bank, consumer preferences and their ultimate satisfaction. Therefore, banks should continuously strive to meet the consumers' expectations, demands and requirements in order to maintain their own identity.

REFERENCES

Aarma, A., & Vensel, V. (2001). Banks' retail customer satisfaction and development of bank-customer relationships. In Vensel, V., & Wihlborg, C. (Eds.), *Estonia on the Threshold of the European Union: Financial Sector and Enterprise Restructuring in the Changing Economic Environment*. Tallinn Technical University.

Al-Ashban, A. A., & Burney, M. A. (2001). Customer adoption of tele-banking technology: the case of Saudi Arabia. *International Journal of Bank Marketing*, 19(5), 191–200. doi:10.1108/02652320110399683

Aladwani, A. (2001). Online banking: A field study of drivers, development challenges, and expectations. *International Journal of Information Management*, 21, 213–225. doi:10.1016/S0268-4012(01)00011-1

Awamleh, R., Evans, J., & Mahate, A. (2003). Internet Banking in Emergency Markets. *Journal of Internet Banking and Commerce*, 8(1). Retrieved from www.arraydev.com/commerce.

Barrett, M. (1997). Playing the Right Paradigm. *Bank Marketing*, 29(9), 32–39.

Beatty, A. (1998). *Online Business: Internet and Electronic Payments*. Mallesons Stephen Jaques Solicitors, Sydney, Retrieved from www.ecomlaw.com/articles

Bughin, J. (2003). The Diffusion of Internet Banking in Western Europe. *Electronic Markets*, 13(3), 251–258. doi:10.1080/1019678032000108329

Burr, W. (1996). Wir informationstechnik die bankorganisation verandern konnte. *Bank und Markt*, 11, 28–31.

Carlson, J., Furst, K., Lang, W. W., & Nolle, D. E. (2001). *Internet Banking: Market Developments and Regulatory Issues*. Paper Presented at the Society of Government Economists Conference 2000, Washington D C.

Centeno, C. (2004). Adoption of Internet Services in the Acceding and Candidate Countries, Lessons from the Internet Banking Case. *Telematics and Informatics, 21*(4), 293–315. doi:10.1016/j.tele.2004.02.001

Chung, W., & Paynter, J. (2001). *An Evaluation of Internet Banking in New Zealand. Department of Management Science and Information Systems.* Auckland, New Zealand: The University of Auckland.

Constantine, G. (2000). *Banks provide internet on ramp.* Hoosier Banker, Indianapolis, March, USA.

Daniel, E. (1999). Provision of electronic banking in the UK and the Republic of Ireland. *International Journal of Bank Marketing, 17*(2), 72–82. doi:10.1108/02652329910258934

Datamonitor, (2003), *European Retail banks 2003.* Retrieved February 14th 2008, from www.datamonitor.com/industries/research

De Young, R., & Rice, T. (2004). How do Banks make Money? A Variety of Business Strategies. *Federal Reserve Bank of Chicago Economic Perspectives, 28*, 52–68.

Devlin, J. F. (1995). Technology and Innovation in Retail Business Distribution. *International Journal of Bank Marketing, 13*(4), 19–25. doi:10.1108/02652329510082915

Diniz, E. (1998). Web Banking in the USA. *Journal of Internet Banking and Commerce*, from www.arraydev.com/commerce

Dourish, P., & Redmiles, D. (2002). *An approach to usable security based on event monitoring and visualization.* Paper presented at proceedings of the 2002 workshop on new security paradigms (pp.75-81), New York.

Durkin, M. (2004). In Search of the Internet Banking Customer, Exploring the Use of Decision Styles. *International Journal of Bank Marketing, 22*(7), 484–523. doi:10.1108/02652320410567917

eMarketer, (2004). *Can Online Banking Reach Widespread US Adoption.* Retrieved 12th March 2007, from www.emarketer.com

Ennew, C., & Watkins, T. (1992). Marketing Strategy and the Marketing Mix in Financial Services. In Baker, M. (Ed.), *Perspectives on Marketing Management, 2.* Chichester, UK: John Wiley & Sons.

Filotto, U., Tanzi, P. M., & Saita, F. (1997). Customer Needs and Front Office Technology Adoption. *International Journal of Bank Marketing, 15*(1), 13. doi:10.1108/02652329710155679

Finextra, (2005b). *Online Banking Services Key to Bank Selection.* Retrieved 20th January 2008, from www.finextra.com

Finextra, (2005c). *Web Banking Growth Stalls in Canada.* Retrieved 20th January 2008, from www.finextra.com

Fox, S. (2002). *Online Banking.* Retrieved 22nd April 2008, from www.pewinternet.com

Furst, K., Lang, W. W., & Nolle, D. E. (2002). Internet Banking. *Journal of Financial Services Research, 22*(1/2), 95–117. doi:10.1023/A:1016012703620

Ghose, T. K. (1987). *The Banking System of Hong Kong.* Singapore: Butterworths.

Gurau, C. (2002). E-banking in transistion economies: The case of Romania. *Journal of Financial Services Marketing, 6*(4), 362–379. doi:10.1057/palgrave.fsm.4770065

Guru, B., Shanmugam, B., Alam, N., & Perera, C. J. (2003). An Evaluation of Internet Banking Sites in Islamic Countries. *Journal of Internet Banking and Commerce, 8*(2), from www.arraydev.com/commerce

Hertzum, M., Juul, N. C., Jorgensen, N., & Norgaard, M. (2004). Usable security and ebanking: Ease of use vis-a-vis security. *Technical Report*, from www.ruc.dk

Howcroft, B., Hamilton, R., & Hewer, P. (2002). Consumer Attitude and the Usage and Adoption of Home Banking in the United Kingdom. *International Journal of Bank Marketing, 20*(3), 111–121. doi:10.1108/02652320210424205

Infoline, I. (2000). *Electronic Fund Transfer and Clearing System.* Retrieved 25th February 2008, from www.indiainfoline.com

Jeevan, M. T. (2000). *Only banks – No bricks.* Voice and Data.

Jesse, H. (1996). *The Impact of Technology and Changing Distribution Strategies on Workforce Planning within Australian Financial Industry over the Next Decade.* Melbourne: Australian Institute of Banking and Finance.

Kalakota, R., & Frei, F. (1998). Frontiers of online financial services. In Cronin, M. J. (Ed.), *Banking and Finance on the Internet.* New York: John Wiley and Sons Inc.

Kass, R. (1994). Looking for the link to customers. *Bank Systems and Technology, 31*(2), 64.

Kerem, K., Lustsik, O., Sorg, M., & Vensel, V. (2003). *The development of e-banking in a EU candidate country: An Estonian case.* Proceedings of International Atlantic Economic Society Conference, Vienna, March 11-17.

Kolodinsky, J. M., Hogarth, J. M., & Hilgert, M. A. (2004). The adoption of electronic banking technologies by US consumers. *International Journal of Bank Marketing, 22*(4), 238–259. doi:10.1108/02652320410542536

Legris, P., Ingham, J., & Collerette, P. (2003). Why people use information technology? A critical review of the technology acceptance model. *Information & Management, 40,* 191–204. doi:10.1016/S0378-7206(01)00143-4

Liao, S., Shao, Y. P., Wang, H., & Chen, A. (1999). The adoption of virtual banking: An empirical study. *International Journal of Information Management, 19,* 63–74. doi:10.1016/S0268-4012(98)00047-4

Luarn, P., & Lin, L. H. (2004). Towards an understanding of the behavioural intention to use mobile banking. *Computers in Human Behaviour,* 1-19.

Marshall, J. J., & Heslop, L. A. (1988). Technology Acceptance in Canadian Retail Banking: A Study of Consumer Motivation and Use of ATMs. *International Journal of Bank Marketing, 6*(4), 31–41. doi:10.1108/eb010836

Mia, M. A. H., Rahman, M. A., & Uddin, M. M. (2007). E-Banking evolution, status and prospects. *Coastal Management, 35*(1), 36–48.

Milligan, J. W. (1997). What do Customers want from you? Everything. *US Bankers Magazine, 107*(12), 38–45.

Mishra, R. (2001). *Internet Banking in India.* Retrieved 10th June 2008, from www.banknetindia. com/banking/ibkg.htm

Mols, N. (1998). The behavioural consequences of PC banking. *International Journal of Bank Marketing, 16*(5), 195–201. doi:10.1108/02652329810228190

Nathan, L. (1999). *Community banks are going online. Community and Banking.* Federal Reserve Bank of Boston.

Neuman, W. L. (1997). *Social Research Methods: Qualitative and Quantitative Approaches.* Boston: Allyn and Bacon.

Pohjola, M. (2002). The new economy: Facts, impacts and policies. *Information Economics and Policy, 14,* 133–144. doi:10.1016/S0167-6245(01)00063-4

Pyun, C. S., Scruggs, L., & Nam, K. (2002). Internet Banking in the U.S., Japan and Europe. *Multinational Business Review, 10*(2), 73–81.

Rao, G. R., & Prathima, K. (2003). *Internet Banking in India*. Retrieved 15th February 2008, from www.mondaq.com

Roth, A. (2001). *Middle East Web could draw US Bankers*. Retrieved 8th February 2008, from www.itp.net/features

Sathye, M. (1999). Adoption of internet banking by Australian consumers: An empirical investigation. *International Journal of Bank Marketing, 17*(7), 324–334. doi:10.1108/02652329910305689

Shao, G. (2007). The Diffusion of Online Banking: Research Trends from 1998 to 2006. *Journal of Internet Banking and Commerce, 12*(2), from www.arraydev.com/commerce

Shih, Y., & Fang, K. (2004). The use of decomposed theory of planned behaviour to study internet banking in Taiean. *Internet Research, 14*(3), 213–223. doi:10.1108/10662240410542643

Singh, A. M. (2002). *Internet Banking: To Bank or Not To Bank. Where is the Question?* Durban: University of Durban Westville.

Stamoulis, D. S. (2000). How banks fit in an internet commerce business activities model. *Journal of Internet Banking and Commerce, 5* (1), from www.arraydev.com/commerce

Steyen, P., & Chan, E. (2003). *Over Half a Million Hong Kong People Visited an Internet Banking Site in January 2003*. Retrieved 10th February 2008, from www.neilson-netratings.com

Straeel, H. (1995). Virtual banking: gearing up to play the no-fee retail game. *Bank Systems and Technology, 32*(7), 20–22.

Suganthi, B., & Balachandran, G. (2001). Internet Banking Patronage: An Investigation of Malaysia. [from www.arraydev.com/commerce]. *Journal of Internet Banking and Commerce, 6*(1), 23–32.

Talmor, S. (1995). New Life for Dinosaurs. *The Banker, 145*, 75–78.

Tedeschi, B. (2005). Banks see Online Gain via Updated Cash Sites. *International Herald Tribune*, 1-2.

Today, C. R. M. (2003a). *New eMarketer Interactive Banking Report Released*. Retrieved January 12th, 2008, from www.crm2day.com

Today, M. (1998). Service Excellence Company of the Year – Winner Financial Services Category: First Direct. *Management Today, 10*, 55–56.

United Nations Conference on Trade and Development, (2000). *E-commerce and development report 2000*, United Nations, New York & Geneva.

Varma, Y. (2001). Banking: The network is the bank, Public Sector: why the lag? Dataquest, January 29th. www.dqindia.com/content/top_stories/301012904.asp

ADDITIONAL READING

Black, N. J., Lockett, A., Winjklhofer, H., & Ennew, C. (2001). The adoption of internet financial services: A qualitative research. *International Journal of Retail and Distribution Management, 29*(8), 390–398. doi:10.1108/09590550110397033

Chan, S., & Lu, M. (2004). Understanding internet banking adoption and use behaviour: A Hong Kong Perspective. *Journal of Global Information Management, 12*(3), 21–43.

Cooper, R. B., & Zmud, R. W. (1990). Information technology implementation research: A technological diffusion approach. *Management Science, 36*(2), 123–139. doi:10.1287/mnsc.36.2.123

Gan, C., Clemes, M., Limsombunchai, V., & Weng, A. (2006). A logit analysis of electronic banking in New Zealand. *International Journal of Bank Marketing, 24*(6), 360–383. doi:10.1108/02652320610701717

Gartner, A. (2003b). *Online banking goes mainstream in US. Nua Internet Surveys*. Scope Communications Group.

Gerrard, P., Cunningham, J. B., & Devlin, J. F. (2006). Why consumers are not using internet banking. *Journal of Services Marketing, 20*(3), 16–28. doi:10.1108/08876040610665616

Gronroos, C. (2001). *Service Management and Marketing: A Customer Relationship Management Approach*. Chichester: Wiley.

Herington, C., & Weaven, S. (2007). Can banks improve customer relationships with high quality online services? *Managing Service Quality, 17*(4), 404–427. doi:10.1108/09604520710760544

Hernandez, J. M. C., & Mazzon, J. A. (2007). Adoption of internet banking: Proposition and implementation of an integrated methodology approach. *International Journal of Bank Marketing, 25*(2), 72–88. doi:10.1108/02652320710728410

Hoffman, D. L., Novak, T. P., & Peralta, M. (1999). Building customer trust online. *Communications of the ACM, 42*(4), 80–85. doi:10.1145/299157.299175

Holak, S. L., & Lehmann, D. R. (1990). Purchase intentions and dimensions of innovation: An exploratory model. *Journal of Product Innovation Management, 7*, 59–73. doi:10.1016/0737-6782(90)90032-A

Igbaria, M., & Chakrabarti, A. (1990). Computer anxiety and attitudes towards microcomputer use. *Behaviour & Information Technology, 9*(3), 229–241. doi:10.1080/01449299008924239

Karahanna, E., Straub, D. W., & Chervany, N. L. (1999). Information technology adoption across time: A cross-sectional comparison of pre-adoption and post-adoption beliefs. *Management Information Systems Quarterly, 23*(2), 183–213. doi:10.2307/249751

Karjaluoto, H., Mattila, M., & Pento, T. (2002). Electronic banking in Finland: Consumer beliefs and reactions to a new delivery channel. *Journal of Financial Services Marketing, 6*(4), 346–361. doi:10.1057/palgrave.fsm.4770064

Kassim, N. M., & Abdulla, A. K. M. A. (2006). The influence of attraction on internet banking: An extension to the trust-relationship commitment model. *International Journal of Bank Marketing, 24*(6), 424–442. doi:10.1108/02652320610701744

Kelle, U., & Laurie, H. (1998). Computer use in qualitative research and issues of validity. In Kelle, U. (Ed.), *Computer-aided Qualitative Data Analysis: Theory, Methods, and Practice* (pp. 19–28). Thousand Oaks, California: Sage publications.

Kolodinsky, J., Hogarth, J. M., & Shue, J. F. (2000). Bricks or clicks? Consumer adoption of electronic banking technologies. *Consumer Interests Annual, 46*, 180–184.

Kuisma, T., Laukkanen, T., & Hiltunen, M. (2007). Mapping the reasons for resistance to internet banking: A means-end approach. *International Journal of Information Management, 27*(2), 75–85. doi:10.1016/j.ijinfomgt.2006.08.006

Moore, G. C., & Benbasat, I. (1991). Development of an instrument to measure the perceptions of adopting an information technology. *Information Systems Research, 2*(3), 173–191. doi:10.1287/isre.2.3.192

Mukherjee, A., & Nath, P. (2003). Assessing users' subjective quality of experience with the World Wide Web: An exploratory examination of temporal changes in technology acceptance. *International Journal of Human-Computer Studies*, *54*(6), 877–901.

Polatoglu, V. N., & Ekin, S. (2001). An empirical investigation of the Turkish consumers' acceptance of internet banking services. *International Journal of Bank Marketing*, *19*(4), 156–165. doi:10.1108/02652320110392527

Ribbink, D., Riel, A., Liljander, V., & Streukens, S. (2004). Comfort your online customer: Quality, trust, and loyalty on the internet. *Managing Service Quality*, *14*(6), 446–456. doi:10.1108/09604520410569784

Roig, J. C. F., Garcia, J. S., Tena, M. A. M., & Monzonis, J. L. (2006). Customer perceived value in banking services. *International Journal of Bank Marketing*, *24*(5), 266–283. doi:10.1108/02652320610681729

Rotchanakitumnuai, S., & Speece, M. (2003). Barriers to internet banking adoption: A qualitative study among corporate customers in Thailand. *International Journal of Bank Marketing*, *21*(6/7), 312–323. doi:10.1108/02652320310498465

Srinivasan, S. S., Anderson, R., & Ponnavolu, K. (2002). Customer loyalty in e-commerce: An exploration of its antecedents and consequences. *Journal of Retailing*, *78*(1), 41–50. doi:10.1016/S0022-4359(01)00065-3

Tan, M., & Teo, T. S. H. (2000). Factors influencing the adoption of internet banking. *Journal of the Association for Information Systems*, *1*(5), 22–38.

Teo, T. (2001). Demographic and motivation variables associated with internet usage activities. *Internet Research: Electronic Networking Applications and Policy*, *11*(2), 125–137. doi:10.1108/10662240110695089

Tornatzky, L. G., & Klein, K. J. (1982). Innovation characteristics and innovation adoption implementation: A meta-analysis of findings. *IEEE Transactions on Engineering Management*, *29*(1), 28–45.

Wang, Y. S., Wang, Y. M., Lin, H. H., & Tang, T. I. (2003). Determinants of user acceptance of internet banking: An empirical research. *International Journal of Bank Marketing*, *14*(5), 501–519.

KEY TERMS AND DEFINITIONS

Automated Teller Machines (ATM): Banking transactions that occur between the bank and the customers in a public space without the need for a bank teller through a computerized telecommunications device.

Automation of Banking Services: In the banking context, automation of banking services is evident by introducing e-banking service delivery channels which increased comfort as well as quick and continuous access to the information by customers.

E-Banking: Banking transactions that occur between the bank and the customers through means other than physical bank branches.

Internet Banking: A form of banking that allows customers to perform their banking transactions over the internet through a bank's website.

Mobile Banking: A form of banking that allows customers to perform their banking transactions with the help of mobile telecommunication devices.

Service Delivery Channels: In the banking context, service delivery channels are the distribution channels through which consumers can interact with the banks.

Telephone Banking: A form of banking that allows customers to perform their banking transactions over the telephone.

Chapter 2
Efficient Anonymous and Non-Repudiation E-Payment Protocol

Sattar J. Aboud
Iraqi Council of Representatives, Iraq

ABSTRACT

There are many proposals which offer anonymous and non-repudiation e-payment protocols. But they have the drawbacks that the anonymity can be misused fraudulently to perform a perfect crime. Currently, the hot research concentrates on the accepting of e-payment protocols where the anonymity of the coins is cancelable via a trusted authority in the case of criminal entities. In the chapter the author suggests an efficient protocol for e-payment schemes that offers a good level of security with appreciate to its efficiency. The proposed protocol prevents the blind office and the bank from impersonating an entity, so that the entity could not repudiate it when the entity misused a coin. Another benefit is that it is constructed from efficient cryptography schemes so that its security can simply be analyzed. The strength of this scheme is in its easiness. So, the author claims that the suggested protocol is more efficient than the existing schemes, since it allows to both a blind office and a bank to impersonate an entity to find and to spend a coin without to be noticed. It might cause a repudiation difficulty where the entity can repudiate his bad activities by proposing that both the bank and the blind office acted inaccurately. Other relevant issues related to the new protocol will be discussed in the section of the security of the scheme.

INTRODUCTION

Internet is designed to allow computers to easily interconnect and to assure that network connections will be maintained even when various links may be damaged, but this versatility also makes

DOI: 10.4018/978-1-61520-635-3.ch002

it easy to compromise data security and privacy protection for e-commerce application.

E-payment systems allow people to carry out commercial activities in an electronic domain. There are many electronic payment systems that have been proposed in recent years (Liu *et al.*, 2001). A secure e-payment systems protecting privacy can be seen as a protocol involving a customer, a shop and a bank. It is goal to transfer money in a secure way from the customer's account to the shop's account. E-payment systems are conventionally divided into those that are on-line and those that are off-line, one can distinguish between on-line payments systems where all parties, the customer, the shop and bank need to be connected on-line, and off-line payments system, where each interaction during the protocol requires two communicating parties only (Camenisch, & Stadler, 1996).

E-payment is a subject of great economic, political and research and Security is an important factor for the wide acceptance of the electronic commerce services. There are many proposals discussed the e-payment protocols which enable anonymity services to protect user's privacy, Protocols relying on traditional trusted parties easily guarantee exchanges, but are inefficient -because a trusted party must be part of every transaction and expensive because a trusted party wants to be paid for each transaction.

Anonymity of the participant's is an important requirement for electronic commerce, in particular for payment systems, because anonymity could be in conflict with law enforcement, currently the researches concentrate on accepting of e-payment protocols where the anonymity of the coins is cancellable via a trustee in case of criminal entities. Most of current systems have drawbacks that the anonymity can be misused by fraudulent to perform a perfect crimes like blackmailing or money laundering and do not provide the non-repudiation service which prevent users from repudiate the misusing of the coins like denying, double-spending.

The idea of anonymous payment scheme was introduced in 1982 (Chaum, 1983). In fact this anonymity might be misused by fraudulent to perform a perfect crime (Solms & Naccache, 1992). For instance stealing of the private keys, money laundry, and blackmailing of coins. The uses of blindfolded protocols in the banks are

considered as a modern threat (Liu *et al.*, 2001). To avoid these threats the payment schemes must offer anonymity method which accepts the tracing of coins in any of the states mentioned above by an authorized trusted authority. The first scheme that is stopping blackmailing and money laundry was suggested in (Brickell *et al.*, 1995). However, there are some proposals (Camenisch, 1996; M'Raihi, 1996; Jacobson & Youg, 1997) to prevent these threats. Every scheme needs the participation of the trusted authority in the opening of the bank account, and also in the withdrawal of coins. The only scheme that does not need trusted authority participation excepting the anonymity has just suggested in (Binh, 2007). But, it is unable to stop extortion threats and the employ of blindfolding schemes. These threats are just prevented in the scheme of (Hohenberger, 2006), which is also not efficient as it needs the trusted authority interaction in e-payment schemes. In case that one of these threats is needed, they require an on-line e-payment scheme among user, shop, and trusted authority to stop the spending of illegitimate coins.

Chaum, Fiat and Naor proposed a practical electronic cash system, using the blind signature paradigm to provide privacy and security for all involved parties (Chaum *et al.*, 1988). However, while protecting the honest customer's privacy in fact the perfect anonymity obtained through the usage of blind signature also open doors for misuse by fraudulent to perform a perfect crime as mentioned in (Solms, & Naccache, 1992). Brickell, Gemmell and Kravitz proposed a new scheme to avoid threats obtained from using a perfect anonymity like blackmailing and money laundry by involving an authorized trustee during withdrawal that can revoke anonymity of certain transaction as needed (Brickell *et al.*, 1995).

The concept of anonymity-revocable payment systems, sometimes called fair payment system, that enables the trustee to revoke customer's anonymity in cooperation with the bank, but the customer's privacy cannot be compromised by the bank nor by the payee, even if they collaborate (Chaum *et al.*, 1988). Every scheme needs the participation of the trusted authority in the opening of the bank account, and also in the withdrawal of coins. The only scheme that does not need trusted authority participation excepting the anonymity has just suggested by Binh (2007).

It is easier to implement the on-line system than off-line system since most of the checking can be done on-line. The most difficult task for off-line system is the detection of double-spending. When double-spending is suspected; the participant's identity must be traceable as suggested in (Kanniainen, 2001, Song & Korba, 2004), but it is the on-line payment system, in (Binh, 2007) they proposed a new e-payment system which possess recoverability and untraceability simultaneously and still remains off-line. There are many systems build high trusted relations between a bank, user and blind office, these trusted relations may lead both blind office and bank to exploitation these relations to impersonate the user without being noticed (Micali, 2003, NCSC-TG-017, 2000). He proposed system that avoids blind office and bank from impersonating user, so the user could not repudiate the coin abuse (Song & Korba, 2004).

However, in any e-payment scheme there are two requirements.

1. The entity need to have anonymous e-payment service
2. The bank needs to ensure that the e-payment scheme will not be abused.

For example, when double spending is suspected; the related participant's identity must be traceable (Kanniainen, 2001). There are numerous papers are suggested employing blind signature schemes to design an e-payment protocols, which satisfies the needs of both the banks and the entities (Zheng & Chen, 2003; Kungpisdan *et al.*, 2004; Yang Li and Li J, 2006).

We propose a secure payment system that allows anonymity by trusted authority in the case of any extortion attacks. Therefore we employ a blind office as a pseudo identity escrow agency. The scheme based on the hypothesis of high trust relations (NCSC-TG-017, 2000; Abe & Fujisaki, 1996; Micali, 2003) between a bank, user and blind office, since both blind office and bank can impersonate user without being noticed.

The problem with the current protocols are that a difficulty resultant from these trust relations when user can repudiate his bad activity (C.S.I, 2002; Jacobson & Wetzel, 2003; Song & Korba, 2004) by claiming that no need to trust both blind office and bank. In this situation it is hard for an unbiased judge to adjudicate between the three entities. The main benefit of the proposed protocol is to avoid blind office and bank from impersonating user, so that user could not repudiate that the entity has abused a coin. Other significant benefits of this scheme are modular, simple design that easy to understand, to apply and to analyze with concern to security needs, for the security analysis we benefits from the modular design of the propose scheme using well known public key encryption schemes. In addition, the proposed scheme is multi-purpose as it allows the integration of multi spendable and divisible coins and supports the challenge semantics. However, the objectives of the chapter are:

1. To modify the existing schemes that is non-repudiation, which when it has to make judge to determine which one to abuse bank, user or blind office. This need encountered in other payment schemes (Trappe & Washington, 2006).
2. Introduce an amendment in the current protocols to provide three characteristics of anonymity, non-repudiation and traceability.
3. To develop an efficient e-payment scheme with anonymity method that achieves prevention of any type of extortion attacks.

BACKGROUND

With the increasing impact of intangible merchandise in worldwide economies and their immediate delivery at small cost, traditional payment systems tend to be more costly than the modern methods. Online service can be worth of value of money smaller than compared with the smallest value of money in physical world. There are two methods of running e-payment systems.

1. On-line payment: in which vendor checks the payment sent by purchaser with a bank before serving the purchaser.
2. Off-line payment: in which double spending must be prevented, and consequently, no on-line link to the bank is needed.

The e-payment schemes can be sub-divided into two groups according to the on-line requirements (Mu, *et al.,* 2001).

1. Payments by transaction method: in which single payment does not need previous arrangements between purchaser and vendor.
2. Payments by account method: in which purchaser and vendor should have system account with bank and certain type of agreement between both before carrying out of real payment transaction.

The payment by transaction can further be divided into two subgroups.

1. The credit card payment transaction: is tailored for large-charge payment of some hundreds or even thousands of dollars. In contrast, net money transaction is usually low-value payment with difficult transaction cost and on-line features, similar to the thought of the e-payment transaction. The drawback of the credit card payment transaction is the fee of transactions, particularly from the perspective of the vendor

that have to pay some bills to the clearing house according to the contract agreement with them. This certainly will have straight impact on the cost policy and the interest between the possible customers.
2. The e-payment by small value transactions on service: This is acquiring certain interest from the area of research. A number of important services of e-payment are e-publishing and multimedia service. In these services, due to the small transaction amount, the merchant acquires relatively shopping mall revenue from every transaction.

As a result, expensive calculations such as digital signature should be limited in order to reduce the investments in software applications. In the recent years, e-payments (Van, 2001; Van, 2003; Wang, *et al.,* 2002; Yen *et al.,* 1999) offering a relatively key improvement in the online revenue malls. The foundation of e-payments is to take benefit of the high level of viewers by present content for a low price. Other alternative of this thought is to rating fractions of cents for equally fractional contents sums. The main features in e-payment protocol are less charges of payment amount and high occurrence of transactions on the e-commerce system.

E-PAYMENT PROTOCOL REQUIREMENTS

The e-payment protocol encompasses three participants

1. User: The user (customer) purchases e-currency from the Bank (broker) employing actual money by e-payment. The user can then utilize e-currency to carry out e-payment buy goods.
2. Merchant: The merchant is the databank, provides user with both services and information.

3. Bank: The bank is the trusted authority. It mediates between user and merchant in order to simplify the duties they carry out. In general, the bank acts like a broker but gives the e-coins for the e-payments.

While using e-currency, a shared set of characteristics for an e-payment protocol is:

1. Anonymity: e-cash must not supply any user information; it means that it must be anonymous e-currency transaction.
2. Divisibility: e-cash can be sub-divided since the currency has a basic piece.
3. Transference: e-cash can be transferred to a trusted authority by offering the suitable amount of currency.
4. Over spending detection: e-cash must be used for only once.

The e-payments are stored and then converted to digital form, which caused new difficulties for the development of secure e payment protocol; the payment is simply to be duplicated in contrary to the conventional physical paying instruments. As the digital payment is characterized as simple sequences of bits, nothing in them stops them copying. When a security of the payment protocol is reliant on the method the payments are hidden from unknown, any individual that can have access to payments maybe use them numerous times. We notice that getting anonymous cash transaction is an important issue, and at the same time giving efficiency is another matter. In this chapter, we study a merchant e-payment protocol (Hwang & Sung, 2006); that gives anonymity characteristic using the idea of blinding signature scheme and hash chain. We then introduce an enhancement of the blinding signature scheme used in the protocol for reaching better efficiency without bargaining its security.

RELATED WORKS

This section provides an overview of related work and identifies the fundamental weaknesses of the existing proposed e-payment schemes.

In 1982 Chaum (Chaum, 1983) proposed a scheme entitled "Blind signature for untraceable payment". He aimed at creating an electronic version of money, he introduced the notion of "coins" and "blind signature" which allow a message to be signed without revealing to the signer any information on the message, he claimed a coin cannot be easily traced from the bank to the shop, furthermore, two spending for a same user cannot be linked together and he defined an electronic coin as number with a certificate (signature) produced by the bank, it is withdrawn from the bank, spent by the customer and deposit by the shop. This scheme does not provide transferability and fairness that is might be misused by fraudulent to perform a perfect crime.

In 1988 Chaum, Fiat and Naor (Chaum *et al.*, 1988) proposed a scheme entitled "Untraceable electronic cash", in this scheme they introduced the first practical electronic cash system, using the blind signature paradigm to provide privacy and security for all involved parties and they presented in their approach removes the requirement that the shopkeeper must contact the bank during every transaction.

In 1995 Brickell, peter and David proposed a scheme entitled "Trustee-based Tracing Extensions to Anonymous Cash and the Making of Anonymous Exchange" in this scheme (Brickell *et al.*, 1995) they introduced the electronic payment system which incorporate with trustee to trace the anonymity if it misused but otherwise provably protect user anonymity and they introduced an online anonymous change-making protocol which address a major stumbling block for anonymous payment system to exchange anonymously one set of coins for another set of coins of equal total value, but different denominations. The system protection against multiple-spending of electronic money and other fraud remains intact.

In 1995 Stadler, Piveteau, Camenisch proposed a scheme entitled "Fair Blind signature" (Stadler. *et al.,* 1995). In this scheme They proposed a new type of blind signatures called fair blind signature which used to design a payment systems protecting privacy, the proposed scheme allow to meet the requirements of all parties, it is guarantee the anonymity of the payment customer's but it helps the trustee to revoke anonymity when it required (e.g. for legal reasons) and it provides a solution against money laundering and blackmailing. This system cannot list all of coins owned by a particular user.

In 1996 Jan, Ueli, Stadler proposed a scheme entitled "Digital payment system with passive anonymity revoking trustee" (Camenisch, & Stadler, 1996). In this scheme They proposed the efficient anonymous payment system in which a trustee is neither involved in payment transaction nor in the opening of an account, but only in case of a justified suspicious transaction, a trustee is completely passive unless he is asked to revoke the anonymity of a customer, also it can be used in on-line or off-line payment system, they introduce the concept of Fairness for (non transferable) e-payment.

In 1996 M'Raihi proposed a scheme entitled "Cost Effective Payment Scheme with privacy Regulation" (M'Raihi, 1996). In this scheme introduced a new electronic money methodology: sub-contracting the blinding to a trustee using an identity-based piece of information to achieve provable privacy and security by combines the usage of a pseudonym, strongly linked to user's with the delegation of public-key, but it like previous trustee-based schemes do not protect the bank against bank-robbery where an attacker obtains the secret keys of the bank and showed how to prevent against this attack.

In 2001 Liu, Wei and Wong proposed a scheme entitled "Recoverable and Untraceable E-cash" (Liu *et al.,* 2001). In this scheme they proposed that an e-cash protocol which support recoverability and un-traceability properties of e-cash systems simultaneously, such that it allows users to recover their lost e-cash while maintaining anonymity provided that they have not double-spent their e-cash, their system still off-line and it combines the advantage of a debit-based and credit-based systems together.

In 2004 Song and Korba proposed a scheme entitled "How to Make e-Cash with Non-Repudiation and Anonymity" (Song & Korba, 2004). In this scheme They proposed that an e-cash system in which a one-time public key (temporary anonymous) is embedded in the partial blind signature to provide the non-repudiation services against the problem exist in e-cash systems like denying, losing, misusing, stealing and double-spending and they also demonstrate that the combination of partial blind digital signature and anonymous digital signature make the e-cash systems more robust and fair than before. This scheme depends on high trust relation between bank, user and trustee so the bank and the trustee can impersonate the user without being noticed.

In 2005 Binh proposed a scheme entitled "Fair Payment System with Online Anonymous Transfer" (Binh, 2007). In this scheme he proposed e-cash system that support anonymous transfer and fairness using Group signature protocol and he provide a flexible and privacy fundamental to e-commerce while providing an avenues for law enforcement to expose the users who abuse the system for illegal activities, the proposed protocol can deal with off-line payment and micro payment, but is unable to stop extortion threats and the employs of blindfolded schemes.

In 2006 Hwang and Sung proposed their protocol entitled study of e-payment based on one-way hash chain (Binh, 2007) which gives user anonymity by implementing a blinding signature scheme using elliptic curve encryption scheme (Koblitz, 1987).

In 2008 Marina proposed a scheme entitled "Improved Conditional E-Payments" (Marina, B., 2008). In this scheme she depends on the "conditional e-payment" that introduced by shi et al. she proposed in her scheme that a payer obtains an electronic coin and can transfer it to a payee under a certain condition, in her work she formalized the security of a conditional e-payment scheme and gives a solution based on CL-signatures and she completely avoids cut-and-choose techniques also eliminate the need for the bank to be involved in all conditional transfer protocols by making the protocol off-line

THE GENERAL E-PAYMENT SCHEME

In this section we will describe the general e-payment scheme which is appropriate for both the existing protocols and the suggested protocol. However, it includes five entities a user U, a blind office O, a bank B, a judge J, and a shop S. It works as follows:

- U Obtains a coin C signed blindly by B.
- B Keeps a relations proof among U's real identifier ID and pseudo identifier PID.
- O Participated in the blind signature, holds another relations proof among PID and C.
- To spend C, U proofs to S that he has information of secret key x according to C.
- If C is misused, for example double spending, B and O will work together to construct a link among ID and C, and J will be participated in this procedure to judge.

Assume that U and B both have an exponent key type signatures denoted by (S_U, V_U) and (S_B, V_B) respectively, such that V_U is known to B and V_B is known to U, O and S. Assume also that O has an exponent public-key cryptosystem, denoted by (E_o, D_o), such that E_o is known to U and B, J could be verified all the schemes. A potential implementation for these cryptosystems is RSA scheme.

The coin contains three fields which are as follows:

1. The exponent key denoted by y for a public key type signature scheme. The corresponding secret signature key is represented by x.
2. The information field i having some pertinent data concerning C, for example its value and expiry dates.
3. The bank's digital signature on both y and i.

There are two different methods of counting i in bank's signature scheme. As follows:

- i could be concatenated with y via O before finding a blinded exponent key represented by y^-
- i Could be added via bank using another signature key based on the information which is being denoted.

In fact, we need the digital signature scheme of the bank to have some feature, that is $S_B(m_1) * S_B(m_2) = S_B(m_1 * m_2)$ which keeps for RSA. Certainly this is usually not preferable property for a digital signature scheme, and for this reason the RSA must always be employed with a special redundancy function or a one-way hash function (Department of Commerce, 1994; Menezes, *et al.*, 1997; Douglas, 2006). In the proposed scheme, we are going to employ a one-way hash function presented by $h(m)$ for the message m with S_B. We will refer to a blinding function by F, and use it as an inverse to the digital signature scheme. Thus $S_B(F(m_1)m_2) = m_1 * S_B(m_2)$, for each m_1, m_2, but when bank digital signature scheme is RSA, then F is just exponentiation employing the public verification key.

THE PROPOSED PROTOCOL

In this section we will introduce the proposed protocol which is as follows:

THE GENERAL PROTOCOL

1. The user U and B generate a shared secret s.
2. Then B signs a one way hash function of s, namely $S_B(h(s))$ which is employed to build PID by concatenating it with $E_o(s)$.
3. Also B keeps a relation proof among ID and s, which we indicate by $\{ID, s\}$. It is a digital signature on $h(s)$ employing S_U.

The Withdraw Protocol

The steps of the proposed protocol for withdrawing a coin work as follows, in which all messages exchanged between B and U are supposed to be encrypted with s when the communication channels between them are insecure.

1. U Picks x randomly, calculate y and then send $E_o(y)$ to O.
2. Both U and O generate a shared w, by employing the Diffie-Hellman scheme (Rivest *et al.,* 1978).
3. O Calculates $y^- = F(w) * y$ and passes it to U.
4. U Proves y^-, and then passes B a message signed employing S_u. This message is invented of s, y^-, O's name and other uses data, for instance the present time and a time stamp, to guarantee that the innovation and uniqueness of the signature is provable.
5. B Holds U's signature scheme, withdraws a true coin from U's account, and then responds to U by $T = E_O(S_B(y^-))$. Then U sends T to O.

6. O Recovers T to get $S_B(y^-)$, then un-blinds $S_B(y)$ to build C, and then passes C to U. Next O keeps $\{PID, C\}$, which contains a record of PID and two public key encryption values, that is the public key encryption value of T with s and the public key encryption value of $E_B(y)$ with s.

The Spending Protocol

To spend C use the following steps:

1. U Sign a message which is created via S as a challenge, to prove U knows x.
2. S Claims a true coin back from B later.
3. If C is double spending, B will request a tracing steps in which B and O work together to construct a link among C and ID, relied on $\{ID, s\}$ and $\{PID, C\}$.

The proposed protocol has three major properties compared with the existing protocols.

1. O Cannot spend C, because does not know x.
2. U Together create a arbitrary w, it guarantee that both O and U can not separately influence the value of w, and therefore both U and O cannot get more than one coin from a one blind signature.
3. B Holds U's signature on y^- as a relationship evidence amongst ID and y^- indicated by $\{ID, y^-\}$. It guarantees that U and B cannot discuss who published x.

For example, in the M'Raihi protocol[6] the bank can connect ID with y^-, it is yet likely for U to reject accountability for C since he has no concept concerning the relationship among y and y^- when creation a contribution to this connection since he is blinded too.

Example: First we must determine the public and private keys for each participant in the protocol.

The Bank

1. Randomly choose two prime numbers $p = 263, q = 347$ (Using Miller-Rabin test)
2. Compute $n = p * q = 263 * 347 = 91261$
3. Compute
    $\theta(n) = (p - 1)(q - 1) = 262 * 246 = 90652$
4. Randomly choose an odd number e in the range $1 < e < \theta(n)$ and relatively is a co-prime to $\theta(n)\varnothing$ that is the $\gcd(e, \theta(n)) = 1$. Thus, we choose $e = 1547$
5. Compute $d = e^1 \bmod \theta(n)$ using Euclidean algorithm) as follows: $1547^{-1} * 32991 \bmod 91261 = 90652$
6. So, bank public key is $(n = 91261, e = 1547)$ and the bank private key is $(\theta = 90652, d = 32991)$

The Blind Office

1. Randomly choose two prime numbers $p = 13, q = 17$ (Using Miller-Rabin test)
2. Compute $n = (p = 13 * q = 17 = 221$
3. Randomly choose an odd number e in the range $1 < c < \theta$ which is co-prime to $\theta(n)$ that is $e \in Z^*_{\theta(n)}$ so $\gcd(e, \theta(n)) = 1$. Suppose we choice $e = 19$
4. Compute
    $\theta(n) = (p - 1)(q - 1) = 12 * 16 = 192$
    Thus, we choose $e = 19$
5. Compute $d = e^{-1} \bmod \theta(n)$ (Using Euclidean algorithm) Thus $d = 19^{-1} \bmod 221 = 192$
6. So, blind office public key is $(n = 221, e = 19)$ whereas blind office private key is $(\theta(n) = 192, d = 91)$.

The User

1. Randomly choose two prime numbers $p = 23, q = 29$. (Using Miller-Rabin test)
2. Compute $n = 23 * 29 = 667$
3. Compute
    $\theta(n) = (p - 1)(q - 1) = 22 * 28 = 616$
4. Randomly choose an odd number e in the range $1 < e < \theta(n)$ which is co-prime to $\theta(n)$ so $\gcd(e, \theta(n)) = 1$. Thus, we choose $e = 61 (e \in z^*_{616})$
5. Compute $d = e^{-1} \bmod \theta(n)$ using Euclidean method. So $e * d \equiv 1 \bmod \theta(n)$ $d = 101 * e = 61 \bmod 667 = 616$
6. So, user public key is $(n = 667, e = 61)$ while user private key is $(\theta(n) = 616, d = 101)$

The General Protocol

The bank B signs $h(s)$ using RSA signature scheme. Note that we assume for simplicity $h(s) = s$.

Signature Generation

Suppose the message m to be signed is share secret $s = m$ 49

$$s_B = m^d \bmod n_B$$

$$= 49^{32991} \bmod 91261 = 90029$$

To verify s_B we will compute the value $v_B(s)$ as follows:

$$v_B = s_B^e \bmod n_B$$

$$= 90029^{1547} \bmod 91261 = 49$$

Table 1. The User U and the Bank B generate shared secret s using Diffie-Hellman protocol and fast exponentiation

User U	Bank B
U, B exchange a prime p and a generator g, such that $p > g$ and g is primitive root of p. Suppose that $g = 7$, $p = 53$	
U generates a random number: x_U suppose $x_U = 6$ (Secret)	B generates a random number: x_B suppose $x_B = 9$ (Secret)
$y_U = g^{x_U} \bmod p$ $y_U = 7^6 \bmod 53 = 42$	$y_B = g^{x_B} \bmod p$ $y_B = 7^p \bmod 53 = 43$
U receives $y_B = 43$	B receives $y_U = 42$
$s = y_B^{x_B} \bmod p$ $s = 43^6 \bmod 53 = 49$	$s = y_U^{x_B} \bmod p$ $s = 42^9 \bmod 53 = 49$

To Encrypt (s)

The user U must use the office O public key $(n_O = 221, e_O = 19)$ to encrypt the message $m = s$.

$$c = m^{e_O} \bmod n_o$$

$$= 49^{19} \bmod 221 = 179$$

Using fast exponentiation
To verify the above value we will compute $d_O(s)$ as follows:

$$v_O = c^d \bmod n_O = 179^{91} \bmod 221 = 49$$

The user U will construct the *PID* by concatenating $s_B(s)$ with $e_O(s)$

$$PID = s_B(s) \,||\, e_O(s)$$

$$PID = 90029 \,||\, 179$$

The bank B keeps $s_U(s)$ as a relation among $U'sID$ and $s \{ID's\}$. So, $s_U(s)$ is

$$s_B = s^d \bmod n_B$$

$$= 49^{101} \bmod 667 = 170$$

To verify the above value we will compute the $v_U(s)$ as follows:

$$v_U(s) = s_B^e \bmod n_B$$

$$= 170^{61} \bmod 667 = 49$$

The Withdraw Protocol

1. The user U picks randomly $x = 3$ and $g = 2$
2. Calculates $y = g^x \bmod p$ where p is prime and $g \in z_p^*$ has order of q So,
   $$y = 2^3 \bmod 23 = 8$$

3. Computes $e_O(y) = y^d \bmod n_O$
   $= 8^{19} \bmod 221 = 70$ and then sends
   $e_O(y)$ to O

4. Both user U and office O generate a shared $w = 3$ using Diffie-Hellman

5. Office O calculates $y^- = f(w) * y$ and pass it to the user U *as follows*

$$y^- = f(3) * 8$$

Note that because of the bank digital signature scheme is RSA, f is exponentiation employing the public verification key, so $f(w) = v_B(w)$. Now we will compute $v_B(3)$ as follows:

$$v_B(3) = m^e \bmod n_B$$

$$3^{1547} \bmod 91261 = 10510$$

To verify the result we will compute the $s_B(v_B(3))$ as follows:

$$s_B(v_B(3)) = v_B^d \bmod n_B$$

$$= 10510^{32991} \bmod 91261 = 3$$

Then we will compute $y^- = f(w) * y$

$$= 10510 * 8 = 84080$$

Note: we assume that both O and U encrypt and decrypt the exchanged y^-

1. The user U will do same steps that done by O to calculate y^- then he will pass it to B the message contains $\{s, y^-, O's\ name, time\ stamp\}$ signed by them using s_U

2. The bank B holds $U's$ signature scheme, withdraw a true coin C from a $U's$ account,

then responds to $U's$ by $T = e_O(s_B(y^-))$. B will compute $s_B(y^-)$ as follows:

$$s_B(y^-) = y^{-d} \bmod n_B$$

$$= 84080^{32991} \bmod 91261 = 14986$$

We will verify $v_B(s_B(y^-))$ as follows:

$$v_B(s_B(y^-)) = s_B(y^-)^e \bmod n_B$$

$$= 14986^{1547} \bmod 91261 = 84080$$

Note that we assume both office O and bank B encrypt and decrypt the exchanged $s_B(y^-)$. Here, O must un-blinds the received message $s_B(y^-)$ to get $s_B(y)$

The Un-Blinding $s_B(y^-)$

$$s_B(y) = w^{-1} * s_B(y^-) \bmod n_B$$
$$= 3^{-1} * 14986 \bmod 91261 = 60841 * 14986 \bmod 91261 = 65836$$

To verify our claim is true, we will compute the $s_B(y)$ as follows:

$$s_B(y) = m^d \bmod n$$

$$8^{32991} \bmod 91261 = 65836$$

Then we will verify $v_B(s_B(y))$ as follows:

$$v_B(s_B(y)) = s_B(y)^e \bmod n$$

$$= 65836^{1547} \bmod 91261 = 8$$

We note that the values of $s_B(y)$ are equal in both ways when compute the value of $s_B(y)$ so it is satisfied our claim.

SECURITY OF THE SCHEME

For the security evaluation we gain from the modular design of proposed scheme employing well known cryptography schemes. Though, all possible threads can be shown to be avoided. The security analysis is clearly controlled as we avoided interaction between the methods as much as possible. We now plan the proofs that the novel scheme has several security characteristics. However, we assume that all entities B, U, O, J and S, do not conspire with every other one.

Theorem 1: U can not get C without the participation of bank and O.

Proof 1: to get C without bank and O be participated, U should be able to calculate $S_B(y^-)$ from y^- or from $E_O(S_B(y^-))$, each of which is supposed to be infeasible.

Theorem 2: The entity who is the publisher of secret key x can only be spending a valid coin pertinent to x.

Proof 2: it is computationally infeasible to decrypt x from given y even with other allied known data, because the secret key x is known just to its publisher and is not disclosed to any other person. So, the acquaintance of x is needed to spend C, the outcomes follows.

Theorem 3: O cannot masquerade as U to B or to S.

Proof 3: To impersonate U to B, O should find U's digital signature on the y^- selected by O, which is supposed to be infeasible. To impersonate U to S for spending, O should be acquainted with both C and x. As U is able to prove y^-, O cannot blind U and then get bank's digital signature scheme on y^- according to his private x. So, it is infeasible for O to find C and its equivalent x.

Theorem 4: When the bank impersonate U to get and to spend C, he cannot claim that U published the coin.

Proof 4: To verify $\{ID, y^-\}$, the bank required U's digital signature on y^- such a digital signature cannot be computed even with O's cooperation, when U is not participated in the coin creation.

We conclude this discussion with a following consequence. When a coin with a relationship of $\{ID, C\}$ is abused, U cannot repudiate accountability for this misuse because this assumption is depending on theorems 2, 3, and 4. The real coin with a relationship of $\{ID, C\}$ holds by both B and O should be related to a secret key x in which published by U and as a result U is the only entity able to spend C.

CONCLUSION

We introduced an efficient e-payment protocol with three characteristics of anonymity, non-repudiation and traceability. It is one of the first protocols that achieve prevention of any type of extortion threads. On account of its high security and efficiency, it can be gauged for two key applications of secure internet e-payment and efficient e-purse, where the efficiency and security requirements are completely different. In the chapter we described a possible repudiation difficulty in current payment protocols and suggested an alternative protocol to conquer the difficulty. The primary benefit of the new protocol is that both B and O cannot impersonate U to find and to spend C without being discovered. Thus if U misuses C, he cannot repudiate it via proposing that it is performed by both B and O. This benefit is at the user computational cost are more burdensome than for the existing protocols, since the user requires to make pre- calculations of the digital signature scheme when employing digital signature scheme for spending C.

REFERENCES

Abe, M., & Fujisaki, E. (1996). *How to Date Blind Signatures*. Advances in Cryptology (pp.244-251), (ASIACRYPT '96. Binh D. Vo, (2007), *A Fair Payment Scheme with On-line Anonymous Transfer* (pp.3-27) MS.c Thesis, MIT.

Brickell, E., Gemmell, P., & Kravitz, D. (1995). Trustee-based Tracing Extensions to Anonymous Cash and the Making of Anonymous Exchange. In *Proceeding of 6th International Conference of ACM-SIAM SODA* (pp. 457-466).

Camenisch, M., & Stadler, M. (1996). Digital Payment Systems with Passive anonymity-revoking trustees. *Computer Security-ESORICS 96, (Lecture Notes in Computer Security 1146 pp.33-34)*. New York: Springer-Verlag.

Chaum, D. (1983). *Blind Signature for untraceable payments. Advances in Cryptology, Crypto '82* (pp. 199–203). New York: Plenum Press.

Chaum, D., Amost, F., & Moni, N. Untraceable Electronic Cash, *Advances in Cryptology - CRYPTO '88, (LNCS 403, pp. 318-327)*.

C.S.I. 2002, Cyber Crime Bleeds U.S Corporations, Survey Shows, Financial Losses from Attacks Climb for Third Year in row, www.gocsi.com.

Department of Commerce. National Institute of Standards and Technology, (1994). Digital Signature Standard. *Federal Information Processing Standard Publication 186*, USA.

Douglas, R. Stinson, (2006). Cryptography and Practice (pp.232-254). Hartford, CT: CRT Press

Hohenberger, S. (2006), *Advances in Signatures Encryption and E-Cash from Bilinear Group (pp.95-142)*, PhD Thesis, MIT.

Hwang, M. S., & Sung, P. C. (2006). A study of micro-payment based on one-way hash chain. *International Journal of Network Security*, 2(2), 81–90.

Jacobson, M., & Youg, M. (1997), Applying Anti-Trust Policies to Increase Trust in a Versatile E-Money System. In *Proceeding of International Workshop on Financial Cryptography*, (21 pages).

Jacobson & Markus Wetzel. (2003). Security Weaknesses in Bluetooth, Retrieved from www.bell.labs.com.

Kanniainen. L., (2001). The Perfect Payment Architecture. *Technical Document Mobey Forum*, Retrieved from www.mobeyforum.

Koblitz, N. (1987). Elliptic Curve Cryptosystems. *Mathematics of Computation, 48*, 203–209.

Kungpisdan, S., Srivnivasan, B., & Le, P. D. (2004), A Secure Account-Based Mobile Payment Protocol. In *Proceedings of the International Conference on Information Technology: Coding and Computing, (ITCC '04)*.

Li, Y., & Li, J. (2006). Application Study on Public Key Cryptography in Mobile Payment. In *Proceeding of the 5th WSEAS International Conference on Information Security and Privacy*, Venice, Italy, November 20-22.

Liu, J. K., Wei, V. K., & Wong, S. H. (2001). Recoverable and Untraceable E-Cash, EUROCON' 2001. *Trends in Communications, International Conference on Information Technology, 1*, 342-349.

M'Raihi, D. (1996). Cost Effective Payment Schemes with Privacy Regulation: Advances in Cryptology. *ASIACRYPT 96, ([)*.New York: Springer-Verlag.]. *Lecture Notes in Computer Science, 1163*, 266–275. doi:10.1007/BFb0034853

Marina, B. (2008). *Improved conditional e-payment. Department of Computer Science and Engineering* (pp. 18–19). University of Notre Dame.

Menezes, P. Van. Oorschot, & Vanstone S, (1997). *Handbook of Applied Cryptography* (pp.321-358), Hartford, CT: CRT Press.

Micali, S. (2003), Simple and Fast Optimistic Protocols for fair e-exchange.In *proceeding in International Conference of 22nd Annual ACM Symposia. On Principles of Distributed Computing (PODC'03)*(pp. 12-19).New York: ACM Press

Mu, Y., Nguyen, K. Q., & Varadharajan, V. (2001). A fair electronic cash scheme. In *Proc. of the International Symposium in Electronic Commerce,(LNCS 2040, pp. 20-32.)*New York: Springer-Verlag, NCSC-TG-017.(2000).*A Guide to understanding Identification and Authentication in Trusted Systems*, U.S National Computer Center.

Rivest, R., Shmir, A., & Adlman, L. (1978). A Method for Obtaining Digital Signatures and Public Key Cryptosystems. *Communications of the ACM, 21*, 294–299. doi:10.1145/359340.359342

Solms, V., & Naccache, D. (1992). Blind Signatures and Perfect Crimes. *Computers & Security, 11*,581–583.doi:10.1016/0167-4048(92)90193-U

Solms, V., & Naccache, D. (1992). Blind Signatures and Perfect Crimes. *Intl. J. Computers & Security, 11*, 581–583. doi:10.1016/0167-4048(92)90193-U

Song. R., & Larry Korba, (2004). How to Make E-cash with Non-Repudiation and Anonymity, In *Proceedings of the International Conference on Information Technology: Coding and Computing, (ITCC'04*, 167-172).

Stadler, M., Piveteau, J. M., & Camenisch, J. (1995). Fair blind signature. In Proc. EURO-CRYPT 95,(LNCS,Vol 921, pp. 209–219). New York: Springer-Verlag

Trappe W., & Lawrence Washington, (2006). *Introduction to Cryptography with Coding Theory, 2nd Edition*,(pp.287-295), Upper Saddle River, NJ: Prentice Hall.

Van Someren, N. (2001). The practical problems of implementing Micromint. In *Proc. of the International Conference of Financial Cryptography*,(LNCS 2339,pp.41-50).New York: Springer-Verlag.

Van Someren, N., Odlyzko, A., Rivest, R., Jones, T., & Scot, D. G. (2003). Does anyone really need micropayments? *Proceeding of the International Conference of Financial Cryptography, (LNCS 2742,pp.69-76)*. New York: Springer-Verlag.

Wang, C., Chang, C., & Lin, C. (2002). A new micro-payment system using general payword chain. *Electronic Commerce Research Journal, 2*(1-2), 159–168. doi:10.1023/A:1013360606669

Yen, S., Ho, L., & Huang, C. (1999). Internet micro-payment based on unbalanced one-way binary tree. *In Proc. of the International Conference of Cryptec'99*, 155-162.

Zheng, X., & Chen, D. (2003). Study of Mobile Payments System. Proceedings *of the IEEE International Conference on E-Commerce, (CEC'03)*.

ADDITIONAL READING

Baddeley, M. (2004). Using e-cash in the new economy: An economic analysis of micro-payment systems. *Journal of Electronic Commerce Research, 5*(4).

Chien, H., Jan, J., & Tseng, Y. (2001). RSA-based partially blind signature with low computation, In *Proceeding of the International Conference in Parallel and Distributed Systems*, (pp. 385–389), USA.

Foo, E., & Boyd, C. (1998). a payment scheme using vouchers, In *Proceeding of the International Conference of Financial Cryptography,(LNCS 1465, pp.103-121)*.New York: Springer-Verlag.

Glassman, S., Manasse, M., Abadi, M., Gauthier, P., & Sobalvarro, P. (1995). The Millicent protocol for inexpensive electronic commerce. In Proceeding *of the International World Wide Web Conference,* (pp. 603–618), Sebastopol, CA: O'Reilly.

Hubaux, J., & Buttyan, L. (2003). A micro-payment scheme encouraging collaboration in multi-hop cellular networks. In *Proceeding of Financial Cryptography,* (LNCS 2742, pp.15-33) New York: Springer-Verlag.

Kim, S., & Lee, W. (2003). A Pay-word-based micro-payment protocol supporting multiple payments. In *Proceeding of the International Conference on Computer Communications and Networks,* (pp. 609-612).

Mu, Y., Nguyen, K., & Varadharajan, V. (2001). A fair electronic cash scheme, In *Proceeding of the International Symposium in Electronic Commerce, (LNCS 2040, pp.20-32).* New York: Springer-Verlag.

Rivest, R. (1997), Electronic lottery tickets as micro payments, In *Proceeding of the International Conference of Financial Cryptography, (LNCS 1318, pp.307-314).* Springer-Verlag, Someren N, Odlyzko A, Rivest R, Jones T and Scot D, (2003), does any*one really need micro payments, in proceeding of the International Conference of Financial Cryptography,* LNCS 2742, Springer-Verlag, pp. 69-76.

Wang, C., Chang, C., & Lin, C. (2002). a new micro-payment system using general pay-word chain, Electronic Commerce. *Research Journal,* 2(1-2), 159–168.

Yen S, Ho L and L Huang L, (1999), *Internet micro-payment based on unbalanced one-way binary tree*, In Proceeding the International Conference of Cryptec'99, 155-162, 1999

KEY TERMS AND DEFINITIONS

Anonymity: E-cash must not supply any user information; it means that it must be anonymous e-currency transaction.

Bank: The bank is the trusted authority. It mediates between user and merchant in order to simplify the duties they carry out. In general, the bank acts like a broker but gives the e-coins for the e-payments.

Divisibility: E-cash can be sub-divided since the currency has a basic piece.

E-Payment System Goal: is to transfer money in a secure way from the customer's account to the shop's account.

E-Payment System: is a scheme that allows people to carry out commercial activities in e-domain.

Internet: is a tool designed to allow computers to easily interconnect and to assure that network connections will be maintained even when various links may be damaged.

Merchant: The merchant is the databank, provides user with both services and information.

Off-Line Payment: In which double spending must be prevented, and consequently, no on-line link to the bank is needed.

On-Line Payment: In which vendor checks the payment sent by purchaser with a bank before serving the purchaser.

Over Spending Detection: E-cash must be used for only once.

Payments by Account Method: In which purchaser and vendor should have system account with bank and certain type of agreement between both before carrying out of real payment transaction.

Payments by Transaction Method: In which single payment does not need previous arrangements between purchaser and vendor.

Secure E-Payment System: is a protecting privacy scheme that can be seen as a protocol involving a customer, a shop and a bank.

The Credit Card Payment Transaction: Is tailored for large-charge payment of some hundreds or even thousands of dollars.

The E-Payment Payment by Small Value Transactions on Service: This is acquiring certain interest from the area of research. A number of important services of e-payment are e-publishing and multimedia service.

Transference: E-cash can be transferred to a trusted authority by offering the suitable amount of currency.

User: The user (customer) purchases e-currency from the Bank (broker) employing actual money by e-payment. The user can then utilize e-currency to carry out e-payment buy goods.

Section 2
The Strategies

Chapter 3

Electronic Banking as a Strategy for Customer Service Improvement in the Developing Economy

Asma Mobarek
Stockholm Business School, Sweden

ABSTRACT

The objective of the chapter is to present a brief review of E-banking services especially in the developing economies, highlighting the major challenges of E-banking with a guideline or recommendations to address those challenges. Technology has introduced new ways of delivering banking to the customer. Developed countries (DC) customers of the E-Banking services are fully aware of the services but the customer's in the developing economies still lag behind. It is clearly seen that delivery channels are lacking in meeting the demands of the customer by not making them aware of e-banking and using obsolete or not too up-to-date technology. I would thus conclude that banks in the developing countries should drown themselves in all the intricacies regarding e-banking to determine ways that will affect the customers in and use it to their maximum benefit. The other issue is that there are very few or no banking facilities in the rural areas and furthermore, access to the internet is close to impossible in these areas therefore awareness and utilization of these services is very little or none at all. At last but not the least is that Banks must adapt to the electronics age. Consumers demand it. Economics drives it. Banks must exploit it.

DOI: 10.4018/978-1-61520-635-3.ch003

INTRODUCTION

The value of banking services must now be judged and seen through customer perceptions of service quality and overall satisfaction. By focusing on customer service in terms of service quality and by using e-banking which permits well designed and structured automated applications, banks can deliver quality customer service. Equally important is the ability of the bank to customise customer service to meet raised customer profiles. Being able to listen to customers is crucial for the bank. So customer service must be an indicator of excellent bank performance in which e-banking plays a significant function

Technology has introduced new ways of delivering banking to the customer. Developed countries (DC) customers of the E-Banking services are fully aware of the services but the customer's in the developing economies are still lag behind. It is clearly seen that delivery channels are lacking in meeting the demands of the customer by not making them aware of e-banking and using obsolete or not too up-to-date technology.

Banks in the DC are faced with a number of important questions, for example how to take full advantage of new technology opportunities, how e-developments change, and the ways customers interact with the financial services provider etc. One of the important aspects of recent discussion on E-banking is the customer relationships. Creating close relationships with the customers is one way of instilling awareness of the available electronic banking services, which in turn promote utilization. Poor customer service in the banking industry in developing countries have resulted in high numbers of customer complaints about poor quality of banking services, negative perception and low customer satisfaction. This has in turn resulted in customers switching between banks in the industry and making customer retention difficult.

The objective of the chapter is to present a brief review of E-banking services especially in the developing economies, highlighting the major challenges of E-banking in the developing Economies with a guideline or recommendations to address those challenges.

I would thus conclude that banks in the developing countries should drown themselves in all the intricacies regarding e-banking to determine ways that will affect the customers in and use it to their maximum benefit. The other issue is that there are very few or no banking facilities in the rural areas and furthermore, access to the internet is close to impossible in these areas therefore awareness and utilization of these services is very little or none at all. Most of the people in developing countries reside in rural areas and this reflects that there is no awareness and utilization of electronic banking services. At last but not the least is that Banks must adapt to the electronics age. Consumers demand it. Economics drives it. Banks must exploit it. Hence, it is imperative for banks to align their strategies in response to customers' needs and developments in technology.

The rest of the chapter is organized as follows: section 1.1 discusses the evolution of E Banking; section 1.2 presents the advantages of E-banking. Section 1.3 highlights the major challenges of E-Banking especially in the developing economies, section 1.4 prescribes recommendation to overcome the challenges and finally section 1.5 reports the conclusions.

EVOLUTION OF E-BANKING

Technological developments have brought new opportunities for banks. The evolution of the e-banking industry can be traced to the early 1970s. Banks began to look at e-banking as a means to replace some of their traditional bank functions, for two reasons. Firstly, branches were very expensive to set up and maintain due to the large overheads associated with them. Secondly e-banking product/ services like ATM and electronic fund transfer were a source of differentiation for banks that utilized them. Being in a fiercely competitive industry, the ability of banks to differentiate themselves on the basis of price is limited.

E-banking is the newest delivery channel for banking services. In recent years, internet banking usage has become one of the most important e-commerce environments (Wang, Y. et al., 2003). Sohail and Shanmugham (2003) pointed out that a bank's promotional efforts indeed facilitate awareness of internet banking adoption and its benefits. Technology has introduced new ways of delivering banking to the customer, such as ATMs and Internet Banking. Hence, Banks have found themselves at the forefront of technology adoption for the past three decades. Increasing labor costs in the 1960s placed pressure on labor intensive industries like banking to look forward automating some of their functions. Barclays Bank was the first to envisage the potential of ATMs, and introduced the first ever ATM in 1967. Initially, ATMs were not sophisticated, and served only as cash dispensers. Originally, banks offering an ATM service achieved an advantage over their competitors (O'Hanlon et al., 1993). There was scant understanding of the customers' needs or expectations and the role of ATMs large in bank's retail delivery system was vague (Violano et al., 1992). In the early market stage, ATM was a product based on a radical technological innovation, and did not represent a solution to a customer need at that point in time. In the mid-1970s, features like cash balance inquiry, deposits and funds transfer that permitted these customers to conduct the majority of their routine transactions without visiting a bank branch (O'Hanlon et al., 1993). By the late 1980s, ATMs were viewed as a generic service, a commodity with no competitive advantage. Since then Internet Banking has been able to successfully cross the chasm as a complete service within the financial service industry. According to the Gartners Group's 1999 report, there has been

a rapid growth in online PC banking in the USA; from just over 0 million in 1999 to the projected 35 million by the year 2003 with a rapid shift in internet access (Barto, 1999). Consumer growth in some European countries such as Germany, Norway and Sweden has been similar (Bons, 1999; Slywotzky, 2001). In an attempt to solidify and expand customer relationships and stay ahead of the competition, banks are turning to the next generation of personalized online services-internet banking portals and mobile banking (Saatcioglu et al., 2001). However, this dynamic revolution needs to spread out to the world economy. Berg et al, (2001) mentioned that awareness is greatly influenced by the level advertising by the sales and marketing departments and the banking services are not easy to advertise.

However, the evolution of internet banking is now a well-accepted approach in the developed economy. Essinger. (1992) found that electronic payment system originated because the general public wanted a more convenient and rapid means of assessing their bank accounts. He concludes that the electronic payment systems arena will become even more interesting and challenging than it has in the past, as financial institutions strive to plan and implement electronic payment system, which meet the needs of existing customers and attract new customers. Similarly, O' Mahony et al, (1997) stated that the unstoppable growth of the internet & the tidal wave of electronic commerce that follows in it's indicate that electronic methods will be supplant conventional payments in the years to come. Chou and Chow, (2000) pointed out that in 1999, seven million US households used online banking (at the time, this represented approximately one-fifth households with online capabilities). Since that time, this numbers have increased significantly, and they are expected to increase considerably in the years ahead, for instance, are said to attract more than 10,000 new users daily. Earlier studies done on customer service in banks in Botswana, a developing country also revealed that some of the causes of poor customer service are negligence and transaction errors; long queues in banking halls; unreliable ATMs; long processing time; high cost of banking services; as well as inaccessible management teams (Bareki, 2004).

ADVANTAGES OF E-BANKING

The advantages or benefits of using e-Banking are as follows: retention of customers, developing a new customer base, and capturing greater share of depositor assets; offering low-cost checking and high-yield certificates of deposit; providing attractive possibilities for remote account access including availability of inquiry and transaction services around the clock; worldwide connectivity; easy access to transaction data; and direct customer control of international movement of funds without intermediation of financial institutions. The advantages or benefits of using e-Banking can be pointed out as follows:

1. Internet banking is a means of retaining increasingly sophisticated customers, developing a new customer base and capturing a greater share of depositor assets.
2. Since internet banks generally have lower operational and transactional costs than do traditional brick-and-mortar banks, they are often able to offer low-cost checking and high-yield certificates of deposit
3. E-banking is quick, more convenient, and easily accessible; hardly any queuing problems, efficient, economy of time, convenient, immediate information on account status, time-saving, less taxing than going to the bank, do not have to face sometimes impolite bank employees. It is safer, more comfortable.
4. E-Banking provides a variety of attractive possibilities for remote account access including availability of inquiry and transaction services around the clock; worldwide connectivity; easy access to transaction

data, both recent and historical; and direct customer control of international movement of funds without intermediation of financial institutions in customer's jurisdiction.

In summary, optimal usage of e-banking usage enables a bank to increase their market share, improove customer service, reduce operational costs, beat competiton, and meet globalised market needs.

MAJOR CHALLENGES

The introduction of electronic banking promises to expand the banks' markets for new products and services. On the pessimistic side, although banks have always been exposed to risks such as fraud and error, the magnitude of those risks and the swiftness with which they can crop up have changed dramatically due to the banks' dependence on the technological advance in computers and telecommunication systems. The challenges of E-banking industry can result into the problems listed below when it is poorly implemented.

1. Loss of confidence due to unauthorized activity on customer account.
2. Disclosure or theft of confidential customer information to unauthorized parties commonly referred to as hackers.
3. Failure to deliver on marketing promises.
4. Failure to provide reliable service due to high frequency as well as long period of service disruptions resulting from technology breakdown.
5. Customer complaints resulting in difficulties in usage of e-banking and the failure of the institution help desk to resolution the problems.
6. Confusion between the services provided by the financial institution and those provided by other organizations linked to the banks website.

Since electronic money is becoming a popular means of payment, this raises policy concerns for central banks, which are the overseers of payment systems, managers of monetary policy, regulators of the financial system, and issuers of currency. Electronic money developments also bring in some consumer protection issues, and gives rise to competition between traditional banks and non-bank issuers of electronic cash. The accessibility of bank information through computer terminals and telephones improves customer services and internal operations but, at the same time, it increases the risks of error and abuse of the bank's information. There is a possibility of information getting lost and/or intercepted and ultimately falling in the hands of criminals. It is, therefore, the responsibility of banks to ensure that security is adequate to guard against unauthorised access to customer information. Operational risks can arise from customer misuse, and from inadequately designed or implemented electronic banking and electronic money systems. Other disadvantages originate from organisational and legal implications of electronic banking for banks.

Criminals have discovered that crime can be carried out with fewer risks through the use of computers than when using traditional ways of bank robberies and other crimes; this is a direct result of technological development. It is imperative, therefore, for regulators and bankers to review systems and procedures used to combat money laundering and to monitoring electronic banking activities so as to manage new risks and challenges brought-out by rapid technological changes. The challenges presented by electronic banking and electronic money laundering include, but are not limited to, risk management challenges; strengthening KYC requirements especially for electronic products and services; setting up the necessary infrastructure to attract electronic banking and developing national strategies to combat money laundering; capacity building for supervisory authorities and addressing problems brought about by informal financial sector. Electronic banking offers a number of risk management challenges for the supervisory authorities.

The Internet is everywhere and global by nature. It is an open network accessible from anywhere in the world by unknown parties, with routing of messages through unknown locations and via fast evolving wireless devices. Therefore, it significantly magnifies the importance of security controls, customer authentication techniques, data protection, audit trail procedures, and customer privacy standards. The above risk challenges could also exacerbate money laundering activities. For example, the rolling out of new business in a very short time frame could lead to banks attracting business from criminals because the screening process would not have been thorough. It is also possible that outsourcing arrangements with third parties, most of whom may be unregulated, could result in banks having relationships with companies controlled by criminals. The accessibility of the Internet worldwide also provides an opportunity for electronic money laundering, which threatens to be a menace in the digital age. It is, l. therefore, important that less developed countries to ensure that banks in their jurisdictions adhere to the risk management principles for electronic banking, which are grouped into three broad areas of board and management oversight, security controls, and legal and reputational risk management. The informal financial sector is very active in many countries and because it is regulated in most developing countries, the region could still become a safe shelter for launderers once comprehensive anti-money laundering measures are applied to the formal financial sector. It is, therefore, important that an anti-money laundering legislation be extended to all sectors of the economy and those guidelines for electronic banking activities should apply to both banking and non-banking entities.

Khalfan, AlRefaei and Al-Hajery (2006) assessed factors influencing the adoption of internet banking in Oman using a descriptive case study analysis. This topic was chosen in order to extend the current investigation into the implications of internet banking in today's world. But more specifically, the study aimed to present a systematic discussion of the issues underlying the slow adoption of IT in the Omani banking sector. This is contrary to the reality that banks were gradually becoming more aware of the importance of e-banking in this era were the internet has emerged as a key competitive arena for the future of financial services. The main aims of the research were to find out the main factors inhibiting the adoption of electronic commerce; in the Omani banking sector; and find out if the banking technical infrastructure is supportive to the building of EC applications. The main findings of the study are summarized as follows: Lack of formulating a wide Information System (IS) or Information Technology (IT) definition and strategy in the organization, as confirmed by 78% of respondents who indicated that their organizations did not develop a formal IT strategy. Acceding to researchers, this hampered adoption of new innovative IT technologies since such technologies would require a clear vision of the road ahead, coupled with a focused IT strategy aligned with the overall business strategy of the organisation. Lack of sufficient IT educational degrees and IS/IT background since only 3 respondents out of 25 (12%) holding senior IT positions had IS/IT background. It was these three respondents with IS/IT degrees that had IT strategy in their computing departments. The implication here is that senior IT positions held by people with different educational degrees would not help the banking sector to adopt, develop and implement new innovative technology because of the lack of comprehension and understanding of IT technology. Some factors existing within the banking industry (or industrial factors) were identified as inhibiting the incorporation of electronic commerce by that business. These included slow adoption of e-ecommerce by banks in the Arab Gulf region

where they were 'quite slow' to launch e-banking; customer insecurities, technology investment costs and a lack of market-readiness have all conspired to make e-banking 'unattractive' Lack of IT managers' commitment and support for e-banking in Oman banks who felt the new technology was not suitable for Oman environment. On the basis of these cases, it can be concluded that challenges facing banks in adopting e-banking in developed and emerging markets are not the same. This is because where as in developed markets it is personal and e-banking characteristics which influence the adoption; it is not so in emerging markets like Oman where internal organisational factors play a role.

The advantages & disadvantages of E-banking is a contemporary issue of research. Sampson, (1998) identified that with the advance of information and growing competition; banks are fighting to personalize their services to customers. Warwick, (1998) emphasizes that the emergence of electronic fund transfer (EFTs) system is the most important monetary development of our age. It is in fact reforming the banking world, facilitating new ways of conducting business, and creating new financial giants, and might divorce the government from cash. Warwick further states that this development can prevent crime by eliminating cash because every crime, even those that do not directly involve crime has an ultimate cash connection. However, Bernstein and Claps, (1999) pointed out that utilization of banking services is more or less a strategy that entails treating individual customers as market segments of one. Fruin (2001) stated that a bank can provide the customer with convenient, inexpensive access to the bank 24 hours, seven days a week. Although critically important, the benefits of this new technology and accompanying procedures and others do not. This raises the question of utilization vis-à-vis awareness. In this way, benefits may be seen as a necessary but insufficient condition toward understanding utilization and awareness. In spite of the promise of customer value, some people have doubts about or even feel negatively towards some services provided by commercial banks (Kambi & Nunes, 2001).

However, Rotchanakitumnuai and Speece, (2003) state that though banks are very interested in internet banking they are concerned with the risks connected with procedures for transactions over the Internet. The security solutions of the future are therefore major concern for banks. If customers distrust the security it may create multiple problems. Banks will find it hard to launch Internet banking services if demand is low because of security doubts. There are 3 security aspects in a transaction: content confidentiality, integrity and authentication and non-repudiation. These aspects are treated independently with various and often disparate standards. It is recommended that security be provided at all levels: client interface, transport and internal systems. Similarly, Joseph and Stone, (2003) suggested that the basic requirements are to prevent the risk are: customer and financial institution have to authenticate each other; private data have to be encoded. Cryptographic algorithms used need to have certain characteristics; no third party should be able to quickly get access to messages or even to diver financial transactions; a digital signature is necessary to get binding legal contracts. Moreover, Solomon (1997) claims that for client interface and transport, security is currently mainly ensured by the use of cryptographic instruments and by the set up of private financial network. Also, private networks are another solution to secure transactions. These networks can be used for corporate banking and retail banking. The net banking, thus, is now more of a customer rather than an exception in many developed countries due to the fact that it is the cheapest way of providing banking services. However, Foreman (2008) pointed out the disadvantages of E-banking services and concluded that although ATMs are helpful in our lives; frequent use of ATMs can be invitation to uncontrolled spending. Some people find it impossible to resist impulse purchase if they

have access to cash. He goes to say that 80% of all banks impose a surcharge if a non customer uses their ATM.

Bamber *et al* (2001) have highlighted that the three main objectives of financial regulation and supervision of financial institutions are to sustain systematic stability, maintain the safety and soundness of financial institutions, and protect consumers. Two types of regulation could be used to address the above objectives, namely, prudential regulation and conduct of business regulation. Prudential regulation focuses on the solvency, safety and soundness of financial institutions; whereas the conduct of business regulation focuses on how financial firms conduct business with their customers, with emphasis on information disclosure, honesty and integrity of the firms. Both types of regulation cover consumer protection issues. The KYC policies and procedures are the main tools used by financial institutions to combat money laundering. Sound KYC policies and procedures can ensure the safety and soundness of financial institutions. Failure to have KYC policies and procedures could lead to reputational, operational, legal and concentration risks for banks. On a related point, the reliance of electronic banking on information technology has created complex operational and security loopholes, which could be exploited by criminals to perpetrate crime. Penetration of banks' computer systems by criminals could compromise the KYC policies and procedures that the banks would have established, and ultimately the safety and soundness of the financial institution. In light of the above, regulation and supervision are essential for both anti-money laundering measures and electronic banking activities.

Electronic banking continues to be adopted by banks, retailers and customers because of the advantages it has over traditional banking. Some issues such as legal obstacles and security loopholes will take time to overcome. However, electronic banking is still developing and regulation should be done cautiously to avoid stifling innovation and creativity. Regulation is costly to the regulated firms and sometimes it can be so stringent that it becomes a barrier to innovation and entry by new firms. It is important that the regulatory regime provides an environment that would promote the development of electronic banking and also deter illegal activities.

RECOMMENDATIONS

The perception of E-banking services is defined in different ways. Claessens et al, (2001) contended that electronic finance especially online banking and brokerage services have reshaped the financial landscape around the world. Furthermore, these electronic financial services, whether delivered online or through other remote mechanisms, have spread quickly in recent years and that these services are more than just delivery channels they are a completely different way of providing financial services. In addition, Schneider, (2001) illustrated that Customers Relationship Management is essentially about better managing all aspects of a company's relationship with its customers that includes better knowing your customer as the first step, while the second is to utilize that knowledge to more effectively target and serve your customers. Drucker, (2002) mentioned that banking is not about money; it is about information. Today, competition in the financial industry is more intense than ever. Moreover, Xu et al (2002) pointed out that the best way to attain maximum utilization of the services by your customers is to thoroughly know your customers and serve them effectively by better targeting their individual characteristics and needs.

In order to ensure e-Banking is successfully introduced and adopted, the following Key Success Factors (KSFs) must be considered by any bank wishing to use it. The FFIEC IT Handbook (http://www.sciencedirect.com) accessed 24/11/2008 outlines some of them.

1. **Availability of Informational and Transactional Websites:** These are KSFs since they provide the infrastructural support to e-banking activities. Informational websites provide customers access to general information about the financial institution and its products or services. Transactional websites on the other hand provide customers with the ability to conduct transactions through the financial institution's website by initiating banking transactions or buying products and services. Banking transactions can range from something as basic as a retail account balance inquiry to a large business-to-business funds transfer.

2. **E-Banking Components:** Since e-banking systems can vary significantly in their configuration depending on a number of factors, financial institutions should choose their e-banking system configuration, including outsourcing relationships based on four factors. These are: strategic objectives for e-banking; second; scope, scale, and complexity of equipment, systems, and activities; third; technology expertise and finally; security and internal control requirements

3. **Management of E-Banking Risks:** These risks are categorised into transactional/operations; credit; liquidity, interest rate, price/market; compliance/legal; strategic; and reputation risks. Those risks associated with e-banking technologies and these ought to be managed effectively if objectives and benefits of using them are to be realised.

CONCLUSION

It can be concluded e-banking is a future competitive strategy in banking. But it is not easy to have it adopted by both customers and bank staff especially in the emerging market. I would say that the key to providing a successful electronic banking system is in listening to the target market, identifying what they want from a system and then selecting the system which provides this functionality through the technology they require. Since software is by its nature a dynamic medium so banks must ensure that the system they purchase or develop is able to adapt, to incorporate new technologies and also new services. I recommend that banks must pay attention to these questions that customers must be concerned about regarding internet banking: Can the bank offer a wide range of products and services over the web? Can the customer effect funds transfer between accounts? Is it secure to transact over the Web? Can the customer get access to other websites such as shopping malls through the bank? Also, in total I would recommend the selected banks in the developing country to pay more attention to developing internet and tele-banking services as they are not yet thoroughly developed and thus, they can be exploited to the benefit of the bank. Banks should try and publicize the e-banking services it provides through advertisements, publications, though its website, by means of pamphlets/brochures and encouraging bank employees to talk about it with the customers. Also, attention should be paid to different types of customers such as young and old customers, risk-takers and skeptical customers, regular and irregular customers. Banks should conduct research to obtain information on how best to deal with the different types of customers it serves.

REFERENCES

Bamber, R., Falkena, H., Llewellyn, D., & Store, T. (2001). *Financial Regulation in South Africa. Revonia.* South African Financial Sector Forum.

Bareki, A. (2004). *The cost and quality of banking services and their impact on performance of the banking industry in Botswana using Standard charter Bank as a Case Study,* Unpublished MBA dissertation, Faculty of Business Law, De Montfort University, UK

Barto, G. L. (1999). *E-Banking 1999: New Model of Banking Emerges.* Stamford, CT: Gartner Group.

Berg, T., Janowski, W., & Sarner, A. (2001). *Personalization: Customer Value Beyond the Web.* Stamford, CT: Gartner.

Bernstein, M., & Claps, C. (1999). *Web Personalization- Possibilities, Problems, and Pitfalls.* Stamford, CT: Gartner Group.

Bons, A. (1999). *Internet Banking: Early Stage Experiences.* Kingston, RI, USA: University of Rhode Island.

Bons, A. (1999). *Internet Banking: Early Stage Experiences.* Kingston, RI, USA: University of Rhode Island.

Chou, D., & Chow, A. Y. (2000). A guide to the internet revolution in banking. *Information Systems Management, 17*(2), 51–57. doi:10.1201/1078/43191.17.2.20000301/31227.6

Claessens, S., Glaessner, T., & Klingbiel, D. (2001). *Electronic finance: A new approach to financial sector development.* World Bank Discussion Paper No.431.

Drucker, P. F. (2002). *Managing in the Next Society.* New York: St Martin's Press.

Essinger, J. (1992). *Electronic Payment System: Winning New Customer.* UK: Chapman and Hall. Imprint by Thompson Corporation.

Fonseca, I., Hickman, M., & Marenzi, O. (2001). *The Future of Wholesale Banking: The Portal.* Commercial Lending Review. Boston, summer.

Fruin, J. (2001). What is CRM? *InfoTech Update, 2,* 5–6.

Gerrard, P., & Cunningham, J., B. (2003). The diffusion of Internet banking among Singapore consumers. *International Journal of Bank Marketing, 21,* 16–28. doi:10.1108/02652320310457776

Ibbotson, P., & Moran, L. (2003). E-banking and the SME/ bank relationship in Northern Ireland. *International Journal of Bank Marketing, 21,* 94–103. doi:10.1108/02652320310461474

Joseph, M., & Stone, G. (2003). An empirical evaluation of US bank customer perceptions of the impact of technology on service delivery in the banking sector. *Journal of Retail and Distribution Management, 31,* 190–202. doi:10.1108/09590550310469185

Kambil, A., & Nunes, P. F. (2001). Personalization? No Thanks. *Harvard Business Review, 79*(4), 32–34.

Kapulos, A., Ellis, N., & Murphy, W. (2004). The Voice of the Customer in E-banking Relationships. *Journal of Customer Behaviour, 3,* 27–51. doi:10.1362/147539204323074592

Khalfan, A. M. S. AIRRefaei, Y.S.Y,& Al-Hajery M.,(2006). 'Factors influencing the adoption of internet banking in Oman: a descriptive case study analysis', In *International Journal Financial Services Management, 1* (2/3), 155-163.

Lymperopoulos, C., & Chaniotakis, I. E. (2004). Branch employees' perceptions towards implications of e-banking in Greece. *Journal of Retail and Distribution Management, 32,* 302–311. doi:10.1108/09590550410538006

Mattila, M., Karjaluoto, H., & Pento, T. (2003). Internet Banking adoption among mature customers: early majority or laggards? *Journal of Services Marketing, 17,* 514–528. doi:10.1108/08876040310486294

O'Hanlon, J., & Rocha, M. (1993). *Electronic Banking for Retail Customers.* London: Banking Technology Ltd.

O'Mahony, D., Peirce, H., & Tewari, H. (1997). *Electronic Payment System.* Artech House Computer Science Library.

Rotchanakitumnuai, S., & Speece, M. (2003). Barriers to Internet banking adoption: a qualitative study among corporate customers in Thailand. *International Journal of Bank Marketing, 21,* 312–323. doi:10.1108/02652320310498465

Saatcioglu, K., Stallaert, J., & Whinston, A. B. (2001). Design of a Financial Portal. *Communications of the ACM, 44,* 6. doi:10.1145/376134.376151

Sampson, S. E. (1998). Gathering Customers Feedback via the internet: Instruments and Prospects. *Industrial Management & Data Systems, 98*(2), 71–82. doi:10.1108/02635579810205511

Schneider, I. (2001). Getting to Know You. *Bank Systems & Technology, 38*(10), 20–24.

Sergent, C. (2000), *Impact of E-banking on Traditional services.* Retrieved from www.encyclopedia.com/doc/1027-sergent.html.

Singh, S., & Chhatwal, S. S., Yahyabhoy, T., M., & Heng, Y., C., (2000). Dynamics of Innovation in E-banking. Retrieved February 15, 2007, from *School of Computing, National University of Singapore* in the website http://csrc.lse.ac.uk/asp/aspecis/20020136.pdf

Slywotzky, A. J. (2001), Revving the Engines of Online Finance. Cambridge, MA: MIT Sloan Management Review, Cambridge, Summer.

Sohail, M., & Shanmugham, B. (2003). E-Banking and Customer Preferences in Malaysia: An Empirical Investigation. *Information Sciences, 150*(4), 207–217. doi:10.1016/S0020-0255(02)00378-X

Solomon, E. H. (1997). *Virtual Money.* New York: Oxford University Press.

Suh, B., & Han, I. (2000). Effect of trust on customer acceptance of Internet banking. Retrieved February 15, 2007, from *Graduate School of Management, Korea Advanced Institute of Science and Technology* in the website http://afis.kaist.ac.kr/download/inter_jnl031.pdf

Violano, M., & Van Collie, S. (1992). *Retail Banking Technology: Strategies and Resources that Seize the Competitive Advantage*. New York: John Wiley and Sons, Inc.

Wang, Y., Lin, H., & Tang, T. (2003). Determinants of users acceptance of Internet Banking an Empirical study. *International Journal of Service Industry Management, 14*(5), 501–519. doi:10.1108/09564230310500192

Warwick, D. R. (1998). *Ending Cash: The Public benefits of federal Electronic Currency*. Westport, Conn.: Quorum Books.

Xu, Y., Yen, D. C., Lin, B., & Chou, D. C. (2002). Adopting Customer Relationship Management Technology. *Industrial Management & Data Systems, 102*(8), 442–452. doi:10.1108/02635570210445871

ADDITIONAL READING

Azam, M. Shah (2005). Adoption of Personal Computer in Bangladesh: The Effects of Perceived Innovation Characteristics. In *Proceeding of the 2nd International Conference of the Asian Academy of Applied Business (AAAB)*. Indonesia: AAAB.647-655.

Bakta, N. C., & Sarder, M. M. R. (2007). *Online Banking: Bangladesh Perspectives*. Paper prepared for presentation at the XVI Biennial Conference.

Bunker, D. J., & MacGregor, R. C. (2000). Successful generation of information 20 technology (IT) requirements for small/medium enterprises (SM E's): Cases from regional Australia. In *Proceedings of the SMEs in a Global Economy*(pp. 72-84). 2000, Wollongong, Australia. Celik, H. (2008). What Determines Turkish customers' acceptance of internet banking? *International Journal of Bank Marketing, 26*(5, 353-370.

Claessens, S., & Glaessner, T. (2002). E-Finance in Emerging Markets: Is Leapfrogging Possible? *Financial Markets Institutions & Instruments, 11*(1), 1–125. doi:10.1111/1468-0416.00001

Dholakia, R. R., & Kshetri, N. (2004). Factors Impacting the Adoption of the Internet among SMEs. *Small Business Economics, 23*, 311–322. doi:10.1023/B:SBEJ.0000032036.90353.1f

Gehling, R., & D. Turner, (2007), Defining the proposed factors for small business online banking: Interviewing the IT professionals. Journal *of Financial Services Marketing 12*(3), 189-196. 21

Guglani, S. (2001). Future of E-Finance for SMEs. A Paper Presented in Expert Group Meeting on Improving Competitiveness of SMEs in Developing Countries: Role of Finance, including E-Finance to Enhance Enterprise Development, Geneva, 22-24. 1-16.

Hawkins, R., & Prencipe, A. (2000). *Business-to-Business E-Commerce in the UK: A Synpaper of Sector Reports Commissioned by the Department of Trade and Industry*. London: DTI.

Hernandez, J. M. C., & Mazzon, J. A. (2007). Adoption of internet banking: proposition and implementation of an integrated methodology approach. *International Journal of Bank Marketing, 25*(2), 72–88. doi:10.1108/02652320710728410

Humphrey, J., R. Mansell, D. Paré & H. Schmitz (2003). The Reality of E-commerce with Developing Countries. Media@LSE.

Kapurubandara, M. & R. Lawson (2007). SMEs in Developing Countries Need Support to Address the Challenges of Adoption e-commerce Technologies. *20th Bled eConference eMergence*.

Kartiwi, M., & MacGregor, R. C. (2007). Electronic Commerce Adoption Barriers in Small to Medium-Sized Enterprises (SMEs) in Developed and Developing Countries: A Cross-country Comparison. *Journal of Electronic Commerce in Organizations, 5*(3), 35–51.

Laukkanen, T. (2006). Customer-perceived value of e-financial services: a means-end approach. *International Journal of Electronic Finance*, *1*(1), 5–17.

Lin, C.-Y. (2008). Determinants of the adoption of technological innovations by logistics service providers in China. *International Journal of Technology Management and Sustainable development, 7*(1).

Molla, A., & Licker, P. S. (2005). E-commerce adoption in developing countries: a model and instrument. *Information & Management*, *42*, 877–899. doi:10.1016/j.im.2004.09.002

Polatoglu, V. N., & Ekin, S. (2001). An empirical investigation of the Turkish consumers' acceptance of internet banking services. *International Journal of Bank Marketing*, *19*(4), 156–165. doi:10.1108/02652320110392527

Rotchanakitumnuai, S., & Speece, M. (2003). Barriers to Internet banking adoption: a qualitative study among corporate customers in Thailand. *International Journal of Bank Marketing*, *21*(6/7), 321–323. doi:10.1108/02652320310498465

Sukkar, A. A., & Hasan, H. (2005). Toward a Model for the Acceptance of Internet Banking in Developing Countries. *Information Technology for Development*, *11*(4), 381–398. doi:10.1002/itdj.20026

Tan, M., & Teo, T. S. H. (2000). Factors influencing the adoption of Internet banking. *Journal of the AIS*, *1*(5), 1–42.

KEY TERMS AND DEFINITIONS

Challenges of E-Banking: E-banking adoption might need to tackle the dispute of customer service within the banking industry it can as well be the cause of poor customer service since it can result into the problems if it is poorly implemented

Customer Service: This defines banking products and services rendered to customers by interacting with them. Customer perceptions of quality service, customer needs, service expectations and service customisation are important in customer service.

Customers: This refers to both individual and corporate or business customers who hold accounts with the bank and those who process transactions with the bank.

E-Banking Adoption: The process by which customers and the bank accept and start using e-banking technologies in accessing banking services.

E-Banking: It means automated delivery of banking products and services directly to customers through electronic, interactive communication channels. It is also strategy for improving customer service.

Strategy: A set of rules or a management framework for implementing and managing e-Banking products and services.

Chapter 4

Factors Influencing KM Strategic Alignment in the Banking Sector:
The Case of Persian Gulf Countries

Jafleh Hassan Al-Ammary
University of Bahrain, Bahrain

ABSTRACT

In today's business environment, knowledge is increasingly recognized as the most important and valuable asset in organizations and a key differentiating factor in business. Therefore, many organizations are positioning themselves strategically based on their tangible and intangible internal resources, and their capabilities rather than on their products and services. However, in order for an organization to be successful in the exploitation of knowledge assets to drive competitive advantages, a holistic approach that spans Knowledge Management (KM), business strategy, and organizational and human factors should be used. The aim of this study is to investigate the effect of some factor on KM Strategic Alignment between KM and business strategy in the banking sector at Persian Gulf Countries. The results have indicated factors such as knowledge sharing, trust, openness to change, IT infrastructure and skills, and existence of CKO are strongly correlated to the strategic alignment between KM and business strategy. Thus, managers in the Persian Gulf banking sectors should adopt new rules using flexible organizational culture, reforming and redesigning their organizational structure, and incorporating an advanced information technology in their operations for competitive advantage.

INTRODUCTION

In today's business environment, knowledge is increasingly recognized as the most important and valuable asset in organizations and a key differentiating factor in business (Stewart et al.,

DOI: 10.4018/978-1-61520-635-3.ch004

2000; Murray, 2000). Some experts consider knowledge to be perhaps the only sustainable competitive advantage (Williams, 2008). Teece (2000) argued that the competitive advantage of organizations depends on their ability to build, utilize, and protect difficult to intimate knowledge assets. For this reason, many organizations are positioning themselves strategically based on their tangible and intangible internal resources, and their capabilities rather than on their products and services (Zack, 2002 a, b; Jashapara, 2004; Murray, 2000; Kankanhalli et al., 2003). It is also recognized that competitive advantage based on resources and capabilities is more important in contributing to superior performance and sustainability than just solely based on products and market positioning (Prahalad & Hamel, 1990; Zack, 2002a; Jashapara, 2004).

However, in order to an organization to be successful in the exploitation of knowledge assets to drive competitive advantages, a holistic approach that spans Knowledge Management (KM), business strategy, and organizational and human factors should be used (Cedar, 2003). Thus, KM should be aligned with business process, organizations, and IT to continuously capture, maintain, and reuse the key information, and arbitrates the strategic knowledge assets that improve business performance (Cedar, 2003). When such alignment is established, the KM system will be directed towards the goal and objectives of the organization which will build and enhance its long term competitive advantages. The lack of such strategic alignment leads to poor strategic planning, which results in misallocation of resources (Cascella, 2002; Luftman, Papp & Brier, 2002) and ultimately poor organizational performance. Therefore, KM Strategic Alignment (KMSA) should be allocated at a high priority of the organizational agenda for organization seeking sustaining their competitive advantage. The alignment is a complex topic as it includes KM, business strategy, human resources and IT. There are many factors embedded in the organization context and culture that may affect the strategic alignment and so the organization performance. Therefore, organizations simply can't enhance the KMSA without adopting new rules using flexible organizational culture, reforming and redesigning its management style and structure, and incorporating an advanced information technology in their operations for competitive advantage (Choi, 2003).

Considerable researches have been devoted to investigate the importance of the alignment between KM and business strategy (Jones, 2000; Smith & McKeen, 2003; Zack, 1999; Aidemark & Sterner, 2002; Davenport, 1999; Sabherwal & Sabherwal, 2003; Sunassee & Sewry, 2002, Al-Ammary, 2008). However, few researches attempted to explore the contingency and antecedent factors which guide KMSA. Then, there is a need for more research into the factors that affect KMSA.

RESEARCH OBJECTIVES

The aim of this study is to investigate the effect of some factor on KM Strategic Alignment between knowledge strategy and Business Strategy KMSA-BS in the Persian Gulf Countries. In addition the study will investigate the effect of KMSA-BS on the organizational performance.

This study focuses on Persian Gulf countries for two reasons. First, knowledge considered by many experts as a powerful driver of economic growth through higher productivity. Knowledge could help the region to expand the scope of human independencies and enhance the capacity to guarantee those independencies through good governance (AHDR, 2003). Second, as developing countries, there is a need for a context specific model for KM, KM strategy, and KMSA-BS in such countries. It was noted that most of the available models and frameworks proposed to guide KM and its issues in organizations are based on skills, practices and studies in Western industrialized countries (such as USA and UK). Most of these countries are already becoming knowledge economies. In addition, most of the models have not considered the national environments, regions and specific local organizational factors that could affect KM and its performance. A study done by Al-Ammary and Fung (2007) provide a more comprehensive picture of the current situation of KMSA-BS at the Persian Gulf banking sectors.

They found that Persian Gulf banks have begun realize the strategic importance of knowledge as the competitive edge for their organizations; and that they need to enhance the strategic alignment between their KM initiatives and their organizational strategy. However, they are still not aware to many aspects of KMSA-BS, such as the role of CKO, the importance of aligning different aspects of knowledge strategy, and the importance of a flexible and supportive culture for knowledge creation and sharing. Al-Ammary (2008) in her study highlighted the importance of investigating some of the contingency factors. She revealed that to proposed KMSA framework for Persian Gulf countries, factors such as the organizational, technological, cultural and environmental factors that may differentiate these countries from other parts of the world should be considered.

RESEARCH BACKGROUND

KM Strategic Alignment

Knowledge is claimed by many researchers to have an enabling role in the formulation of successful strategies and achieving the organizational overall objectives (Snyman & Kruger, 2004; Zack, 2002 b; Jones, 2000; Maier & Remus, 2002). Academics and researchers also advocated that the true power of knowledge lies in its ability to positively influence, and enable the business strategy. Zack (2002 a, b), for instance, suggested that the vital role of knowledge and its management should be reflected by the organizational related strategies in order to achieve the organizational desired competitive advantage.

Furthermore, it is recognized that the effective use of knowledge to drive competitive advantage depends upon using a holistic approach that spans five key business considerations: Knowledge Management (KM), business strategy, technologies, organizational culture, and human factors (Cedar, 2003). Hamid (2003) argued that the

effective management of KM system involves managing the entire system, people, structure, processes, culture, and technology to ensure there is holistic collaboration and participations in all the KM processes.

The concept of alignment in the KM field is complex as it addresses both KM and organizational strategies. The complexity of the organizational strategy is related to the market place uncertainty, market share, profit growth, customer retention, and competition (Bawany, 2001). KM is complex as it touches human behaviors, attitudes and capabilities, business philosophies, operations and practices, and complicated technologies (Wiig, 1997). Building on the existing investigation and discussion of the IT strategy alignment, many research has been conducted to investigate many of the issues related to the concept of alignment in KM. such as the different perspectives of KM strategic alignment; and the performance significance of them on the organizational performance (Zack, 2002 a, b; Sabherwal and Sabherwal, 2003; Asoh, 2004; Shih & Chiang, 2005; Bloodgood & Morrow, 2003; Al-Ammary, 2008).

Jashapara (2004) declared that KM can be considered from different perspectives: strategy, HR process, and IT or IS strategy. The strategic perspective of KM aims at helping organization in achieving its goals by making the factor knowledge productive (Uit Beijerse, 2000). HR process perspective of KM, on the other hand, highlights the human dimension of developing knowledge in individuals, teams and organizations which occurs through different learning processes, and the IT or IS strategy focus on the IT methods, instruments and tools, that are used to contribute to the promotion of core knowledge processes (Mertins et al.; 2003). Accordingly, three different types of KM strategic alignment are identified: KM and business strategic alignment KMBS-SA, KM and IS strategic alignment – KMIS-SA, and KM and HR strategic alignment – KMHR-SA. The alignment between KM and business strategy or IS strategy can be considered as strategic alignment (Abou-

Zeid, 2003), while the alignment between KM and the IT strategy, HR, or organizational environment can be considered as operational (or functional) alignment. The main concern of operational KM is to connect people to the process of distribution and transfer of knowledge, while the strategic KM is aimed at linking organizational knowledge with the organizational structure and business strategy.

Wiig (1997) admitted that the focus of KM has changed from an operational perspective for the purpose of improving efficiency and quality, to a strategic perspective for the support of enterprise innovation and broad effectiveness. Therefore, the current research study focuses on the KM strategic alignment between knowledge strategy and business strategy (KMBS-SA). This alignment has been extensively discussed and emphasized by academics and researchers in the KM and management disciplines (Zack, 1999, 2002 a, b; Marier & Remus, 2002; Sabherwal & Sabherwal, 2003; Carrillo et al., 2003; Abou-Zeid, 2003; Asoh, 2004; Snyman & Kruger, 2004). Jones (2000) stated that knowledge-based strategy requires the organization first understand the business needs, in term of technical, human and structural aspects, as bad choices or decision hurt the organizational productivity. Thus in order to formulate a KM strategy, KM manager needs to be fully conversant with all aspects of the business strategy. Business manager, however, should be able to articulate the organization knowledge-related activities with the organization strategic activities and strategic plan.

Although some research have made an attempt to provide definitions for the KMSA (Zack, 2002 a, b; Asoh, 2004; Abou-Zeid, 2003; Evans, 2003; Maier & Remus, 2002), they tended to focus on KMBS-SA. Most of these definitions have overlooked the alignment between KM and IS strategy, HR strategy and the organization's environmental elements. Al-Ammary (2008) has provided a definition for KMSA-BS based on the available definitions provided by the literature. According to her, KMBS-SA can be defined as "*the degree*

to which knowledge resources and capabilities provided by the knowledge strategy, is supporting and supported by the strategic and intellectual requirements of the business strategy in order to manage the strategic and knowledge gap".

Factor Influencing KM Strategic Alignment

While there are several studies have been done to investigate the critical success factors that may affect KM, little were attempted to investigate the factors that may affect KMSA. The concept of KMSA-BS is very complex as is clearly manifested in the definition mentioned previously. Thus, to identify the factors that may influence KMSA-BS, many aspects should be considered include: knowledge resources, KM, knowledge strategy, business strategy, and organization in general should be considered. Albert (2009) stated that an elementary success factor of knowledge management (KM) is to have a common understanding of the terms "knowledge management" and "knowledge sharing" and how they apply to their situation and needs. Then the factors influence KMSA-BS can be identified based on their effect on knowledge, and knowledge strategy, business strategy, and business environment in general. Accordingly, many factors can be identified such as IT, human factors, culture, organizational structure, management style, knowledge management styles, leadership and etc.

APQC (1996) identified four enablers in the KM include: strategy and leadership, culture, measurement, and technology. However, Albert (2009) identified six organizational factors that considered critical for KM and its environment. These factors include culture, leadership, organizational intent, knowledge processes, organizational structure and technology infrastructure. Hasanali, (2002) alternatively, stated that the success of KM initiative depends on many factors that can be categorized into five primary categories: leadership, culture, structure, roles and responsibilities,

IT infrastructure, and measurement. However, Holsapple and Joshi (2000) have developed a framework that organized these factors into three categories: managerial influences, resource influences, and environmental influences. In addition, Holsapple and Joshi have identified some environmental factors which include those factors that exist outside the organization and have a direct influence on its activities. These factors include the governmental, economic, political, social, and educational factors.

In general, it can be concluded that factors that may influence KMSA-BS are include but not limited to: Culture, leadership, organizational structure, IT infrastructure, management styles, and strategy.

Factors Influencing KMSA-BS in Persian Gulf Countries

Many of the above mentioned factors that may influence KM and so KMSA are manifested in the environment of Persian Gulf organizations. The Persian Gulf region in general is considered as changing, fast-growing and socio-cultural context. There are many factors embedded in the Persian Gulf countries context that call for a specific model for implementing KM and enhancing the strategic alignment in their organization. Among these factors are: nation and organizational culture, IT infrastructure and skills, business strategy, organizational structure and management styles. Therefore, in this section, factors that may influence KMSA-BS in the Persian Gulf organization will be investigated.

The organizations in the Persian Gulf countries are characterized by many factors. These include Islamic Sharia, Arabic language, climate and geographic location, scarcity of IS professionals, IS market maturity and cultural values independently and collectively. Kassem and Habib (1989) have asserted that the organizations in the Persian Gulf countries tend to have a reasonable degree of specialization, a low degree of coordination because

of excessive personal authority and extensive use of committees and a high degree of centralization of decision making.

Family and government ownership is a common phenomenon in the Arab and Persian Gulf organizations and especially banking industry (El-kharouf, 2000; Cader, 2003). In many cases, the members of the groups of families (ownership) of the organization or the bank are often directly involved in management (Limam, 2001). This structure of ownership affects the strategic orientation, the quality of implementation of corporate governance, and the quality of management and control (El-kharouf, 2000). Moreover, the ownership (groups of family) of banks in most of the Persian Gulf countries is reluctant to distribute and share information with banks. This attitude influences the lending decision processes and the financial position of the bank, and most importantly, its assets (El-kharouf, 2000).

On the other hand, business strategies in Persian Gulf organizations are constrained by environmental forces, inadequacy of government proceedings and policies as well as insufficient reaction of the organization due to their weak internal capabilities (Cader, 2003). Organizational structure in most of the Arab organization including the Persian Gulf can be characterized by "authoritarian-paternalistic". Following this type of organizational structure has brought about the overwhelming of the higher power distance culture (Cader, 2003).

Most importantly, the Arab culture is one of the more complex culture and social systems in the world (Straub, et al., 2001). Persian Gulf countries symbolize modern states with an Islamic spirit. The most noticeable face of the Islamic culture is Arabic language. For Muslim language is not just a symbol of a common heritage but also a holy language (Abdul-Gader, 1997). Persian Gulf countries culture is also differentiated by the Bedoaucracy characteristics such as the tribal and familial social structure. The bedoaucracy model highlights the importance of Bedouin culture in the Persian Gulf organizational setting (Abdul-Gader, 1997).

Although the Persian Gulf countries have a well established IT infrastructure in most organizations, they still lack the skilled and capable people. The problem of localization of labor force (replacing the skilled expatriate labors by local unskilled labors) has vital implications on the IT efficiency and effectiveness. It is also found and especially in the UAE, that organizations are punished if they do not comply with this law (Islam, 2003). Moreover, Straub, et al., (2001) stated that cultural conflicts between the organization and management style of western and Arab institutional leaders and workers have impacted the system development process and produced unsuccessful approaches to computer use and policy.

Al-Ammary and Fung (2006) found that the culture in the Persian Gulf banks promote the self-actualization, foster the human to human contact, and sharing knowledge. These types of culture would likely to decrease the resistance in the transfer of knowledge and enhance the individual and organizational knowledge creation (Ladd & Ward, 2002; Syed-Ikhsan & Rowland, 2004). However, the bureaucratic-authoritarian culture that described the organizational culture in most of Persian Gulf banks has a great effect on the interpersonal communication. Such culture encourages the dependency and diminishes the relational channel and so it's likely to discourage the transferring and sharing of knowledge within the bank (Ladd & Ward, 2002; Ladd & Heminger, 2003).

Furthermore, it has been found that "knowledge is power" is a common culture in the Persian Gulf countries. Most of the knowledge owners consider their knowledge as their private power that has to be guarded to protect their positions in the bank (Al-Ammary & Fung, 2007). This finding is consistent with Zack (1999) who argued that the most critical problem facing knowledge management is seeing knowledge as power. Al-Shammari (2008) clarify that this type of culture

word prevent employee in the Arab word from cooperate in sharing their knowledge with other colleagues.

Finally, Al-Ammary and Fung (2007) results implicitly revealed that the CKO is an unknown position in the participating banks. It was also found that the responsibilities of CKO or KM manager are mainly assigned to CIO, IT director or the Head of the IT department. Thus, managers in Persian Gulf countries have little awareness about the roles played by CKO and how these roles are distinguish from the roles of CIO (Al-Ammary and Fung, 2007).

RESEARCH MODEL

Based on the research objectives and the above discussion, the research model on the factors affecting KMSA-BS was developed as shown in Figure (1). The research model depicted in Figure 1 illustrates the relationship between two types of factors that have an effect on KMSA-BS which include: Contextual Factors (IT Infrastructure and skills, Management style, and existence of CKO) and factors related to the organizational Culture (knowledge sharing, openness to change, and trust). Moreover, the model demonstrates the relationship between KMSA-BS and the organizational performance.

RESEARCH HYPOTHESES

Contextual Factors

IT infrastructure and skills: The focus on knowledge and its management has led to an increased attention towards IT as one of the most important sources of competitive advantages (Johannessen et al., 2000). The role of IT in KM is a vital consideration for any company wishing to exploit emerging technologies to manage their knowledge assets and a critical success factor in the development of an effective KM system (Egbu & Botterill, 2002).

The relationship between KM and IT has been approached from the capabilities of IT infrastructure and from the processes of KM (Okunoye, 2003). Junnarkar and Brown (1997) discussed the role of IT in KM as a mechanism to facilitate knowledge creation and transfer. This role lies in the new IT capabilities to support communication and collaboration in order to enable collaborative learning (Alavi & Leidner, 1999). According to Manasco, (1996), the critical role of IT lies in the ability to support communication, collaboration, and search for knowledge and information dynamically instead of just getting information from static repositories of best practices. Studies by APQC (1997) consider technology as a significant enabler for KM and organizations embarking on KM initiatives must establish a suitable IT infrastructure in order to successfully accomplish the goals of the organization. Therefore, the following hypothesis is developed:

H1: *There is a positive relationship between the IT infrastructure and skills and KM strategic alignment in the banking sector at Persian Gulf countries.*

Figure 1. Research model

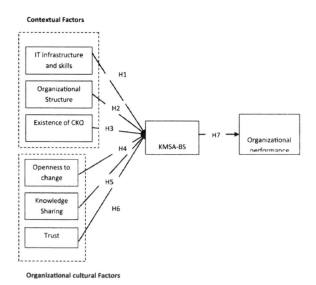

Organizational structure: Organizational structure influences information flows as well as the context and nature of human interaction (Millar (1987). Consequently, organizational structure will influence KM and its implementation. Therefore, organizations must adopt organizational structures that facilities or spaces for employees to informally share knowledge which would improve the environment for KM (Clavercorte's, et al, 2007; Albers, 2009).

For instance, organization with bureaucratic structure, which discourages interpersonal communication, is likely to diminish relational channel and discourage the pursuit of individual knowledge (Ladd and Ward, 2002). Then, such organization need to incorporate certain process such as equity, accountability, clarity of objectives, coordination as well as through-out decisions (Cader, 2003) to support the development of its strategic knowledge. Hence, we hypothesized that:

H2: *There is a positive relationship between Organizational structure and KM strategic alignment in the banking sector at Persian Gulf countries.*

Existence of CKO: Knowledge management success requires a holistic approach, of strategy, technology and human recourses. Hence, organization needs an effective leader with technical, business and social skills. CKO is someone who can lead an enterprise-wide knowledge management program. CKO is considered as the main tools with which organization can improve the effectiveness of their knowledge process (Leitch & Rosen, 2001). Eral and Scott () argued that appointing a CKO is one way of spurring, directing, and coordinating a knowledge management program. Organizations are investing in many aspects of knowledge management without appointing a CKO. Instead, they assigned the role of CKO to professional in other areas, such as IT, human resources, and marketing (Padova, 2009; Liebowitz, 2002). Assigning such position to those who do not have the expertise and leadership to support a serious KM programmer, the outcome of knowledge management strategies often fails (Liebowitz, 2002). Therefore, the following hypothesis is developed:

H3: *There is a positive relationship between the Existence of CKO and KM strategic alignment in the banking sector at Persian Gulf countries.*

Factors of the Organizational Culture

Culture dose play an important role in the success of a knowledge management efforts. Culture is regarded as the key factor since it determines the effects of other variables such as technology and management techniques on the success of knowledge management (Syed-Ikhsan & Rowland, 2004). Vital researches in the area of knowledge management have revealed that knowledge sharing, transferring or creating can only work if the culture of the organization promotes it (Stoddart, 2001; Syed-ikhsan & Rowland, 2004).

The current research focuses on the organizational culture. The organizational culture can be studied from many dimensions include reward system, trust, openness to change, and sharing knowledge. Albert (2009) revealed that culture is one of the most critical element in implementing KM and that the ideal KM culture is characterized by trust, openness to change, teamwork, collaboration, and risk taking. Moreover, Suarez (2006) reveals that organizations would need to be as flexible so that trust, communications, knowledge sharing and collaboration can take place.

Therefore, three dimensions which could have the most impact on the strategic alignment between business strategy and knowledge strategy will be investigated in the current research. These include: openness to change, knowledge sharing, and trust.

Openness to change: An organization whose culture is characterized by openness to change/ innovation would likely "foster human-to-human

contact and stress similarities between individuals" (Ladd & Ward, 2002). According to Gurteen (1999) openness to change means "seeing the world in a different way".

Organizations most opened are the ones that are getting the larger benefit from KM. Such culture would allow knowledge to flow smoothly within the organization, engage further with other organizations, and make interactions much richer and worthy (Suarez, 2006). This probably encourage knowledge worker to seek and find ways to share what they know with others (Suarez, 2006). In addition, this type of culture promotes humanistic orientation, affiliation, achievement, self-actualization, task support, task innovation, and hands-on management (Ladd & Ward, 2002). Self-actualization, for instant, is likely to increase individual knowledge (Ladd & Ward, 2002). Ladd and Ward (002) found that openness to change/ innovation culture nature tended to increase an organization's ability to transfer knowledge (Ladd & Ward, 2002). Consequently, the following hypothesis is developed:

H4: *There is a positive relationship between Openness to change culture and KM strategic alignment in the banking sector at Persian Gulf countries.*

Knowledge sharing: Usoro, et al, (2006) define knowledge sharing as a "process of communication between two or more participants involving the provision and acquisition of knowledge". Then, the relational channels in organizations that are not encouraging culture of knowledge sharing are not well developed (Ladd & Heminger, 2003). As such channels prevent the organization from sharing and transferring their knowledge and ultimately building their knowledge capabilities and competencies. Al-Shammari (2008) in his study conducted on Arab countries concluded that successful implementation of a KM strategy requires a major shift in organizational culture and commitment at all levels of an organization. Having such actions, organizations will be able to initiate a focus on people and methods to enhance learning, improve communication, and encourage knowledge sharing instead of knowledge hoarding (Al-Shammari, 2008). Therefore, the following hypothesized:

H5:*There is a positive relationship between Knowledge sharing culture and KM strategic alignment in the banking sector at Persian Gulf countries.*

Trust: Davenport and Prusak (1999) stress on the importance of trust in KM and state that trust must be promoted through frequent face-to-face meeting. Trust or interpersonal trust which is defined by Renzt (205) as "the willingness of a party to be vulnerable" is an essential part of knowledge sharing. Trust increases knowledge sharing through reducing fear of losing one's unique value and improves willingness to document knowledge (Renzt, 2005). However, it has been observed that may knowledge owners reluctance to make their knowledge and expertise available through knowledge repository. Instead, they prefer to share it within a controllable, trusted group under conditions negotiated for the specific situation and partners (Dignum & Eijk, 2007).

The influence of trust in general on KM and knowledge sharing has been studied by many researchers (Wang et al., 2003; Renzt, 2005). Wang et al. (2003) in his study, attempted to investigate the relationship between trust and KM by examining how the benefits obtained from knowledge sharing change as trust level change. The results suggest that the benefit obtained from knowledge sharing increases as trust level increase (Wang et al., 2003). Renzt (2005) on the other hand, has provided a better understanding of that relationship by demonstrating that fear of losing one's unique value and knowledge documentation have a mediating effect on the relationship between trust in management and knowledge sharing. Therefore, the following hypothesis is developed:

H6:*There is a positive relationship between Trust culture and KM strategic alignment in the banking sector at Persian Gulf countries.*

KM Strategic Alignment and Organizational Performance

The impact of KMBA-SA on the performance and the organization competitive advantage have been revealed by many researchers (Zack, 2002 b; Stewart et al., 2000; Snyman & Kruger, 2004; Tiwana, 2002; Maier & Remus, 2002; Seeley, 2002). Hansen, et al. (1999) however, drew attention to the importance of the alignment between business strategy and the strategies of KM at both the strategic and operational strategic levels. While at the strategic level the alignment between KM and business strategy or KMBS-SA is vital for enhancing the strategic decision making processes, the organization needs to practice effective operational KM to ensure that it brings all the required knowledge to execute their strategies (Hansen, et al., 1999).

Furthermore, the organization's fundamental capabilities relating to its culture, technology and system, and management need to be supported and leveraged by the knowledge assets (Hasan and Handzic, 2003). In order to gain competitive knowledge, organizations need to be able to enhance what they know and predicate what they must know and to recognize the kind of value it intends to provide and to whom. Thus, an organization needs to capitalize on what they know and need to align their strategic goals and the strategies of KM (Snyman & Kruger, 2004). Dunnick (1996) argued that the existing objectives set by the organization for serving customers and beating competitors needs to be linked to the new organizational intellectual capital (intellectual resources and capabilities), otherwise all the organizational learning, technical capabilities and skills, or knowledge-based processes are "mere costly diversions". Then the following hypothesis is developed:

H7:*There is a positive relationship between KM strategic alignment and organizational performance in the banking sector at Persian Gulf countries.*

RESEARCH METHODOLOGY AND DATA COLLECTION

The following section presents details on the study of the proposed research model of the factors affecting KM strategic alignment at the GCC banking sector using path analysis

Sample

Banking sector in the Persian Gulf countries was deemed to be appropriate for this research due to their high information intensity. The Persian Gulf countries comprise of six Arab states. These include the Kingdom of Saudi Arabia, Kingdom of Bahrain, Kuwait, Qatar, United Arab Emirates and Oman. Since this study aimed at investigating a situation in Persian Gulf banks, the selection of banks was made on one main premise according to which they must be embedded Arabian culture, management style, and organizational structure that may affect its operation, strategies and performance. Therefore, only the local banks that are operating in the Persian Gulf environment were selected. However, foreign banks have been excluded from the list due to the different style of operation and management in these banks. Accordingly, 100 banks were selected which present most of the local banks in the Persian Gulf countries. Table 1 shows the types and number of participated banks. These banks comprise four types: commercial, investment, specialist and Islamic banks.

Instrument

In gathering information pertaining to the current study, a questionnaire was used as the main instrument for data collection. Questionnaire was developed to measure factors (variables) given in the research model depicted in Figure 1: Trust, Knowledge sharing, Openness to change, IT infrastructure and skills, Organizational structure, Existence of CKO, KMSA-BS and Organizational performance. The questionnaire also contained a section on demographic variables (personnel information) dealing with bank's name, respondent age, experience, qualification, and function. Other section consists of 54 items measuring eight variables. Items in questionnaire were developed by selecting from other scales with no modifications, with modification and framed by the investigator. Five-points itemized scale was used for the purpose with rating of one for strongly disagree and rating of five for strongly agree.

Table 1. Sample description: banks types

Country	No. Local banks				Total number of banks
	Commercial	Investment	Specialist	Islamic	
Kingdom of Saudi Arabia KSA	6	7	4	2	19
United Arab Emirate UAE	9	7	3	6	25
Kuwait	3	3	2	4	12
Oman	4	2	3	0	9
Qatar	2	2	2	3	9
Kingdom of Bahrain	10	9	2	5	26
Total number in each type	34	30	16	20	100

To capture openness to change/innovation and sharing knowledge, FOCUS questionnaire (Muijen et al., 1999) was used. Seven modified item were selected to measure openness to change and five items were selected to measure knowledge sharing. To measure the construct of trust, six items were adopted from (Rempel, Holmes & Zanna, 1985) measurement. Eight items were used to measure KMSA-BS which adopted from (Al-Ammary, 2008). The adopted instrument to measure the organizational performance in this research was based on the performance instruments used by Morgan (2003), Sin et al. (2006) and Sabherwal and Chan (2001). This instrument is a synthesized measure which was made using combination of traditional accounting-based items, market growth, profitability, company reputation, and product-service innovation. To measure IT infrastructure and skill, organizational structure and existence of CKO, the descriptions of these three concepts given in the literature were used. Accordingly, 20 items were developed: seven items for IT infrastructure and skills, six items for organizational structure and seven items for existence of CKO.

ANALYSIS AND RESULTS

200 copies of questionnaire were distributed to the selected banks. A total of 87 were returned in a form eligible for the analysis. Twelve of the questionnaires were dropped because they had incomplete answers. The overall response rate for this study was 43.5%. This response rate considers being relatively high, as the respondents were managers who supposed to be too busy to answer questionnaires.

The internal consistency reliability was assessed by calculating Cronbach alpha values. The results of the reliability test conducted for the study constructs are summarized in Table 2. All alpha scores were above 0.7, which suggest an acceptable of reliability. The means and standard deviations of all the variables of the study are summarized in Table 2. To analysis the data both descriptive, correlation and multiple regression were used.

The results in Table 3 show the profile of the respondents. The results demonstrate that most of the respondents were male (82%). This may reflect some aspects of Persian Gulf culture. As such, the strategic positions in the banking sectors mostly occupied by male, specifically in Saudi Arabia and Qatar. Another important point to be highlighted is that only 2% of the respondents were CKO.

A multiple regression analysis was employed to identify which factors made significant contributions to predicting KMSA-BS. The results in Table 4, have demonstrated that openness to change, sharing knowledge, trust, existence of CKO and IT Infrastructure and skills are posi-

Table 2. Respondents profile

	No. of Items	Mean	SD	Reliability
Organizational performance	8	4.5	0.9	0.91
KMSA-BS	8	4.4	0.9	0.75
Existence of CKO	7	4.1	1.1	0.701
IT Infrastructure and skills	7	3.9	1.2	0.69
Organizational structure	6	3.8	1.3	0.7
Knowledge sharing	5	4.2	.87	0.87
Openness to change	7	3.7	1	0.82
Trust	6	4.1	.9	0.85

Table 3. Respondents profile

	Frequency	Percentage
Gender		
Male	72	83%
Female	15	17%
Age Mean: 38.2 SD: 6.5		
Position		
Chief Executive Officer	22	25.28%
Chief Information Officer	19	21.8%
Chief Knowledge Officer	2	2.3%
IT managers/ Head of IT	31	35.6%
Others	13	14.9%
Educational level		
Master	20	23%
Bachelor degree	46	53%
Secondary school	21	24%

** p<0.01, ***p<0.001

tively and significantly (p <0.01 and P< 0.001) affected KMSA-BS (β=0.236, β=0.261, β=0.331, β=0.301, and β=0.345, respectively). However, organizational structure has no significant effect on KMSABS (β=0.095). The adjust R squared value was 0.620 which indicates that factors of openness to change, sharing knowledge, trust, existence of CKO and IT Infrastructure and skills explain 62.0% of the total variance of KMSA-BS.

A correlation analysis was conducted to assess the relationship between KMSA-BS and organizational performance. The results shown in Table 5 indicate that there is a significant correlation between KMSA-BS and organizational performance (r=0.412, p=.001).

DISCUSSION AND CONCLUSION

This study tried to contribute to the research efforts concerning KM strategic alignment in organization in general and the Arab countries specifically. The study has investigated the effect of some contextual factors (IT Infrastructure and Skills, Management styles, and Lack of CKO) and factors related to organizational culture such as openness to change, sharing knowledge, and trust. In addition, the relationship between the KMSA-BS and performance was examined.

The first indication of the result is that KMSA-BS is strongly correlated with organizational performance. Thus, Persian Gulf countries need to establish an alignment between KM and business strategy in order to move their KM systems in a direction that holds promise for long-lasting competitive advantage. Otherwise, they may lose

Table 4. Results of multiple regression analysis for factors affecting KMSA-BS

Independent variable (s)	KMSA-BS Organizational performance		
	$R^2 = 0.620$, F= 27.616 ***		
	β	t	Sig.
IT Infrastructure and Skills	0.345	2.746	.000***
Existence of CKO	0.301	2.667	.000***
Organizational Structure	0.095	0.931	.876
Openness to Change	0.236	2.117	.004**
Knowledge Sharing	0.261	2.154	.003**
Trust	0.331	2.654	.000***

Table 5. Correlation between KMSA-BS and organizational performance

Independent Variable	Organizational performance
KMSA-BS	r = 0.412 0.008***

*** $p < 0.01$

many opportunities. As such, organizations may fall into the trap of attempting to explicate knowledge that is not explicable and failing to explicate knowledge that should have been converted from tacit to explicit (Tiwana, 2002).

The second indication of the result is that contextual factors of IT infrastructure and Skills and existence of CKO have shown a significant contribution on KMSA-BS. However, the result shows that organizational structure has no effect on KMSA-BS in the banking sector at Persian Gulf countries. Furthermore, the results show that all the organizational culture factors have a significant contribution on KMSA-BS. Hence, organizations in Persian Gulf countries should put more emphasis on all aspects of the organizational culture. For example, the implementation of the Basle Committee on Banking Supervision (BCBS) by the Persian Gulf banking industry in addition to their participation in the WTO require a cultural change and consequently a completely different orientation in the way they are managed (El-Kharouf, 2000). Moreover, the globalization and liberalization and emerge of the knowledge economy raises the concern regarding the applicability and reliability of the management styles and organizational structure followed by the Persian Gulf organizations. El-kharouf, (2000) asserted that the Persian Gulf organizations and especially banks require a strategic reorientation or "Cultural Revolution" in the way they are doing and managing their business. The participation, cooperation, coordination, and empowered teamwork of employees should be reform to cope with the emerged management techniques and information technology.

Finally, the results of the current research revealed that organizations at Persian Gulf countries paid little attention to CKO as just 2.3% of the participants were CKO. The reason behind the lack of CKO in such countries is the misconception on understanding KM concept and Information System Management (MIS) among the IT managers. Although, there are many KM projects have been implemented in the Persian Gulf banks intended to create and disseminate knowledge in the bank; they are still considered as an advanced MIS (Al-Ammary, 2008). Managers in such countries need to fist take away the misconception on KM and MIS concepts, and then they will realize the important of appointing positions such CKO or at least KM manager.

REFERENCES

Abdul-Gader, A. H. (1997). Information system strategic for multinational companies in Persian Gulf Countries. *International Journal of Information Management*, *17*(1), 3–12. doi:10.1016/S0268-4012(96)00038-2

Abou-Zeid, E. S. (2003). Developing business aligned knowledge management strategy. In *E Coakes, Knowledge management current issues and challenges* (pp. 156–172). Hershey, PA: IRM Press.

Aidemark, J., & Sterner, H. (2003), A framework for strategic balancing of knowledge management initiatives. In *Proceeding of the 36th Hawaii International Conference on System Sciences (HICSS'O3)*, 6-9 Jan. 2003, Hawaii, USA

Al-Ammary. Jaflah Hassan (2008). *Knowledge Management Strategic Alignment in the Banking Sector at the Gulf Cooperation Council (GCC) Countries*, PhD. Dissertation, University of Murdoch, Perth, Australia

Al-Ammary, J., & Fung, C. C. (2007). Knowledge Management in the Gulf Cooperation Council (GCC) Countries: a Study on the Alignment between KM and Business Strategy. In Cader, Y. (Ed.), *Knowledge Management Integrated – Concepts and Practice* (pp. 187–211). Australia: Heidelberg Press.

Al-Shammari, M. (2008). Toward a Knowledge Management Strategic Framework in Arab Region. *International Journal of Knowledge Management, 4*(3).

Alavi, M & Leidner DE (1999). Knowledge Management systems: Issues, challenges, and benefits, *Communication of the Association of Information Systems, 1*, Article 7, Feb 1999.

American Productivity & Quality Center (APQC) (1997). *Knowledge Management: Consortium Benchmarking Study Final Report*. Retrieved from. [online: http://www.store.apqc.org/reports/summary/know-mng.pdf]

Arab Human Development Report AHDR. (2003). *Building a knowledge society*. Retrieved from. [online: http://www.undp.org/rbar/ahdr/english2003]

Asoh, D., Belardo, S., & Neilson, R. (2002). Knowledge Management: Issues, Challenges and Opportunities for Governments in the New Economy. In *Proceeding of the 35th Hawaii International Conference on System Sciences (HICSS'O2)*, 5, Hawaii, USA pp. 129.2.

Bawany, S. (2001). *Developing a Knowledge strategy: Aligning knowledge management programs to business strategy*. Retrieved from. [online: http://www.bawany.com.sg]

Bloodgood, J. M., & Morrow, J. L. (2003). Strategic organizational change: Exploring the roles of environmental structure, Internal conscious awareness and knowledge. *Journal of Management Studies, 40*(7), 1761–1782. doi:10.1111/1467-6486.00399

Carrillo, P. M., Robinson, H. S., Anumba, C. J., & Al-Ghassani, A. M. (2003). IMPaKT: a framework for linking Knowledge Management to business performance. *Electronic Journal of Knowledge Management, 1*(1), 1–12.

Cedar, (2003), How Knowledge Management, Drives Competitive Advantage. *Cedar white paper*, released December, Maryland, USA

Choi, Y. S. (2003). Reality of Knowledge Management Success. *Journal of Academy of Business and Economics, 11*(1), 184–188.

Claver-Cortes, E., Zaragoza-Saez, P., & Pertusa-Ortega, E. (2007). Organizational structure features supporting knowledge management processes. *Journal of Knowledge Management, 11*(4), 45–57. doi:10.1108/13673270710762701

Davenport, T. H. (1999). Knowledge management and the broader firm: Strategy, advantage, and performance. In J Liebowitz (Ed.), *Knowledge Management Handbook: 2.1—2.11*, Boca Raton, FL:CRC Press.

Davenport, T. H., & Prusak, L. (2000). *Working Knowledge, how organizations manage what they know*. Boston: Harvard Business School Press.

Dignum, F. P. M., & Eijk, R. M. (2007). *Agent communication and social concept*. New York: Springer. [online: eijk_07_agentcommunication.pdf]

Dunnick, R (1996), Strategy as if knowledge mattered. *Fast company*, Issue 2, [online: www.fastcompany.com/online/02/stratsec.html].

Egbu, C. O., & Botterill, K. (2002). Information Technologies for Knowledge Management: Their Usage and Effectiveness. *ITcon, 7*, 125.

El-Kharouf, Farouk (2000), Strategy corporate governance and the future of the Arab banking industry. *The Arab bank review, 2*, (2), 30-39.

Evans, C. (2003). *Managing for knowledge HR's strategic role*. Oxford, UK: Butterworth Heinemann.

Gurteen, D. (1999), Greeting a knowledge sharing culture. *Knowledge Management Magazine, 2*, (5).

Hamid, J. A. (2003). *Understanding Knowledge Management*. Malaysia: University of Putra Malaysia Press.

Hansen, MT, & Nohria, N & Tierney, Thomas. (1999). What's your strategy for managing knowledge? *Harvard Business Review, 77*(2), 106–116.

Hasan, H., & Handzic, M. (2003). *Australian Studies in Knowledge Management*. Wollongong: UOW Press.

Hassanali, F. (2002), *Critical Success Factor Of Knowledge Management*.Retrieved from [online: www.providersedge.com/docs/km-articles/critical_success_factor_of_KM.pdf

Holsapple, C. W., & Joshi, K. D. (2000). An investigation of factors that influence the management of knowledge in organizations. *The Journal of Strategic Information Systems, 9*(2/3), 235–261. doi:10.1016/S0963-8687(00)00046-9

Islam, Mazhar M. (2003), Development and performance of domestic and foreign banks in GCC countries.*Managerial finance, 29*, (2-3), 42.

Jashapara, A. (2004). *Knowledge management an integrated approach. Upper Saddle River, NJ: Prentice Hall*. Essex, UK: Pearson Educaion Ltd.

Johannessen, J. A., Olaisen, J., & Olsen, B. (2000). *Mismanagement of tacit knowledge: knowledge management, the danger of information technology, and what to do about it. SKIKT*. Retrieved from. [online: www.program.forskningsradet.no/skikt/johannessen.php3]

Jones, PH (2000), Knowledge strategy: Aligning knowledge programs to business strategy.*Knowledge Management World 2000*, Santa Clara, CA, September 12-15.

Junnarkar, B., & Brown, C. (1997). Re-assessing the enabling role of information technology in KM. *Journal of Knowledge Management, 1*(2), 142–148. doi:10.1108/EUM0000000004589

Kankanhalli, A., Tanudidjaja, F., Sutanto, J., & Tan, B. C. Y. (2003). The role of IT in successful knowledge management initiatives. *Communications of the ACM, 46*(9), 487–505. doi:10.1145/903893.903896

Kassem, M., & Habib, G. (1989). *Strategic Management of Services in the Persian Gulf States*. Berlin, New York, NY: Company and Industry Cases, Walter de Gruyter.

Ladd, A. & Ward, Mark (2002). An investigation of Environment factors influencing Knowledge transfer. *Journal of Knowledge Management Practice*, vol. 3

Ladd, D. A., & Heminger, A. R. (2003). An investigation of organizational culture factors that may influence knowledge transfer. *in Proceedings of the 36th Hawaii International Conference on System Sciences*

Leibowitz, J. (2002). The role of the chief knowledge officer in organizations. *Research and Practice in Human Resource Management, 10*(2), 2–15.

Leitch, J. M., & Rosen, P. W. (2001). Knowledge Management, CKO, and CKM: The Keys to Competitive Advantage. *The Manchester Review, 6*(2&3), 9–13.

Limam, I. (2001), A comparative study of GCC banks technical efficiency. *Economic Research Forum ERF working paper*, No. 200119, Retrieved from [online: http://www.erf.org.eg].

Luftman, J., Papp, R., & Brier, T. (1999). Enablers and inhibitors of business-IT alignment. *Communications of the association for information system, 1,* (3es), Article No. 1.

Maier, R., & Remus, U. (2002). Defining process-oriented knowledge management strategies. *Knowledge and Process Management, 9*(2), 103–118. doi:10.1002/kpm.136

Manasco, B. (1996). Leading firms develop knowledge strategies. *Knowledge Inc, 1*(6), 26–29.

Mertins, K; Heising, P & Alwert, K (2003). Process-oriented knowledge structuring. *Journal Of universal computer science, 9,* (6), 542-550.

Miller, K. R. (1978). Structural organization in the photosynthetic membrane. In Akoyunoglou, G. (Ed.), *Chloroplast Development* (pp. 17–30). Amsterdam: Elsevier Press.

Morgan, R. E., & Strong, C. A. (2003). Business performance and dimensions of strategic orientation. *Journal of Business Research, 56*(3), 163–176. doi:10.1016/S0148-2963(01)00218-1

Muijen, van; Koopman, Pul, Witte, Karel De; Cock, Gaston; Lemoine, Calaude;& Bourantas, Dimitri (1999). organizational culture: the FOCUS Questionnaire. *European Journal of Work and Organizational Psychology, 8.*

Murray, P. (2000). Designing business from knowledge management. In C Despres, D Chauvel,(eds.) *The present and the promise of knowledge management.*(pp. 171-194).Boston: Butterworth-Heinemann, Boston, MA.

Okunoye, A. (2003). Large-scale Sustainable Information Systems Development in Developing Country: The Making of an Islamic Banking Package. [ACIT]. *Annals of Cases on Information Technology, V,* 168–183.

Padova, A. (2009). *Concerns of CKO. Inside-knowledge.* Retrieved from. [online: www.ikmagazine.com]

Prahalad, C. K., & Hamel, G. K. (1990). The core competence of the corporation.In MH Zack (Ed.), *Knowledge and Strategy* (pp.41-62).Boston: Harvard business review, May-June, Butterworth-Heinemann.

Rempel, J. K., Holmes, J. G., & Zanna, M. (1985). Trust in close relationships. *Journal of Personality and Social Psychology, 49,* 95–112. doi:10.1037/0022-3514.49.1.95

Renzt, B. (2006). Trust in management and knowledge sharing: the mediating effects of fear and knowledge documentation. *Special Issue on Knowledge Management and Organizational Learning, 36*(2), 206–220.

Sabherwal, R., & Sabherwal, S. (2003). *How do knowledge announcement affect firm value? A study of firm pursuing different business strategies.* Working paper University of Missouri, [online: http://misrc.umn.edu/workshops/2003/fall/Sabherwal_100303.pdf].

Seeley, C. P. (2002). Establishing a business-driven strategy igniting knowledge in your business processes. *Knowledge Management Review, 5*(4), 12–15.

Shih, H. A., & Chiang, Y. H. (2005). Strategic alignment between HRM, KM, and corporate development. *International Journal of Manpower, 26*(6), 582–605. doi:10.1108/01437720510625476

Sin, L. Y. M., Tse, A. C. B., Chan, H., Heung, V. C. S., & Yim, F. H. K. (2006). The effects of relationship marketing orientation on business performance in the Hotel Industry. *Journal of Hospitality & Tourism Research (Washington, D.C.)*, *30*, 407–426. doi:10.1177/1096348006287863

Snyman, R., & Kruger, C. J. (2004). The interdependency between strategic management and strategic knowledge management. *Journal of Knowledge Management*, *8*(1), 5–19. doi:10.1108/13673270410523871

Stewart, K. A., Baskerville, R., Storey, V. C., Senn, J. A., Raven, A., & Long, C. (2000). Confronting the assumptions underlying the management of knowledge: an agenda for understanding and investigating knowledge management. *ACM SIGMIS Database*, *31*(4), 41–53. doi:10.1145/506760.506764

Stoddart, L. (2001). Managing internets to encourage knowledge sharing opportunities and constraints. *Online Information Review*, *25*(1), 19–28. doi:10.1108/14684520110366661

Straub, D. W., Loch, K. D., & Hill, C. E. (2001). Transfer of Information Technology to Arab world: A test of cultural influence modeling. *Journal of Global Information Management*, *9*(4), 6–28.

Suarez, Luis (2006), Enabling Knowledge sharing- a matter of cultural and organizational changes?- The role of communities. *Social computing evangelist*

Sunassee, N., & Sewry, D. A. (2002), A theoretical framework for knowledge management implementation", In *Proceeding of 2002 annual research conference of the South African insiture of computer scientists and information technologists on Enablement through technology, (SAICSIT), Port Elizabeth, South Africa*, (pp. 235-245).

Syed-Ikhsan, Syed Omar S. & Rowland, Fytton. (2004). Knowledge management in a public organization: a study on the relationship between organizational element and the performance of knowledge transfer. *Journal of Knowledge Management*, *8*(2), 95–111. doi:10.1108/13673270410529145

Teece, D. (2000). *Managing intellectual capital: organizational, strategic and policy dimensions*. Oxford, UK: Oxford University Press.

Tiwana, A. (2002). *The Knowledge Management Toolkit: Orchestrating IT, Strategy, and Knowledge Platforms* (2nd ed.). Upper Saddle River, NJ: Prentice Hall.

Uit Beijerse, R. P. (2000). Knowledge management in small and medium-sized companies: knowledge management for entrepreneurs. *Journal of Knowledge Management*, *4*(2), 162–179. doi:10.1108/13673270010372297

Usoro, A. (2006). *An investigation into trust as an antecedent to knowledge sharing in virtual communities of practice*. Computing and Information System.

Victor, Cascella (2002).Efective Strategic Planning. *Quality Progress, 35*, (11).

Wang, Y., & Vassileva, J. (2003)Bayesian Network Trust Model in Peer-to-Peer Networks. *In Proceedings of Second International Workshop Peers and Peer-to-Peer Computing*, July 14, Melbourne, Australia.

Wiig, K. M. (1997). Knowledge Management: where did it come from and where will it go? *Expert Systems with Applications*, *13*(1), 1–14. doi:10.1016/S0957-4174(97)00018-3

Williams, Randy (2008). Critical success factors when building knowledge management system. *Share Point Magazine*, December

Zack, M. H. (1999). Developing a knowledge strategy. *California Management Review*, *41*(3), 125–145.

Zack, M. H. (2002a), A strategic pretext for knowledge management. *Proceeding of the Third European Conference on Organizational Knowledge, Learning and Capabilities*, Athens, Greece, April 5.

Zack, M. H. (2002b). Developing a Knowledge strategy. In Choo, C. W., & Bontis, N. (Eds.), *The strategic management of intellectual capital and organizational knowledge* (pp. 255–267). Oxford, UK: Oxford University press.

KEY TERMS AND DEFINITIONS

KM: Knowledge management (KM) comprises a range of practices used in an organization to identify, create, represent, distribute and enable adoption of insights and experiences. Such insights and experiences comprise knowledge, either embodied in individuals or embedded in organizational processes or practice. KM efforts typically focus on organizational objectives such as improved performance, competitive advantage, innovation, the sharing of lessons learned, and continuous improvement of the organization. KM efforts overlap with organizational learning, and may be distinguished from that by a greater focus on the management of knowledge as a strategic asset and a focus on encouraging the sharing of knowledge. KM efforts can help individuals and groups to share valuable organizational insights, to reduce redundant work, to avoid reinventing the wheel per se, to reduce training time for new employees, to retain intellectual capital as employees turnover in an organization, and to adapt to changing environments and markets (McAdam & McCreedy 2000) (Thompson & Walsham 2004).

KMSA: KM Strategic Alignment (KMSA) is alignment allocated at a high priority of the organizational agenda for organization seeking sustaining their competitive advantage. When such alignment is established, the KM system will be directed towards the goal and objectives of the organization which will build and enhance its long term competitive advantages. Organizations simply can't enhance the KMSA without adopting new rules using flexible organizational culture, reforming and redesigning its management style and structure, and incorporating an advanced information technology in their operations for competitive advantage.

Organizational Culture: Organizational culture is an idea in the field of Organizational studies and management which describes the psychology, attitudes, experiences, beliefs and values (personal and cultural values) of an organization. It has been defined as "the specific collection of values and norms that are shared by people and groups in an organization and that control the way they interact with each other and with stakeholders outside the organization. This definition continues to explain organizational values also known as "beliefs and ideas about what kinds of goals members of an organization should pursue and ideas about the appropriate kinds or standards of behavior organizational members should use to achieve these goals. From organizational values develop organizational norms, guidelines or expectations that prescribe appropriate kinds of behavior by employees in particular situations and control the behavior of organizational members towards one another.

Persian Gulf Countries: The Persian Gulf, in the Southwest Asian region, is an extension of the Indian Ocean located between Iran and the Arabian Peninsula. Persian Gulf region embraces countries Iran, Bahrain, UAE, Qatar, Kuwait, Iraq, Oman, Saudi Arabia.

Chapter 5
Internet Banking Strategy in a Highly Volatile Business Environment:
The Nigerian Case

Abel E. Ezeoha
Ebonyi State University, Nigeria

ABSTRACT

Internet banking strategy can be generally very challenging, but more challenging in an economic environment infested with high degree of corruption, insecurity, bad governance, poverty, and financial system instability. Due to its global nature, Internet banking, under such situation, is threatened by the easiness at which off-line crimes are transmitted into online businesses, and the difficulty in building trusts and confidence in online business relationships. Using the Nigerian case, this chapter aims at establishing some theoretical link between offline country image and Internet banking reputation. The chapter summarizes the structural and regulatory challenges in the Nigerian banking system. It represents and relates the country's socioeconomic conditions with its Internet business reputation; and lays down past regulatory and global efforts to control the menace of the Nigerian version of Internet frauds. The last two sections of the chapter, respectively, suggest some future research direction and conclude the chapter.

INTRODUCTION

The volume of activities passing through the Internet has been on the increase since the start of the 21st Century. Production of goods do not in actual sense take place in the Internet, but basic services such as marketing, research and development, financial services, education and

DOI: 10.4018/978-1-61520-635-3.ch005

others are presently at the mainstream of Internet business development. Incidentally, as the volume of Internet-based business activities increases, so also has the rate of growth in frauds and crimes committed with the aid of cyber facilities and networks. Although the spread of this version of frauds defiles geographical definitions, most of such frauds are linked to certain countries that are believed to be the rallying points and bases of cyber criminals. While some of the linkages are traceable to the sources of cyber frauds and the identities of the perpetrators, others are based on the hardcore image of the affected countries. Hence, a country that is criminally notorious in the eyes of the international community may find it difficult exonerating itself of the allegations of being a base for cyber fraudsters.

Efforts on research and regulation at the moment are targeted at addressing the question of whether a country's Internet business reputation is as a result of its hardcore image. The problem arising from this controversy is also heightened by the fact that while Internet activities are borderless, regulation is in most cases country-based and country-specific. Each country has a territorial authority on the structure and nature of laws governing the operations of businesses within its jurisdiction. Laws that are meant to govern domestic operations thus prove inadequate in controlling borderless Internet businesses. Some of the identifiable regulatory gaps have thus helped to increase the prevalence of Internet banking frauds in the global scene.

The Nigerian 419 ranks among the top cyber frauds in the world. This is evidence in the fact that an experiment using any of the search engines to link Nigeria and Internet businesses would commonly yield results that relate to 419 frauds. This strong online link between Internet business fraud and Nigeria has not only threatened the country's e-business reputation, but has also negatively influenced the country's international online business dealings. Part of the growing concerns on Nigerian Internet frauds is that it is the persistent negative hardcore reputation of the country that is responsible for its bad Internet image; and in view of this perspective, nationals of other countries found it convenient to use the Nigerian identity as a way of concealing their dirty deals. Undoubtedly, before Internet usage took a centre stage in the country in the mid-1990s, the country ranked high in terms of corruption, poverty, conflicts and bad governance. The business environment is also held globally as one of the most unsafe and unstable. The financial system, specially, was infested with high cases of frauds, distresses and failure, especially between the early 1980s and December 2005. Although some major economic and political reforms have taken place in the country since 1999, there are still trails of these negative global impressions about the country. These hardcore impressions have essentially resulted to some difficulties in making meaningful distinction between fraud perpetrated by Nigerians from Nigeria and those perpetrated by alleged Nigerian nationals overseas, and between Internet frauds actually committed by Nigerian nationals (irrespective of their places of residence) and those committed by other nationals that hide under the Nigerian impression.

The above notwithstanding, the Nigeria government and public have shown reasonable concerns on the continued high ranking of the country in Internet frauds. Because of the accepted premises that a country's governance and safety index influence the level of capital inflows and (a) its business competitiveness, government over the years has come up with various initiatives to fight Internet crime. Most of the initiatives stretch from general to specific cyber-related regulations and guidelines. Popular among them are: The Money Laundering Act of 1995 (repealed by the Money Laundering Act of 2004) and the Advanced Fee Fraud (419) Act of 2006. There is also the set of Guidelines on Electronic Banking in Nigeria. The government has equally evolved some specialised institutional structures to fight internet-related frauds to change the image of the country abroad. Some of such structures are the Economic and Financial Crimes Commission (EFCC) formed in 2003, the Independent and Corrupt Practices (and Other Related Offences) Commission (ICPC), as well as the increased surveillance roles of the Central Bank of Nigeria (CBN). At the same time, series of judicial reforms have taken place between 1999 and date. The reforms are basically targeted at facilitating and sanitising the judicial processes to make them acceptable and reliable in the eyes of the international community.

Several factors have joined to undermine these domestic efforts. First is the fact that the intents and contents of most of the regulations bordering on the control of Internet frauds predate the emergence of Internet businesses in the country that is, the existence of a wide gap between Internet banking advances and existing banking laws and regulations in the country. This creates a situation where the laws fail to address most of the issues relating to Internet business dealings. The second reason is the continued perception of the global community that every Internet fraud that bears the tag "419" or "advance fee fraud" is made in Nigeria. The implication caused by the latter is that in most cases, global efforts against Internet frauds are misdirected and sometimes wasted, as a result of some mistaken identities. Going down the history, it is established that the first major international attention on Internet fraud was raised in 1994 when Russian hacker Vladimir Levin and his accomplices in St. Petersburg used the Internet to electrically break into Citibank's mainframe systems in New York to transfer US$11 million from several Citibank accounts to their own accounts at banks in Finland, Israel, and California (O'Brien, 2002). Again, the effectiveness of the local laws and their enforcement institutions is challenged by the fact that Internet businesses are naturally borderless and so require collaborative efforts to resolve. Although frauds are branded, sometimes, according to their countries of origin, the prevalent and spread are usually not country decimated.

This chapter aims specifically at exploring the possibility that one of the greatest reasons for the persistent cases of the Nigerian version of Internet frauds could be the inability of the global community to make out meaningful difference between hardcore country image and Internet banking reputation. This is against the backdrop of an apparent positive linear relationship between rising cases of 419 frauds on one hand, Internet fraud control investments by both the Nigerian government and its development partners and

increasing surveillance mounted by different countries against Nigerian Internet frauds, on the other hand.

BACKGROUND ISSUES IN THE NIGERIAN BANKING SYSTEM

The Nigerian Banking Environment: Structure and Regulation

Although banking was in place in Nigeria from 1892, conventional banking business actually commenced in 1952, when specific regulatory frameworks were put in place for the licensing and operation of banking in Nigeria. Since then, regulation has been within the sole discretion of the central government. Thus, unlike the case in the United States and other countries operating federal system of government, the states in Nigeria have no hands in regulating or licensing banks. Structurally, there are five key institutional agents in the country's banking industry – namely the Central Bank of Nigeria, which is the apex regulatory institution; the Nigerian Deposit Insurance Corporation; the deposit money banks (made up of both commercial and merchant banks); the development finance institutions, which are generally owned by the central government; and the micro-finance banks (formerly known as community banks).

Before December 2005, there were about 89 deposit money banks in the system, 8 development finance institutions, and a host of community banks. The dominant players in the industry are however, the deposit money banks – the commercial and merchant banks. Trends in the number of such banks indicate a good deal of inconsistency, with the introduction of structural adjustment programme (SAP) in 1986 causing some tremendous increase from 40 in 1985 to 120 in 1992. SAP brought with it an extensive deregulation of the Nigerian economy; created opportunities for outright evasion of banking and financial laws in the country; and made it possible for some new banks to survive and prosper by mainly buying and selling foreign exchange (Uche, 2000). Thus, a discussion of structural development in the Nigerian banking system is usually not complete without due mention of SAP and its impacts on the country's economy.

The adjustment programme loosened conditions for the granting of bank licenses and at the same time created a lot of instability in the banking system. As expected, most of the banks that took advantage of the lapses created by SAP could not survive the then competitive heat in the industry. Explaining further some of the causes of the distress, the Central Bank of Nigeria (2001, p.28) argued that in a bid to take advantage of the relaxation in the requirements for granting of banking licenses, promoters borrowed funds on short-term basis to float banks, and only for the new banks to be stripped of the capital shortly after the acquisition of licenses. The end result was usually an early collapse of such banks. The distress trend continued unabated and resisted regulatory measures and institutions on the ground. As a way of preventing the spread, the Central Bank of Nigeria in 1991 placed embargo on the licensing of more banks in the country. This lasted until 1998 when the embargo was finally lifted.

Another policy thrust of government that is worth mentioning is the coming into force of universal banking practice. The adoption of universal banking system in the country in 2001 erased completely the usual regulatory and operational differences between merchant and commercial banking in the country. The desperation at which this system of banking was introduced and the fragility in the regulatory framework at the time of the introduction joined to expose banking in Nigeria more to system abuses and vulnerability (Uche, 2001). Little attention was paid on resolving the likely regulatory overlaps that were inherent in an environment of universal banking. The system at the time became highly infested with visible degree of rigidity and systemic inefficiency. The

banking industry thus suffered from structurally vulnerable due to frauds and abuses, up to December 2005.

In recognition of the dangerous effects of excess freedom occasioned by SAP, the Nigerian government in 1996 discontinued the implementation of the SAP programme, and then tightened regulations and other intervention measures. Rather than instilling sanity in the system, the new measures resulted to series of distress and failure cases, especially among the smaller banks that had low capital bases and less competitive power, and incidentally were then in the majority. This situation caused further exposure of the industry to high incidences of frauds and insider-abuses. Some of the deficiencies, as identified above are illustrated in the following section.

Pre-Consolidation Features of the Nigerian Banking Industry

Rigidities in Bank Ownership Structure

Ownership structures of banks in Nigeria have taken some various dimensions since 1892. Between 1982 and 1972, the structure was foreign dominated. The Nigerian government took advantage of the 1972 and 1976 Indigenisation Policy, which was meant to transfer a majority ownership of economic resources in the country to Nigerians, to take over the top three banks in the country erstwhile foreign owned; and by 1986, government had substantially increased its equity holding in those banks by as much as 75 percent. The abolition of the Indigenisation policy and of course the adoption of the structural adjustment programme led to a reversal of structure. Most private investors were granted licenses to operate banks. Government equally sold off its holdings in the big banks. This was the case up until December 2005, when an industry consolidation was concluded among banks. The industry consolidation, introduced and enforced by the Central Bank of Nigeria between July 2004 and December 2005, did not change much the post-SAP ownership structure. This is so considering that at the conclusion of the exercise in 2005, out of the 25 banks left in the system, 20 were still owned by Nigerians private investors, only 4 by foreign private investors, and just one partially by the Nigerian government (see Table 1). In addition, the high level of ownership concentration among the banks, which itself is a historic feature, is not altered by the exercise.

Lack of Market Access

Another interesting ownership-related factor that impacted on how banking was conducted in Nigeria is that before 2005, less than half of the banks were publicly quoted. A good number of the banks were privately and closely held, with thick family and personal links (Ezeoha, 2007). This trend is more amplified in the argument of the governor of the Central Bank of Nigeria that due to cultural environment and peculiar individual mindset, many Nigerians would prefer to own 100 percent of barely nothing by way of family businesses rather than 1 percent of something (Soludo, 2004). The problems caused by this include lack of access to the capital market and very high information asymmetry. Majority of the banks relied on public sector deposits and could get involved in all sorts of illegal and unprofessional dealings to attract funds. Again, because of their absence in the capital market, most of the banks were shut-off from the public, and so could

not garner enough public confidence required to run efficiently.

Uneven Distribution of Size and Structure of the Industry

Before 2004, the banking industry was made of too many small banks that were neither well capitalized nor better managed. The industry was controlled by just about 5 out of the 89 banks, who controlled up to 50 percent of the total assets, total credits and total capitalization of the industry. The other 84 banks were relatively small banks that were used by their owners to run personal businesses including trading in foreign exchange, money laundering, and chasing of public sector accounts (Soludo, 2004).

Deficiency in the Intermediation Process

There is even at date abnormality in the intermediation structure of banks in the country. This is especially the case in the areas of deposits and lending where most of the deposits are of short-term, and where the capacity of the banks to grant long-term loans is hampered by near lack of long-term deposits in the system. The economic impact was that between 1992 and 2003, the average of currency outside the banking system stood at about 47 percent (Ezeoha, 2007). This situation has not changed much, especially as the banking density, at about 35,000 Nigerians per bank

Table 1. Ownership structure of Nigerian banks (%)

Ownership	Year							
	1991	2000	2001	2002	2003	2004	2005	2006
Private Nigeria	63.1	87.6	86.5	86.7	86.5	86.5	86.5	84.0
Government	25.9	1.1	1.1	1.1	1.1	1.1	1.1	0.0
Foreigners	11	11.2	12.4	12.2	12.4	12.4	12.4	16.0
Total	100.0	100.0	100.0	100.0	100.0	100.0	100.0	100.0

Central Bank of Nigeria Annual Reports and States of Accounts [Various Years]

branch[1], remains comparably among the highest in the world. Because of lack of basic infrastructures, most Nigerian rural areas and semi-urban communities are still without the presence of banks.

High Prevalent of Frauds and other Sharp Practices

Frauds and sharp practices were, before December 2005, very common features of the banking industry in Nigeria (see Tables 3 and 4). Essentially, bank frauds assume various forms in the country. The most prevalent of such crimes among banks, however, have been those relating to fraudulent transfer and withdrawals of funds – taking as much as 38.36 percent, 52.16 percent and 31.21 percent of the total amounts involved bank frauds, respectively, during the years 2004, 2003 and 2002 (Nigerian Deposit Insurance Corporation, 2004). Other popular versions of frauds in the system were presentation of forged cheque, granting of unauthorized credits, posting of fictitious credits, cheque and cash defalcation, outright theft and bank robbery.

Regulatory Inconsistency

The industry, up until date, is also heavily regulated. It contends with not only numerous regulations, but also very inconsistent regulatory trends. Areas mostly regulated are minimum capital requirements, interest rates, prudential requirements, lending policies and so on. The industry has had to face numerous regulatory agencies whose roles often suffer a great deal of overlapping and conflicts of interest.

High Mortality Rates

The high frequency of bank failure and distress, which culminated from the above-mentioned factors, was another significant feature of the banking industry in Nigeria before end-2005. In essence, this trend has remained the prevailing reason for

the numerous regulatory changes recorded in the country's banking system since 1952.

No doubt, the 2004/2005 banking consolidation exercise succeeded in resolving some of the daunting problems. Despite this claim, some of the challenges, such as high fraud rates, bank robbery, deficiency in the intermediation process, among others, are still visibly present in the system.

Some Regulatory Imperatives in the Banking Industry

More than market dynamisms, the Nigerian banking industry has more been shaped by regulations (Ezeoha, 2007). Banking regimes in the country are defined along eras of regulatory changes such as: the stage of Liaises-fair banking (1894 – 1952); the stage of limited banking regulations (1952-1958); the regime of intensive regulations (1958-1986); era of structural adjustment or banking deregulation (1986-997); and then the indirect control regime (1998 to date) (Ojo, 1991; Oguleye, 1999; Uche, 2000; and Ezeoha, 2007). Similarly, the structure of banking regulation in the country comprises of comprehensive laws governing banking practices; the prudential guidelines that are meant to guarantee sound-banking practice; the monetary policy guidelines; and other specialised laws. The era of banking legislation came into effect in 1952, following the enactment of Banking Ordinance of 1952, with its major provisions as: provisions for holding a valid license prior to the establishment of a banking business; laid down standards and procedures for conducting banking business; and prescribed minimum capital and reserve structure for banks. The 1952 Ordinance was reviewed comprehensively in 1958, 1969, 1991 and 1999. The series of reviews bordered essentially on licensing of banks, opening and closing of bank branches, the autonomy of the Central Bank of Nigeria, corporate governance, and minimum capital requirements for banks. Some authors on the Nigerian banking system have equally argued that persistent records of bank distress and failure in the country ignited most of the reviews, especially at the dawn of the 1980s (Ezeuduiji, 1997; and NDIC, 1994).

Of essence is the 1991 Banks and Other Financial Institutions (BOFI) Decree (now Act) of 1991. The BOFI Decree No. 25 of 1991, supported with the Central Bank of Nigeria Decree No. 24 also of 1991, consolidated the positions of the various amendments of the country's banking laws; laid foundation for the evolution of a more stable monetary and credit system and an efficient banking system; and close several loopholes that existed in the system due to increased complexities in the ways and manners of doing business (Ajayi, 1991; Oke 1991; Ezeoha & Uche, 2006). Also, subsequent changes to the 1991 banking law followed suit in 1997, with an amendment for a reasonable autonomy to the CBN, broadening of the scope of CBN authority by bringing in development banks and other financial institutions within the Bank's control, as well as increasing the minimum capital base of banks. There was also an amendment of the BOFI Decree in 1998, which sort to grant full autonomy to CBN by allowing the Bank to report directly to the presidency, instead of through the Minister of Finance, and allowing its Governor to issue banking licences or to impose, vary or revoke conditions subject to which the licences were issued. In 1999, following some rigidity still prevalent in the banking system, the Nigerian government undertook another comprehensive overhaul of the Nigerian banking law. This gave birth to the Banks and Other Financial Institutions Act of 1999.

Other ancillary laws that relate to banking in Nigeria are, among others, the Money Laundering Decree No. 3 of 1995 and the Failed Bank Decree of 1990. The Money Laundering Decree came into effect as a result of high level of financial malpractices and frauds witnessed from the beginning of the 1990s. In other to save the image of the country from crimes arising from money laundering (which banks were key media for such crime), the Decree compelled banks to disclose deposits with them beyond a stipulated amount. On the other hand, the Failed Banks (Recovery of Debts) and Financial Malpractices in Banks Decree 18 of 1994 came as a result of the increasing incidences of bank failure in Nigeria between the late 1980s and the early 1990s. The Decree created a tribunal (section 1 (1)) and section 3 (1) empowered it to try offences specified in the BOFID and the Nigeria Deposit Insurance Corporation Decree, as well as offence relating to the business or operation of a bank under any enactment.

There is also Central Bank of Nigeria Monetary Policy Circular. The monetary policy circulars of the CBN cover wide variety of monetary policy issues, including those that affect the supply and flow of bank credit. The first of such circulars was issued in 1969, and has since then being very effective instrument for controlling the liquidity and credit flow in the economy. Major areas covered by the circular are the reserve requirements, prudential requirements, capital funds adequacy ratios, and credit and foreign exchange policies. The Prudential Guideline, which is an appendage to the monetary policy circular, was originally set out in 1990. It usually outlines criteria for classifying banks' credits according to "performing" and "non-performing" assets, and the percentage to be provided for each class out of bank profits.

Although, the BOFI and the official banking circulars do not have explicit provisions relating electronic banking transactions in Nigeria, greater portion of the Money Laundering Act is dedicated to tackling 419 frauds. In effect, the Money Laundering Act and the Electronic Banking Guidelines seem to be the only legal instruments focusing on Internet banking transactions in the country at present.

Internet Banking Development in Nigeria

Internet banking is synonymous with electronic-banking, and has been defined as "the use of magnetically encoded plastic cards at terminals outside a regular bank location for cheque cashing, deposits and other money transfer functions" (The New Webster's Dictionary of the English Language, 1992). Essentially, Internet banking is beneficial to both banks and customers. To the banks, this banking system helps in the reduction of transaction and information costs.[2] To the customers, it offers opportunity to reduce the scale of information asymmetry between banks and customers. By comparing different bank portals, for instance, a customer is able to compare product lines and other important decision factors. It follows therefore that development in Internet banking has in the main been propelled by both the desire of banks for cost-efficient services and customers' need for improved banking services. In the case of Nigerian banks, the desire was a more inducing factor considering that from the late 90s, banks had started suffering serious deterioration in their levels of operating efficiency. On the average, the efficiency ratios of banks witnessed a downward trend from 77.9 percent in 1999 to as low as 49.0 percent in 2003 (Central Bank of Nigeria, 2002) – signifying a speedy rise in operating cost over and above operating income.

Generally, according to the Comptroller's Handbook (1999), Internet banking development takes the stages of:

1. The informative Stage: which is the basic level of Internet banking, and involve a bank having its marketing information on products and services on a stand-alone server.
2. The transaction Stage: that is a stage where Internet banking system allows some interaction between the ban*k*'s systems and the customer, and may be carried out through electronic mail, account inquiry, loan applications, or static file updates (name and address changes).
3. Transaction Stage: here Internet banking allows customers to execute transactions such as accessing accounts, paying bills, transferring funds, etc.

The fourth level that has been captured in the emerging Internet banking development trends is the virtual banking stage, which allows banks to exist and operate without a physical address.

In the case of Nigeria, all the banks have advanced through the first two stages – the informative and communicative stages. They all have functional web addresses; and they all advertise through the Internet. Although most of their customers lack Internet access, there is in existence reasonable degree of interactions between the banks and the customers with the aid of mobile telephone. As a result of high level of illiteracy and poverty in the country, banking practices are still evolving through the communicative stage.

Except with the use of mobile phone access, there are no structured electronic banking services taking place among Nigerian banks at the transaction stage. This is not surprising because the fragility of Internet banking demands that the market participants should be offered reasonable degree of legal protections. Where such protection is lacking, the confidence and zeal to participate will correspondingly be very low. The vulnerability of the Nigerian Internet business environment and lack of adequate regulatory protections on Internet business transactions have therefore not allowed banks to progress well enough beyond the communication level. In its 2002 survey on the use of e-banking by banks in Nigeria, for example, the Central bank of Nigeria discovered that majority of the banks were using physical security as their mode of e-banking control – a measure found very unimaginable in a highly volatile banking environment like Nigeria (Central bank of Nigeria, 2002; Chiemeka & Evwiekpaefe, 2006).[3] Nevertheless, a handful of transactions, involving some few larger banks and their privileged customers still take place through the Internet. Also, the electronic banking guidelines in

Nigeria generally do not permit the establishment, operation or existence of virtual banking system either through the Internet or in any other form. Paragraph 4.2 of the Guidelines out rightly bans virtual banks or banks that exist only in cyberspace from operating in the country; and stipulates that only banks, which are licensed, supervised and with physical presence in Nigeria, are permitted to offer electronic banking services to Nigerians.

Outside the clearer picture painted above, there is little understanding of the meaning and intents of Internet banking, both among banks and the regulatory agencies. There are for instances frivolous claims by all the banks that they have full Internet banking facilities, and so offer full Internet banking. While it is not doubtful that the banks have full Internet integrated facilities, what is indeed doubtful is the utilization rates and the level of customer patronage attributable to such facilities. Survey undertaken by the Central Bank of Nigeria, prior to the consolidation exercise, on the scale of Internet banking adoption in the country revealed that of the 89 licensed banks in the country, 17 were offering Internet banking, 24 were offering basic telephone banking, 7 had ATM services, while 13 of the banks were offering other forms of e-banking.[4] The survey did not however capture the nature of banking services being rendered by the 17 banks said to be involved in Internet banking.

At present, after the consolidation, all the 25 emerging banks[5] today offer Internet banking (not beyond the communicative stage), ATM and other forms of electronic banking. This is not surprising because the consolidation exercise offered banks the opportunity to increase their capital bases and be able to update their technological infrastructures. Irrespective of the present development, the benefits of Internet banking are yet to be transmitted into the mainstream of the country's economic activities. The socio-economic structures and infrastructure developments have not significantly kept paste with development in the banking system. Poor ICT adoption rate, epileptic power supply, deficiency in the education system and high poverty rate are among the socio-economic factors that tend to have rubbished the massive investments of banks in IT facilities since 2005. Majority of bank customers in the country, for instance, today do not show enough interest in the level of ICT deployment being undertaken by the banks. Thus, relative to the size of the country's population and economy, very few proportion of banking services take place through the Internet in Nigeria. This explains why branch banking has continued to play dominant role in the system. For security reasons, also, ATM deployments are mainly restricted within bank branches – thereby making nonsense of the real idea of such banking mode. There are also the cases of absence of clearly defined legal framework for Internet banking, leaving banks with inadequate legal cover against frauds and abuses melted on the system by cyber-criminals.

Regulatory Concerns over Internet Banking

The general idea of regulation is built on protection of the system, the economy and the customers (Ezeoha, 2005a). Nevertheless, the nature of Internet and electronic banking in general makes protection more difficult and complicated; and so regulatory requirements in an era of Internet banking should expectedly assume some new dimensions. Internet banking challenges conventional regulatory models in several ways. It increases the easiness at which banks circumvent rules. It also redefines risk structures and exacerbates risk complexities in banks - by introducing entirely new versions of risks relating to transactions, reputation, and strategy. Technically, Internet banking speeds up transactions, creates new competitors and services, alters banking operations and support functions, and expands the reach of financial institutions (Spong, 2000). The system typically runs on a platform of no paper documentation and traditional identity verification processes (Wright,

2002). By its nature, therefore, the introduction of Internet as part of the media of the delivery of banking services makes banks and bank customers more vulnerable to risks of fraud and failure than the normal conventional banking system (Williams, 2002).

One other area Internet banking has influenced regulation is the coverage and jurisdictions of existing banking laws. Conventional regulations require that banks keep to the laws and policies applicable within the national environment. In the case of Internet banking, where most of the available transactions are executed through borderless processes, the issue of jurisprudence becomes a serious matter. Thus, countries that perceive Internet frauds and crimes as country-specific problems make some dangerous mistakes (see for instance Bhargava, 2006). This reflects the warning offered by Williams (2002) that purely national or even bilateral responses are simply inadequate to deal with the problem, considering the dynamics of illegal markets, the activities of criminal enterprises, the reach of criminal networks, and the pervasiveness of money laundering all that are facilitated through Internet banking structures. What, for instance, happens when Internet frauds spread in network of countries are originated from a country where the national government lacks resources and technical capacity to fight such crimes, and where also available regulations are highly inadequate? What would be the effects on global Internet frauds when, for instance, due to corruption and lack of political wills, governments in such a country is unwilling to take decisive action against indigenous criminal organisations?

Indeed, the origin of Internet fraud calls for important regulatory attention. But, the spread of such crime should be of far more concern to regulators and international anti-fraud agencies. This is so because the registration of an Internet site in a country does not automatically translate to a physical attachment of the affected individual or company. For example, a team of cyber criminals may just get an Internet address registered in Nigeria, whereas the actual targets and places of physical operations of the team may be in the United Kingdom.

The above scenario points at the need for some regulatory alignments to enable the existing laws to catch up with the speed of Internet banking development and the arising spread and dynamism of cyber-related crimes. It has been along this line posited that the logic of Internet has already shaped markets and financial institutions for a while, and it is now high time to draw relevant regulatory conclusions from this development (Norgren, 2001). Such conclusions should be based on improving the efficiency of the domestic control instruments as well as collaboration in the international banking jurisprudence. To fight Nigerian 419 frauds, for instance, a foreign government would require a deep understanding of the domestic laws relating to banking in Nigeria and the institutions for enforcing these laws.

The Nigerian Brand of Internet Banking Frauds

It is indeed difficult to separate the coverage of the present Internet business challenges generally from the specifics of Internet banking frauds. In the words of O'Brien (2002, p.319), the real motive of many computer crimes involves the theft of money, and mostly involves insider jobs. Payments or transfer of funds arising from Internet deals are required to be made through banks, given the virtual gap between the parties involved. In which case, most Internet frauds end up as bank fraud, essentially from the point of view of Nigerian banking laws and regulations.

The Nigerian version of Internet fraud has been severally defined, with some inherent similarities cutting across most of the definitions that have so far been offered. Some of the definitions have it that Nigerian Internet fraud is:

1. Collection of fraudulent e-mail messages from Africa and elsewhere around the world (WorldWideSpam.info)
2. An unsolicited email messages from a stranger who promises great wealth — a get-rich-quick scheme (http://www.bsacy-bersafety.com/threat/nigerian_scam.cfm)
3. A scam where the sender requests help in facilitating the transfer of a substantial sum of money, generally in the form of an email. In return, the sender offers a commission, usually in the range of several million dollars (http://www.answers.com/topic/advance-fee-fraud).
4. The Nigerian scam is an advanced fee fraud that was started from Nigeria by Nigerians and has now transcended the Nigerian borders; previously operated via phone and postal mails, the scam has taken advantage of the Internet and its paraphernalia (http://www.nigerianscambuster.com/).
5. An attempt to defraud by sending out large amounts of emails stating that the recipient has inherited a vast fortune, but will need to supply banking account details, or to send payment for fees, before the inheritance can by passed on (http://www.allwords.com/word-Nigerian+scam.html)

The above definitions interestingly suggest that any of such frauds do not necessarily come from Nigeria or be committed by Nigerians before it can be regarded as 419 or advance fee fraud. Nevertheless, most of the broader definitions have suggested that this version of fraud have both Nigerian background and origin. More generally, this brand of fraud is known by numerous names: Advance Fee Fraud, 419 Fraud, the West African Scam, the Nigerian Connection, Nigerian Letter Scam, Nigerian Money Offers, the Nigerian Scam, Yahoo Boys, among others. Perhaps the most specific definition is the one offered by the Nigerian Criminal Code from which the concept "419" originated. According to Section 419 of the Criminal Code Act of the Federal Republic of Nigeria, one guilty of advance fee fraud (or by whatever name it might be called) is "any person who by false pretence, and with intent to defraud, obtains from any other person to deliver to any person anything capable of being stolen, is guilty of a felony … it is immaterial that the thing is obtained or its delivery is induced through medium of a contract induced by false pretence". Section 419(A) of the Criminal Code defines one as being guilty of 419 fraud offence/crime if "by any false pretence or by any means of any other fraud obtains credit for himself or any other person … is guilty of a felony and is liable to imprisonment".

The most popular among Internet frauds globally linked to Nigeria therefore is the 419 frauds. The spread of 419 frauds has indeed remained a big threat to the public confidence in Internet business transactions general; and great source of embarrassment to Nigerian people (Ribadu, 2006). In 1999, for instance, up to US$5 billion had been stolen worldwide through the use of the scheme (Smith et al., 1999). As at 2007, an Internet source placed the figure at an estimate of over 32 billion US$ to date, with as much as US$4.3 billion recorded only in 2007 (http://www.ultrascan.nl/html/419_statistics.html). The amount involved is undoubtedly huge and the destructions are growing – thus, the global attention on the 419 fraud. What is not clear enough is whether it is Nigerians only committing 419-related Internet frauds or if (like every old successive scam like the Dutch fraud, Angolan scam, Spanish and Australian scams) it has been has been widely copied by other nationals wearing Nigerian impression.

This kind of crime is globally understood to be a financial crime in which the criminal lures his victim with attractive offers of a share in huge fortune. The offer is posed as risk-free and tax-free, with the victim being expected to make an initial offer or submit his account information if he wishes to benefit from the deal. The victim is told that the required payment is to enable the *partner* clear grounds and bribe the *other officers* to facilitate the entire transaction.

At the domestic front, 419 offences take far much more baberick forms and unlike the global version are most times committed without the bank. It could be a promise of money-doubling requesting the victim to extend an amount of money for the purchase of chemicals for the printing of millions of currency which the latter would be the major beneficiary. It could also be an appeal for the victim to extend cash to facilitate the clearing of goods impounded or seized by seaport officials Or even more crudely, people pretending to be disabled or to run NGOs in order to attract money from unsuspecting public. Essentially, these crude methods which are prevalent local take place out of the banking system, and so are done mainly on cash basis.

There are thus significant differences in the ways and forms 419 frauds occur domestically and internationally. Because of the geographical disparity in international transactions, international 419 frauds are perpetrated not necessarily in cash, but through banks, who knowingly or unknowingly facilitate payment for such transactions. In some cases, there are allegations of insider involvement to cover the identities and traces of huge amount of cash usually involved. Again, because of its remote nature, 419 frauds at the global level are committed through electronic media such as telephone, e-mail, and Internet. From the point of view of the international community, a report by the Swiss Federal Department of Foreign Affairs (2008), carefully documented the manners the Nigerian Internet frauds take. According to the report, Nigerian scam correspondence could be in the form of letters, fax messages or e-mails; and initiating an attempt to defraud could come in the form of:

1. e-mails sent to people telling them that the sender is a high ranking officer in a bank with knowledge of funds deposited by persons now deceased. The 'funds' are supposedly without bonafide owners and at the risk of being confiscated by the management of the bank if they remain unclaimed within a certain period. The depositors of the funds may be said to have died in a plane crash and the next of kin cannot be traced.

2. e-mails from top government officials (possibly in State oil corporations, or similar organisations) informing the victim of contracts, which were over-quoted with the resultant excess funds being held in the corporation accounts pending the transfer to a 'foreign bank account' The government official may want the victim to provide a bank account to transfer the funds out of the country.

3. e-mail from the widow of a prominent (may be renowned for corruption, e.g. Abacha, Mobutu) asking the recipient to help gain access to her late husband? Wealth which may be tied up in gold coins hidden in trunk box. The box may have been lodged with a security firm that has no knowledge of the real contents.

4. Another example of 419 involves the purchase of gemstones. The victim is contacted by 'officials of a foreign company', which wants to source some raw material from a local company. The victim may be given the contact information of the local company and asked to act as intermediary with an attractive commission. In most cases, the victim buys samples from the 'local company' and is invited to a rendezvous with representatives of the foreign firm. The representatives either never make the meeting, or the samples are disqualified as substandard and the victim is asked to return for more. When the victim returns the products to discover that the seller has disappeared. When the victim is considered trustworthy (meaning he/she is extremely greedy and not likely to be a police informant) the sample is paid for by the foreigner. The profit would be so much that the victim is lured into going for more of the material, this time making a

bigger investment. Some have been known to borrow money in order to buy a greater quantity, but when they return, the foreign investor would have disappeared.

While other forms of Internet frauds are built around the traditional mail order businesses that existed before the advent of commercial Internet usage, the Nigerian version is typically built on the greed of both the fraudsters and their victims. The victims originally show interest and zeal to make unusual and untaxed profits, with little capital. At the start of the purported transaction, there is normally little pressure put on the victim, and so may not be cut in the web if he or she fails to show interest. This explains why till date, non-response to 419 letters remains the best strategy to avoid being a victim of this class of cyber crime.

Causes of Internet Frauds in Nigeria

Certain factors pose as reasons for the growth and persistence of the Nigerian version of Internet frauds. First, Nigerian Internet frauds perhaps persist because the existing local and global measures are not enough. It could also be that the perpetrators have advanced alongside with innovative developments in information and communication technology. Again, Nigerian Internet fraudsters might have had their ways because of the presumption that their acts were preyed on greedy foreign victims. While those fraudsters innovate and perfect their criminal operations on the Internet, existing governance and institutional structures in the country do little to checkmate them. Essentially, some of the remote causes presented as follows:

Lack of Adequate Regulatory Framework

This has been largely pointed at as the major cause of Internet frauds in the country. A Nigerian cyber expert simply chronicled the regulatory environ-

ment of Internet transactions in Nigeria, highlighting the following points (Oyesanya, 2004a):

- Most Nigerian's Internet Systems do not provide the minimum level of Information Assurance.
- Nigerian ISP's and Cybercafe, operate in a highly deregulated Telecommunications Industry, the Internet arrived here impromptu, and in most cases bypasses local Infrastructure. Most Nigerian Internet traffic is non-local, rather, gets routed to VSAT Backbone Providers all around the world. It is a highly decentralized. Operating environment, mostly outside the control of government.
- The Nigeria's Internet environment is properly conducive to electronic Lawlessness. If electricity generation were regular, Nigeria would have become the Las Vegas of Internet vice.
- Domain Name registration in Nigeria is free, and the registration process only requires that you provide a Nigerian address, which by the way, may not be verifiable by the National Postal Service Authority.
- The Nigerian Police simply lacks Internet policing capability. Validating individual identity is also problematic, the National ID Card program became stalled with fraudulent activities, no Centralized Credit checking facility, and Passport issuance is just a matter of paying the right price.
- Self-regulation and corporation between Nigerian Internet Service Providers, cybercafe operator, and local law enforcement agencies, is also non-existence.

Inadequate Cooperation of Banks

Another factor responsible for the persistence in Nigerian Internet fraud is the easy at which banks give fraudsters access to their networks. As stated earlier, it is not possible for cyber frauds to be committed without the aid of the banking system. Unfortunately, in the case of Nigeria, increased competition leads to a situation where banks can do anything to garner deposits. The regulatory authorities do little to enforce existing laws prohibiting the flow of unidentified funds through the banks, and banks have little incentive to reveal the identities of their customers.

Growing Technology Gap between Banks and the Regulatory Authorities

While the regulatory authorities are crawling in an effort to beef up their surveillance mechanisms, banks in the country have taken advantage of the huge capital base bequeathed on them by the 2004 reforms to acquire sophisticated IT facilities. This has in no small measure placed some overwhelming duties on the shoulders of the regulators. As identified by (Oyesanya, 2004b), Nigerian law enforcement agencies are basically technology illiterates; they lack computer forensics training, and often result to conducting police raids on Internet Service sites, mainly for the purpose of extortion. Explaining this gap, Ribadu (2007) also argued that the Nigerian banking industry hurriedly embraced the credit card system without carrying the law enforcement and criminal justice sector along in the capacity to understand the intricacies and multiple dimensions of the problem – a factor he attributed to the currently huge and rising incidence of cybercrime in the system.

The Case of Mistaken Identity by the Global Community

An important question that arises here borders on whether the global community is not missing the point by having a mindset that every Internet fraud case tagged 419 originates from Nigeria and is committed by a Nigerian. Perhaps, most Internet investment and financial frauds committed until date may not be by Nigerians. Some may be from foreigners hiding under the vulnerable Internet

environments in Nigeria. This claim is confirmed by the 2004 revelation by a capture Al Qaeda's operative, Muhammad Naeem Noor Khan, that Nigerian Websites and Email Systems were used by Al Qaeda to disseminate Internet Information, and that terrorist Information flow used Nigeria as its gateway. As argued by Oyesanya (2004a), the choice of Nigeria is simply that of a case of choosing the perfect environment for passing undetected terrorist Internet Information. Nigerian Internet space provides the best electronic cave for Al Qaeda to hide.

Link Between Nigeria's Image and Internet Banking Reputation

An interesting argument in the whole idea of safe Internet banking environment centres on whether bad offline reputation of a country automatically translates to bad online reputation. Is there a direct link between a country's hardcore image and her Internet business reputation? While this begs for empirical investigation, most Internet control measures adopted by developed countries today assume that there is clearly no difference between the two phenomena. Arguments raised here highlight the fact that there could still be a case of mistaken identity; and that part of the causes of failure of prevailing cybercrime control mechanisms could be this mistaken identity.

A Glance of the Hardcore Country Image

No doubt, Nigeria as a country has had very poor approval rating in the global business community. According to the reports of the Transparency International on the country's corruption rating, since 2001, Nigeria has remained very much at the bottom of the corruption perception index (see Table 2). Nigeria is also rated poorly in terms of the safety of its business environment.

In terms of politics and human rights records, the image of Nigeria relative to other countries is

Table 2. Corruption perception index (CPI) of Nigeria, South Africa and Bangladesh

Year	Total No. of Countries	Country Ranking	CPI Score				
		Nigeria	South Africa	Bangladesh	Nigeria	South Africa	Bangladesh
2001	91	2nd	25th	1st	1.0	4.8	0.4
2002	102	2nd	27th	1st	1.6	4.5	1.2
2003	133	2nd	26th	1st	1.4	4.4	1.3
2004	145	2nd	31st	1st	1.6	4.6	1.5
2005	158	3rd	26th	1st	1.9	4.5	1.7
2006	160	7th	33rd	3rd	2.2	4.6	2.0
2007	162	9th	33rd	7th	2.2	5.1	2.0
2008	180	16th	33rd	10th	2.7	4.9	2.1

Source: Compiled from Transparency International Country Reports

not impressive. Since the country's independence in 1960, for instance, the military had ruled with fierce force and instinct for looting of public treasuries and human rights abuses, for about 31 years.[6] In between the military junta leadership, there were seven coups, with some reportedly very deadly. There are widespread allegations that the electoral system even is very deficient and does not give room for the election of credible persons in political offices (Amoda, 2008). These allegations manifest clearly in the ways and manners elections are marred by massive riggings and electoral violence; and in the present popular insistence on electoral reforms. Not surprising, the transformation from military to civilian regime in 1999 has not significantly changed the country's global rating and perception, especially as it concerns public sector corruption. It is also not surprising that between 2001 and 2004, the country retained a position as the second most corrupt country in the world. She was 3rd in 2005. Although the statistics improved between 2006 and 2008, there may still not be any much improvement in real terms, especially considering that these periods covered small countries that were ruled like family businesses and the devastated economies

of Sudan, Afghanistan and Iraq.[7] The effect of this level of notoriety on the flow of foreign investment in the country has also been well documented (see for instance Doh et al., 2003; Shao et al., 2007)

The Hardcore Image of the Nigerian Banking System

Essentially, the banking system is not insulated from the above image. The industry has passed through some hard times, and has also not enjoyed sound global goodwill. Before 2000, the industry was faced with gross instability; failure and distress occasioned by high prevalence of frauds and insider abuses (Central bank of Nigeria, 2002, 2001a). This condition joins to explain the basis for the unpopular standings of Nigerian banks in the Internet. Domestic public confidence on the banks before 2005 was weakened by seasonal failure cases.[8] Banks in the country are consistently accused of providing media for laundering stolen public money. Bank robbery is also a common phenomenon and a routine occurrence in the country. What has essentially happened is that fraudsters and their criminal insiders in the banks

Figure 1. Trends in the number of reported cases of bank fraud in Nigeria (1994to 2004) (Source: Nigerian Deposit Insurance Corporation [Various Years])

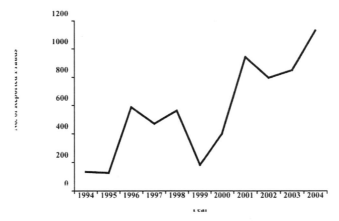

have cashed on the already established bad images. Figure 1, for instance demonstrates visible rise in the number of reported cases of bank frauds in the country during the period 1994 to 2004.

Table 3 shows clearly that fraud was not an industry wide phenomenon, as it looked like just some few banks were dedicated to frauds and fraudulent activities during the periods 1990 to 2004. An average of 90.7 percent of the total frauds committed by banks in the country within the period came from just 10 banks. Essentially, as shown in Table 4, most of the frauds (an average of about 67.1 percent (between 2000 and 2004) were perpetrated by managers and senior officers of banks.

On first principle, because of the above image record before 2004, foreign countries and their nationals found convenient in avoiding dealings with Nigerian banks. This justification is premised more on the fact that even before the adoption of Internet business transactions in the country, dubious Nigerians had invented and perpetrated the act of 419 frauds through telephones and postal mails. That the notoriety of these offline frauds and criminal acts creep into the online Internet business system cannot therefore be a baseless suspicion.

The Nigerian Internet Business Image

Since Internet deals are characteristically cross-border by nature, cash payment or bulk cash transfers are impossible without the aid of banks. In which case, Internet frauds generally cannot exist without the instrumentality of the banking system. Banks are needed to complete every form of Internet business transactions. This is why discussions on Internet banking frauds go hand-in-hand with Internet businesses generally. As inferred by Ezeoha (2005a), Nigeria has a high reputation for Internet-related frauds in the world, referred to, at the international scene as the headquarters of Advance Fee Fraud (419). The international image is an offshoot of the earlier incidences that inflicted the industry up till the late 90s, when bank frauds, forgeries, money laundering, insider abuse and erosion of public confidence constituted a set of disturbing issues to regulators, international development partners, bank customers and policy makers in general, in Nigeria.

Before the start of cyber-related businesses in Nigeria in the early 90s, electronic crimes were already gaining their grounds. As at then, ICT development was at its embryonic stage, as

Table 3. Frauds concentration in 10 Banks

Year	Total No. of Banks in Operation	% Of frauds By 10 Banks	% Of Frauds by Others	Total
1990	107	97.3	2.7	100
2000	90	93.35	6.65	100
2001	90	93.47	6.53	100
2002	90	88.9	11.1	100
2003	89	92.02	7.98	100
2004	89	85.88	14.12	100
Average (2000-2004)	90	90.724	9.276	100

Nigerian Deposit Insurance Corporation Annual Reports [Various Years]

telephone was a very privileged facility found only in corporate and government offices. Very few institutions and individuals had access to computer, and Internet was virtually unheard of. Shortage in communication facilities was caused mainly by government's monopoly and excessive control in the sector. 419 frauds were committed and prosecuted like every other crime in the country. The international version of this crime was committed through the telephone and postal mailing system. There was at that stage not much about Internet business or Internet frauds. With the liberalisation of the information and com-munication sector in the late 1990s, many digital network organisations sprang up. By the beginning of 21 Century, access to computer and telephone facilities had improved. International fraudsters then saw the development as a good opportunity to expand their network of frauds.

The coming into force of the Internet infra-structure was a huge boost to the electronic structures already on ground. According to a local newspaper source in 2004, for instance, the rate of cyber crime in Nigeria quickly outgrew the rate of Internet usage in the country (Fanawopo, 2004). As at then, according to the same source,

Table 4. Distribution of bank staff involved in frauds

Staff Category	Year						
	1990	2000	2001	2002	2003	2004	Average 2000-2004
Managers/Supervisors	13.7	26.8	36.2	18.8	23.6	41.0	29.3
Officers, Accountants/ Executive Assistant	10.8	20.5	39.5	56.5	38.7	33.7	37.8
Clerks/Cashiers	49.6	27.8	19.7	15.3	23.6	15.9	20.5
Typists/Technicians/ Stenography	1.9	4.1	-	-	-	4.7	4.4
Messengers/Drivers/Cleaners/ Security Guards/Stewards	16.3	16.4	3.3	4.7	6.6	3.9	7.0
Temporary Staff	0.5	1.6	1.3	4.7	7.6	0.8	3.2
Unclassified	7.2	2.8	-	-	-	-	2.8
Total	100.0	100.0	100.0	100.0	100.0	100.0	100.0

statistics from an intelligence brief of the Verisigh's Internet Security had ranked Nigeria as 56th out of 60 countries in embracing Internet usage but third, in the fraud attempt category. From a struggle to get letters mailed to local and overseas victims, 419ers (as they are locally called) cashed on the easiness, speed and wide coverage offered by Internet access to expand their scope of activities. Today, this Nigerian version of Internet fraud, as revealed in Table 5, has become one of the top global concerns on the safety and welfare of cyber community. Its ranking ranged from 1st to 3rd positions in terms of the amount of loss per person (see Table 5). The Nigerian Internet fraud came first among the top ten Internet frauds, under the same measure, in the years 2000, 2002, 2005 and 2006.

The above sections reveal some good deal of consistency between Nigeria's hardcore country image and the country's Internet business reputation. Over the years 2000 to 2007, the country has ranked uniformly top among the most corrupt nations in the world, with its banking system heavily infested with cases of frauds, distress and failure. The prevalence of poverty and economic hardship, occasioned by several years of systemic corruption in governance, is also another visible feature of the Nigerian state (Ezeoha, 2005b). All these join to support the claim that the country's bad Internet banking or business reputation is not a mere coincidence. This conclusion perfectly agrees with the argument provided by Chuhan (2006) that "deep deprivation weakens the capacity of states to combat organised crime, arm conflicts, terrorism, and the spread of diseases, and can severe economic, environmental, public health, and security consequences for neighbouring states and the global community". A corrupt system provides incentives for the misuse of innovations in digital technologies. At the same time, a weak banking system, such as the case in Nigeria, submits itself to vulnerability arising from such misuse and end up facilitating fraudulent transactions perpetrated through the Internet. Thus, efforts to control cyber crime should revolve around the enactment and enforcement of laws that would boost the level of sanity in the banking system. The Nigerian government, as shown in the next section, has severally tried this approach.

Laws Relating to Internet Banking in Nigeria

Unmonitored Internet banking activities can actually distort the predictability of funds flows in and out of the banking system. At the same time, weak Internet banking regulation influences the overall level of frauds and corruptions at the national level, by providing channels for easy laundering and flow of stolen money from both public officers and corrupt businessmen. This trend is capable of complicating monetary policy management at the macroeconomic level and then operational risk and liquidity management at the individual bank level. Under such situation, it becomes very difficult to control inflation, pricing system and protect the value of the local currency. The need for special regulations to guard Internet banking arises because of the inherent and unique opportunities and threats. The challenges include the introduction

Table 5. Average loss per person arising from the Nigerian internet frauds 1999-2007

Year	Amount of Loss Per Person (US$)	Position Among World Top 10
1999	0	0
2000	3,000	1st
2001	5,957	2nd
2002	3,864	1st
2003	5,496	2nd
2004	3,000	2nd
2005	5,000	1st
2006	5,100	1st
2007	1,922	3rd

Source: US Federal Bureau of Intelligence (FBI) Internet Crime Reports [For the various years] and National White Collar Crime Centre

of new versions of risks in bank management[9]; exposure to frauds, and creation of opportunities for arbitrary circumvention of banking laws. In the area of risk, in addition to the usual credit, interest rate, liquidity, price, and foreign exchange risks that are inherent in bank management, Internet banking heightens other forms of banking risks such as transaction, compliance, strategic and reputation risks (Comptroller's Handbook, 1999). According to the Handbook, transaction risk is the current and prospective risk to earnings and capital arising from fraud, error, and the inability to deliver products or services, maintain a competitive position, and manage information; compliance risk is the risk to earnings or capital arising from violations of, or nonconformance with, laws, rules, regulations, prescribed practices, or ethical standards; strategic risk is the current and prospective impact on earnings or capital arising from adverse business decisions, improper implementation of decisions, or lack of responsiveness to industry changes; and reputation risk is the current and prospective impact on earnings and capital arising from negative public opinion.

Because of its remote nature, Internet banking makes banks vulnerable; and also breaches the principle of secrecy upon which bank-customer relationship is originally built. This explains why it is highly challenging to regulate this system of banking with conventional laws and policies (Wallsten, 2003). Although, Nigeria does not yet have dedicated Internet banking laws, two closely related regulatory instruments governing the activities of banks and their customers in the Internet are the Money Laundering Law and the Advanced Fee Fraud Act. There is also the more direct set of guidelines on electronic banking released in 2004.

The Money Laundering Law

The money laundering law in the country is originally referred to as the Money Laundering (Prohibition) Decree No. 3 of 1995, repealed by the Money Laundering (Prohibition) Act of 2004.

The law was enacted mainly to criminalize the act of money laundering, and to impose responsibilities on financial institutions by requiring them to embark on measures that will ensure proper knowledge of their customers and the nature of their business through pre-transaction and operational requirements (Central Bank of Nigeria, 2002). The major provisions of the law that links it closely to the fight against Internet frauds can be seen in Table 6.

Due to its nature, the provisions of the Money Laundering Act are primary enforced by the Nigerian Drug Law Enforcement Agency (NDLEA). The law is however linked to the overall Internet banking regulatory frameworks in the country because frauds committed through Internet usually involve huge amount of money; and such funds expectedly are transmitted and laundered through the banking system by fraudsters. A source put it that the average loss per person arising from the Nigerian money offer (or 419 frauds) stood at US$5,957 as at 2001 – a figure that place this version of fraud second among all categories of Internet frauds. The major focus of the Act, in this regard, is that tracking down the origins of funds allegedly from proceeds of illegal transactions (such as 419, drug trafficking and terrorism sponsorship) is as good as tracking down the culprits. While this may be effective from the point of view of prosecuting offenders, its capacity to deterred 419 fraudsters is doubtful in that banks are traditionally known for not having the incentive to reveal the identities of their profile "customers". O'Brien (2002) also remarks that bank frauds involving the use of Internet and computer networks may be concealed by banks because of the fear of scaring away customers and provoking shareholders complaints.

The Advanced Fee Fraud and Other Fraud Related Offences Act

The Advance Fee Fraud and Other Fraud Related Offences Decree (No. 13 of 1995) was first enacted on 1 April 1995 and later comprehensively amended as The Advance Fee Fraud and Other Fraud Related Offences Act of 2006. Its main intent was the proscription of three forms of conduct: obtaining property by false pretences, obtaining benefits by false pretences and doubling, washing or minting of currency. Because of its lack of democratic flavors and the complain that it was against the principles of fairness and justice expected of all international criminal proceedings, as well as against the provisions of Chapter V of the Nigerian Constitution, the Decree was amended in 2006 and renamed the Advance Fee Fraud and Other Related Offences Act of 2006. Section 1 of the new Act defines as being guilty of *advance fee fraud* any person who by any false pretence and with intent to defraud:

a. Obtains, from any other person, in Nigeria or in any other country for himself or any other person;
b. Induces any other person, in Nigeria or in any other country, to deliver to any person; or
c. Obtains any property, whether or not the property is obtained or its delivery is induced through the medium of a contract induced by the false pretence, commits an offence under this Act.

Interestingly, Section 4 provides that "a person who by false pretence, and with the intent to defraud any other person, invites or otherwise induces that person or any other person to visit Nigeria for any purpose connected with the com-

Table 6. Some relevant provisions of the Nigerian money laundering law

Section	Provision
Sections 2(1) and 2(2)	Which require that a transfer to or from foreign country of funds or securities of a sum greater than $10,000 or its equivalent be reported to the Central Bank of Nigeria; and that such report shall include an indication of the nature and amount of the transfer, and the names and address of the sender and receiver of the funds or securities
Section 5(1)	Which requires that a financial institution shall verify its customer's identity and address before opening an account for, issuing a passbook to, entering into a fiduciary transaction with, renting a safe deposit box to or establishing any other business relationship with the customer?
Section 6(1b&c)	Which requires a special surveillance on the part of a financial institution to seek information from the customer as to the origin and destination of funds, the aim of the transaction and the identity of the beneficiary – for funds surrounded by conditions of unusual or unjustified complexity and funds appear to have no economic justification or lawful objective.
Section 7	Which requires a financial institution or designated non-financial institution to preserve and keep at the disposal of regulatory authorities the record of a customer's identification for a period of at least 5 years after the closure of the customer's accounts or the severance of relations with the customer?
Section 9(1)	Which requires a financial institution to develop programmes to combat the laundering of the proceeds of a crime or other illegal act – with some of such programmes including (a) the designation of compliance officers at management level or at its headquarters and at every branch and local office, (b) regular training programme for its employees, (c) the centralisation of the information collected, and the establishment of an internal audit unit to ensure compliance with and ensure the effectiveness of the measures taken to enforce the provisions of the law.
Sections 10 & 11	Section 10 makes it mandatory for a financial institution or designated non-financial institution to report to the regulatory agencies transactions involving certain amount of money; while section 11 holds directors or top officers of such institutions liable under the law for conspiring with the owner of laundered funds, and provide for the subjections of such officers to criminal proceedings for all offences arising there from.
Sections 14 &15	Which defines one as being guilty of money laundering offences if the person converts or transfers resources or properties derived directly or indirectly from illicit traffic in narcotic drugs and psychotropic substances or any other crimes or illegal act, with the aim of concealing or disguising the origins of funds or resources arising there from; or the person collaborates in concealing or disguising the genuine nature, origin, location, disposition, movement or ownership of such funds or resources.

Sources: Extracted from the relevant sections of the Money Laundering (Prohibition) Act of 2004

mission of an offence under this Act commits an offence and is liable on conviction to imprisonment for a term not more than 20 years and not less than seven years without the option of a fine". On the deliberate involvement of banks or bank officers in the act of advance fee frauds, section 7 subsection 3 provides for the prosecution of a bank or its officers under a situation where "as a result of negligence, or regulation in the internal control procedures, a financial institution fails to exercise due diligence as specified in the Banks and Other Financial Institutions Act, 1991 as amended or the Money Laundering (Prohibition) Act, 2004 in relation to the conduct of financial transactions which in fact involve the proceeds of unlawful activity"

Other interesting areas of the Advance Fee Fraud Act include:

1. Section 12(1) which requires that any person or entity providing an electronic communication service or remote computing service either by e-mail or any other form shall be required to obtain from the customer or subscriber full names and addresses;

2. Section 12(2) which provides that "any person or entity providing the electronic communication service or remote computing service either by e-mail or any other form, who fails to comply with the provisions of subsection (1) of this section, commits an offence and is liable on conviction to a fine of N 100,000 and forfeiture of the equipment or facility used in providing the service";

3. 3. Section 13(1) which requires that any person or entity who in the normal course of business provides telecommunications or Internet services or is the owner or person in the management of any premises being used as a telephone or Internet cafe or by whatever name called shall be registered with the Economic and Financial Crimes Commission; and shall maintain a register of all fixed line customers which shall be liable to inspection by any authorized officer of the Commission; and submit returns to the Commission on demand on the use of its facilities; and

4. Section 13(2) which requires that "any person whose normal course of business involves the provision of non-fixed line or Global System of Mobile Communications (GSM) or is in the management of any such services, shall submit on demand to the Commission such data and information as are necessary or expedient for giving full effect to the performance of the functions of the Commission under this Act";

Unlike the Failed Bank Act that provides series of options of fines for individuals or groups that breach the provisions of the law, most offences under the Advance Fee Fraud and Other Related Fraud Offences Act do not have options of fine. The jail sentences for the latter range from 7 to 20 years; and it does not matter whether the offence is committed in Nigeria or outside the country. This indeed shows the level of seriousness attached to the prevalence of advanced fee frauds by the Nigerian government. The coming into force of the EFCC has equally boosted the enforcement status of the act. Despite its elaborate provisions and strictness, however, the Advance Fee Fraud Act does not cover well enough the online version of 419 frauds. Such omissions create situations where attempt to enthrone safe Internet banking has been publicly viewed as being too extra-judicial and self-benefiting.

The Central Bank of Nigeria Guidelines on Electronic Banking

The Central Bank of Nigeria (CBN) Guidelines on Electronic Banking in Nigeria, released in August 2003, has elaborate provisions on how to use electronic media in the deployment and delivery of banking services/products. The goal of the guidelines, as specified by the CBN is to inform the future conduct of financial institutions in e-banking in the country. Specifically, paragraph 1.1 of the guidelines, which focus on standard for computer networks and Internet, require that:

1. Networks used for transmission of financial data must be demonstrated to meet the requirements specified for data confidentiality and integrity.
2. Banks are required to deploy a proxy type firewall to prevent a direct connection between the banks back end systems and the Internet.
3. Banks are required to ensure that the implementation of the firewalls addresses the security concerns for which they are deployed.
4. For dial up services, banks must ensure that the modems do not circumvent the firewalls to prevent direct connection to the bank's back end system.
5. External devices such as Automated Teller Machines (ATMs), Personal Computers, (PC's) at remote branches, kiosks, etc. permanently connected to the bank's network and passing through the firewall must at the minimum address issues relating to non-repudiation, data integrity and confidentiality. Banks may consider authentication via Media Access Control (MAC) address in addition to other methods.
6. Banks are required to implement proper physical access controls over all network infrastructures both internal and external.

At the same time, the provisions under paragraph 1.4.3 center specifically on Internet banking. The provisions make it compulsory for banks to put in place procedures for maintaining the bank's Website, which should ensure the following:

a. Only authorized staff should be allowed to update or change information on the Web site;

b. Updates of critical information should be subject to dual verification (e.g. interest rates).
c. Website information and links to other Websites should be verified for accuracy and functionality.
d. Management should implement procedures to verify the accuracy and content of any financial planning software, calculators, and other interactive programs available to customers on an Internet Website or other electronic banking service.
e. Links to external Websites should include a disclaimer that the customer is leaving the bank's site and provide appropriate disclosures, such as noting the extent, if any, of the bank's liability for transactions or information provided at other sites.
f. Banks must ensure that the Internet Service Provider (ISP) has implemented a firewall to protect the bank's Website where outsourced.
g. Banks should ensure that installed firewalls are properly configured and institute procedures for continued monitoring and maintenance arrangements are in place.
h. Banks should ensure that summary-level reports showing web-site usage, transaction volume, system problem logs, and transaction exception reports are made available to the bank by the Web administrator.

Another provision that borders on the Internet mode of bank services delivery, as contained in paragraph 1.4.8 of the guidelines, requires Internet Service Providers (ISPs) to exercise due diligence to ensure that only websites of financial institutions duly licensed by the CBN are hosted on their servers; and that ISPs that host unlicensed financial institutions would be held liable for all acts committed through the hosted websites. Unfortunately, the efficiency of local ISPs is not even trusted by the local banks. This leads to a situation where most of the banks resort to subscribing to foreign

ISPs that are by implication out of the jurisdiction of the Central Bank of Nigeria.

Despite its extensive requirements on strategies for ensuring safe and fraud-free Internet banking development in the country, the E-banking Guidelines have also been criticised by Ezeoha (2005a) on the ground that:

1. It does not have adequate and effective provisions to check the growing popularity of Internet banking against the backdrop of growing sophistication in technology related crimes and frauds – by not laying emphasis on the four key areas where Internet banking may have regulatory impact, which include: changing the traditional lines upon which existing regulatory structures are laid; handling concerns about existing public policy issues; changing the nature and scope of existing risks; and rebalancing regulatory rules and industry discretion;
2. It omitted some of the original key recommendations of the Committee that drafted the Guidelines – specifically as it regards paragraph 6.1 of the Committee's report, which among others recommended that all banks intending to offer transactional services on the Internet/other e-banking products should obtain an approval-in-principle from CBN prior to commencing these services.
3. It fails to explicitly recommend a standard that allows banks to examine potential threats that may already be in existence in each individual financial institution's current network.
4. It omits the major realities unique in the Nigerian context – including the poor state of basic information technological infrastructure in the country; the fact that most ISPs are located outside the country; and that Internet banking proper is still at its embryonic stage of development in the country.

The effectiveness of the Guidelines to guarantee smooth and effective Internet banking development in the country may be constrained because of its rigidity on who should render Internet banking in Nigeria. Paragraph 4.2, for instance, emphasizes that only banks, which are licensed, supervised and with physical presence in Nigeria, are permitted to offer electronic banking services in Nigeria, and that virtual banks are not to be allowed. The Guidelines also gives indications that the products/services can only be offered to residents of Nigeria with a verifiable address within the geographic boundary of Nigeria; any person residing physically in Nigeria as a citizen, under a resident permit or other legal residency designation under the Nigerian Immigration Act; any person known herein as a "classified person" who neither is temporarily in Nigeria. The Guidelines go further to indicate that the e-banking service should be offered in Naira only; and that where such a service is to be provided in foreign currency, it should be to only the holders of ordinary domiciliary accounts, and conform with all other foreign exchange regulations. The above provisions, no doubt, can affect the speed and easiness at which Internet banking in the country can be globally integrated. As demonstrated by Guasch and Hahn (1999), Carlson et al. (2001) and Norgren (2001), excessive regulation of Internet banking, especially in developing countries, threatens the speed and efficiency of Internet banking development. They caution that regulations must be able to take into consideration the level of administrative expertise and resources available, as well as the structural capacity of the banking institutions operating in the countries.

The realities of the above arguments against the effectiveness of the E-banking Guidelines to guarantee sound and efficient Internet banking in the country are not contestable. At the same time, its effectiveness in protecting the local Internet banking network is doubtful. Not much also can the guidelines do in the present quest to launder the country of its persistent bad Internet business reputation. The whole implication is that with a good number of holes identifiable in the only specialised regulatory instrument that guides Internet banking in the country, Nigeria can be emerging towards an unregulated Internet banking development.

The enforcement mechanisms of the above laws, as stated above, was originally weak, and in the case of banks, the CBN was overburdened by several professional and technical duties, including the management of the nation's economy. The policing structure in the country was and is still overstretched. Thus, the electronic business environment generally was left un-regulated between the periods 1998 and 2004. It was in recognition of the growing damages caused by clear lack of specialised regulations on Internet banking and the weakness inherent in the existing law enforcement structures that the Nigerian government establishment the ICPC and the EFCC. While the Central Bank of Nigeria lacks the ICT capacity to supervise the electronic banking operations of the post-consolidation mega banks in the country, the only active enforcement agency remains the EFCC, which is most times accused of operating outside the law and using extra-judicial processes in their fight against cybercrimes and other forms of frauds. The danger has not only reported in the low level of domestic confidence on banks and on Internet business, but has helped the international community to directly interpret the country's Internet image as an offshoot of its age-long hardcore bad reputation.

The Role of the Economic and Financial Crimes Commission

According to Section 46 of the EFCC Establishment Act of 2004, the anti-graft agency is charged with the responsibilities of investigating, preventing and prosecuting offenders who engage in:

i. Money laundering, embezzlement, bribery, looting and any form of corrupt practices;

ii. Illegal arms deal, smuggling, human trafficking, and child labour;

iii. Illegal oil bunkering, and illegal mining;

iv. Tax evasion, foreign exchange malpractices and counterfeiting of currency;

v. Theft of intellectual property and piracy, open market abuse, dumping of toxic wastes, and prohibited goods.

It is also mandated to identify, trace, freeze, confiscate or seize proceeds derived from terrorist activities. The agency has it as a duty to enforce the criminal and penal codes in the Country's Criminal Law and to enforce the money laundering and 419 laws. Presently, as indicated above, the EFCC is the only active and outstanding fraud-enforcement agency in the country – enjoying the supports of both the national government and the international community. Since its formation, the agency has formatted strong collaborative relationship with international governments and agencies – examples of which include a working relationship with the United States Secret Service; the FBI; the SOCA in Britain; the Amsterdam Police, as well as the Australian police (Ribadu, 2007).

Among the acclaimed achievements of the Commission since its establishment in 2003, according the immediate past chairman, Ribadu (2006) are:

1. Cleansing of the Banking Sub-sector – Including its contribution in the sanitization of the banking sector through investigation and prosecution of Chief Executives and other officials for Money Laundering and other frauds. Bank failures, which were rampant in the past, have now become outdated.

2. Prosecution and Conviction of Corrupt Top Public Officers – including the successfully prosecuted and secured convictions against top government functionaries, including the former chief law enforcement officer of the nation, the Inspector-General of Police (IGP); and its investigative efforts leading to the removal from office and prosecution of

a president of Senate, a governor, ministers, parliamentarians, chief executives of banks, etc.

3. Record Convictions for '419', Money Laundering and Terrorism – including a record of 56 convictions on corruption, money laundering, oil pipeline vandalisms and related offences; and the seizure and freezing of assets well over $5 billion from corrupt officials, their agents and cronies.

4. Recovery and Return of Proceeds of Crime – involving that prosecution and conviction of kingpins including the celebrated US$242 million case involving a Brazilian bank. Much of the amount has been recovered and returned to the bank in Brazil; the recovery and return of the sum of US$4 million to a victim of 419 in Hong Kong and has seized and returned over US$500,000 to sundry US citizens; and the return of $1.6 million to a victim in Florida.

5. Setting up of the Financial Intelligence Unit and Taking Action Against Terrorist Financing – including the establishment of the Nigerian Financial Intelligence Unit (NFIU), which essentially helped in the: detection of suspicious transactions in financial institutions; coordination and the implementation of the National Strategy Plan Against Money Laundering and Terrorist Financing.

6. Partnership with Microsoft against Internet Scam and Identity Theft – involving collaborative efforts of EFCC to deploy technology to combat cyber crimes, with Microsoft.

7. Capacity Building for Law Enforcement and Judicial Officials – Including the establishment of a state- of-the-art Training and Research Institute in the country, for the training of its officials.

The coming into force of EFCC no doubt brought some new live into the country's crime law enforcements programmes. At some quarters before the end of 2007, the operations of the agency

were likened to those of the FBI or the CIA in the US. Then, a common palace in the country was that *the fear of EFCC is the beginning of wisdom* to public officers, banks' chief executives, cyber criminals and their accomplices. The agency became an active catalyst in the war against Nigerian Internet frauds. As usually in Nigeria, politics seems to have crept into the structure of this important anti-graft institution. In 2007, for instance, the pioneer chief executive, Dr. Nuhu Ribadu, was disgraced out from office, demoted from the office of Assistant Inspector General of Police (AIG) to Assistant Commissioner of Police, and latter in 2008 finally sacked from the Nigerian police. By doing that, the Nigerian government demonstrated little regards for the achievements and global partnerships built by EFCC in fighting cyber crimes emanating from Nigeria (or from Nigerians), under the leadership of Dr. Nuhu Ribadu.

Some Past Global Efforts to Fight Nigerian Internet Banking Frauds

The first global attempt to fight Internet frauds originating from Nigeria was recorded in 1998, when, according to Smith et al. (1999) the Nigerian Advance Fee Fraud Prevention Bill was introduced into the United States Senate. The bill was intended to highlight the problem, inform the public that the arising risks there from, and to enable government actions to be taken to facilitate the prevention (Smith et al., 1999).

Two approaches to curbing the spread of Internet frauds have subsequently emerged. First is to offer assistances to countries where cases of such frauds are prevalent. The second approach is to isolate or blacklist the originating countries. The first approach has proved more successful because of the terrain of the global Internet community and the near impossibility of defining participatory limits in Internet usage. While most European countries have adopted the second model, the United States government has mostly strived to offer assistances to countries to fight cyber crimes at both domestic and international fronts. Since 1998, as indicated above, the American government and corporations have evolved measures not only to mitigate and control the prevalence of 419 frauds of Nigerian origin, but has also helped develop fraud fighting structures in Nigeria. Past and on-going fraud prevention measures by the US government include:

1. The institution of a Working Group by the US Senate to develop policies and plans to combat international Nigerian crime by supporting the task forces; helping to select task force cities and assuring that the task force cities carry out the mission of the NCI; and addressing policy issues, such as privacy and discovery in criminal cases.

2. The ADNET arrangement, which serves as a network arrangement on ground for storage and retrieval of data on Nigerian crime. It is part of the duties of the Working Group to educate Internet users on how to effectively apply ADNET.

3. The designation of the US Secret Service, in 1998, as the lead investigative agency for Nigerian crime. Through the Secret Service Internet website, and its Financial Crimes Division in its Washington headquarters, the Secret Service acts as a central repository for complaints above Nigeria fraud (Buchanan and Grant, 2001).

4. The efforts by the FBI in training law enforcement agencies in Nigeria and Ghana. In 2005 for instance, Cyber Division FBI supervisors conducted training in Ghana and Nigeria, and deployed agents to Nigeria for extended temporary duty assignments to actively work with Nigerian law enforcement regarding top targets identified in Operation Relief.

5. The formation of an African Working Party on Information Technology Crimes formed under the auspices of Interpol.

6. The signing of agreement in 2005 between the Nigerian government and Microsoft that required their working together to end Internet crimes. According to Neil Holloway (President Microsoft Europe) "it is the first-ever agreement Microsoft has signed with an African country to aid law enforcement efforts. Microsoft's aid will include providing information to law enforcement in addition to training. The company has already been working with Nigerian authorities over the last three to six months. We think we have a responsibility to make an impact in this particular area" (B Blogger, October 21, 2005).

Other global measures against advance fee Internet frauds, which Nigeria has adopted include signing up to United Nations Conventions such as the UN Convention against Transnational Organized Crime (adopted on 15 November 2000), the UN Convention against Corruption (opened for signatories in December 2003), the UN Convention Against Illicit Traffic in Narcotic Drugs and Psychotropic Substances (adopted on 31 May, 2001), and the UN Convention for the Suppression of the Financing of Terrorism. These conventions are argued to be capable of providing a disciplined and prudent approach to government decision-making, and of affording the country an opportunity to gain global experiences in Internet regulations and policy (Ezeoha, 2006). Nigeria also submits herself to the membership of a 26-member anti-Spam group called the London Action Plan. There is also the Cybercrime Convention of the European Council adopted in November 2001 as the first major international agreement to regulate on juridical and procedural aspects of investigating and prosecuting cybercrimes, particular as it efforts to prevent illegal intervention into the work of computer systems.

Interestingly, these measures have proved very successful in several dimensions. The assistance of the US in training and equipping EFCC, for instance, has resulted to arrest and prosecution of high-caliber cyber criminals in the country. However, the US model has one significant flaw, which borders on ways and manners the Nigerian 419 fraud is defined. Foreign law enforcement agencies, including those of the US, see the Nigerian 419 fraud as *the version of cyber crime that originate from Nigeria and is committed by Nigerians*. This can be likened to defining *Euro Loan* as loan granted in Europe by a European bank. In actual fact, not all 419 frauds originate from Nigeria and not all are committed by Nigerians. Yes, it is easier for a foreign national to use the Nigerian identity as a way of shielding traces and trails. A stronger mindset and mis-definition of the scope and content of 419 Internet frauds could mislead enforcement agents and may be part of the difficulties currently encountered in tracking down Internet fraudsters. There is, thus, need for most of the global strategies to be redefined. The US model that has worked very well need to be built around a new definition of Internet fraud dynamisms.

This chapter lays strong support to the earlier claim that off-line frauds were traditional features of the Nigerian business and banking practices; and that fraudsters took advantage of the economies of scales offered by Internet to expand the dimension and scope of their crimes. It also infers that the Nigerian version of Internet frauds may have been copied and duplicated in other countries by nationals order than Nigerians, as a way of taking advantage of the globally bad image of the country.

FUTURE RESEARCH DIRECTION

This chapter has mainly drawn attention to how the socio-economic situation in a country may have influenced the Internet business reputation. In the case of Nigeria, which is chronically deficient in terms of the quality of governance and the condition of the banking system, the Internet reputation has been expectedly very poor – with the Nigerian version of Internet frauds ranking between first and second among the top ten types of Internet frauds. This situation has raised a lot of national and international concerns, at the national level, various regulatory frameworks have been put in place to fight cybercrimes and other related offences. At the international level, most countries have just ignored any form of online dealings with Nigerians (legitimate or otherwise); others (such as the US) have invested much in directly controlling the menace of 419 and in assisting the anti-graft agencies in the country. Unfortunately, most of these efforts have yielded little results, especially as 419 cases persist.

The persistency in the rising level of 419 frauds gives room for more meaningful studies in the area. Commissioning expert and intelligent researches on Internet usage in Nigeria, is a clear way the regulatory authorities, international communities and the Nigerian government particularly can assist in enlightening and educating Nigerians on the need to support sound Internet environment in the country (Ezeoha, 2006). In addition to the theoretical revelations made in this work, further researches are needed in the following areas.

i. The fact that Internet businesses have little geographical attachments call for some empirical investigation of the relationship between a country's hardcore image and its online reputations. This would help in efficient channelling of efforts and resources for Internet fraud control. The present situation where strategies are based on assumptions and prevailing national images looks sub-optimal.

ii. We have inferred here that most times, payments for Internet business transactions are made through the banking system thus drawing a theoretical conclusion that every Internet fraud automatically amount to Internet banking fraud. This however would require some empirical validation. Researches here would centre on the degree and nature of Internet banking intermediation.

iii. Future researches can also going to focus on the possibility of Internet regulatory convergence among countries. This would be targeted at resolving the problem of jurisprudence that normally challenges global Internet business regulations.

iv. Future Internet banking studies would also centre on investigating and modelling Internet frauds and the global impact of each class of fraud at each stage in the life cycle. This is capable of helping to resolve problems associated with the geographical spread of Internet frauds, and the speed at which the nationals of one country can copy fraud originating from another country.

v. Research need would also arise in the area of investigating how banking industry consolidation or reforms increase or reduce the rate of Internet or electronic-crimes in banks.

vi. Finally, more complex studies would be required to examine the joint effects of poverty, banking system development, quality of public governance, literacy rate, corruption, and regulation impact on Internet banking development in general, and Internet banking frauds in particular.

CONCLUSION AND RECOMMENDATION

As long as there have been banks, there have also been governments to set rules for them (World Bank, 2002:79). An efficient banking system development requires sound and prudent regulatory frameworks. In the absence of strong rules that guide the conducts of banks and customers, frauds are bound to persist. In Nigeria, most banking developments predated regulation, with the latter used most times as contingent tool to solve problems as they arise. This reason explains the prevalent of bank frauds, distress and failure in the country's banking industry. In addition, bad governance, corruption, poverty, insecurity and the likes have historically hindered economic growth

and development in the country. The fact that Internet business generally requires high degree of security and trust to thrive leaves everyone in doubt over how such innovation can survive in the Nigerian environment.

This chapter lays strong support to the earlier claim that off-line frauds were traditional features in the Nigerian business and banking practices; and that fraudsters took advantage of the economies of scales offered by Internet to expand the dimension and scope of their crimes. It emphasises that rising incidences of 419 frauds have negatively affected the process of Internet banking in the country. As a way of taking advantage of the globally bad image of the country, nationals of other countries might have copied and duplicated the Nigerian version of Internet frauds. The chapter stresses that the case of mistaken identity arising from the above may have been responsible for the resistance of 419 frauds to both domestic and global measures. To resolve this problem, therefore, the following measures have been preferred.

1. To be able to domestically fight the scourge of 419 frauds in the system, the regulatory authorities need to, as a matter of urgency, update their IT infrastructure, train their personnel and mount intensive surveillance mechanism to match the advancement in the technology. At the international scene, the authorities should be able to build effective and functional collaborative networks that allow for smooth sharing of information, software resources and other anti-graft facilities.

2. Banking and financial regulations need to be kept abreast with the technological development in the banking industry. In the past, little efforts were made to resolve background issues before the adoption of technological innovations in the system. In a volatile business environment like Nigeria, this strategy weakens the banking structure and creates lapses to be taken advantage of by criminals (The World Bank, 2002).

3. There is need to change the Internet security policies of major countries such as the United States of America and Britain from focusing on how to prevent the incursion of Nigerian cyber-criminals to supporting the development of local institutions that facilitate internet business operations. Banks must be offered enough incentives to prevent and report crimes committed through their system networks.

4. Restrictive model of Internet businesses regulation is no longer enough. While it is good to form some multilateral conventions on Internet-related businesses, strengthening the international banking laws and getting countries to be bonded by the laws might prove more effective.

5. At present, the only dedicated Internet banking framework in Nigeria – the Electronic Banking Guidelines, enjoys little backing of the country's legal system. This makes its provisions only enforceable by the Central bank of Nigeria. The Nigerian government, through the required legislative process, would have to inculcate the provisions of the Guidelines into the Banks and Other Financial Institutions Act to accord them full legal weight and make them enforceable by the judiciary and other anti-graft agencies in the country.

6. There is also need to restructure the entire Internet business environment, not only in Nigeria, but also in most other developing economies. This would include formalizing the processes of securing ISP license, commercial and private cyber cafes and other IT facilities that aid Internet business services. In this sense, providing infrastructure and acquiring necessary software, especially by banks, need to be supported with reasonable investments in increasing the access of the banking public to more secured and structured internet banking facilities. In the developed countries, using public Internet cafés to transact Internet banking and other

forms of sensitive financial transactions is practically discouraged. Unlike what obtains in the developed countries, access to computer and Internet in most developing countries is most times available through commercial providers. This makes nonsense of the issue of security.

7. The fact that Internet banking frauds can be committed with a great deal of anonymity creates a high need for increase collaborative efforts at bank levels, among international regulatory and anti-graft agencies, and by foreign governments. Such collaborations would be capable of improving the quality of regulation, as well as the quality of Internet banking practices among banks.

8. As is the case in US and other countries, the Nigerian government should put in place dedicated system for data collection and research to effectively track down the movement of funds arising from Internet businesses involving Nigerians and originating from Nigeria. One way of doing this may be to institute a Police Electronic Crime Laboratory to compliment the Internet Fraud Complaint Centers that have been put in place by the EFCC. Such a laboratory can serve as repository or databank for documentation of the volume of Internet business activities and fund flow structure. Such facility is capable of assisting the law enforcement agencies in tracking down Internet fraudsters and in better management of the country's Internet banking reputations overseas.

9. The Nigerian government should also increase effort to address the rising incidence of poverty in the country by ensuring that available resources are invested in projects that impact directly on the lives of ordinary Nigerians. Similarly, there is also need to discourage public corruption, which has grown in widths and breaths since the return of democratic governance in 1999. Jobs need to be created as a way of granting the

teeming youths alternative and legal means of livelihood.

10. Finally, more meaningful investments need to be made in the area of education and public enlightenment. Effective public education on Internet banking, Internet frauds and their regulatory implications, as earlier posited by the US House Committee on Energy and Commerce (2001), are necessary ways of handling and controlling the spread of financial crimes on the net. No doubt, a system of private-public sector involvement is required here to give such educational programme meaningful direction and allow for its proper coordination.

REFERENCES

Ajayi, O. (1991). *The Regulation of banks and financial institutions*. Lagos, Nigeria: Greyhouse African Resources Development Project.

Amoda, J. M. (2008, October 7). Transparency international's annual corruption perception index. *Vanguard Newspaper* (Lagos, Nigeria).

Bhargava, V. (2006). Curing the cancer of corruption. V. Bhargava (Ed), *Global issues for global citizens: an introduction of key development challenges* (pp.341-369). Washington DC: The World Bank.

Buchanan, J. and & Grant, A. J. (2001, November). *Investigating and prosecuting Nigerian fraud*. United States Attorneys' Bulletin, (pp. 39-47).

Central Bank of Nigeria. (2001a). *The effects of economic crimes in the financial industry* (pp. 55–63). Central Bank of Nigeria Banking Supervision Annual Report.

Central Bank of Nigeria. (2001b). *Bank licensing* (pp. 27–29). Central Bank of Nigeria Banking Supervision Annual Report.

Central Bank of Nigeria. (2002). *Banking supervision annual report. Lagos*. Central Bank of Nigeria Research and Publication Department.

Central Bank of Nigeria. (2003, August), Guidelines on electronic banking in Nigeria. Retrieved February 27 2009 from http://www.cenbank.org/OUT/PUBLICATIONS/BSD/2003/E-BANKING.PDF

Central Bank of Nigeria (Various Dates). Annual reports and statement of accounts, Lagos.

Chiemeke, S. C., Evwiekpaefe, A. E., & Chete, F. O. (2006). The adoption of internet banking in Nigeria: an empirical investigation. *Journal of Internet Banking and Commerce, 11*(3). Retrieved 8 February 2009 from http://www.arraydev.com/commerce/jibc/

Chuhan, P. (2006). Poverty and inequality. In Bhargava, V. (Ed.), *Global issues for global citizens: an introduction of key development challenges* (pp. 31–50). Washington, DC: The World Bank.

Comptroller's Handbook. (1999, October). *Internet banking. comptroller of the currency. Administrator of National Banks*. Retrieved February 8 2009 from http://www.occ.treas.gov/handbook/intbank.pdf

Doh, J. P., Rodriguez, P., Uhlembruck, K., Collins, J., & Eden, L. (2003). Coping with corruption in foreign markets. *The Academy of Management Executive, 17*(3), 114–127.

Ezeduiji, F. U. (1997). Bank failures in Nigeria: causes and dimensions. *Central Bank of Nigeria Bullion, 21*, 17–22.

Ezeoha, A. E. (2005a). Regulating internet banking in Nigeria: part 1 – problems and phallenges. *Journal of Internet Banking and Commerce, 10*(3). Retrieved February 23 from http://www.arraydev.com/commerce/JIBC/2006-02/abel.asp

Ezeoha, A. E. (2005b). Increasing incidence of poverty in Nigeria: an impact assessment of the government's economic reform programme. *Journal of Social Development in Africa, 22*(2), 112–131.

Ezeoha, A. E. (2006). Regulating internet banking in Nigeria: part 2 – some success prescriptions. *Journal of Internet Banking and Commerce, 11*(1). Retrieved February 23 2009 from http://www.arraydev.com/commerce/JIBC/2006-04/Nigeria-2_F.asp

Ezeoha, A. E. (2007). Structural effect of banking industry consolidation in Nigeria: a review. *Journal of Banking Regulation, 8*(2), 159–176. doi:10.1057/palgrave.jbr.2350044

Ezeoha, A. E., & Chibuike, U. C. (2006). Rethinking monetary and fiscal policies in Nigeria. *Journal of Sustainable Development in Africa, 8*(2), 93–105.

Fanawopo, S. (2004, August 2). Federal government moves to enforce cyber crimes laws. *The Sun Newspaper*, (Lagos, Nigeria).

Federal Government of Nigeria. (1990). *Criminal code act*. Laws of the Federation of Nigeria.

Federal Government of Nigeria. (1991). *Banks and other financial institutions decree No 25*. Lagos, Laws of the Federation of Nigeria.

Federal Government of Nigeria. (1995). *Advance fee fraud and other fraud related offences decree No. 13 of 1995*. Lagos, Laws of the Federation of Nigeria.

Federal Government of Nigeria. (1995). *Money laundering (prohibition) decree No. 3 of 1995*. Lagos, Laws of the Federation of Nigeria.

Federal Government of Nigeria. (2004). *Money laundering (prohibition) act of 2004*. Abuja: Laws of the Federation of Nigeria.

Federal Government of Nigeria. (2006). *Advance fee fraud and other fraud related offences act of 2006*. Abuja: Laws of the Federation of Nigeria.

Gkoutzinis, A. A. (2006). *Internet banking and the law in euro – regulation, financial integration and electronic commerce*. Cambridge, UK: Cambridge University Press. doi:10.1017/CBO9780511494703

Library of Congress. (2008, July). Federal research division country profile: Nigeria. Retrieved February 8 2009 from http://lcweb2.loc.gov/frd/cs/profiles/Nigeria.pdf.

National Consumers League. (2002). *Internet fraud statistics*. Retrieved February 27 2009 from (www.nclnet.org/shoppingonline)

Nigerian Deposit Insurance Corporation (for Various Years). Annual reports and statements of account.

Norgren, C. (2001, June). *Impact of the internet in the functioning and regulation of markets*. Paper presented at Public Documents of the XXVIth Annual Conference of the International Organization of Securities Commissions (IOSCO), Stockholm, Sweden.

O'Brien, A. J. (2002). *Management informational system – managing information technology in the e-business enterprises* (5th ed.). Boston: McGraw-Hill Irwin.

Ogunleye, E. (1999). A review of banking activities and its regulatory framework in Nigeria. *Nigerian Deposit Insurance Quarterly, 9*(4), 35–36.

Ojo, M. O. (1991). Deregulation in the Nigerian banking industry: a review of appraisal. *Central Bank Nigeria Economic and Financial review, 29*(1), pp.1-6.

Oke, B. A. (1994). Regulations of bank and other financial institutions with special reference to the regulation of discount houses in Nigeria. *Central Bank Nigeria Economic and Financial Review*, *3*(1), 3–15.

Oyesanya, Y. (2004a, August 4). *Nigeria: heaven for terrorist Internet communication? The Nigerian Village Square*. Retrieved February 15 2006 from http://www.nigeriavillagesquare.com

Oyesanya, Y. (2004b, July 13). *Review of central bank guidelines for electronic banking*. The Nigerian Village Square. Retrieved February 27 2009 from http://www.nigeriavillagesquare.com

Research Markets Brochure. (2009), *Nigerian internet user survey*. Retrieved February 8 2009 from http://www.researchandmarkets.com/reports310872

Ribadu, N. (2006, May 18). *Nigeria's struggle with corruption*. Paper presented to US Congressional House Committee on International Development, Washington DC.

Ribadu, N. (2007, July). *Cybercrime and commercial fraud: a Nigerian perspective, Modern Law for Global Commerce*. Paper presented to a Congress to celebrate the Fortieth Annual Session of UNCITRAL, Vienna.

Shao, J., Ivanov, P. C., Podobnik, B., & Stanley, H. E. (2007). Quantitative relationships between corruption and economic factors. *The European Physical Journal B – Condensed Matter and Complex System, 56*(2), pp.1434-6028

Singer, D. D., Ross, D., & Avery, A. (2005). The evolution of online banking. *Journal of Internet Banking Business*, *2*(Spring).

Smith, R.G., Holmes, M. N., & Kaufmann, P (1999, July). *Nigerian advance fee fraud, trends and issues in crime and criminal justice*, Australian Institute of Criminology, Canberra, No. 121.

Soludo, C.C. (2004, August 6). Guidelines and incentives on consolidation in the Nigerian banking industry. Thisday Newspaper (Lagos, Nigeria)

Spong, K. (2000). *Banking regulation: its purposes, implementation and effects* (5th ed.). Division of Supervision and Risk Management, Federal Reserve Bank of Kansas City.

Swiss Federal Department of Foreign Affairs. (2008). *Economic report on business and economy in Nigeria*. Retrieved February 8 2009 from http://www.eda.admin.ch/eda/en/home/reps/afri/vnga/ref_bufor/busnga.html

Transparency International, National Integrity System, Country Study Reports [For Various Years] Retrieved from http://www.transparency.org/publications/publications

Uche, C. U. (2000). Banking regulation in an era of structural adjustment: the case of Nigeria. *Journal of Financial Regulation and Compliance, 1*(2), 157–169. doi:10.1108/eb025040

Uche, C. U. (2001). The adoption of universal banking in Nigeria. *Butterworths Journal of International Banking and Financial Law, 16*(9), 421–428.

Uche, U. C. (1998). The adoption of money laundering law in Nigeria. *Journal of Money Laundering Control*, (pp. 220-228).

United Nations. (2005, April 19). Eleventh UN congress on crime prevention and criminal justice. (BKK/CP/08). Bangkok Thailand, Committee 1, 2nd and 3rd Meetings.

Wallsten, S. (2003). *Regulation and internet use in developing countries (No. 2979)*. World Bank Policy Research Paper, The World bank Development Research Group.

Williams, P. (2002). *Organized crime and cybercrime: implications for business*. CERT Coordination Center.

Wright, J. D. (2002, May). *Electronic banking: new developments and regulatory risks*. Paper present at the International Monetary Fund (IMF) Conference – Washington D.C.

ADDITIONAL READING

Akani, C. (2002). *Corruption in Nigeria: the Niger Delta experience*. Nigeria: Fourth Dimension Publishers.

Bank of International Settlement. (2003). Risk management principles for electronic banking. *Basel Committee on Banking Supervision.* July http://www.bis.org/publ/bcbs98.pdf (accessed November 10, 2009)

Brands, S. A. (2000). *A review of rethinking public key infrastructures and digital certificates and privacy*. Cambridge, MA: MIT Press.

Brunet, P., & Tiemtoré, O. and & Vettraino-Soulard, M. (2004). Ethics and the internet in West Africa: toward an ethical model of integration. *Africa World Press/IDRC.* http://www.idrc.ca/en/ev-9437-201-1-DO_TOPIC.html (accessed November 10, 2009).

Buchanan, J. and & Grant, A. J. (2001). Investigating and prosecuting Nigerian fraud. *United States Attorney's Bulletin. 49*(6). pp. 39-47 http://www.justice.gov/usao/eousa/foia_reading_room/usab4906.pdf. (accessed November 11, 2009).

Bwalya, K. J. (2009). Factors affecting adoption of e-government in Zambia. *Electronic Journal of Information System in Developing Countries. 38*(4), pp.1-13 http://www.ejisdc.org/ojs2/index.php/ejisdc/article/viewFile/573/286. (accessed November 11, 2009).

Carlson, J., & Furst, K. and & Nolle, D. E. (2001). Internet banking: market developments and regulatory issues. *A Paper Presented to Society of Government Economists Conference 2000, The New Economy: What Has Changed, and the Challenges for Economic Policy.* Washington DC. November 17.

Catan, T., & Peel, M. (2003). Bogus websites, stolen corporate identities: how Nigerian fraudsters steal millions from western banks. *The Financial Times.* March 3. p.21.

Central Bank of Nigeria (2003). Report of the technical committee on electronic banking. *Central Bank of Nigeria Research Department.* Abuja. February.

Chang, Y. T. (2006)., *Dynamics of internet banking: lessons from Korea, CCP Policy Brief,* ESRC Centre for Competition Policy: University of East Anglia, U.K. April http://www.uea.ac.uk/polopoly_fs/1.104498!ccp_06-3_pb.pdf. (accessed November 10, 2009).

Crede, A. (1998). International banking and the internet. In Cronin, M. J. (Ed.), *Banking and Finance on the Internet,* New York: *John Wiley & Sons*. New York.

Financial Crime Sector report (2004)., *Countering financial crime risks in information security.* November http://www.fsa.gov.uk/pubs/other/fcrime_sector.pdf. (accessed November 10, 2009).

Gkoutzinis, A. A. (2006). *Internet banking and law in Europe: regulation, financial integration and electronic commerce.*: New York: Cambridge University Press. New York

Gkoutzinis, A. A. (2009). *Internet banking and the law in Europe - regulation, financial integration and electronic commerce.*: London: Cambridge University Press. London

Glickman, H. (2005). The Nigerian "419" advance fee scams: prank or peril? *CJAS/RCEA,* Vol. *39*(3),:460-490.

Goldface-irokalibe, I. J. (2007). *Law of banking Nigeria*. Sulfolk, VA: Malthouse Press.

Han, K. S., Noh, M. H. (1999-2000). Critical failure factors that discourage the growth of electronic commerce. *International Journal of Electronic Commerce*. Winter, Vol. 4, No. (2), pp. 25-43.

Hardy, D. C. (2006). Regulatory capture in banking. *IMF Working Paper.* No. WP/06/34, January, http://www.imf.org/external/pubs/ft/wp/2006/wp0634.pdf. (accessed November 11, 2009).

Hedley, S. H. (2005). *The law of electronic commerce in the UK and Ireland*. United Kingdom: Taylor & Francis.

Huang, J.; Makoju, E.; Newell, S. and & Galliers, R. D. (2003). Opportunities to learn from failure with electronic commerce: a case study of electronic banking. *Journal of Information Technology*, 18,.pp. 17–26

Huang, W.-X. (2007). *Institutional banking for emerging markets: principles and practice*. New York: John Wiley & Sons.

Jdibua, J. I. (2006). *Modernization and the crisis of development in Africa: the Nigerian experience*. Aldershot: Ashgate Publishing.

Luo, G. (2009). E-government, people and social change: a case study of China. *Electronic Journal of Information System in Developing Countries*. 38(3): pp.1-23 http://www.ejisdc.org/ojs2/index.php/ejisdc/article/viewFile/511/285. (accessed November 11, 2009).

Mols, N. P. (1998). The behavioral consequences of PC banking. *International Journal of Bank Marketing*, *16*(5), 195–201. doi:10.1108/02652329810228190

Norton, J., & Walker, G. (2000). Banks: fraud and crime, 2nd edition: Informa maritime and Professional. http://www.informaprofessional.com/publications/books/banks_fraud_and_crime (accessed November 11, 2009).

Ojomo, A. J. (2001). Advance fee fraud and Nigeria's image: Paper 1. *Proceedings of the First National Seminar on Economic Crime*, Abuja.

Peel, M. (2006). *Nigeria-related financial crime and its links with Britain: an African program report: Chatham New Jersey*. Chatham House.

Radha, V., & Gulati, V. (2004). Preventing technology based bank frauds [JBC]. *Journal of Internet Banking and Commerce*, *9*(1), 132–145.

Ramakrishnan, G. (2001). Risk management for internet banking. *Information Systems Control Journal*, 6, http://www.isaca.org/Template.cfm?Section=Home&CONTENTID=17424&TEMPLATE=/ContentManagement/ContentDisplay.cfm (accessed November 11, 2009).

Reed, C., & Walden, I. and & Edgar, L. (2000). *Cross-border electronic banking, 2nd edition. Informa Maritime and Professional*http://www.informaprofessional.com/publications/books/cross-border_electronic_banking (accessed November 10, 2009).

Salawu, O., & Salawu, M. K. (2007). The emergence of internet banking in Nigeria: an appraisal. *Information Technology Journal*, *6*(4), 490–496. doi:10.3923/itj.2007.490.496

Sha, M. H., & Khan, S. and & Xu, M. (2005). A survey critical success factors in e-banking, http://www.iseing.org/emcis/EMCIS2005/pdfs/18.pdf (Accessed 12 November, 2009)

Smith, D. J. (2008). A culture of corruption: everyday deception and popular discontent. In *Nigeria*. New Jersey: Princeton University Press.

Smith, R., Holmes, M., & Kaufmann, P. (1999). Nigerian advance fee fraud. *Trends & Issues in Crime and Criminal Justice No. 121*, Australian Institute of Criminology, Stein, H.; Ajakaiye, D. O. I.; and & Lewis, P. (2002). *Deregulation and the banking crisis*. In *Nigeria: a comparative study*. New York: Palgrave Macmillan.

Till Angels Govern, T. A., Barth, J. R., & Caprio, G. and & Levine, R. (2009). *Rethinking bank regulation.*: London. Cambridge University Press.

UNODC. (2005). *Crime and development in Africa*. www.unodc.org/pdf/African_report.pdf (accessed November 11, 2009).

World Bank. (2009). Combating money laundering and the financing of terrorism: a comprehensive training guide. 1 to 7. http://go.worldbank.org/YKW58M9BH1 (accessed November 12, 2009).

Yakubu, J. A. and & Oyewo, A. T. (2000). Criminal Law and Procedure in Nigeria: Malthouse. Nigeria.

KEY TERMS AND DEFINITIONS

Banking Regulation: Formal, conventional and public laws and policy guidelines governing the conduct of banking businesses within a definable geographical scope.

Deregulation: This is the process of reducing the authority and influence of government in the conduct of businesses within an economic sector. It also has to do with the transfer of economic power from government to the private sector or from a controlled system to a market-based system.

Electronic Banking: Electronic banking refers to a method of banking that de-emphasizes physical movements of cash and near-cash items in financial transactions. Popular media for electronic banking include automatic teller machine (ATM), the mobile phone, internet, credit cards, etc.

Internet Banking: Internet banking refers to the use of internet websites as a platform for the conduct of banking businesses.

Internet Fraud: Internet fraud is any kind of fraud that is committed with the aid of internet facilities or components. Such fraud relies on either email scam, websites, chat rooms, and other available protocols in the internet.

Reputation: The level of confidence or perception people have about the functioning or behavior of a system or the operations of a business entity. There are offline reputation (perception on the physical behavior) and online reputation (perception about the virtual behavior).

Virtual Banking: Virtual banking is a banking system that relies wholly on the internet and other remote electronic protocols. A virtual bank, for instance, has no physical or verifiable address, and so exists entire on the internet.

ENDNOTES

1. At about a population of 140 million and estimated total number of branches of banks in Nigeria at 4,000 as at end-2008, the banking density is: 140 million divide by 4,000 – that is 35,000 persons per bank branch.

2. According to Singer, et al. (2005), the Internet has an absolute cost advantage in providing financial products and services, potential for enhancing the value of these products and services by making them more convenient for consumers to acquire, empowering consumers to make better choices, and personalizing those products and services to their individual needs.

3. This was against other better security control methods such as authentication, firewalls, cryptography, digital signature, digital certificate, secured socket layer (SSL), public key infrastructure (PKI), and so on.

4. The number and popularity of ATM usage in the country has however grown astronomi-

cally over the past years. From just 3 ATM in 2000, the number rose to 68 in 2002, and as at January 2009 stood at about 7,200.

5   The number of banks in the country has further shrunk from 25 to 24 at the end of 2007, and 23 banks at the end of 2008. There are expectations that larger banks with huge capital base would continue to prospect to buy over relatively smaller one – thus giving rise to a situation where the number would further reduce.

6   The military ruled from 1964 to 1978; and then from 1984 to May 1999. Democratically elected governments have only been in power from 1960 to 1963; and from May 1999 to date. Describing the impact of the military rule, Ribadu (2007) argued that decades of military autocracy cemented a practice where the networks of criminality hid behind con-

sensual agreements of illegality concealed from the public and shielded by bayonets.

7   Examples of such countries include: Chad, Haiti, Myanmar, Somalia, Turkmenistan, and Uzbekistan.

8   The rising rate of bank failure at the time was such that between 1995 and 2000, the Central bank of Nigeria had revoked the licenses of up to 33 banks. The highest number of annual revocation was 26 recorded in 1998; 2 licenses were revoked each in 1994 and 1995; and 3 were revoked in 2000 (Central Bank of Nigeria, 2001b, p.27)

9   The inherent nature of Internet banking in eliminating paper documentation and traditional identity verification processes clearly introduces new dimensional risks and regulatory challenges (Wright, 2002).

Section 3
The Models

Chapter 6
Business Model of Internet Banks

Jean-Michel Sahut
Amiens School of Management, France

ABSTRACT

Internet is not simply one more distribution channel among the multi-channel strategies used by the financial industry; it is fostering new "e-Business Models" such as Internet-primary banks. However, in spite of its strong development potential, this type of bank has often achieved a weak breakthrough onto this market and shows modest financial results. The goal of this chapter is to study the "e-Business Model" of Internet-primary banks and to determine if it can perform better than the "Business Model" of a traditional bank.

INTRODUCTION

The development of Information and Communication Technologies, and more specifically Internet, has increased competition in the banking sector and brought about the separation of production from the distribution of financial services and products. The arrival of Internet has given a new dimension to the convergence and the deconstruction of the value chain by making it possible to lower information costs, and by reducing barriers to entry into the financial sector.

Convergence has taken place on three levels:

DOI: 10.4018/978-1-61520-635-3.ch006

- convergence of offers; by widening their product range, banks and insurance companies have entered into direct competition,
- convergence of the sub-sectors of the financial industry; banking, insurance and asset management activities increasingly overlap,
- financial institutions and non-finance actors have become more closely linked

Previously, deconstruction came mainly from the offer side, i.e. from the emergence of new entrants (e.g. consumer credit). With Internet, it comes from the demand side: customers can choose the best supplier depending on their preferences (e.g. real estate loans, online brokering). With the appearance of banks which mainly sell their services by Internet (Internet-primary banks), the major competitive advantage of traditional banks - a network of local branches - has been diminished for certain types of customer. These customers have been attracted by the prospect of accessing their accounts and carrying out bank transactions 24 hours a day, seven days a week without having to go anywhere, and sometimes with a better quality of service than was offered by a bank branch. Online brokers were the first to offer private individuals the opportunity to invest on the stock exchange via Internet. Moreover, the vast majority of Internet-primary banks charge lower account administration fees than those charged by traditional banks. This has often been used as an argument to attract customers in a nearly saturated market.

The goal of this chapter is to study the "Electronic Business Model" of Internet-primary banks and to determine if it can outperform the "Business Model" of a traditional bank. After having defined the Business Model and e-Business Model (e-BM) concepts, we will analyze the e-BM of online banks as an economic model through the study of its revenue sources, costs incurred, and how it creates value for customers. Then, we will question its strategic development prospects. Lastly, we look at Internet's impact on performance in the case of both traditional institutions as well as Internet-primary banks.

BUSINESS MODELS IN THE FINANCIAL SECTOR

Business Models and Electronic Business Models

The objective of this section is to better understand the "Business model" (BM) concept. Many papers have already been written which attempt to clarify this concept due to its dynamic dimension. We

will look at how this concept has been applied to electronic services: the "Electronic Business Model" (e-BM).

One of the first workable definitions of this concept was provided by Timmers (1998). He defines a BM as being:

- the architecture for product, services and information flows including a description of the model's various business actors and their roles;
- a description of the potential benefits for each business actor involved;
- a description of the sources of revenue.

Other writers have since expanded this idea. Linder and Cantrell (2000) state: "It's a rich, tacit understanding about how all the pieces work together to make money". These authors confirm this vision of BMs by the fact that 62% of the company directors they interviewed found it difficult to describe their BM over and above its success[1]. While for Loilier and Tellier (2001), a BM can be likened to a firm's value creation method.

In fact, defining what a BM is can be a difficult exercise because this concept is associated with dynamic dimensions such as value creation, competitiveness and organizational change. Porter (2001) in particular described this concept as "fuzzy", "superficial", and "theoretically difficult to grasp". Magretta (2002) specifies that the usual error with respect to BMs is to regard them as being a strategy: "Business modeling is the managerial equivalent of scientific method - you start with a hypothesis, which you can test in action and revise when necessary". For this author, the BM describes in system form, how the firm manufactures and sells a service or a product. Equally, for Afuah and Tucci (2003), the BM is a basket of activities which allows a business to earn money in a sustainable way. Along the same lines, Demil et al. (2004) approach it as an intermediate concept used to make strategies operational. They define the BM as all the choices which a firm makes in order to generate revenue. Whatever definition you choose, it is important to dissociate the concept of BM from that of strategy and to regard it as a dynamic concept which is constantly reconsidered according to market conditions, technology, regulations, inter-company relations, etc.

The development of ICTs, and specifically the Internet, has generated new activities resulting either from technological innovation (for example Internet portals), from the deintegration of value chains (e.g. loan comparison sites), or from new channels (e.g. online brokers). These activities then brought about the appearance of new BMs or redefined those which already existed (Applegate, 2001). For example, Internet strengthens the Research and Development function (a support service according to Porter's value chain concept) by helping in the collective design of products between sites and participants in the value system, by listing the concepts accessible to all the branches of the business and by giving access in real-time to all the sales and services databases. Also, Internet makes it possible to reduce order transmission times by automating both customer and supplier contacts and enables a truly integrated management system to be put in place. The impact of such practices on work efficiency creates an additional added value for the firm (Porter, 2001).

The term "Electronic Business Model" (e-BM) has since appeared to qualify the BM of these new activities. As the concept is derived from that of BMs, it is also difficult to define and can be understood in different ways. This is why many authors have tried to define it using a heuristic approach, in other words starting from their observations of the market. The result has been a wide diversity of studies which cover both the number of e-BMs identified and their characteristics: Timmers (1998) counted eleven different types, Loilier and Tellier (2001) counted five and Rappa (2001) nine.

Even if many similarities are identified, convergence between these typologies started to take place in 2001 with the analysis of value creation.

Indeed, Timmers (1998) has a vision which focuses on the internal dynamics of e-BMs and on their interaction with the environment. As for Mahadevan (2000), he prefers a "macro" vision in which e-BMs depend on the types of relations which exist between actors from the same market. Applegate's article (2001) marks a transition by putting forward a very precise classification of e-BMs concerning value creation for the e-BM (sources of differentiation, revenue and costs incurred), but the value created for customers is not a central issue. It wasn't until Novak and Hoffman's article (2001) that the different dimensions of e-BMs were brought closer together. Novak and Hoffman present "Customer Model Integration" in which the definition of an e-BM is jointly linked to both value models for customers and revenue models.

More precisely Novak and Hoffman identify the twelve value models shown in Table 1.

However, these revenue or value models created for customers cannot be regarded as exhaustive for two primary reasons:

- Given the difficulty of defining only one typology of e-BM, it is possible to present as many models as there are combinations of sources of revenue; the appearance of a new e-BM means the existence of new original combination of sources of revenue, even the creation of a new element for generating revenue;
- It would seem that revenue sources other than those presented by Novak and Hoffman can exist, for example the sale of customer data (e-mail, addresses, purchasing behavior, etc), a purchase made in a store following the consultation of the product on Internet, etc.

Moreover, the type of activity strongly influences the structure of an industry (Porter, 2001). As a result e-BMs are very different from one sector to another. Hereafter, we will look at the

Figure 1. Values, revenues and customer model integration

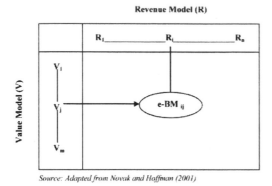

Source: Adapted from Novak and Hoffman (2001)

financial sector and at the different e-BMs which characterize it, and more specifically, at Internet banks.

Typology of E-Business Models for Financial Services

Due to their apparent contradictions, it is difficult to come to any firm conclusions on the positioning of Internet-primary Banks compared to more general e-BMs. On the other hand, if one focuses on the specific sector of financial services, a greater convergence of e-BMs can be clarified by studying the work of Muylle (2001) and Sahut (2001) and Horsti et al. (2005).

Between these different e-BMs for financial services, there exist several forms of exchange, partnership and strategic alliances. In particular, portals offer virtual banking agencies, aggregators and financial actors in general a space to advertise and be referenced. Moreover, certain portals

Table 1. Value models for customers (Novak & Hoffman, 2001)

Value Models	Value created for the customer	Example of e-BM
Brokerage	Facilitates bringing buyers and sellers together (B2B, B2C or C2C).	VerticalNet PaperExchange.com
Content	Meets all types of customers' information needs.	About.com
Search	Targets the information the customer is looking for.	Google.com
Incentive	Gives customer access to certain services and products after they have accumulated points (loyalty scheme)	Beenz.com MyPoints.com Webmiles.com
Freeware	Customers are given free access to software which is useful to them.	Blue Mountain Freemerchant.com
Communication	Provision of an e-mail service or free computer-to-phone calls.	Net2phone
Control	Pressure from customer groups concerning protection of their private life, intellectual property rights of content and the boycott of unethical content is a source of customer value.	Anonymizer Copyright Agent
Outsourcing	The customer is directly connected by Internet-ERP to the producer for greater control over his requirements.	I Print.com servicelane.com
Entertainment	The concept is based on the offer of information specific to a field of specific interest.	Sportingbet.com eMode
Transaction	The customer benefits from access to stores not (or not easily) accessible geographically.	Retromodern.com
Affiliate	This model is mainly for SMEs which want to make themselves known on the web. Payment for advertising costs is limited to the number of clicks to their ad banner.	Amazon.com Art.com PayTrust American Express
Community	Provides like-minded people with range of services relating to their center of interest as well as services for putting people in contact and exchanging information (forum, email, etc)	Epinions.com Participate.com

develop co-branding strategies (coproduction) by coming together with certain producers to produce or sell joint services.

Thus while calling into question the comparative advantages of traditional actors, the financial service sector on Internet has become very competitive and obliges actors to innovate by creating alliances, partnerships or mergers making it possible to build up new comparative advantages, to catch up with competitors, or to break into new markets. The movement which recently saw a consolidation of online brokers in Europe illustrates this phenomenon. Between 2002 and 2006, 22 brokers were taken over or merged in France (Les Echos, n° 19783, 30/10/2006).

Moreover, it is difficult to understand the financial equilibrium of e-BMs because not only have they brought about new commercial concepts but, above all they have provided a new logic for value

creation. In the start-up phase, companies in the e-business field generate large negative free cash flows for a certain length of time, before turning round and progressing exponentially. This type of cycle which is more marked than for traditional industries can be explained in particular through the theory of the network economy (Shapiro and Varian, 2003). In fact, the main specificities of e-BMs which develop in an economy based on networks show that:

- *profitability is only achieved by developing the use of a good or product* (one speaks about "an experience good") because the consumers are not motivated to buy or carry out transactions on line when they have doubts about the quality of the products or the operation's level of security. Once the "reputation" of the e-BM has been

Table 2. Typology of e-BMs for financial services

Type	Characteristics	Revenue Created	Value Model
Vertical Portal Financial Portal [MUY 01] **Portals** [SAH 01]	They mainly offer general or specialized information services in several fields. Some have created "personal finance spaces", like Yahoo with "Yahoo Finance", which proposes, in addition to informational services, transaction services (credit card, account aggregation, advice about stock market investments, etc).	Advertising, Affiliation, Commission, Sale of products and services.	Brokerage; Content; Search, Communication; Community; Affiliate, Transaction.
Aggregator [MUY 01] Aggregators: • **Brokers** • **Quoters** [SAH 01]	These are sites whose role is to act as online intermediary between different actors. "Quoters", contrary to brokers, do not carry out the transaction, they are infomediaries which bring business to virtual agencies, or compare offers for consumers.	Brokers: Sale of products and services. Quoters: Commission, Advertising, Affiliation.	Brokers: Content, Transaction. Quoters: Content, Brokerage.
Speciality manufacturer [MUY 01] **Suppliers** [SAH 01]	These are producers of financial services (like Visa, equity funds, traditional banks, etc) which distribute them through their own network, or external networks (resale or co-branding).	Commission, Sale of products and services.	Outsourcing, Transaction.
Company sites [Company web sites [MUY 01] Virtual agencies (banks, insurance, or broking on line) [SAH 01]	These are online banking, investment or insurance services. The sites with the best performance offer, in addition to advanced information and transaction services, customer relations management services (tools to help in decision-making, online advice, development of personalized products, etc). The main difference with brokers/aggregators is that they are not satisfied to aggregate the existing offer. They mainly sell products in their brand.	Product sales and services, Commission, Advertising.	Outsourcing, Transaction, Content, Brokerage, Community.

made, this type of psychological barrier decreases;

- *profitability is determined by "the attention" paid to the e-BM.* In fact, Internet provides an important mass of information with rapid, permanent and inexpensive access. Many BMs therefore try to benefit from this by setting up an informational website. Thus, gradually, competition in the physical markets has moved onto Internet. However, there are so many websites for companies selling the same products that saturation has been reached: far from increasing their visibility, these companies have provoked an "attention shortage". It is therefore imperative for an online bank wishing to "grab the attention" of customers from other banks already offering Internet Banking services, to propose superior value to that offered by its competitors. This requires big investment (in the development of services and the acquisition of customers) and explains the high level of negative free cash flows suffered by e-BMs at the beginning of their life cycle;
- *profitability depends on the technological infrastructure and the capacity to give added value to the offer on Internet.* In fact, contrary to a BM, e-BMs are characterised by the high costs of technological infrastructure (computers, software, data-base servers, computer maintenance, network equipment, etc.). This technological infrastructure can be the basis for the acquisition of a competitive advantage as soon as it improves capacity for storing, researching, sorting, filtering and sending out information (Applegate 2001). It increases, at the same time, the value of the information itself (and the service provided to the customers in general). But the high fixed cost that technology represents can not be amortized until a critical number of cus-

tomers has been reached. However, such an acquisition takes a long time to achieve.

Lastly, we can notice that the profits expected by Internet Banking services are more indirect, in other words they come from efficiency to the detriment of productivity in value. Even before the appearance of Internet banks, Rowe (1994) had noticed that the IT expenditure of French banks was increasing faster than productivity. He saw this phenomenon as confirmation of "the Solow paradox".

Should we therefore call into question Internet's productivity and its contribution as a channel of distribution? Will the traditional banks continue to perform the same with or without Internet? What are an online bank's real prospects for profitability?

IMPACT OF INTERNET BANKS ON PERFORMANCE

After having analyzed different e-BMs, their sources of revenue, their costs and their method of creating value, we study the profitability of Internet banking services.

The few studies which have looked into this aspect are divided into two categories: those interested in the introduction of Internet banking services on the profitability of traditional banks (known as click-and-mortar), those comparing the performance of Internet banks with other banks.

The first studies tried to show whether or not the introduction of Internet banking services in traditional banks in the USA increased their profitability (Egland et al, 1998; Carlson et al, 2000; Furst et al, 2002). But, these services represented too small a proportion of the activity to really influence the profitability of these banks. Similarly, Sullivan (2000) showed that the multichannel banks of the 10th Federal Reserve District do not appear more profitable on average when they have a transactional website. In Italy, Hasan et al. (2005) demonstrate a positive relationship, over the 1993–2001 period, between Internet adoption and the profitability of click-and-mortar banks.

More recently, Degado et al. (2007) studied the impact of the adoption of Internet Banking services on the performance of 72 commercial banks in Spain over the period 1994-2002. They conclude that the effects of this adoption take time to appear and result in a fall of overhead expenses. One needs 1 year and a half to notice a significant increase in ROA (return on assets) and three years for ROE (return on equity). In this context, Internet is used more as a complementary channel than as a substitute to the physical branches.

These contrasting conclusions are debatable because they are based on average results obtained at the beginning of the development of these services. Thus they depended more on the customers' adoption of Internet than on the real contribution of Internet Banking services on the overall profitability of the bank. In fact, these studies have mainly highlighted the problems of measuring the profitability of these services.

The second wave of studies tried to free themselves from these limits by defining a broader measurement of the performance of Internet banks compared to that of the other banks. We are going to concern ourselves mainly with this second type of study. But beforehand, we will look at performance measurement in the banking sector.

How to Measure Profitability?

Demirguc-Kunt and Huizinga (2000) highlight that "the approach to profitability in banking and finance is characterized by its complexity and its multiform aspect". They explain their analysis through five main points:

- *The merging of "raw material", "money deposited", "final product" and "money loaned"*: the fungibility of money makes it more complicated to calculate profitability due to the difficulty of dissociating resources from their uses;

- *The impossibility of establishing provisions of profitability in the short term* because of the existence of several uncertainties which are part of bank-customer relations (loan prepayment, litigation, change of address, etc.);

- *The difficulty in establishing profitability per product* because traditional banking is based on linked product sales which have high indirect costs;

- *The strong regulation (or commoditization) of some products:* an innovation in the banking sector cannot be patented and can easily be copied;

- *The strong constraint of rigidity of costs in banking* which are mainly "overhead costs" and indirect. Defining the profitability of a product, a customer segment or a center of responsibility (branch, area, etc) is a complicated task and depends on method of indirect cost allocation.

For all these reasons, banks performances are assessed ex-post starting from general accounting indicators such as the level of deposits, the losses on loans, the ROA (return on assets) or the ROE (return on equity). But, in the case of a comparison of the performance of newly created Internet banks with that of traditional banks, these indicators (ROA and ROE) are not very relevant because the net income can be negative (because the activity is starting up), and they do not take into account other elements such as "possible market power" (Shepherd et al., 1999).

Among the other methods used, the most famous is the profit efficiency model (DeYoung, 2005). This method allows us to identify between the technology-based scale effects and the technology-based experience effects, showing whether the profitability gaps evaporate as Internet banks grow larger, gain experience and capture economies of scale.

For Cyree et al. (2008): *"Profit efficiency indicates how well management produces outputs for a given input mix along with other market characteristics and is measured as the distance from the best-practice frontier".* Moreover, this methodology captures "technology-based experience" and "technology-based scale" effects.

Do Internet Banks Give a Superior Performance?

On the basis of the idea that "experience" could be a determinant of cost reduction and production efficiency, DeYoung (2001) presented a first comparison of the ROA between newly chartered banks (newly created traditional banks) and Internet banks (Internet-primary banks) between 1997 and 1999. He notes that the Internet-primary banks show significantly lower profits than those achieved by the newly chartered banks because of difficulties generating deposit accounts and higher non-interest expenses. The gap is very wide during the first two years but is reduced quickly thanks to technology experience effects. The growth rate of the Internet-primary banks declines to meet that of the newly chartered banks. The banks then progress at the same rate except for the deposit-to-asset ratio. The maturity effects are similar for the two types of bank. Lastly, Internet-primary banks, just like the newly chartered banks, can only reach the same profitability (ROA) as traditional banks at the end of approximately 10 years of activity (DeYoung, 2001).

In a second study, DeYoung (2005) confirms these results by using the profit efficiency model. He shows that the Internet-primary bank startups tended to underperform the branch bank startups over the period 1997-2001 in the USA. This seems to call into question the viability of the Internet bank e-BM. One can conclude from this that the success of an Internet bank is only possible if it reaches a sufficient level of economy of scale and has efficient management practices, particularly for cost management.

The more recent results from Cyree et al. (2008), which study the performance of Internet-primary banks and newly chartered traditional banks from 1996 to 2003, provide more details of these performance gaps with certain conflicting conclusions to the studies of DeYoung (2001, 2005). Their univariate analysis shows that Internet-primary banks have lower ROA, ROE, loan losses, and net-interest margin, compared to newly chartered traditional banks. But, they indicate that the Internet-primary banks are more profit efficient than the newly chartered traditional banks.

In fact, several elements can justify the performance gap of Internet banks with traditional banks especially when starting up (Les Echos n° 19586, 18/01/2006):

- *Incompressible structural costs:* These are expenses inherent to all banking activities and are mainly composed of high fixed charges and costs of IT development. In the case of Axa Banque, these IT costs account for 30% of total operating costs,
- *A high turnover of advisers and the difficulty of arranging schedules spread over 12 or even 24 hours to man a hot-line,*
- *A very high cost of customer acquisition:* For Axa Banque, this cost must not exceed 300 euros per customer recruited to be profitable. This stumbling block can only be overcome with a diversification of customer recruitment methods, loss leaders, and precise customer targeting.

On the other hand, other factors are favorable to the development of online services including (Les Echos n° 19586, 1/18/2006; EFMA, 2007):

- *the specific characteristics of customers who use on line banks:* 20% are on average expert users in Europe (48% in the Netherlands). This clientele is autonomous in decision making, they are mainly men, managers, with a high income who subscribe regularly to financial products on line;

- *Internauts are more profitable than non-internaut customers:* In the case of Axa Banque, their internaut customers bring in 15% more revenue than the non-internaut customers as soon as they join and achieve the target revenue after 18 months instead of 30 months on average;

- *the potential of productivity for online banks is higher than that of the traditional bank:* in the case of Axa Banque, the productivity by employee is 405 customers (which is a higher performance than the average French bank) with a productivity potential which can reach double that of a traditional bank;

- *the structure of the net banking income from an online bank is very different from that of a traditional bank:* for example, Axa Banque draws 70% of its net banking income from payment methods. The remaining 30% comes from the banking offer (credit, savings and stock exchange transactions) which have strong development potential;

- *the backing of a big group* means that certain costs can be minimised by benefiting from a phenomenon of material synergy (compensation operations, debit and credit cards, etc.) and intangible synergy (experience, notoriety, etc.). For example, the Midland Bank provided First Direct with a back office of 7 000 ATMs in Great Britain which was the basis of its success. The risk of the cannibalisation of channels, competition between the online bank and the mother company (traditional bank) is low because the banks attract a different clientele.

In fact, these studies and research show that the success of an online bank is mainly conditioned by:

- *Building a strong competitive advantage* which lies in access to customers and a good understanding of their behaviour and tastes. Many banks believed that the competitive advantage depended on the technology used; however, technological advances are very quickly copied. This advantage makes it possible to control the cost of acquiring a new clientele. The support of an institution delivering financial services (insurance, supermarkets, banks, etc), the creation of an attractive loss leader (savings accounts with a high interest rate like ING Direct, etc) or an innovating service (for example: online brokers at the end of the 90s, etc) are the main means of building up a competitive advantage;

- *The difficulty of maintaining continuous investments without making profits* forces certain online financial operators to merge with each other. This was specially the case of certain online brokers who, when they started dealing on the stock exchange, were able to collect large funds. But, as their period of investing at a loss lengthened, they had difficulties accessing other investments. The only way out for those in most difficulty was to merge. One finds several examples in the case of online banks such as the absorption of ZeBank by Egg (which gave it access to the French market), the merger of First-e (Ireland) and Uno-e (Spain), etc;

- *A strong brand* which inspires trust from potential customers and which also helps reduce the cost of acquiring new customers.

These conditions highlight the difficulty of creating an online bank for actors from outside the banking sector.

CONCLUSION

In conclusion, we have shown that the dynamic of the financial services sector on Internet is intensifying and that a certain structuring of the sector can be observed. Indeed, the actors are looking for new "revenues-created values" combinations following the example of online brokers, such as Schwab, who have become information providers for the portals, and are trying to reach a critical size via mergers and strategic alliances.

However, the shape of an e-BM specific to online banks hasn't clearly emerged. Despite the strong development potential of online banks, their survival as a specific e-BM can be questioned because of their weak breakthrough onto the international and national markets and their modest financial results. The most successful actors have concentrated on market niches, like ING Direct in Europe.

One can question the capacity of online banks, as e-BMs, to remain banks which are virtual, independent and generalist. In this case, it is extremely probable that they will have to develop their own physical sales network (like Schwab) or enter into partnerships with traditional establishments. Otherwise, they are likely to disappear or be absorbed by traditional banks and become gradually integrated into their multi-channel strategy.

REFERENCES

Afuah, A., & Tucci, C. (2003). *Internet Business Models and Strategies*. New York: McGraw-Hill.

Applegate, L. M. (2000). *Emerging e-Business Models: Lessons from the Field*. Boston: Harvard Business School Press.

Berger, A. N., Demsetz, R. S., & Strahan, P. E. (1999). The consolidation of the financial services industry: Causes, consequences, and implications for the future. *Journal of Banking & Finance, 23*(2-4), 135–194. doi:10.1016/S0378-4266(98)00125-3

Carlson, J., Furst, K., Lang, W., & Nolle, D. (2000) Internet Banking: Markets Developments and Regulatory Issues. *Office of the Comptroller of the Currency, Economic and Policy Analysis Working Papers* 2000-9.

Cyree, K.B., Delcoure, N., & Dickens, R. (2008). An examination of the performance and prospects for the future of internet-primary banks.*Journal of Economics and Finance*, June.

Delgado, J., Hernando, I., & Nieto, M. J. (2007). Do European Primarily Internet Banks Show Scale and Experience Efficiencies? *European Financial Management, 13*(4), 643–671. doi:10.1111/j.1468-036X.2007.00377.x

Demil, B., Lecoq, X., & Warnier, V. (2004).Le business model: l'oublié de la stratégie? *13th AIMS Conference,* Normandie, 2-4 June.

Demirguc-Kunt, A., & Huizinga, H. (2000), Financial structure and bank profitability. *World Bank, Policy Research Working Paper Series* 2430.

DeYoung R. (2001), The financial progress of pure-play internet banks *Bank for International Settlements, Monetary and Economic Department, BIS Papers n°7*, 80-86.

DeYoung, R. (2005). The Performance of Internet-Based Business Models: Evidence from the Banking Industry. *The Journal of Business, 78*(3), 893–947. doi:10.1086/429648

EFMA (2007). *Online consumer behaviour in retail financial services*, with Novametrie, Capgemini and Microsoft, EFMA Studies, December

Egland, K. L., Robertson, D., Furst, K., Nolle, D. E., & Robertson, D. (1998). Banking over the Internet. *Office of the Comptroller of the Currency. Currency Quarterly, 17*, 25–30.

Essayan, M., Rutstein, C., & Wetenhall, P. (2002). *Activate and Integrate: Optimizing the Value of Online Banking*. Boston: Boston Consulting Group.

Furst, K., Lang, W. W., & Nolle, D. E. (2002). Internet banking. *Journal of Financial Services Research*, *22*, 95–117. doi:10.1023/A:1016012703620

Hasan, I., Zazzara, C., & Ciciretti, R. (2005). Internet, Innovation and Performance of Banks: Italian Experience. *unpublished manuscript*.

Hensman, M., Van den Bosch, F. A., & Volberda, H. (2001). Clicks vs. Bricks in the Emerging Online Financial Services Industry. *Long Range Planning Journal*, *34*, 33–235.

Hernando, I., & Nieto, M. J. (2007). Is the Internet delivery channel changing banks' performance? The case of Spanish banks. *Journal of Banking & Finance*, *31*(4), 1083–1099. doi:10.1016/j.jbankfin.2006.10.011

Horsti, A., Tuunainen, V. K., & Tolonen, J. (2005). Evaluation of Electronic Business Model Success: Survey among Leading Finnish Companies. *Proceedings of the 38th Annual Hawaii International Conference on System Sciences*, Volume 7.

Linder, J., & Cantrell, S. (2000). *Changing Business Models: Surveying the Landscape*. Accenture Institute for Strategic Change.

Loilier, T., & Tellier, A. (2001). *Nouvelle Economie, Net organisations*. Paris: EMS Eds.

Magretta, J. (2002). Why Business Models Matter? *Harvard Business Review*, (May): 90–91.

Mahadevan, B. (2000). Business Models for Internet-based e-Commerce: An anatomy. *California Management Review*, *42*(4), 55–69.

Muylle, S. (2001). e-Business in Financial Services", KPMG, Retrieved from http://www.e-investments.be/KPMG.pdf.

Novak, T.P., & Hoffman, D.L. (2001). Profitability on the Web: Business Models and Revenue Streams. *eLab Position Paper, Owen Graduate School of Management, Vanderbilt University*, January: 9-18.

Porter, M.E. (2001). Strategy and the Interne. Boston: *Harvard Business Review*, June.

Rappa, M. (2001) Business models on the Web. Retrieved from http://digitalenterprise.org/models/models.html.

Rowe, F. (1994). *Des Banques et des Réseaux: Productivité et Avantages Concurrentiels*. ENSPTT-Economica, janvier: 246-247

Sahut, J.M. (2000), L'impact de l'Internet sur les métiers de la banque. *Les Cahiers du Numérique*, septembre: 158-162.

Sahut, J.M. (2001). Vers une révolution du secteur bancaire ? *La Revue du Financier* n°131, 34-38.

Sahut, J. M. (2004). Why does SSL dominate the e-payment market? *Journal of Internet Banking and Commerce*, *9*(1).

Shapiro, C., & Varian, H. R. (2003). Information rule. *Ethics and Information Technology*, *5*(1).

Sullivan, RJ (2000), How has the adoption of internet banking affected performance and risk in banks? *Federal Reserve Bank of Kansas City, Financial Perspectives, December*: 1-16.

Timmers, P. (1998). Business models for electronic markets. *Electronic Markets*, *8*(2), 2–8. doi:10.1080/10196789800000016

ADDITIONAL READING

Berry L., A., Parasuraman, V., & Zeithaml V. (1990). *Delivering Quality Service: Balancing Customer Perceptions and Expectacions*. The Free Press, March.

Chen, S.-H., & Chen, H.-H. (2009). The empirical study of customer satisfaction and continued behavioural intention towards self-service banking: technology readiness as an antecedent. *International Journal of Electronic Finance*, *3*(1). doi:10.1504/IJEF.2009.024270

Claessens, S., Glaessner, T., & Klingebiel, D. (2002). Electronic Finance: Reshaping the Financial Landscape Around the World. *Journal of Financial Services Research, 22*(1), October, Available at SSRN: http://ssrn.com/abstract=382932

Dong, J., & Bliemel, M. (2008). Strategies for Increased Integration of Online and In-Branch Services of Banks in Canada. *Journal of Internet Banking and Commerce, 13*(3).

Ghobadian, A. (1994). Service Quality: Concepts and Models. *International Journal of Quality & Reliability Management, 11*(9). doi:10.1108/02656719410074297

Ghobadian, A., Speller, S., & Jones, M. (1994). Service quality: concepts and models. *International Journal of Quality & Reliability Management, 11*(9). doi:10.1108/02656719410074297

Giordani, G., Floros, C., & Judge, G. (2009). Internet banking services and fees: the case of Greece. *International Journal of Electronic Finance, 3*(2). doi:10.1504/IJEF.2009.026359

Krostie, J. (1996). *Using Quality Function Deployment in Software Requirements Specification. Andersen Consulting and IDI*. Oslo, Norway: NTNU.

Liljander, V., van Rien A., & Pura M. (2002). *Customer Satisfaction with e-Services: The case of an Online Recruitement Portal*. Published in the Yearbook of Services Management 2002 – e-Services.

Migdadi, Y. K. A. (2009). Quantitative Evaluation of the Internet Banking Service Encounter's Quality: Comparative Study between Jordan and the UK Retail Banks. *Journal of Internet Banking and Commerce, 14*(1).

Sahut, J. M. (2006). Electronic wallets in danger. *Journal of Internet Banking and Commerce, 11*(2).

Sahut, J. M. (2008). Internet Payment and Banks. *International Journal of Business, 13*(4).

Sahut, J. M. (2008). A TAM extension for e-wallet adoption: The case of Moneo. *Journal of Internet Banking & Commerce, 13*(1).

Sahut, JM. (2008). On-line Brokerage in Europe: Actors & Strategies. *Journal of Internet Banking and Commerce, 8*(1), June 2003

Sahut, J. M., & Hrnciar, H. (2003). Problématique de la qualité des services d'Internet Banking. *Gestion, 2000*(2).

Sahut, J. M., & Jegham, M. (2008). ICT acceptation: The case of CRM project. *Gestion, 2000*(2).

Sahut, JM., & Kucerova, Z. (2005). Improving End-User Experience via Quality Performance Evaluation: Internet Banking Case. *La revue du Financier*, October.

Sahut, J. M., & Kucerova, Z. (2005). Enhance Internet Banking Service Quality with Quality Function Deployment Approach. *Journal of Internet Banking and Commerce, 8*(2).

Schaechter, A. (2002)., Issues in Electronic Banking: An Overview. *IMF Policy Discussion Paper No. 02/6*, Washington: International Monetary Fund.

Settlements, Bank for International (2001), Electronic Finance: *A New Perspective and Challenges*. BIS Paper No. 7, November, Available at SSRN: http://ssrn.com/abstract=1187567

Tam, Ch. T. W., Leung, T. K. P., & Wong, Y. H. (2003). An integrated model of online customer loyalty. [Brussels, Belgium.]. *Proceedings of ABAS International Conference, 2003*(July), 11–13.

Van Riel, A. C. R., Liljander, V., & Jurriens, P. (2001). Exploring consumer evaluation of e-services: a portal site. *International Journal of Service Industry Management, 12*(4).

KEY TERMS AND DEFINITIONS

Bank Performance: Any of many different mathematical measures to evaluate how well a company is using its resources to make a profit (Farlex dictionary).

Business Model: all All the choices which a firm makes in order to generate revenue.

Click-and-Mortar Banks: traditional Traditional banks.

Distribution Channel Strategy: the The route by which a product or service is moved from a producer or supplier to customers (bnet dictionary).

Electronic Business Model: qualify Qualify the BM of electronic activities.

Information and Communication Technology (ICT): "is an umbrella term that covers all technical means for processing and communicating information. While this technically encompasses pre-digital technologies, including paper-based writing, it is most often used to describe digital technologies including methods for communication (communication protocols, transmission techniques, communications equipment, media (communication)), as well as techniques for storing and processing information (computing, data storage, etc.) The term has gained popularity partially due to the convergence of information technology (IT) and telecom technology." (Wikipedia)

Online Banking: A system allowing individuals to access to remote bank services, via the internet and/or phone.

Profitability: The ability to earn a profit.

Pure Player Banks: All the bank activity is only accessible via Internet oand/or phone.

ENDNOTES

1   Study carried out by Accenture Institute for Strategic Change.

Chapter 7
Toward a Conceptual Framework for Verification and Analysis of Effective Factors in Successful Implementation of Electronic Banking

Mirza Hassan Hosseini
Payame Noor University, Iran

Ali Ghorbani
Payame Noor University, Iran

ABSTRACT

Nowadays, e-banking plays an important role in e-society and human life. Imagine an e-society without e-banking is not possible. The e-banking is considered as an enabler factor to e-business, e-commerce, e-government and other e-initiatives. Despite the pivotal role of e-banking in our lives, yet a comprehensive conceptual model of electronic banking success factors has not been provided by the researchers. The present chapter is trying to provide a comprehensive conceptual model by categorizing factors affecting implementation of electronic banking. In this regards, the factors affecting implementation of electronic banking was classified based on Co-structural factors, Content factors and Context factors. We called this conceptual model as the Tri-Category (3C) Model. The questionnaire used for gathering data. The results showed that there is a positive relationship between successful implementation of e-Banking and attention to Co-structural, Content and Contextual factors. At the end of chapter, several recommendations have been offered to implementing successful E-banking.

DOI: 10.4018/978-1-61520-635-3.ch007

INTRODUCTION

The new technologies in the banking services are a part of rapid changes in the way of life and thinking. The aware banks toward these new changes are fundamental for their performance improvement (Danciu, 2008). Among such technologies were the growing number of technology-based remote access delivery channels and payment systems, such as automated teller machines that displaced cashier teller; the telephone, represented by call centers that replaced the bank branch; the Internet that replaced snail mail; credit cards and electronic cash that replaced traditional cash transaction; and shortly, interactive television that will replace face-to-face transaction (Kamel & Hassan, 2003).

The potential of E-Banking was well recognized a decade ago (Booz & Hamilton, 1997; Deloitte Consulting, 2000) when key institutions began to align the product delivery mix with new technology and explore and exploit new approaches to their business (Chi et al, 2007). It is widely believed that the impact of e-commerce enables banks to provide an inexpensive and direct way of exchanging information and to sell or buy products and services. Burr defines E-banking as "an electronic connection between the bank and the customer in order to delivering, managing and controlling the financial interactions" (Lustsik, 2004, p. 9).

E-banking is developed in two forms: One also called automation of banking; the banks services offer through electronic system. In this system, the branches are equipped with computer and bank staffs use them. There is no change in the banking infra-structures (Bayat, 2002). On the other hand in form two; banks offer their service only through electronic channels, without having a physical branch. These types of banks are called as virtual bank, bank without branches, or pure internet banks (Scratchier, 2002).

E-banking advantages can be viewed by two approaches: (a) Through customer's point of view: the high speed of offering services, easy to use, availability and accuracy, removing time and place limitations; (b) Through bank point of view: Competitive Advantage, Customer Retention and Attraction, etc (Zolia, 2000). Recognizing those advantages, banks have early and aggressively moved offerings to the internet, e.g. before the internet bubble, a 100% growth rate in new on-line bank ventures was witnessed in Western Europe alone, according to eMarketer (eMarketer, 2000)

To be successful, E-banking requires that high percentage of bank customers would be able to connect to the bank and receive their favorite services. However, these services require the installation of specific telecommunication networks or application software, which can be costly and lack user accessibility and flexibility (Chi et al, 2007).

E-banking initiated in the years 1993-1994 in Iran. The initial efforts to information exchange network between banks (shetab) generated by three public banks in the year 2000. Then, the central bank initiated shetab system with the aim of creating connection among banks (Bahramian, 2003). Commercial banks in Iran have been quick to realize the importance of E-banking to competitive advantage. Since the 2001, they have continuously innovated through technology-enhanced products and services, such as multi-function automatic teller machines (ATMs), electronic share application, tele-banking, TV-banking, electronic transfers, electronic cash cards, and Internet-based e-banking. It can be claimed that me have stepped into the E-banking world.

Research Problem: The Iranian banking industry is undergoing rapid change and becoming intensely competitive. Traditional and new players both are trying to protect their customer base. The advances in information technology are becoming an important factor to the future development of banking industry (Kannabiran & Narayan 2005).

According to ICTna, "only 7.5% of Iran banking network customers had possibility to internet buying at the end of 2008" (ICTna, 2008) but the emergence of new private-sector banks in the country e.g. Pasargad, Saman, Eghtesad Novin and Parsian has changed the scenario drastically, as the business model of these new banks revolved around a strong IT backbone. Almost all of these banks costumers have Credit Card, can buy form internet (ICTna, 2008). Emergence and success over the last several years have put competitive pressure on many of the state-owned banks to look at IT as a strategic necessity to remain competitive (Kannabiran & Narayan 2005). Therefore understanding the success factors in e-banking is important for senior management of banking related organizations because it would help them improve their e-banking implementation process.

The Purpose of Research: In an attempt to find out how some banks were successful in Iran, this chapter is to recognize the effective factors in successful implementation of E-banking in Iran's banking system, what key lessons came out of their experience which could be generalized and as result to propose alternatives which seem to be fruitful in successful implementing of E-banking by others.

Research Hypotheses: This research has tested three hypotheses in the form of Tri-Category (3C) Model for recognizing and ranking effective factors in successful implementation of E-banking as follow:

- There is a meaningful relation between Co-structural factors and successful implementation of E-banking in Iran's banking system.
- There is a meaningful relation between Content factors and successful implementation of E-banking in Iran's banking system.
- There is a meaningful relation between Contextual factors and successful implementation of E-banking in Iran's banking system.

CONCEPTUAL FRAMEWORK

Since 1960 and specially after proposing general systems theory, it seems less likely that a theorist would not use clarification of theory relation with these three fundamental concepts in management, i.e., human, organization and society or environment (Mirzaei & Amiri 2002).

Tri-Category Model is one of logical models in classifying models. All organizational concepts, events and phenomena can be studied, analyzed in the frame of this three dimensions (Mirzaei, 1998).

Co-Structure (Organizational) dimension of organization means all of elements, physical and non-human factors, and conditions of the organization which are bounded together through special order and regulation and constitute frame, cover, or physical and material body of the organization. In fact, Co-structure dimension contain non-alive factors of the organization (Sarlak & Mirzaei 2005; Mirzaei, 1998). According to Damanpour these factors are variables such as theories are: functional differentiation (the number of different functional units in an organization), specialization (different areas of expertise in an organization), professionalism (professional knowledge including employees' education and experience), formalization (the degree to which rules and procedures are followed in an organization), and centralization (whether decision making is centralized or distributed) (Damanpour, 1987).

Individuals do not passively accept and use technology. In contrast, they actively enact technologies in different ways. They can use it minimally, maximally, or improvise in ways that are hard to anticipate (Gwebu & Wang, 2007). Human (Content) dimension of organization means human and its behavior in the organization which are bounded together through special patterns, behavioral norms and unofficial communications and constitutes the main content of the organization and are regarded as, in fact, alive factors of the organization (Mirzaei, 1998).

Environmental (Context) dimension includes all extra-organizational factors and conditions surrounding the organization and constitute main systems of the organization such as customers, government, markets and other environmental elements of the organization (Mirzaei, 1998). Researchers in information technologies and organizational studies have long pointed out that an identical technology can be enacted differently in different organizational context (Boudreau & Robey, 2005; Vinnem & Liyanage 2008). They adopt this dimension not only is the most important and main dimension but also creates the other two ones and general growth and survival of the organization depends upon it (Mirzaei, 1998). Damanpour and Gopalakrishnan (1998) focus on the dynamism of the environment and further classify environmental dynamism into two components: environmental stability and environmental predictability. These two components have resulted in four combinations of environment characteristics: stable and predictable, stable and unpredictable, unstable and predictable, unstable and unpredictable (Gwebu & Wang, 2007). Researchers adopt a less deterministic view and propose that both human agency and the social context within which a technology operates play an important role in the outcome of the technology (Vinnem & Liyanage 2008; Gwebu & Wang, 2007).

Considering research literature and also special problems of Iran's bank regarding successful implementation of E-banking; this research has been tried to give comprehensive summary of indexes or sub-variables of literature which were pointed out in more than 30 foreign and domestic researches, summarized and classified in the form of Tri-Category (3C) Model (Co-structure, Content, and Context dimensions). Therefore it can be said that independent variables of the research include Co-structural, Content and Context factors. We can refer to successful implementation of E-banking as a dependent variable. Table 1 presents conceptual frame of research through demonstrating each factors of model and indexes of each factor.

MATERIALS AND METHODS

Research Methodology: In terms of its purpose this is an descriptive-explorative study and regarding the utilization, it is a applied research.

Instrument: Articles, books, thesis, and information websites has been used for data collection in literature reviewing and conceptual fundamentals of research. Questionnaire and interview have been used in order to study and adjust factors obtained through research literature. For measuring responders view point about factors affecting successful implementation of E-banking, designed 24 items using Likert 5-point ranking spectrum (ordinal) which rated from strongly disagree to strongly agree. Some questions were put at the section 2 of the questionnaires in order to obtain some descriptive information about responding individuals and the rate their bank use E-banking. The questionnaires with research model were given to 15 of E-Banking experts (including those who are responsible to E-banking affairs at banks, governmental organizations and college masters) after readying and were confirmed by them after some partial displacements in effective factors classifying and simplifying some questions.

Validity & Reliability: To be more assured about "questionnaire validity", At the first step the questionnaire was distributed among 9 banks (13 individuals) which were in different levels considering implementation of E-banking by using of "concurrent validity" and ambiguous questions were edited at the next edition of questionnaire. Cronbach α correlation were used for evaluation of reliability of the questionnaire through using 13-person (9 banks) preliminary sample. Reliability all over the questionnaire was 0.89 and for Co-structural, Content and Context factors was 0.85, 0.94 and 0.88, respectively.

Data Analyzing Procedure: Chi-Squire Test (for testing statistical hypotheses) and Friedman analysis of variance test (for ranking dimensions of Co-structural, Content and Context factors) was used for data analysis procedure (Azar and Momeni 2001). The results obtained at 0.05 α level in this research. SPSS software and Excel software was used for hypotheses testing and ranking of factors respectively.

Statistical Population: Research statistical population has been made by experts and managers of IT and E-banking in banks of Iran; but because of their expansion they were restricted to experts of

Table 1. Tri-Category (3C) Model; Factors affecting successful implementation of E-banking in Iran's banking system

Effectives	Indexes	Researcher/year
Co-Structur	Security of IT systems in E-banking	Daniel, Story, (1997) - Wallman, (1999), Regan, Macaluso, (2000) - Turban, Lee, King, Shung, (2008) - Enos (2001) - Shah, Khan, Xu, (2006) - Sarlak, Abolhasani, Forozandeh, Ghorbani (2009)
	Telecommunication, software, hardware and technical infra-structures	Dejpasand (2006) - Ferguson (2000) – Sachs (2000) - Toufaily, Daghfous, Toffoli, (2009) - Shah, Khan, Xu, (2006)
	Financial sources for investing in E-banking infra-structures	Toufaily, Daghfous, Toffoli, (2009) - Shah, Khan, Xu, (2006) - Sarlak, Abolhasani, Forozandeh, Ghorbani (2009) - Rao, Metts, Monge (2003) - Kuzic, Fisher and Scollary (2002)
	Drawing of the Internet market map for the e-banking strategy	Dejpasand (2006) - Stamoulis (2000) - Toufaily, Daghfous, Toffoli, (2009) - Eid, Truman and Ahmed (2002)
	Presenting a comprehensive website, contain: Corporate profile, product and pricing information, interest rates, and application forms etc	Stamoulis (2000) - Riggins (1999) – Rao, Metts, Monge (2003) – Darch, Lucas (2002)
	Using branding for highlighting E-banking systems	Cooper, Lichtenstein, Smith, (2009) – Yousafzai, Pallister, Foxall (2005)
	Transforming internal foundations to be effective and integrated in order to provide each customer with unique offerings	El Sawy, Malhotra, Gosain, Young (1999) - Enos (2001) – Franco, Klein, (1999) - King, Liou (2004) - Shah, Khan, Xu, (2006) - Shah, Ahmed, Meckel, Shah (2008)
Content	Educated and efficient staff in E-banking context	Sotudeh, (2003) – Sachs (2000) - Toufaily, Daghfous, Toffoli, (2009) - Al-Hajri (2008) - Shah, Khan, Xu, (2006) - Sarlak, Abolhasani, Forozandeh, Ghorbani (2009)
	A user-friendly web-interface and appropriate promotion	Turban, Lee, King, Shung, (2008) - Riggins, (1999) - Shah, Khan, Xu, (2006) – Kuzic, Fisher and Scollary (2002) - Eid, Truman and Ahmed (2002)
	Positive view of point into E-banking and existence of innovation motivation among staff and management of bank	Kehzadi (2002) - Dejpasand (2006) - Riggins, (1999) - Al-Hajri (2008) - Shah, Khan, Xu, (2006)
	Enough knowledge and cognition of staff on opportunities and benefits of E-banking	Toufaily, Daghfous, Toffoli, (2009) - Shah, Ahmed, Meckel, Shah (2008) - Sarlak, Abolhasani, Forozandeh, Ghorbani (2009)
	Efficient and very quick customer service	Jayawardhena, Foley (2000) – Orr (2004) - Kuzic, Fisher and Scollary (2002) - Eid, Truman and Ahmed (2002)
	Planning toward training (e.g. ICDL courses) and updating knowledge and skills of staff	Sotudeh (2003) - Amini (2006) - Darch, Lucas (2002) - Eid, Truman and Ahmed (2002) – Sargazi (2008)
	The data gathered about the customer with any interaction, for good understanding needs and wants of customers	Sotudeh (2003) - Franco, Klein, (1999) - Regan, Macaluso, (2000) - Storey, Thompson, Bokma, Bradnum (2000) - Shah, Khan, Xu, (2006)
	Support of head management from implementation of E-banking	Dejpasand (2006) - Turban, Lee, King, Shung, (2008) - Sarlak, Abolhasani, Forozandeh, Ghorbani (2009) - Amini (2006) - Kuzic, Fisher and Scollary (2002) - Eid, Truman and Ahmed (2002) - Amini (2006) – Sargazi (2008)

continued on following page

Table 1. Continued

Effectives	Indexes	Researcher/year
Context	Regulations convenience related to E-banking	Kehzadi (2002) – Kannabiran and Narayan (2005) - Sarlak, Abolhasani, Forozandeh, Ghorbani (2009) - Sargazi (2008) - Kuzic, Fisher and Scollary (2002)
	Convenience and customer accessibility to web based services (e.g. computer, high speed internet etc)	Crede (1999) – Sarrafizadeh (2005) – Cooper, Lichtenstein, Smith, (2009) – Al-Hajri (2008) - Amini (2006)
	Strategic aiming and movement toward E-banking in country	Rao, Metts, Monge (2003) – Sargazi (2008) - Eid, Truman and Ahmed (2002)
	Codifying standards and indexes related to E-banking	Sarlak, Abolhasani, Forozandeh, Ghorbani (2009) - Eid, Truman and Ahmed (2002)
	Existence of appropriate culture toward E-banking in society (trust)	Sachs (2000) – Enos (2001) - Yousafzai, Pallister, Foxall (2005) - Darch, Lucas (2002) - Eid, Truman and Ahmed (2002)
	Perceived usefulness by customer (customer awareness)	Sachs (2000) - Al-Hajri (2008) - Sargazi (2008) - Shah, Ahmed, Meckel, Shah (2008) - Amini (2006)
	Threatening of technological environment and competitors executing E-banking	Toufaily, Daghfous, Toffoli, (2009) - Sarlak, Abolhasani, Forozandeh, Ghorbani (2009) - Rao, Metts, Monge (2003)
	Coordination and cooperation with the other banks in E-banking context	Amini (2006) - Rao, Metts, Monge (2003) – Sargazi (2008) - Kuzic, Fisher and Scollary (2002) - Eid, Truman and Ahmed (2002)

(N=318 bank), the most advanced bank at the field of E-banking. Applying simple random method, questionnaires distributed between 90 Pasargad bank dimensions throughout the country at winter 2009 (This value was derived through computing formula mentioned by (Azar & Momeni, 2001).

RESULTS

Outcomes of study characterized that 81.1% of the responders are man and 18.9% of them are woman. According to Figure 1, surveying the education level of responders demonstrates that most of responders hold bachelor degree. Also surveying age of responders demonstrates that their mean age is 34.89 (See Figure 2).

The questionnaire outcomes of study manifests that majority of the responders had less than 10 years work experience in the banking (See Figure 3).

The results of data analysis for testing statistical hypotheses presented in Table 2 demonstrates that the amount of testing statistics is more than critical value in all three hypotheses.

Figure 1. Education level of responders

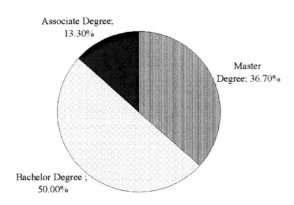

Figure 2. Scale of responders ages

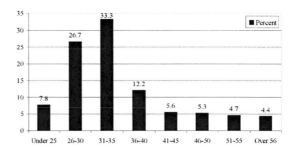

Figure 3. Work experience of responders

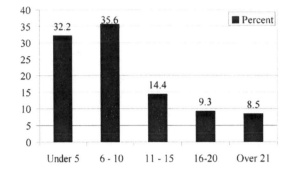

Test of First Hypothesis: The results obtained through using Chi-Squire Test demonstrate that testing statistic for the first hypothesis is 37.089, shows a significant difference in critical value, i.e., 28.86. Therefore, the first hypothesis is supported and at confidence level of 95% it can be claimed that the null hypothesis accepted, in other word "There is a meaningful relation between Co-structural factors and successful implementation of E-banking in Iran's banking system" (Table 2).

Test of Second Hypothesis: Considering results obtained in the Table 2 by using Chi-Squire Test, testing statistic for the second hypothesis 45.444, is more than critical value, i.e., 33.92. Therefore, the second hypothesis is supported, too and at confidence level of 95% it can be claimed that the null hypothesis accepted, in other word "There is a meaningful relation between Content factors and successful implementation of E-banking in Iran's banking system" (Table 2).

Test of Third Hypothesis: Considering results obtained by using Chi-Squire Test in the table 2,

testing statistic for the second hypothesis is 44.000 and since it is more than critical value, i.e., 42.55, therefore, the third hypothesis is supported like the two others and at confidence level of 95% it can be claimed that the null hypothesis accepted, in other word "There is a meaningful relation between Contextual factors and successful implementation of E-banking in Iran's banking system" (Table 2).

Considering Table 2 using Friedman analysis of variance test demonstrate that from the highest to the lowest, Co-structural, Context and Content factors occupy ranks one to three, respectively, in the case of effectiveness intensity on successful implementation of E-banking in Iran's banking system.

Ranking of factors Indexes: In this part, more minor factors (indexes) including each factor are ranked by using Friedman analysis of variance test. Accordingly, ranking of Co-structural factors indexes offered as Table 3, Content factors indexes as Table 4 and Context factors indexes as table 5.

DISCUSSION

We conducted a surveying study to get insights into relation between Co-stuctural, Content, Context factors, and the successful implementation of E-banking and found that there is a meaningful relation between these tree factors and successful implementation of E-banking in Iran's banking system.

Each phenomenon should provide some non-alive and physical conditions and elements in order to reach its goals. Co-structure dimension

Table 2. Summarized stages of statistical testing of research hypotheses and their ranking

Hypothesis No.	Critical value	Asymp. Sig	D.F	Chi-Square Testing Statistic	Test Result	Population Mean	Rank mean	Rank
1	28.86	0.005	18	37.089	H_0 Accepted	3.25	2.19	First
2	33.92	0.002	22	45.444	H_0 Accepted	2.97	1.79	Third
3	42.55	0.037	29	44.000	H_0 Accepted	3.14	2.02	Second

Table 3. Ranking of co-structural effective indexes

Index (barrier)	Rank Mean	Rank
Transforming internal foundations to be effective and integrated in order to provide each customer with unique offerings	4.50	1
Financial sources for investing in E-banking infra-structures	4.43	2
Telecommunication, software, hardware and technical infra-structures	4.09	3
Security of IT systems in E-banking	3.82	4
Presenting a comprehensive website, contain: Corporate profile, product and pricing information, interest rates, and application forms etc	3.81	5
Drawing of the Internet market map for the e-banking strategy	3.74	6
Using branding for highlighting E-banking systems	3.59	7

Table 4. Ranking of content effective indexes

Index (barrier)	Rank mean	Rank
A user-friendly web-interface and appropriate promotion	5.34	1
Efficient and very quick customer service	4.84	2
The data gathered about the customer with any interaction, for good understanding needs and wants of customers	4.76	3
Enough knowledge and cognition of staff on opportunities and benefits of E-banking	4.74	4
Support of head management from implementation of E-banking	4.32	5
Positive view of point into E-banking and existence of innovation motivation among staff and management of bank	4.20	6
Educated and efficient staff in E-banking context	4.01	7
Planning toward training (e.g. ICDL courses) and updating knowledge and skills of staff	3.78	8

Table 5. Ranking of context effective indexes

Index (barrier)	Rank Mean	Rank
Strategic aiming and movement toward E-banking in country	5.40	1
Perceived usefulness by customer (customer awareness)	5.15	2
Convenience and customer accessibility to web based services (e.g. computer, high speed internet etc)	5.11	3
Coordination and cooperation with the other banks in E-banking context	4.99	4
Threatening of technological environment and competitors executing E-banking	4.91	5
Regulations convenience related to E-banking	4.83	6
Existence of appropriate culture toward E-banking in society (trust)	4.78	7
Codifying standards and indexes related to E-banking	3.57	8

of E-banking is one of the main tools in helping the bank for its implementation. It is evident that implementing of E-banking will not be possible without creating non-human and material factors and substructures. Therefore, existence of infra-structures such as financial sources, security, Transforming foundations and etc. makes it necessary that these infra-structures and systems be in correspondence with methods and different kinds of intra-organizational systems. As a result, strength of Co-structural factors as one of the main E-banking successful implementation was expected. Acceptance of the first hypothesis of this research is an evidence for the above-mentioned matters.

Although E-banking implementation is not possible in case of lack of Co-structural and physical factors of the bank, it can be claimed that human is the reason for evolution and advancement of all materials. A creature with different views, character, values, needs and cultures and each of them find different solution for fulfilling their different needs. In implementation of E-banking, human should not be regarded as a non-alive thing on whom we have dominance and its behavior can be affected through using of physical rules. This is human and its relationships in the bank joining with behavioral norms, unofficial communications and special patterns constitute the main content of intra and extra bank. Therefore, Support of head management, knowledge of staff, efficient customer services and etc. can be regarded as serious factors in E-banking implementations. This is the reason for confirmation of Content factors hypothesis.

If Co-structural variables are supposed as independent variables and Content variables as dependant ones, the Context variables will be regarded as mediatory ones. And if Content variables are supposed as independent ones and Co-structural variables as dependent variables, Context variables will constitute hidden variables. In both cases, these variables will be regarded as "extra organizational" variables and will change Co-structural and Content factors, unwillingly. This br dimension anch will not only results in survival and growth of the other two dimensions but also creates these two dimensions in the organization. Therefore, factors such as Coordination with the other banks, technological environment, customer accessibility to web based services, and etc., should be considered for successful implementing of E-banking. As it seems these factors lead to confirmation of Context factors in this research.

A review on research literature and studies done in the field of this research makes it clear that most researchers have carried out case-by-case study in order to find independent variables of the research, and finally have presented a list of E-banking implementation factors which constitutes the main fundamentals of this research. Some researcher examine only one dimention of E-banking success factors e.g. Shah et al (2006) Investigated only organizational success factors in e-Banking and exctracted some indexes; or Yiu et al (2007) tried to make sense of Internet Banking in Hong Kong from angle the influences of perceived usefulness, perceived ease of use, perceived risk and personal innovativeness in information technology (Technology Acceptance Model). TAM model are used frequently to exploring E-banking usability by researchers.

Moreover it seems that classifying of scholars who have studied the set of success factors in the form of multiply categories, does not hold required comprehensiveness and makes it impossible to put most variables in these categories. for example Toufaily et al (2009) offered a conceptual model of the adoption of E-banking involed organizational variables, strategic variables and structure variables. We believe Tri-Category (3C) Model is more flexible than this model. Maybe most comprehensive reserch in this field is accomplished by Stamoulis (2000), suggest an internet commerce market structure model charts the Internet commerce market, by categorizing the role that they various participants, including banks, play in this market (Technology providers, Content providers, Context providers and Enablers). It is possible to concord content providers with Content dimension and context Providers with Context dimension. However in our research Co-structure dimension include most broader factors, technology providers have been studied in this frame, but "Enablers" didn't offer as independent dimention in this research and it's indexes investigated under three dimentions.

CONCLUSION AND RECOMMENDATIONS

This research has been tried to give comprehensive complex of effective factors by research literature; summarized and classified factors belike affecting successful implementation of E-banking in the form of Tri-Category (3C) Model and these examined on successful banks of Iran implementing E-banking. The findings demonstrate that three main dimensions of Co-structural, Context and Content factors lead to successful implementation of E-banking in Iran's banking system respectively. In ranking of Co-structural factor indexes, following indexes occupy the first three ranks of the dimension:

1. Transforming internal foundations to be effective and integrated in order to provide each customer with unique offerings;
2. Financial sources for investing in E-banking infra-structures;
3. Telecommunication, software, hardware and technical infra-structures.

In ranking of Content factor indexes, following barriers occupy the first three ranks of the dimension:

1. A user-friendly web-interface and appropriate promotion;
2. Efficient and very quick customer service;
3. The data gathered about the customer with any interaction, for good understanding needs and wants of customers.

In ranking of Contextual factor indexes, following indexes constitute the most important three ranks of the dimension:

1. Strategic aiming and movement toward E-banking in country
2. Perceived usefulness by customer (customer awareness)
3. Convenience and customer accessibility to web based services (e.g. computer, high speed internet etc).

Considering research results, taking Co-structural factor as the most important factor affecting successful implementation of E-banking in Iran's banking system into account, it is recommended related organizations pay more attention to this effective and try on improving them.

Some of important factors in this research includes different aspects whose study and their analysis is considered as essential needs of E-banking implementation. Among them we can refer to;

- Security of IT systems in E-banking
- The data gathered about the customer with any interaction, for good understanding needs and wants of customers
- Enough knowledge and cognition of staff on opportunities and benefits of E-banking
- Strategic aiming and movement toward E-banking in country
- Perceived usefulness by customer (Customer Awareness)

RESEARCH LIMITATIONS

1. Necessity of personal attending for filling of questionnaire
2. Geographically distribution of banks
3. Little cooperation of some responders

4.   This study has been done on a private bank in Iran and expansion of results to other country must be used with prudence.

REFERENCES

Al-Hajri, S. (2008). The Adoption of e-Banking: The Case of Omani Banks. *International Review of Business Research Papers, 4*(5), 20–128.

Amini, A. (2006). *Investigating Barriers And Challenges of E-banking Development and Improvement in Parsian Bank of Iran,* M.Sc dissertation, Shahid Beheshti University, Iran.

Azar, A., & Momeni, M. (2001). *Statistics and its Application in Management.* Tehran, Iran: SMT Publication.

Bahramian, Y. (2003). A Short Perusal for E-Banking Birth in Iran. *Journal of Bank Va Eghtesad,* N. 50, 52-53.

Bayat, Gh.R. (2002). Electronic Banking, Choice or Committal! *Elm Va Ayandeh, 1*(2), 52–58.

Boudreau, M.-C., & Robey, D. (2005). Enacting integrated information technology: A human agency perspective. *Organization Science, 16*(1), 3–19. doi:10.1287/orsc.1040.0103

Cooper, V., Lichtenstein, Sh., & Smith, R. (2009). Successful Web-based IT Support Services: Service Provider Perceptions of Stakeholder-oriented Challenges. *International Journal of E-Services and Mobile Applications.* Hershey, PA: Idea Group Publishing, *1* (1): 1-20.

Crede, A. (1999). Electronic Commerce and Banking Industry: the requirement and opportunities for new payment system using The Internet. *Science policy research unit university* p 27. Retrieved January 5, 2009, from http://jcmc.indiana.edu/vol1/issue3/crede.html

Damanpour, F. (1987). The adoption of technological, administrative, and ancillary innovations: Impact of organizational factors. *Journal of Management, 13*(4), 675–678. doi:10.1177/014920638701300408

Daniel. E. & Story, Ch. (1997). *Online Banking: Strategic and Management challenges.* Long rang planning. *30* (6), 890-898.

Darch, H. & Lucas, T. (2002). Training as an E-Commerce Enabler. *Journal of Workplace Learning, 14* (4), 148-155. Dejpasand. F., (2006). *Cash Electronic Transmission and E-banking.* Tehran, Commerce Ministry Publication, 178-209.

Eid, R., Truman, M., & Ahmed, A. M. (2002). A Cross Industry Review of B2B Critical Success Factors. *Internet Research, 12*(2), 110–123. doi:10.1108/10662240210422495

El Sawy, O. A., Malhotra, A., Gosain, S., & Young, K. M. (1999). IT-Intensive Value Innovation in the Electronic Economy: Insights from Marshall Industries. *Management Information Systems Quarterly, 23*(3), 305–335. doi:10.2307/249466

Ferguson. R. W., (2000, October). *Information Technology in Banking and Supervision,* At the Financial Services Conference, Online Banking Report, Piper Jaffray Equity Research, Available at: www.pjc.com/ec-ie01.asp?team=2 [Accessed 15 September 2008]

Gwebu, K. L., & Wang, J. (2007). The Role of Organizational, Environmental and Human Factors in E-learning Diffusion, *International Journal of Web-Based Learning and Teaching Technologies, 2* (2), 59-78., Hershey, PA: Idea Group Publishing, Information and Communication Technology News Agency, (2008). *Investigating The Rate of E-banking Usability in Iran,* Retrieved March 23, 2009, from http://www.ictna.ir/report/archives/016012.html [Accessed 23 March 2009]

Jayawardhena, C., & Foley, P. (2000). Changes in the Banking Sector – the Case of Internet Banking in the UK. *Internet Research: Electronic Networking Applications and Policy, 10*(1), 19–30. doi:10.1108/10662240010312048

Kamel, Sh., & Hassan, A. (2003). Assessing The Introduction of Electronic Banking in Egypt Using the Technology Acceptance Model, In: M. Kosrpw-Pour (Ed), *Annals of Case on Information Technology,* 5, 1-25, Hershey, PA: Idea Group Publishing.

Kannabiran, G., & Narayan, P. C. (2005). Deploying internet banking and e-commerce - case study of a private - sector bank in India. *Information Technology for Development, 11*(4), 363–379. doi:10.1002/itdj.20025

Kehzadi, N. (2002). *E-Banking: Prerequisites, Limitations and its Implementing Methods in Iran,* Paper presented at 11th Annual Conference of Monetary and Financial Policies, Tehran.

King, S. F., & Liou, J. (2004). A Framework for Internet Channel Evaluation. *International Journal of Information Management, 24*(6), 473–488. doi:10.1016/j.ijinfomgt.2004.08.006

Kuzic, J., Fisher, J., & Scollary, A. (2002, June). Electronic Commerce Benefits, Challenges and Success Factors in the Australian Banking and Finance Industry. In S. Wrycza (Ed.), *Tenth European Conference on Information Systems,* (pp. 1607-1616). Gdansk, Poland.

Liao, Z., & Choeung, M. T. (2002). Internet based E-banking and Consumer altitudes: an empirical study. *Information & Management, 39*(4), 283–295. doi:10.1016/S0378-7206(01)00097-0

Lustsik, O. (2004). *Can E- Banking Services be Profitable?* University of Tartu - Faculty of Economics & Business Administration Working Paper Series; Issue 30, p3-38. Retrieved January 24, 2009, from http://connection.ebscohost.com/content/article/1037621009.html;jsessionid=B45ED229D0A55C9679323C87043C07A7.ehctc1

Mirzaei, H. (1998, May). Toward a conceptual scheme for verification and Analisys of effective effective factors in "Work ethics" and social dicipline in organization. In *Proceedings of the 2th Conference on Investigating Methods of Conscience and Social Discipline Implementation,* Tehran, Islamic Azad University, 305-329.

Mirzaei, H., & Amiri, M. (2002). Developing a Three Dimensional Model for Analysis of Philosophical Bases and Fundamental Substructures of Management Theories. *Management Knowledge, 15*(56), 3–21.

Orr, B. (2004). E-Banking job one: Give customers a good ride. *American Bankers Association Banking Journal, 96*(5), 56–57.

Rao, S. S., Metts, G., & Monge, C. A. (2003). Electronic Commerce Development in Small and Medium Sized Enterprise: A Stage Model and its Implications. *Business Process Management Journal, 9*(1), 11–32. doi:10.1108/14637150310461378

Regan, K., & Macaluso, N. (2000. October). Report: *Consumers Cool to Net Banking.* e-Commerce Times, Retrieved November 18, 2008, from http://www.linuxinsider.com/story/4449.html?wlc=1249845342

Riggins, F. J. (1999). A Framework for Identifying Web-based Electronic Commerce Opportunities. *Journal of Organizational Computing and Electronic Commerce, 9*(4), 297–310. doi:10.1207/S153277440904_4

Sachs. J. D. (2000). *Readiness for the Networked world: A Guide for Developing Countries,* Center for International Development at Harvard University, (pp. 62-85). Retrieved January 7, 2099, from http://ictlogy.net/bibciter/reports/projects.php?idp=206

Sargazi, K. Z. (2007*). Investigating Deterrent Factors of E-banking Fixing and Development in Sistan Baluchestan State,* M.Sc dissertation, Sistan and Baluchestan University, Iran.

Sarlak, M.A., & Abolhasani, H., A., Forozandeh. D., L., & Ghorbani, A. (2009). Investigating on E-commerce Acceptance Barriers in Dried Fruits Producing- Exporting Companies of Iran. *World Applied Sciences Journal, 6*(6), 818–824.

Sarlak, M.A., Mirzaei, A., H. (2005). A Review of Organizational Epistemology: Evolution Process, Schools and Management Applications, *Peyke Noor Journal (Quarterly),* Special issue on management, 3 (3), 21-35.

Sarrafizadeh. A. (2005). *IT in Organization,* Tehran, Mir Publication.

Scratchier, A. (2002). Issues in electronic banking: an overview. *International Monetary Funds, 2*(6), 1–26.

Shah, M. H., Ahmed, W., Meckel, M., & Shah, M. A. (2008). *Organisational Barriers in e-Banking: A Case from UK Banking Industry,* In Proceedings of the 7th Annual ISOnEworld Conference, June 2-4, Las Vegas, NV.

Shah, M. H., Khan, S., & Xu, M. (2006). A Survey of Critical Success Factors in e-Banking. *European Journal of Information Systems,* Retrieved Desember 5, 2008, from http://www.csgstrategies. com/download.php?id=302

Sotudeh, S. M. (2003). E-banking: Success Ways, Challenges and Threats. *Bank Magazine, 14,* 27–31.

Stamoulis, D. S. (2000). How Banks fit in an Internet Commerce Business Activities Model, *Journal of Internet Banking and Commerce,* No. 1, Retrieved December 11, 2009, from http:// www.arraydev.com/commerce/jibc/0001-03.htm

Storey, A., & Thompson, J. B. Bokma, & Bradnum, A. J. (2000, August). *An Evaluation of UK and USA Online Banking and WebSites,* Paper was presented at the Association for Information Systems 2000 Americas Conference on Information Systems, Long Beach, California. Vol. 2: 723-728.

Toufaily, E., Daghfous, N., & Toffoli, R. (2009). the Adoption of "E-banking" by lebanese banks: Success and Critical factors. *International Journal of E-Services and Mobile Applications, 1*(1), 67-93. Hershey, PA: Idea Group Publishing, Enos, L. (2001). Report: *Critical Errors in Online Banking.* E-Commerce Times, April 11, Retrieved December 6, 2008, from http://www.ecommercetimes. com/perl/story/8867.html

Turban, E., Lee, J., King, D., & Chung, H. M. (2008). *Electronic Commerce: a Managerial Prspective, 5re Edn.* London: Prentice Hall.

Victor, D. (2008). *The New Technologies Extension in Banking: The Case of E-Banking in the Romanian Practice.* Academy of Economic Studies, Bucharest Romania, 723-727. Retrived May 14, 2009, from http://steconomice.uoradea.ro/ anale/volume/2008/v3-finances-banks-accountancy/130.pdf

Vinnem, J. E., & Liyanage, J. P. (2008). Human-Technical Interface of Collision Risk Under Dynamic Conditions: An Exploratory learning Case from the north sea, edited by Bernd Carsten Stahl, *International Journal of Technology and Human Interaction,* Idea Group Publishing, *4* (1), 35-47.

Wallman, S. (1999). *The Information Technology Revolution and its Impact of Regulation and Regulatiory structure* (1st ed.). Booking - Wharton Papers on Financial Services.

Yiu, C. S., Grant, K., & Edgar, D. (2007). Factors affecting the adoption of Internet Banking in Hong Kong - implications for the banking sector. *International Journal of Information Management, 27*(5), 336–351. doi:10.1016/j. ijinfomgt.2007.03.002

Yousafzai, S. Y., Pallister, J. G., & Foxall, G. R. (2005). Strategies for building and communicating trust in electronic banking: A field experiment. *Psychology and Marketing, 22*(2), 181–202. doi:10.1002/mar.20054

ADDITIONAL READING

Agarwal, R., Rastogi, S., & Mehrotra, A. (in press). Customers' perspectives regarding e-banking in an emerging economy. *Journal of Retailing and Consumer Services.*

Aladwani, A. M. (2001). Online banking: a field study of drivers, development challenges, and expectations. *International Journal of Information Management, 21,* 213–225. doi:10.1016/S0268-4012(01)00011-1

Alawneh, A., & Hattab, E. (2009). E-banking diffusion in the Jordanian banking Services Sector: an Empirical analysis of key factors. *International Journal of Actor-Network Theory and Technological Innovation,* Hershey, PA: Idea Group Publishing, 1(2), 50-66.

Barnes, S. J. (2002). The mobile commerce value chain: analysis and future developments. *International Journal of Information Management, 22,* 91–108. doi:10.1016/S0268-4012(01)00047-0

Bauer, K., & Hein, S. E. (2006). The effect of heterogeneous risk on the early adoption of Internet banking technologies. *Journal of Banking & Finance, 30,* 1713–1725. doi:10.1016/j.jbankfin.2005.09.004

Brown, I., Hoppe, R., & Mugera, P. Newman., P., & Stander, A. (2000). The Impact of National Environment on the Adoption of Internet Banking: Comparing Singapore and South Africa. *Journal of Global Information Management* 12(2),1-26., Hershey,PA: Idea Group Publishing.

Bughin, J. (2004). Attack or convert?: early evidence from European on-line banking. *Omega, 32,* 1–7. doi:10.1016/j.omega.2003.08.002

Calisir, F., & Gumussoy, C. A. (2008). Internet banking versus other banking channels: Young consumers' view. *International Journal of Information Management, 28,* 215–221. doi:10.1016/j.ijinfomgt.2008.02.009

Chan., S.Ch., & Lu, M.T., (2004). Understanding Internet Banking Adoption and Use Behavior: A Hong Kong Perspective. *Journal of Global Information Management,* Idea Group Publishing, *12*(3), 21-43.

Cheng, T. C. E., Lam, D. Y. C., & Yeung, A. C. L. (2006). Adoption of internet banking: An empirical study in Hong Kong. *Decision Support Systems, 42,* 1558–1572. doi:10.1016/j.dss.2006.01.002

Chow, C. K. W., & Fung, M. Y. (2000). Small Businesses and Liquidity Constraints in Financing Business Investment: Evidence from Shanghai's Manufacturing Sector. *Journal of Business Venturing, 15,* 363–383. doi:10.1016/S0883-9026(98)00014-7

Corrocher, N. (2006). Internet adoption in Italian banks: An empirical investigation. *Research Policy, 35,* 533–544. doi:10.1016/j.respol.2006.02.004

Dong, Q., Rodenburg, S. E., Huang, C., & VandeVoort, C. A. (2008). Effect of pre-freezing conditions on semen cryopreservation in rhesus monkeys. *Theriogenology, 70,* 61–69. doi:10.1016/j.theriogenology.2008.02.008

Durkin, M., Jennings, D., Mulholland, G., & Worthington, S. (2008). Key influencers and inhibitors on adoption of the Internet for banking. *Journal of Retailing and Consumer Services, 15,* 348–357. doi:10.1016/j.jretconser.2007.08.002

Eriksson, K., & Nilsson, D. (2007). Determinants of the continued use of self-service technology: The case of Internet banking. *Technovation, 27,* 159–167. doi:10.1016/j.technovation.2006.11.001

Gupta, M., Rao, R., & Upadhyaya, Sh. (2004). Electronic Banking and Information Assurance Issues: Survey and Synthesis. *Journal of Organizational and End User Computing, Idea Group Publishing, 16*(3), 1–21.

Hernando, I., & Nieto, M. J. (2007). Is the Internet delivery channel changing banks' performance? The case of Spanish banks. *Journal of Banking & Finance, 31*, 1083–1099. doi:10.1016/j.jbankfin.2006.10.011

Ho, Ch. T. B., & Wu, D. D. (2009). Online banking performance evaluation using data envelopment analysis and principal component analysis. *Computers & Operations Research, 36*, 1835–1842. doi:10.1016/j.cor.2008.05.008

Jih, W. J., Wong, S. Y., & Chang, T. B. (2005). Effects of Perceived Risks on Adoption of Internet Banking Services: An Empirical Investigation in Taiwan. *International Journal of E-Business Research, Idea Group Publishing, 1*(1), 70–88.

Kuismaa, T., Laukkanena, T., & Hiltunen, M. (2007). Mapping the reasons for resistance to Internet banking: A means-end approach. *International Journal of Information Management, 27*, 75–85. doi:10.1016/j.ijinfomgt.2006.08.006

Laeven, L., & Levine, R. (2007). Is there a diversification discount in financial conglomerates? *Journal of Financial Economics, 85*, 331–367. doi:10.1016/j.jfineco.2005.06.001

Lai, V. S., & Li, H. (2005). Technology acceptance model for internet banking: an invariance analysis. *Information & Management, 42*, 373–386. doi:10.1016/j.im.2004.01.007

Lariviere, B., & Poel, D. V. (2007). Banking behaviour after the lifecycle event of "moving in together": An exploratory study of the role of marketing investments. *European Journal of Operational Research, 183*, 345–369. doi:10.1016/j.ejor.2006.09.051

Laukkanen, T., Sinkkonen, S., & Laukkanen, P. (2009). Communication strategies to overcome functional and psychological resistance to Internet banking. *International Journal of Information Management, 29*, 111–118. doi:10.1016/j.ijinfomgt.2008.05.008

Lee, M. Ch. (2009). Factors influencing the adoption of internet banking: An integration of TAM and TPB with perceived risk and perceived benefit. *Electronic Commerce Research and Applications, 8*, 130–141. doi:10.1016/j.elerap.2008.11.006

Liao, S., Shao, Y. P., Wang, H., & Chen, A. (1999). The adoption of virtual banking: an empirical study. *International Journal of Information Management, 19*, 63–74. doi:10.1016/S0268-4012(98)00047-4

Littler, D., & Melanthiou, D. (2006). Consumer perceptions of risk and uncertainty and the implications for behaviour towards innovative retail services: The case of Internet Banking. *Journal of Retailing and Consumer Services, 13*, 431–443. doi:10.1016/j.jretconser.2006.02.006

Luneborg, J. L., & Nielsen, J. F. (2003). Customer-focused Technology and Performance in Small and Large Banks. *European Management Journal, 21*(2), 258–269. doi:10.1016/S0263-2373(03)00020-3

Makris, M., Koumaras, V., Koumaras, H., Konstantopoulou, A., Konidis, S., & Kostakis, S. (2009). Quantifying Factors Influencing the Adoption of Internet Banking Services in Greece. [Hershey, PA: Idea Group Publishing.]. *International Journal of E-Adoption, 1*(1), 20–32.

Rouibah, K., Thurasamy, R., & May, O. S. (2009). User Acceptance of Internet Banking In Malaysia: Test of Three Competing Models. [Hershey, PA: Idea Group Publishing]. *International Journal of E-Adoption, 1*(1), 1–19.

Shah, M. H., Mohsin, M., Mahmood, Z., & Aziz, R. (2009). Organisational Barriers in Offering E-Banking. [Hershey, PA: Idea Group Publishing.]. *Journal of Electronic Commerce in Organizations, 7*(2), 67–82.

Shah, M. H., & Siddiqui, F. A. (2006). Organizational critical success factors in adoption of e-banking at the Woolwich bank. *International Journal of Information Management, 26,* 442–456. doi:10.1016/j.ijinfomgt.2006.08.003

Shan, T. C., & Hua, W. W. (2006). Service-Oriented Solution Framework for Internet Banking. [Hershey, PA: Idea Group Publishing.]. *International Journal of Web Services Research, 3*(1), 29–48.

Sohail, M. S., & Shanmugham, B. (2003). E-banking and customer preferences in Malaysia: An empirical investigation. *Information Sciences, 150,* 207–217. doi:10.1016/S0020-0255(02)00378-X

Suh, B., & Han, I. (2002). Effect of trust on customer acceptance of Internet banking. *Electronic Commerce Research and Applications, 1,* 247–263. doi:10.1016/S1567-4223(02)00017-0

Tomiuk, D., & Pinsonneault, A. (2001). Costumer Loyalty and Electronic-Banking: A Conceptual Framework. *Journal of Global Information Management, 9*(3), 1–11.

Tsai, W.H., Huang, B.Y., Liu, J.Y., & Tsaur, T.Sh., & Lin., S.J. (in press). The application of Web ATMs in e-payment industry: A case study. *Expert Systems with Applications.*

Vatanasombut, B., Igbaria, M., Stylianou, A. C., & Rodgers, W. (2008). Information systems continuance intention of web-based applications customers: The case of online banking. *Information & Management, 45,* 419–428. doi:10.1016/j.im.2008.03.005

Weir, C. S., Anderson, J. N., & Jack, M. A. (2006). On the role of metaphor and language in design of third party payments in E-banking: Usability and quality. *International Journal of Human-Computer Studies, 64,* 770–784. doi:10.1016/j.ijhcs.2006.03.003

Weir, C. S., Douglas, G., Carruthers, M., & Jack, M. (2009). User perceptions of security, convenience and usability for E-banking authentication tokens. *Computers & Security, 28,* 47–62. doi:10.1016/j.cose.2008.09.008

Wendels, T. H., Mahlmann, T., & Versen, T. (2009). Determinants of banks' risk exposure to new account fraud – Evidence from Germany. *Journal of Banking & Finance, 33,* 347–357. doi:10.1016/j.jbankfin.2008.08.005

Williamson, K., Lichtenstein, Sh., Sullivan, J., & Schauder, D. (2006). To Choose or Not to Choose: Exploring Australians' Views about Internet Banking. [Hershey, PA: Idea Group Publishing.]. *International Journal of Technology and Human Interaction, 2*(4), 17–34.

Wresch, W., & Fraser, S. (2006). Managerial Strategies Used to Overcome Technological Hurdles: A Review of E-Commerce Efforts Used by Innovative Caribbean Managers. [Hershey, PA: Idea Group Publishing.]. *Journal of Global Information Management, 14*(3), 1–16.

Young, R. D., Lang, W. W., & Nolle, D. L. (2007). How the Internet affects output and performance at community banks. *Journal of Banking & Finance, 31,* 1033–1060. doi:10.1016/j.jbankfin.2006.10.003

KEY TERMS AND DEFINITIONS

Content Dimension: Human and its behavior in the organization which are bounded together through special patterns, behavioral norms and unofficial communications and constitutes the main content of the organization and are regarded as, in fact, alive factors of the organization.

Contextual Dimension: Include all environmental and extra-organizational factors and conditions surrounding the organization and constitute main systems of the organization such as customers, government, markets and other environmental elements of the organization.

Co-Structure Dimension: All of elements, physical and non-human factors, and conditions of the organization which are bounded together through special order and regulation and constitute frame, cover, or physical and material body of the organization.

ICT: Information and Communication Technology.

Tri-Category Model: A three dimensional model that all organizational concepts, events and phenomena can be studied, analyzed in it's frame.

Section 4
The Technologies

Chapter 8
Introduction to Modern Banking Technology and Management

Vadlamani Ravi

Institute for Development and Research in Banking Technology, India

ABSTRACT

This chapter introduces Banking Technology as a confluence of several disparate disciplines such as Finance (including risk management), Information technology, Computer Science, Communication technology and marketing science. It presents the evolution of banking, the tremendous influence of information and communication technologies on banking and its products, the quintessential role played by computer science in fulfilling banks' marketing objective of servicing customers better at a less cost and thereby reap more profits. It also highlights the use of advanced statistics and computer science to measure, mitigate and manage various risks associated with banks' business with its customers and other banks. The growing influence of customer relationship management and data mining in tackling various marketing related problems and fraud detection problems in banking industry is well documented. Of particular significance is the set of latest trends this chapter presents in terms of biometric ATMs, RFID enabled bank notes, Antiphishing techniques that make Internet banking secure and the applications of Web 2.0 in banking. The chapter concludes by predicting that the Banking Technology discipline is all set for rapid growth in future.

INTRODUCTION

The term "Banking Technology" refers to the use of sophisticated information and communication technologies together with computer science to enable banks to offer better services to its custom-

ers in a secure, reliable and affordable manner and sustain competitive advantage over other banks. Banking Technology also subsumes the activity of using advanced computer algorithms in unraveling the patterns of customer behavior by sifting through customer details such as demographic, psychographic and transactional data. This activity also known data mining, helps

DOI: 10.4018/978-1-61520-635-3.ch008

banks achieve their business objectives by solving various marketing problems such as customer segmentation, customer scoring, target marketing, market-basket analysis, cross-sell, up-sell, customer retention by modeling churn etc. Successful use of data mining helps banks achieve significant increase in profits and thereby retain sustainable advantage over their competitors. From theoretical perspective, Banking Technology is not a single, stand-alone discipline, but a confluence of several disparate fields such as finance (subsuming risk management), information technology, communication technology, computer science and marketing science. Figure 1 depicts the constituents of Banking Technology. From the functional perspective, Banking Technology has three important dimensions. They are as follows: (i) The use of appropriate hardware for conducting business and servicing the customers through various delivery channels and payments systems and the associated software constitutes one dimension of Banking Technology. The use of computer networks, security algorithms in its transactions, use of ATM and credit cards, Internet banking, telebanking and mobile banking are all covered by this dimension. The advances made in information and communication technologies take care of this dimension. (ii) On the other hand, the use of advanced computer science algorithms to solve several interesting marketing related problems such as customer segmentation, customer scoring, target marketing, market-basket analysis, cross-sell, up-sell and customer retention etc. faced by the banks to reap profits and outperform their competitors constitutes the second dimension of Banking Technology. This dimension covers the implementation of a data warehouse for banks and conducting data mining studies on customer data. (iii) Moreover, banks cannot ignore the risks that arise in conducting business with other banks and servicing their customers, for otherwise, their very existence would be at stake. Thus, the quantification, measurement, mitigation and management of all the kinds of risks that banks

face constitutes the third important dimension of Banking Technology. This dimension covers the process of measuring and managing credit risk, market risk and operational risk. Thus, in a nutshell, in the word 'Banking Technology', 'banking' refers to the economic, financial, commercial and management aspects of banking while 'technology' refers to the information and communication technologies, computer science and risk quantification and measurement aspects.

Evolution of Banking

Despite the enormous changes the banking industry has undergone through during the past 20 years – let alone since 1943 – one factor has remained the same: the fundamental nature of the need customers have for banking services. However, the framework and paradigm within which these services are delivered has changed out of recognition. It is clear that people's needs have not changed and neither has the basic nature of banking services people required. But the way banks meet those needs is completely different today. They are simply striving to provide a service at a profit. Banking has had to adjust to the changing needs of societies, where people not only regard a bank account as a right rather than

Figure 1. Different constituents of banking technology

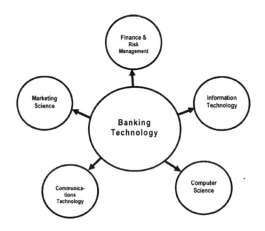

as a privilege, but also are aware that their business is valuable to the bank and, if the bank does not look after them, they can take their business elsewhere (Engler & Essinger, 2000).

Indeed, technological and regulatory changes have influenced the banking industry during the past 20 years so much so that they are the most important changes to have occurred in the banking industry, apart from the ones directly caused by the changing nature of the society itself. In this book, technology is used interchangeably with information and communication technologies together with computer science. The relationship between banking and technology is such that nowadays it is almost impossible to think of the former without the latter. Technology is as much part of the banking industry today as a ship's engine is part of the ship. Thus, like a ship's engine, technology drives the whole thing forward (Engler & Essinger, 2000).

Technology in banking ceased being simply a convenient tool for automating processes. Today banks use technology as a revolutionary means of delivering services to customers by designing new delivery channels and payment systems. For example, in the case of ATMs people realized that it was a wrong approach to provide the service as an additional convenience for privileged and wealthy customer. It should be offered to the people who find it difficult to visit the bank branch. Further, the cost of delivering the services through these channels is also less. Banks then went on to create collaborative ATM networks to cut the capital costs of establishing ATM networks to offer services to customers at convenient locations under unified banner (Engler & Essinger, 2000).

People interact with banks to obtain access to money and payment systems they need. Banks, in fact, offer only what might be termed as a secondary level of utility to customers meaning that customers use the money access that banks provide as a means of buying the things they really want from retailers who offer them a primary level of utility. Customers, therefore, naturally want to get the interaction with their bank over as quickly as possible and then get on with doing something they really want to do or with buying something they really want to buy. That explains why new types of delivery channels that allow rapid, convenient, accurate delivery of banking services to customers are so popular. Nowadays, customers enjoy the fact that their banking chores are done quickly and easily (Engler & Essinger, 2000).

This does not mean that the brick-and-mortar bank branches will completely disappear. Just as increasing proliferation of mobile phones does not mean that landline telephone kiosks will disappear, so also the popularity of high-tech delivery channels does not mean that physical branches will disappear altogether. It has been found that corporate and older persons prefer to conduct their business through bank branches (Engler & Essinger, 2000).

The kind of enormous and far-reaching developments discussed above have taken place along with the blurring of demarcations between different types of banking and financial industry activities. Five reasons can be attributed to it: (i) Governments have implemented philosophies and policies based on an increase in competition in order to maximize efficiency. This has resulted in the creation of large new financial institutions that operate simultaneously in several financial sectors such as retail, wholesale, insurance and asset management (ii) New technology creates an infrastructure allowing a player to carry out a wide range of banking and financial services, again simultaneously (iii) Banks had to respond to the increased prosperity of their customers and to customers' desire to get the best deal possible. This has encouraged banks to extend their activities into other areas (iv) Banks had to develop products and extend their services to accommodate the fact that their customers are now far more mobile. Therefore demarcations are breaking down (v) Banks have every motivation to move into new sectors of activity in order to try to deal with the problem that, if they only offer banking services, they are condemned forever to provide only a secondary level of utility to customers (Engler & Essinger, 2000).

ROLE OF ICT IN BANKING

Technology is no longer being used simply as means for automating processes. Instead it is being used as a revolutionary means of delivering services to customers. The adoption of technology has led to the following benefits: (i) Greater productivity, profitability and efficiency (ii) Faster service and customer satisfaction (iii) Convenience and flexibility (iv) 24 x 7 operations (v) Space and cost savings (Sivakumaran, 2005). Harrison Jr., Chairman and Chief Executive Officer of Chase Manhattan, which pioneered many innovative applications of ICT in banking industry, observed that internet caused a technology revolution and it could have greater impact on change than the industrial revolution (Engler & Essinger, 2000).

Technology has been used to offer banking services in the following ways (Sivakumaran, 2005):

(i) ATM's: ATMs are the cash dispensing machines, which can be seen at banks and other locations where crowd proximity is more. ATMs started as a substitute to a bank to allow its customers to draw cash at anytime and to provide services where it would not be viable to open another physical branch. The ATM is the most visited delivery channel in retail banking, with over 40 billion transactions annually worldwide. In fact, the delivery channel revolution is said to have begun with the ATM. It was indeed a pleasant change for customers to be in charge of their transaction, as no longer would they need to depend on an indifferent bank employee. ATMs have made banks realize that they could divert the huge branch traffic to the ATM. The benefits hence were mutual. Once banks realized the convenience of ATM, new services started to be added.

(ii) The phenomenal success of ATMs had made the banking sector develop more innovative delivery channels to build on cost and service efficiencies. As a consequence, banks have introduced Telebanking, Call Centers, Internet banking and Mobile Banking. Telebanking is a good medium for customers to make routine queries and also an efficient tool for banks to cut down on their manpower resources. The call center is another channel, which captured the imagination of banks as well as customers. At these centers enormous amounts of information is at the fingertips of trained customer service representatives. It meets a bank's infrastructural as well as customer service requirements. Not only does a call center cut down on costs, it also results in customer satisfaction. Moreover, it facilitates 24x7 working and offers the "human touch" that customers seek. Call center has big potential dividends by way of improved CRM and return on investment (ROI).

(iii) With the Internet boom, banks realized that Internet banking would be a good way to reach out to customers. Currently, some banks are attempting to harness the benefits of Internet banking, while others have already made Internet banking as an important and popular payment system. Internet banking is on the rise, as is evident from the statistics. Predictions of Internet banking to go the ATM way have not materialized as much as was anticipated, a lot of reasons can be attributed for the same. During 2003, the usage of Internet as a banking channel accounted for 8.5%. But this was due to the false, unrealistic expectations tied to it. Some of the factors that were detrimental in bringing down or rather not being supportive are low Internet penetration, high telecom tariffs, slow Internet speed and inadequate bandwidth availability, lack of extended applications and lack of trusted environment.

(iv) Mobile banking however is being regarded in the industry as "the delivery channel of future", for various reasons. First and foremost is the convenience and portability afforded. It is just like having a bank in the pocket. Other key reasons include the higher level of security in comparison to the Internet, and relatively low costs involved. The possibility that customers will adopt mobile banking is high considering the exponential growth of mobile phone users worldwide. Mobile banking typically provides services such as the latest information on account balances, previous transactions, bank account debits and credits, credit card outstanding and payment status. They also provide their Online Share trading customers with alerts for pre-market movements and post-market information and stock price movements based on triggers.

Another fallout of the ICT-driven revolution in banking industry is Centralized Banking Solution (CBS). A CBS can be defined as a solution that enables banks to offer a multitude of customer-centric services on a 24x7 basis from a single location, supporting retail as well as corporate banking activities as also all possible delivery channels - existing and proposed. The centralization thus afforded makes "one-stop" shop for financial services a reality. Using CBS, customers can access their accounts from any branch anywhere irrespective of where they physically opened their accounts. The benefits offered by CBS are: (i) Offer a "one-stop" IT management shop (ii) Make banks prepared for current as well as future requirements (iii) Decrease the risks arising from solutions requiring multiple components and multiple vendors (iv) Improve the returns via seamless integration of software and hardware services (v) Provide a greater choice through the availability of an array of technologies (Sivakumaran, 2005).

Information technology has not only helped banks to deliver robust and reliable services to their customers at a less cost but also helped banks take better decisions. Here a data warehouse plays an extremely important role. It essentially involves collecting data from several disparate sources to build a central data warehouse to store and analyze the data. A data warehouse in a bank typically stores both internal data and data pertaining to its competitors. Data mining techniques can then be applied on a data warehouse for knowledge discovery (Hwang et al., 2004). Data warehouse also allows banks to perform time series analysis and online analytical processing (OLAP) to answer various business questions that would put the banks ahead of their competitors.

Apart from the market-driven reasons, compliance-driven reasons are also there behind banks establishing a data warehouse. Base II accord is one such compliance. Basel II is one of the biggest financial shake-ups in recent times, which will eventually lead to new rules and regulations for banking industry worldwide. Banks were supposed to have their processes and systems in place by the start of 2007, which was when the Basel Committee on Banking Supervision planned to implement the Accord. The crux of Basel II is to ensure that financial institutions manage risk so that they have the adequate capital to cover exposure to debt. Banks will have to carry out a fundamental review and overhaul of their processes and systems in order to achieve compliance. Technology will be at the core of their strategies to meet Basel II requirements. The construction of a historical data store is a key IT initiative that must be pursued as on a priority basis within Basel II programs. This will collect up to three years of operational risk data and up to seven years of credit risk data and will act as a stepping-stone towards a 'single customer view' for managing risk at an individual customer level (Porter, 2003).

The next wave in ICT-driven banking resulted in the creation of Society for Worldwide Interbank Financial Telecommunication (SWIFT), which is the financial industry-owned co-operative organization. SWIFT provides secure, standardized messaging services and interface software to 7,650 financial institutions spread over 200 countries. SWIFT's worldwide community includes banks, broker/dealers and investment managers, as well as their market infrastructures in payments, securities, treasury and trade. Establishment of SWIFT is a landmark development in worldwide payment systems in banks and financial institutions. SWIFT through its comprehensive messaging standards offers the financial services industry a common platform of advanced technology and access to shared solutions through which each member can communicate with its counter party. SWIFT works in partnership with its members to provide low-cost, competitive financial processing and communications services of the highest security and reliability. It contributes significantly to the commercial success of its members through greater automation of the end-to-end financial transaction process, based on its leading expertise in message processing and financial standards setting. Thus SWIFT is another important product of the applications of ICT in banking industry (Graham, 2003).

Negative Effects of ICT in Banking and Solutions Offered by ICT

While ICT provides so many advantages to banking industry it also poses security challenges to banks and their customers. Even though Internet banking provides ease and convenience, it is most vulnerable to hackers and cyber criminals. Online fraud is still big business around the world. Even though surveillance cameras, guards, alarms, security screens, dye packs and law enforcement efforts have reducing the chances of a criminal stealing cash from a bank branch, criminals can still penetrate the formidable edifice like banking industry through other means. Using the Internet banking and high tech credit card fraud, it is now possible to steal large amounts of money anonymously from financial institutions from the

comfort of your own home and it is happening all over the world (Graham, 2003).

Further, identity theft, also known as phishing, is one of the fastest growing epidemics in electronic fraud in the world. Identity theft occurs when fraudsters gain access to personal details of unsuspecting victims through various electronic and non-electronic means. This information is then used to open accounts (usually credit card), initialize loans and mobile phone accounts or anything else involving a line of credit. Account theft, which is commonly mistaken for identity theft, occurs when existing credit or debit cards or financial records are used to steal from existing accounts. Although account theft is a more common occurrence than identity theft, financial losses caused by identity theft are on average greater and usually require a longer period of time to resolve (Graham, 2003).

Spam scams involve fraudsters sending spam emails informing customers of some seemingly legitimate reason to log in to their accounts. A link is provided in the email to take the user to a log in screen in their bank site, however the link that is provided actually takes the user to a ghost site, where the fraudster can record their log in details. This information is then used to pay bills and or transfer balances for the fraudster's financial reward (Graham, 2003).

Card skimming refers to the use of portable swiping devices to obtain credit card and EFT card data. This data is rewritten to a dummy card, which is then usually taken on elaborate shopping sprees. As the fraudster can sign the back of the card himself or herself, the merchant will usually be unaware that they have fallen victim to the fraud.

One can curb these hi-tech frauds by using equally hi-tech security mechanisms such as Biometrics and smart cards. The key focus in minimizing credit card and electronic fraud is to enable the actual user of the account to be correctly identified. The notion of allowing a card to prove your identity is fast becoming antiquated and unreliable. With this in mind, using Biometrics to develop a more accurate identification process could greatly reduce fraud and increase convenience by allowing consumers to move closer to a "no wallet" society. The main forms of Biometrics available are (i) Fingerprint identification (ii) Palm print identification (iii) Facial recognition (iv) Iris recognition (v) Voice recognition (vi) Computer recognized hand-writing analysis (Graham, 2003).

Many industry analysts such as the American Bankers Association are proposing that the smart payment cards are finally poised to change the future of electronic payments. The smart card combines a secure portable payment platform with a selection of payment, financial, and non-financial applications. The reach of smart card potentially goes beyond the debit and credit card model. Instead of smartcard, ISO uses the term Integrated Circuit Card (ICC), which includes all devices where an integrated circuit is contained within the card. The benefits provided by smart cards to consumers include (i) Convenience – easy access to services with multiple loading points (ii) Flexibility – high/low value payments with faster transaction times (iii) Increased security. The benefits offered to merchants include (i) Immediate/guaranteed cash flow (ii) Lower processing costs (iii) Operational convenience (Graham, 2003).

CUSTOMER RELATIONSHIP MANAGEMENT (CRM) THROUGH DATA MINING

Despite investing enormously into the ICT paraphernalia for providing better services to customers, banks cannot take their customers for granted. Unlike olden days, the customers have become more demanding. In other words, if customers are dissatisfied with the services of a particular bank, they immediately shift loyalties to its competitors. Hence, like in other businesses such as retail and insurance, banks have made a paradigmatic shift to their marketing strategies. Consequently, the age-old product-focused strategy has given way to customer-focused strategy. Hence, building

profitable and long lasting relationships with customers has become paramount to banks. This is precisely where CRM play a critical role. The main objective of CRM is to make long lasting and profitable relationships with customers.

The successful adoption of IT enabled CRM redefines the traditional models of interaction between a business and its customers both nationally and globally. CRM promises achieving corporate objectives, which involves continuous use of refined information about current and potential customer. With IT and communication technologies, banks can offer their customer a variety of products, lower prices and personalized service. The effective management of information and knowledge is important to CRM for product tailoring and service innovation. It provides a single and consolidated view of the customer, calculating the value of the customer, establishing a strategy for a multi-channel based communication with the customer and designing personalized transactions. CRM together with data mining helps banks improve their marketing policies to attract more customers and thereby increase their profit. Customer knowledge is recognized as an asset. IT is the enabling technology for discovery and management of customer knowledge (CRM in UK ref). With the IT enabled CRM, relationship marketing has become a reality in recent years to gain competitive advantage (Rygielski et al., 2002).

Data mining tools can answer business questions very fast and accurate now due to the information available, but in the past that was time consuming to pursue. The advent of Internet has undoubtedly contributed to the shift of marketing focus, as on-line information is more accessible and abundant. Collecting customer demographic and psycho graphic data and its analysis makes target marketing possible. Knowledge Discovery in Databases (KDD) or Data mining activities can be categorized into three major groups viz., Discovery, Predictive Modeling and Forensic Analysis. Data mining performs analysis that would be too complicated for traditional statisticians (Rygielski et al., 2002). Most of the banks are investing large amount of money to collect and store transactional, demographic and psychographic data of customers. The emphasis is now on how to effectively utilize the customer databases to manage the customer relationship. The potential difficulty of converting data into profits lies in obtaining relevant information from the data and customize the marketing mix policies to satisfy the consumer's wants and needs (Chun qing li et al).

Banks employ data mining for the following tasks: (i) Card marketing. By identifying optimal customer segments, card issuers and acquirers can improve profitability with more effective acquisitions and retention programs, targeted product development and customized pricing. (ii) Cardholder pricing and profitability. Card issuers can take advantage of data mining to price their products so as to maximize profit and minimize loss of customers. They can also perform risk based pricing. (iii) Predictive lifecycle management. Data mining helps banks predict each customer's lifetime value and to service each segment appropriately. (iv) Forensic analysis. It is unusual to employ data mining for forensic analysis in many domains, but in banking it is a common practice, which looks for deviations in the data for fraud detection. Businesses must have to use technology responsibly in order to achieve a balance between privacy rights and economic benefits. Currents CRM solutions are not ensuring customer information privacy fully (Rygielski et al., 2002). (v) Cross-sell/Up-sell. Using data mining, banks can cross-sell or up-sell their products to customers (vi) Customer churn modeling. Customer churn modeling is an important problem for banks and financial institutions to grapple with. Churn happens when existing customers become disgruntled with the some aspects of the service of a given bank and shift loyalties to its competitor. Data mining techniques are extremely useful in identifying potential churners and giving banks early warning signals. Once potential churners are

identified, banks take remedial actions to prevent such customers from leaving. This is because acquiring new customers is time consuming and more expensive than retaining the existing customers. (vii) Anti-money laundering. Money laundering considered a major financial crime, is the process of illegally transferring money from one country to another in an innocuous manner so that it goes undetected by law enforcement agencies. With development of global economy and Internet banking it is predicted that money laundering crimes will become more prevalent, more difficult to investigate and more detrimental to economy and financial systems. The investigation of money laundering crimes involves reading and analyzing thousands of textual documents to generate crime group models (Zhang et al., 2003). The use of international trade to transfer money undetected between countries is an old technique to bypass the government scrutiny. This is achieved by either overvaluing imports or undervaluing exports. This approach of money transfer need not be used to fund terrorist activities but also can be used to evade taxes (Zdanowicz, 2004). Data mining is extremely useful in tackling the problem and techniques like web mining, text mining, collaborative filtering, social network analysis and

Figure 2. Applications of data mining in banking

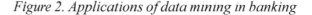

link discovery based on correlation analysis are nowadays used to trace the links between transfer of high value amounts (Zhang et al., 2003). Figure 2 succinctly captures various applications of data mining in banking and finance.

Business process re-engineering is increasingly important as a way for companies to remain competitive. Process orientation combined with IT can yield tremendous performance improvements in companies. The banking sector is also demanding re-engineering due to changes in economic setting, consumer needs and market competition and requires a redesign of current account-oriented and product information technology systems to customer-oriented systems. Majority of current banking IT systems adopt account-oriented approach, thus limiting flexibility either to create strong relationships with their existing customers or to attract new ones with increased marketing efforts. Hence, there is a practical need for re-engineering of both banking business process and their associated Information systems. It was found that object oriented methods are useful for business process re-engineering as they can form a basis for representing banking business process and Information system (Mentzas, 1997).

ROLE OF COMPUTER SCIENCE IN RISK MANAGEMENT IN BANKING

The quantification, measurement, mitigation and management of risks occurring in banks while conducting their business are an integral part of successful and efficient banking operations. Risk is defined as the potential for realization of unwarranted consequences of an event. In view of the foregoing discussion in previous sections, it is clear that IT has become essential for the smooth running of the banks' operations. Even in the area of risk management various areas of computer science are employed like never before and the growth has been tremendous. Various statistical and computer science algorithms are used for quantifying the risk whose information can then be used by the management team in hedging the risk through various countermeasures as applicable. In the banking scenario, risks can be broadly classified into three categories: Credit, Market and Operational risks. Credit risk is the risk of a counter party not meeting its obligations. Various credit-scoring models are developed in order to evaluate the counter party's creditworthiness, whose information can be very valuable when the management takes the decision of whether or not to grant a loan to a counter party.

In the past decade, many modeling alternatives, like traditional statistical methods, non-parametric methods and artificial intelligent techniques have been developed in order to successfully handle credit scoring tasks. Discriminant analysis and logistic regression are the most commonly utilized statistical credit scoring techniques, but often being criticized due to their strong model assumptions and poor credit scoring capabilities. On the other hand, the artificial neural networks are attractive alternatives in handling credit scoring tasks due to its associated memory characteristic, generalization capability. Even with the above-mentioned advantages, neural networks are criticized for long training process in designing the optimal network's topology and difficulties in interpreting the knowledge learnt by the weights of the network. Li et al., (2003) reported that classification trees are more suitable than logistic regression in credit scoring applications. Later, hybrid models involving multivariate adaptive regression splines (MARS) and neural networks (Lee et al., 2005), a new fuzzy support vector machine (Wang et al., 2005), genetic-fuzzy and a neuro-fuzzy classifiers (Hoffmann et al.,), backpropagation neural networks with discriminant analysis (Lee et al., 2002), clustering and neural networks (Hsieh N-C, 2005), radial basis function network with softmax activation function (Sarlija et al., 2006) and two-stage genetic programming (Huang et al., 2005) were proposed for credit scoring problems.

According to the Basel committee, Operational risk is defined as *"the risk of loss resulting from inadequate or failed internal processes, people and systems or from external events"*. This kind of risk is most difficult to anticipate and hence manage because of its unpredictable nature. Many sophisticated methodologies have been proposed in order to quantify operational risk in the recent times. The methodologies range from simple mathematical methods to the sophisticated soft computing methods. Scandizzo (2003) discussed the use of fuzzy logic in the measurement of operational risk. He developed a clustering algorithm based on a fuzzy algebra that produces a ranking of the business units within a financial institution.

Both linear and non-linear models have been developed for the measurement of operational risk. Linear models include regression models, discriminant analysis, etc. The non-linear models, based on artificial intelligence, try to capture the non-linearities in operational risk. Neural networks are an alternative to non-parametric regressions. Bayesian belief networks have attracted much attention recently as a possible solution to the problems of decision support under uncertainty. Bayesian networks provide a lot of benefits for data analysis. The first is due to the fact that the model encodes dependencies among all variables and it also handles missing data. Further, they can be used to learn causal relationships and hence used to gain an understanding of problem domains and to predict the consequences of intervention.

Data mining can be extremely useful in estimating hidden correlations and patterns of losses related to operational risk in large organizations, where these operational losses can be correlated to a number of unimaginable factors. And the simplest correlation techniques might not work efficiently or uncover hidden patterns or correlations. Fuzzy set theory facilitates decision-making where there are vague or subjective judgments as inputs to the decision process. In banks in which less sophisticated techniques have been put in place, fuzzy logic can help in optimizing tasks such

as the classification or ranking of operational risk, or even in allocating a certain capital to complex transactions where a history of losses may be very difficult to collate (Scandizzo, 2003).

Market risk can be broadly classified into interest rate risk, foreign exchange rate risk and liquidity risk. Interest rate risk and foreign exchange rate risk are modeled and predicted by using time series methods, neural networks, decision trees etc.

ROLE OF IT IN DATA STORAGE AND INFORMATION SECURITY IN BANKING

An interesting and useful way of storing information for banks with business presence in several countries is storage area networks (SAN). SAN is a dedicated, centrally managed, secure information infrastructure, which enables any-to-any (n-to-n cardinality) interconnection of servers and storage systems. Using SAN, banks can store their wealth of information in an organized, secure and an easily accessible manner. SAN offers the following advantages: (i) They provide the connectivity of SAN with an ATM or a Gigabit Ethernet (ii) They also facilitate true fiber channel and SCSI (Small Computer System Interface) internetworking and conversion (iii) If a 3rd party copy agent is introduced, then it also reduces the backup lot of them have backups on a daily basis (iv) Another major advantage with SANs is that they can interoperate with RAIDs (Redundant Array of Inexpensive Disks), tape storage and servers (v) They provide a comprehensive web-based and SNMP (Simple Network Management Protocol) management (Tanna, 2002).

Having stored a lot of sensitive and confidential financial data about their customers in information systems, the banks have to worry about making them secure enough, because the customers ultimately trust the banks for the safety of their information. There is a great chance that data being misused when transaction are made on the internet. To avoid such catastrophic developments, the banks must deploy a very powerful and reliable mechanism for securing the data. Some of the ways to introduce security in a bank using cryptographic algorithms are as follows (Tanna, 2002): (i) *Restricted Access*: Allowing only genuine people to enter the bank premises by having a physical security check. This can prevent unwanted people entering into the bank. (ii) *Authentication/Authorization:* This is a standard protocol to verify whether the correct user is accessing the information (authentication by a valid username) and whether he himself is the authorized person who is actually using the information by making him/her to enter a password (authorization) (iii) *Encryption/Decryption of sensitive/crucial data:* The final step in the process would be encode the sensitive data so that irrelevant people do not have access to it, while the data is in transit or when it is stored permanently.

Techniques for making the sensitive data secure are: (i) *Encryption Systems:* These are systems that use various encryption algorithms to secure the information. (ii) *Digital Signatures:* This is a useful technique to secure information when there is a need to transfer critical documents across Networks to combat with snooping and manipulation of the same. The signature is sensitive to the contents of the file and the signature is sent along with the file for verification. E.g. MD5 (iii) *Digital Certificates:* These powers are built in today's browsers like IE and Netscape to employ SSL (Secure Socket Layer) security via *shtml* (Secure HTML) pages. The area of cryptography encompasses several algorithms to ensure safe encryption, decryption and authentication.

ROLE OF IT IN BCP/ DR IN BANKING

Business continuity and disaster recovery planning is very much critical to ensure the successful and continuous operations in banks and financial institutions. Business disruptions occur for both foreseeable and unforeseen reasons. Terrorist attacks, floods, earthquakes, landslides etc., could some of these reasons. While the probability of occurrence of any individual event may be negligibly small, the business impact of disruptions can be immense. To survive, banks must protect their business against crises. This is not simply by taking property and casualty insurance on capital items and human resources, but by preparing comprehensive and robust business continuity plans (BCP) that ensure business operations are resilient, the impact on customer service is minimized, financial losses are reduced and regulatory compliance is maintained in the event of crisis. Customer loyalty, business reputation and public trust must be protected by an effective and actionable BCP when a disaster strikes. Business Continuity Planning is about maintaining, resuming and recovering business operations - not just the recovery of the information system. The planning process should include: risk and business impact analyses; risk management and crisis response action plans; monitoring and testing of operations, regulatory compliance and recovery plans; awareness planning; and periodic reviews and revisions. Physically, banks can have a mirror site, which will act as a hot redundant unit to the original site where disaster may strike and business can be conducted as usual in a seamless way. However, software solutions to BCP are also possible. Software solutions provide support throughout the BCP process, enhancing bank's existing assets and capabilities with proven products and services that help bank in assessing likely impacts, avoiding known risks, planning recovery options, managing and implementing recovery mechanisms, monitoring the health of bank's operations and automating action and awareness activities (http://www3.ca.com/technologies/subsolution.aspx?id=3936).

LATEST TRENDS OF ICT APPLICATIONS IN BANKING AND FINANCE

Biometric ATMS

Traditionally, access to secure locations or sensitive information has been controlled by a card or key and/or a Personal Identification Number (PIN) or a password. Today, many people have PINs and passwords for a variety of devices, from the car radio and mobile phone, to the computer, web-based services and their bank information (Coventry et al., 2003). However, it was realized after some time that all these mechanism are not foolproof. Hence, Biometrics based security mechanisms are increasingly becoming popular. Biometrics refers to methods for uniquely recognizing humans based upon one or more intrinsic physical or behavioral traits. In information technology, in particular, Biometrics is used as a form of identity access management and access control.

Biometrics has found very good applications in ATMs. One of the big issues with the ATM is that ultimately it has to deal with the entire banking population of the world (Coventry et al., 2003) With the biometric enabled ATMs, you do not need to punch those PIN numbers to withdraw money from the ATM anymore. Identification of right user by the use of face recognition technology is the latest form of Biometrics. Since biometric technology can be used in the place of PIN codes in ATMs, it benefits mostly rural and illiterate masses, who find it difficult to use the keypad of ATMs.

Biometric ATM's are the latest inventions to help us avoid fraud and duplication. If somebody steals our card as well as our PIN they can easily withdraw cash from our account. In case of biometric ATM's they cannot simply do this anymore. Usually the PIN for biometric based ATM's is the fingerprint of the cardholder or his eye retina scan etc. These cannot be duplicated and hence they are very safe and secure.

As regards biometric identification technologies, it's not only our fingerprints that are very important. Now, our eyes, hands, signature, speech, and even facial temperature can identify us (Jain et al., 2000). Biometric authentification has become more and more popular in the banking and finance sector (Alaxander von Graevenitz, 2007). While technology continues to evolve and improve, more work is required to address the usability issues which will be key to successful implementation of Biometrics within a general public application such as banking (Coventry et al., 2003).

RFID Enabled Bank Notes

The main goal of Radio Frequency Identification (RFID) systems is to identify objects in an environment by embedding tags onto these objects. A tag is a tiny device capable of transmitting, over a short distance, a unique serial number and other additional data (Avoine, 2004). Radio-frequency identification (RFID) is the use of an object (typically referred to as an RFID tag) applied to or incorporated into a product, animal, or person for the purpose of identification and tracking using radio waves. Some tags can be read from several meters away and beyond the line of sight of the reader. Most RFID tags contain at least two parts. One is an integrated circuit for storing and processing information, modulating and demodulating a radio-frequency (RF) signal, and other specialized functions. The second is an antenna for receiving and transmitting the signal. Radio Frequency Identification (RFID) is a generic term for non-contacting technologies that use radio waves to automatically identify people or objects (www.parallax.com/dl/docs/prod/audiovis/RFID-Reader-v1.2.pdf).

Benefits of using radio frequency identification (RFID) in banks would be high-level client service and help prevent credit card fraud. RFID is a small chip that can contain information about a bank's client and can be implanted in a passbook or credit card (http://www.bankingtechnology. org/RFID_in_Banks.htm). In particular, the European Central Bank (ECB) decided to use some RFIDs to protect Euro banknotes (Avoine, 2004). Although Euro banknotes already include physical security features, ECB believes that RFIDs will add further protection: electronic tags will give governments and law enforcement agency the means to track banknotes in illegal transactions (Avoine, 2004).

Radio Frequency Identification (RFID) is an emerging wireless technology with many potential applications, including supply chain management, personnel tracking and point of sale checkout. Its wide spread adoption raises concerns about known security and privacy vulnerabilities, including the ability of rogue RFID readers to access the unique identifier and data of RFID tags. To prevent the eavesdropping of tag through communication channel, methods like one-way hashing, cryptography and one-time pads have been used; however they do not prevent the clandestine tracking of tags using their unique identifier. (Vartak et al., 2006). Japanese government also plans to embed RFIDs into new 10'000 Yen notes. The central bank and the law enforcement agency, both profiting from this system by enforcing banknote tracking and anti-counterfeiting (Avoine, 2004).

Antiphishing Measure

Companies such as Pay Pal, eBay, Amazon, and most of the banks have been the biggest target for phishing attacks (Patel & Luo, 2007). In the field of computer security, phishing is the criminally fraudulent process of attempting to acquire sensitive information such as usernames, passwords and credit card details by masquerading as a trustworthy entity in an electronic communication. Phishing is a kind of attack in which criminals use spoofed emails and fraudulent web sites to trick people into giving up personal information. (Sheng et al., 2007).

Among all Hong Kong and Singapore banks with official Web sites, it was found that anti-phishing measures only appeared on the Web sites of banks with online banking service (Bose and Leung, 2007). Unlike predicting Spam, there are only few studies that compare machine-learning techniques in predicting phishing. The present study compares the predictive accuracy of several machine-learning methods including Logistic Regression (LR), Classification and Regression Trees (CART), Bayesian Additive Regression Trees (BART), Support Vector Machines (SVM), Random Forests (RF), and Neural Networks (NNet) for predicting phishing emails (Abu-Nimesh et al., 2007).

To avoid the risk of being locked in by phishers, here are few tips (Patel & Luo, 2007):

- Be extremely suspicious of any e-mails with urgent requests for personal information.
- Do not fill out any forms in e-mail messages especially from banks.

Common anti-phishing measures for identity theft in the case of Hong Kong banks included SSL-128 bit encryption, auto-logout, account suspension, and personal digital certificate and firewall was the anti-phishing measure of choice for malware. With regard to phishing emails, there was no bank that had implemented any relevant anti-phishing measure. Singapore banks dealt with identity theft using measures that included SSL-128 bit encryption and auto-logout. All banks had implemented digital server certificates and a number of banks had launched incidence report hotlines (Bose & Leung, 2007).

Web 2.0 in Banking

Actually, there is not a clear-cut definition for Web 2.0 but it typically describes a form of user-to-user communication over the Internet (Heng, 2007). "Web 2.0" refers to the second generation of web development and web design that facilitates information sharing, interoperability, user-centered design and collaboration on the World Wide Web. The advent of Web 2.0 led to the development and evolution of web-based communities, hosted services, and web applications. Examples include social-networking sites, video-sharing sites, wikis, blogs, mashups and folksonomies (http://en.wikipedia.org/wiki/Web_2.0).

Web 2.0 is about moving away from the desktop as the center of computing towards use of the web as a platform. It's also about having a rich, customizable user interface that escapes the traditional limitation of old-school web pages (Rollyson, 2007). Financial services providers need not to adapt to a new era of communication and may turn it into their advantage. Any news can spread uncontrollably through virtual worlds. Web 2.0 inspired inroads into traditional banking seize on the human factor. Interactive Web 2.0 applications such as online diaries (blogs), online libraries (wikis) or virtual worlds have changed the way that consumers gather information. Instead of settling for the role of passive customer, the active Web 2.0 user wants to contribute and discuss the latest news. Financial services providers are realizing that they need to deploy Web 2.0 applications to differentiate themselves for customers and to maximize their reach in the offline and online segments. According to Gartner Research, three-quarters of financial institutions will be using Web 2.0 applications by 2012 (Heng, 2007).

Web 2.0 allows customers to interact the way they want to – by leveraging the social aspect of the Internet to make connections and 2 IBM Global Business Services decisions. To complete in this environment, banks should become a part of their customers' online social networks and understand how to harness their power to create value (Feller & Petit, 2008).

CONCLUSION

This chapter describes in a nutshell the evolution of banking and defines Banking Technology as a consortium of several disciplines namely finance subsuming risk management, Information and communication technology, computer science and marketing science. It also highlights the quintessential role played by these disciplines in helping banks (i) run their day-to-day operations in offering efficient, reliable and secure services to customers (ii) meeting their business objectives of attracting more customers and thereby making huge profits (iii) protect themselves from several kinds of risks. The role played by smart cards, storage area networks, data warehousing, customer relationship management, cryptography, statistics and artificial intelligence in modern banking is very well brought out. The chapter also highlights the important role played by data mining algorithms in helping banks achieve their marketing objectives, fraud detection and anti-money laundering etc.

In summary, it is quite clear that Banking Technology has emerged as a separate discipline in its own right. This chapter also highlights some landmark developments that are noticed, of late, which are biometric ATMs, RFID enabled bank notes, Antiphishing measures that make Internet banking secure and Web 2.0, which make the web interface to the bank highly interactive. As regards future directions, the proliferating research in all fields of ICT and computer science can make steady inroads into the Banking Technology because any new research idea in these disciplines can have potentially great impact on Banking Technology. Some of such areas include cloud computing, virtualization, Green computing etc.

REFERENCES

Abu-Nimeh, S., Nappa, D., Wang, X., & Nair, S. (2007). A Comparison of Machine Learning Techniques for Phishing Detection (pp.60-69). APWG eCrime Researchers Summit, Pittsburgh, PA, USA.

Alaxander von Graevenitz, G. (2007). Biometric Authentication In Relation To Payment Systems And Atms. *Datenschutz und Datensicherheit, 31*(X), 1–3.

Avoine, G. (2004). *Privacy Issues in RFID Banknote Protection Schemes,* In Proceedings of The 6th International Conference on Smart Card Research and Advanced Applications - CARDIS, Toulouse, France, (pp.33-48).

Bose, I., & Leung, A. C. M. (2007). A Comparative Study of Anti-Phishing Preparedness of Hong Kong and Singapore Banks. In *Proceedings of the IEEE Conference on Industrial Engineering and Engineering Management,* (pp. 1893-1897).

Business Continuity Planning for Banking and Finance. retrieved on February 7, 2007 from http://www3.ca.com/technologies/subsolution.aspx?id=3936

Coventry, L., De Angeli, A., & Johnson, G. (2003). *Usability and Biometric Verification at the ATM Interface.* Conference on Computer-Human Interaction, *5* (1), 153-160.

Cruz, M. G. (2002). *Modeling, measuring and hedging operational risk.* London: John Wiley & Sons.

Engler, H., & Essinger, J. (2000). *The Future of Banking, Reuters.* London: Pearson Education, UK.

Feller, W., & Petit, C. (2008). Harnessing *the power of Web 2.0 to rebuild trust in banking.* IBM Institute for Business Value, Retrieved from http://www-935.ibm.com/services/us/gbs/bus/pdf/gbe03117-usen-bank2.pdf

Graham, B. (2003). *The Evolution of Electronic Payments.* BE Thesis, Division of Electrical and Electronics Engineering, School of Information Technology and Electrical Engineering, The University of Queensland, Australia. (http://innovexpo.itee.uq.edu.au/2003/exhibits/s334853/thesis.pdf)

Heng, S. (2007). Implications of Web 2.0 for financial institutions: Be a Driver, Not a Passenger. *Deutsche Bank Research, E-conomics, 63,* 1–11.

Hofmann, F., Baesens, B., Martens, J., Put, F., & Vanthienen, J. (2002). Comparing a genetic fuzzy and neurofuzy classifier for credit scoring. *International Journal of Intelligent Systems, 17*(11), 1067–1083. doi:10.1002/int.10052

Hsieh, N. C. (2005). Hybrid mining approach in the design of credit scoring models. *Expert Systems with Applications, 28*(4), 655–665. doi:10.1016/j.eswa.2004.12.022

Huang, J.-J., Tzeng, G.-H., & Ong, C.-S. (2006). Two-stage genetic programming (2SGP) for the credit scoring model. *Applied Mathematics and Computation, 174*(2), 1039–1053. doi:10.1016/j.amc.2005.05.027

Hwang, H.-G., Ku, C.-Y., Yen, D. C., & Cheng, C.-C. (2004). Critical factors influencing the adoption of data warehouse technology: a study of the banking industry in Taiwan. *Decision Support Systems, 37,* 1–21. doi:10.1016/S0167-9236(02)00191-4

Jain, A., Hong, L., & Pankanti, S. (2000). Biometric Identification. *Communications of the ACM, 43*(2), 91–98. doi:10.1145/328236.328110

Karakostas, B., Kardaras, D., & Papathanassiou, E. (2005). The state of CRM adoption by the financial services in the UK: an empirical investigation. *Information & Management, 42,* 853–863. doi:10.1016/j.im.2004.08.006

Lee, T.-S., & Chen, I.-F. (2005). A two-stage hybrid credit scoring model using artificial neural networks and multivariate adaptive regression splines. *Expert Systems with Applications, 28*(4), 743–752. doi:10.1016/j.eswa.2004.12.031

Li, C., Xu, Y., & Li, H. (2005). An empirical study of Dynamic Customer Relationship Management. *Journal of Retailing and Consumer Services, 12*(6), 431–441. doi:10.1016/j.jretconser.2005.01.003

Li, X., Ying, Y., Tuo, J., Li, B., & Liu, W. (2004). *Applications of classification trees to consumer credit scoring methods in commercial banks.* Proceedings of IEEE International Conference on Systems, Man and Cybernetics, October, 5, 4112-4117.

Mentzas, G. N. (1997). Re-engineering Banking with Object-Oriented Models: Towards Customer information Systems. *International Journal of Information Management, 17*(3), 179–197. doi:10.1016/S0268-4012(96)00060-6

Patel, D., & Luo, X. (2007). *Take a Close Look at Phishing. Information security curriculum development.* Proceedings of the 4th annual conference on Information security curriculum development, ACM, Kennesaw, Georgia, USA, 1-4.

Porter, D. (2003). BASEL II: Heralding the rise of operational risk. *Computer Fraud & Security, 7*, 9–12.

Rollyson, C. S. (2007). Enterprise 2.0: Game-Changer for Investment Banks. Retrieved from http://rollyson.net/download/GHCJ/Adv_Ent20_i-banking.pdf

Rygielski, C., Wang, J.-C., & Yen, D. C. (2002). Data mining techniques for customer relationship management. *Technology in Society, 24*(4), 483–502. doi:10.1016/S0160-791X(02)00038-6

Sarlija, N., Bensic, M., & Zekic-Susac, M. (2006). *A neural network classification of credit applicants in consumer credit scoring.* Proceeding of the Conference on Artificial Intelligence and Applications, Innsbruck, Austria, 205-210.

Scandizzo, S. (2003). Connectivity and measurement of operational risk: An input-output approach. *Soft Computing, 7*, 516–525. doi:10.1007/s00500-002-0236-0

Sheng, S., Magnien, B., Kumaraguru, P., Acquisti, A., Cranor, L. F., Hong, J., & Nunge, E. (2007). *Anti-Phishing Phil: The Design and Evaluation of a Game That Teaches People Not to Fall for Phish.* Symposium on Usable Privacy and Security (SOUPS), Pittsburgh, USA, pp.88-99.

Sivakumaran, M. V. (2005). *Banking Technology Course material, for M.Tech (IT) with Specialization in Banking Technology and Information Security.* IDRBT.

Tanna, G. B. (2002). *SAN and information security in banking.* Buffalo, New York, USA: School of Management, University of Buffalo.

Vartak, N., Patwardhan, A., Joshi, A., Finin, T., & Nagy, P. *Protecting the privacy of passive RFID tags.* Technical Report, TR-CS—6-10, Department of Computer Science and Electrical Engineering, University of Maryland, Baltimore County, USA.

Wang, Y., Wang, S., & Lai, K. K. (2005). A new fuzzy support vector machine to evaluate credit risk. *IEEE Transactions on Fuzzy Systems, 13*(6), 820–831. doi:10.1109/TFUZZ.2005.859320

Zdanowicz, J. S. (2004). Detecting money laundering and terrorist financing via data mining. *Communications of the ACM, 47*(5), 53–55. doi:10.1145/986213.986239

Zhang, Z., Salerno, J. J., & Yu, P. S. (2003). *Applying data mining in investigating money laundering crimes,* SIGKDD'03, Washington DC, USA.

KEY TERMS AND DEFINITIONS

Antiphishing: Also known as identifying and preventing fraudulent process of attempting to acquire sensitive information; associated in the manuscript with ICT applications in banking and finance.

Biometrics: Also known as Methods for uniquely recognizing humans based upon one or more intrinsic physical or behavioral traits; Associated in the manuscript with ICT applications in banking and finance.

Business Continuity Planning (BCP): Similar to Disaster recovery planning.

Customer Relationship Management: Also known as CRM; Similar to Relationship marketing; Associated in the manuscript with customer life cycle management, card holder pricing and profitability, customer segmentation, market basket analysis, cross-sell, up-sell, churn modeling, target marketing, fraud detection and anti-money laundering.

Data Mining: Also known as Knowledge Discovery in Databases (KDD); Similar to statistics, machine learning, artificial intelligence; Associated in the manuscript with credit scoring, bankruptcy prediction, customer life cycle management, card holder pricing and profitability, customer segmentation, market basket analysis, cross-sell, up-sell, churn modeling, target marketing, fraud detection and anti-money laundering.

Delivery Channels: Also known as Money dispensing methods; Associated in the manuscript with ATM, Mobile banking, Smart Card.

Information System: Similar to Database, Decision support system; Associated in the manuscript with data mining techniques for credit scoring.

Internet Banking: Also known as Electronic banking; Similar to Mobile banking; Associated in the manuscript with Payment Systems, Cyber crimes, Fraud detection.

Payment Systems: Also known as: Money paying/transferring methods; Associated in the manuscript with Internet banking, SWIFT, Mobile banking, Credit card, Smart card

RFID: Also known as Identify objects in an environment by embedding RFID tags onto these objects; Associated in the manuscript with ICT applications in banking and finance.

Risk: Similar to Risk management; Associated in the manuscript with Credit Risk, Market risk and Operational risk.

Smart Cards: Also known as Chip card; Associated in the manuscript with Delivery channels, Payment systems.

Chapter 9
Application of RFID Technology in Banking Sector

Lotfollah Forozandeh Dehkordi
Payame Noor University, Iran

Ali Ghorbani
Payame Noor University, Iran

Ali Reza Aliahmadi
University of Science & Technology, Iran

ABSTRACT

Nowadays, the banks are using new technologies to provide better services to customers. One of these new technologies is RFID. In this chapter first a brief introduction presented about RFID technology and its components. Then, some applications of RFID in banking sector such as RFID applications in the cheques between banks, reducing the manual operation, customer relationship management, tracking and tracing, money transferring system, countering counterfeiting, contactless smart cards, people identification, phone banking, establishing security, checking purpose and so on are explained. Finally some of the barriers to technology acceptance by the customers and some methods to data protection and increasing security in RFID systems are described.

INTRODUCTION

Technological developments particularly in the area of information technology are revolutionizing the banking industry. With the development of this technology, Commercial banking is undergoing rapid change.

Radio frequency identification (RFID) is a seemingly simple technique. Data is stored in RFID tags that are attached to objects or located

DOI: 10.4018/978-1-61520-635-3.ch009

in Smart cards, and this data can be read using radio signals and presented on a display by using a suitable reader. The data can then be transmitted automatically to an information technology (IT) system for further processing (Hasen &Gillert, 2008). The appeal of this technology is its convenience and efficiency offered to both the consumers and the merchants. (Banks, Pachano,Thompson & Hanny, 2007)

RFID's ability to perform as an auto-identification technology was first utilized by the Royal Air Force in World War II to differentiate between friendly and enemy aircraft. Friendly planes were equipped with bulky "active" RFID transponders (tags) energized by an attached power supply and interrogated by an RFID transceiver (reader). Applications today rely on similar communication between RFID tag and reader, although the tags (miniscule microchips attached to antennae) are generally "passive," powered by an electromagnetic field emitted by the reader. Radio signals inform nearby readers of a serial number stored on the tag that uniquely identifies any item bearing the tag. (Angell & Kietzmann, 2006). Table 1 shows RFID application fields.

The Auto-ID Center, established in 1999 as an academic research project at the Massachusetts Institute of Technology, developed the architecture for creating a seamless global network of all physical objects (www.autoidlabs.org/aboutthelabs.html). The technology has since been transferred to EPC global (www.epcglobalinc.org), which oversees development of standards for electronic product code (EPC) tags. These tags are used for every imaginable item from clothes to medicine, electronics, food, motor vehicles, books, door locks, and airplanes revolutionizing logistics and supply-chain and inventory management worldwide. (Angell & Keitzmann, 2006)

ELEMENTS OF RADIO FREQUENCY COMMUNICATION

The communication takes place between two devices: a reader that needs the information and a tag that has the information. Before we dive

Figure 1.

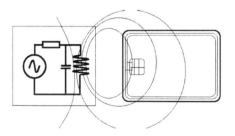

into the physics of communication, let's get on the same page about some concepts that are at the heart of this communication (Sanghera, 2007).

Radio frequency communication uses the EM waves with frequencies from a specific part of the EM frequency spectrum. Therefore, the underlying physics behind RF communication is the same as for any communication that uses electromagnetic waves to carry information.

The four major players that make this communication happen are the following: (Sanghera, 2007)

- Data signal: This is the wave that actually contains the information that needs to be sent to the receiver.
- Carrier signal: This is the wave that carries the data signal.
- Modulation: This is the process that encodes the data signal into the carrier signal and creates the radio wave that is actually transmitted by the antenna to propagate.
- Antenna: This is a device used to transmit and receive signals such as radio waves.

In an RFID system, both the reader and the tag have their own antennas through which they communicate with each other. A tag is also called a transponder because it responds to the reader's attempt to read it, and the reader is also called a transceiver because it receives information from the tag (Sanghera, 2007).

THE APPLICATION OF RFID IN THE CHEQUES BETWEEN BANKS

One of most important application of RFID tags is in the field of issuing cheques between the banks and cheques to the order of banks. As you know when the customer asks for a cheque between the banks, after issuing the cheque and referring of the customer to the destination banks, there, it is necessary to exert a high level of care about controlling the signature and the code number of order cheque. And just for this reason it one of the most difficult posts in the bank. After controlling, the official in charge must make a contact with the source bank to control the accuracy of the sum of the cheque and the code number and in this the cheque is confirmed; but sum issued like the telephones being engaged and things like that make it a time-consuming work. But when the RFID tags are located in the cheque, there is no need for these works and by referring of the customer to the destination back and by placing cheque in front of reader machine, all the information will be visible and easy to control which enhance the speed and safety of the operation.

In 2006 in attempt to fight against counterfeiting the bill and cheque, most of the central banks decided to devise RFID tags in cheque, securities and bonds (Bakhtiari, Alikahani,& Ghasemzadeh, 2008). Placing the RFID tags inside the cheque (called certified cheque) enables the banks and other institutes to enhance the safety of the cheque to a large extent. Each cheque enjoys a special serial for itself and the information in it include the sum of the cheque, the information related to the issuer, the date and other related data. This information in encoded by an advanced algorithm and unlocking it is practically impossible.

RFID readers interrogate multiple tags simultaneously. Every time notes are passed to or from a bank, RFID readers identify and record them, linking this data with the person who presented or received them. The bank has the potential to know not only exactly how much cash is being carried out/in the door but who is carrying it and who carried it previously. By comparing the respective identification numbers to entries in their database (for authentication purposes, of course), the authorities can draw a link between the last recorded holder of the note and the current one. (Angell & Kietzmann, 2006) The information in the cheque can be corrected or cleaned upon cashing the cheque in the bank. Also the validity of cheque can be identified in only several seconds in any branch of bank having the special reader. One of the features of these cheques is their being anti-countering, because it needs physical contact; and since the information and serial number are

Table 1. RFID application fields

	RFID Application Fields	Description
Mainly Object Tagging	**A.** Logistical Tracking & Tracing	Solely identification and location of goods and returnable assets (e.g., pallets or containers)
	B. Production, Monitoring and Maintenance	Smart systems in combination with RFID-Technology to support production, monitoring, and maintenance of goods and processes
	C. Product Safety, Quality and Information	Applications to ensure quality (e.g., sensors to monitor temperature) and product safety (e.g., fight against counterfeiting)
Tagging with Reference or Potential Reference to Individuals	**D.** Access Control and Tracking & Tracing of Individuals	Single function tags for identification and authorisation applications for entry control and ticketing
	E. Loyalty, Membership and Payment	Smart Card based identification and authorisation systems for multifunctional applications (e.g., loyalty, payment, and banking systems)
	F. eHealth Care	Systems for hospital administration and smart systems to support and monitor health status
	G. Sport, Leisure and Household	Sports applications, rental systems (e.g., cars or books), smart home
	H. Public Services	Systems mandated by law or to fulfill public duties (e.g., ID-Cards, Health Insurance Cards, Road Tolling Systems)

Reference: B. Gampl, M. Robeck, M. Clasen

hidden and invisible, their counterfeiting is impossible. Identifying the invalid information stored in chip is easy, since the system announces it in the case the printed information on the cheque and the information stored in chips are not the same. Also identifying the issuer of the cheque is an easy work and certifying the cheque is rapidly done. Even in some cases which the cheque is issued for a certain person in an specific branch, it is possible to record the identity of person on the chip for safety reasons (Bakhtiari, Alikahani,& Ghasemzadeh, 2008, 2008). To increase the safety, the biometric information or identification keys of the user can be placed in the cheque.

THE APPLICATION IN RECEIVING THE BANK DOCUMENT INFORMATION AUTOMATICALLY AND REDUCING THE MANUAL OPERATION

To speed up the bank operation RFID system can be used. For this purpose RFID tags must be located on documents like bankbooks of customers, bonds, and cheques. The readers in bank booths, upon receiving the document from customers by bank teller, just in a moment can enter the information related to the document like date of issuance by the bank, serial number of the document, the name of the owner of the document and related information of the account to system of the bank, and in this way not long time will be spent to enter information manually to the system. According to Dehghan and Ghaderi (2008), this will have two advantages(Dehghan & Ghaderi, 2008)

- The accuracy of the document is certified and maybe the probability of counterfeiting and cheating will decrease to a remarkable degree.
- There is no need to do the operation and record features or account number manu-

ally. And this will increase the speed of operation.

With this information, bank clerks and teller can calculate their own statistics at the end of the day and month about closing the safe and closing the monthly balance sheet easily and with high certainty. By using RFID, the Automatic Teller Machines (ATMs) and Money Counting Machines can even confirm the safety of bills and cheques easily, and count them and then enter their information in user system of bank.

CUSTOMER RELATIONSHIP

Many banks are exploring ways to use RFID technology to better manage and enhance their relationships with their customers, especially their blue-chip clients. The general idea is to provide the customer with a RFID-tagged object, like a card or cheque book, so that the customer can be identified on their visits to the branch. It would also be possible to use the technology to differentiate the level of attention that a privileged customer would receive. For example, if a high-net-worth customer enters the branch, the technology can be used to trigger an alert to the branch manager for his special attention instead of the customer service officer in the normal scenario.(Gupta & Joseph, 2006)

The reader receiving the waves from the tags on customer's document can display the information desired by the customer and in this way the customer can get information about the money in his/her account or his/her account flow or other information which can be possibly defined for the system in later stages. And also by using RFID systems, customers can easily be sure of the safety of the cheques in their hands. This method is especially useful for confirming the travel cheques and identifying the counterfeit cases or stolen one for the customers.

ELECTRONIC TURN TAKING OF CUSTOMERS

RFID tags create virtual identities for the objects to which they are attached, and smart cards equipped with RFID tags do the same thing for persons (Hansen & Gillert, 2008).

Smart cards equipped with RFID can be used to assign turns and order the customers and prevent disorder in the affairs of the bank by standing of customers in front of the booths of the clerks. This can be done when the customers with the documents equipped with RFID tag in their pockets enter the entrance door of bank; the system automatically by welcoming the customer by name assigns a turn with regard to the possible service needed by the customer in related booth. In this way, the aim of customer promotion will be achieved and the only thing the customer will do is to sit down till his/her turn reaches and also there is no need to a machine using paper for turn taking.

TRACKING AND TRACING

Who wouldn't pay to locate misplaced keys, spectacles, gloves, or socks (conveniently tagged by their manufacturers)? (Angell & Kietzmann, 2006) Misplaced documents can prove to be extremely costly for banks and can lead to financial loss and, more importantly, the loss of reputation. RFID can play a significant role in tracking and tracing the most important operational assets of a bank – documents. This would be of particular interest to departments such as: credit administration, which is normally the custodian of security documents; custody services, where securities are held in the physical format; and in retail operations, where the sheer volume of documents processed makes tracking and tracing a difficult operation in itself RFID technology can also be a fraud-preventive tool. (Gupta & Joseph, 2006)

There have been instances when an employee, in collusion with a fraudulent client, has passed on security documents prior to the repayment of dues, thereby passing on the title to the security. (Gupta & Joseph, 2006) To conduct this, RFID readers were located in a strategic position.

By marrying an asynchronous reader with a synchronous mobile phone, the emergent device would be able to read and transfer tag data anywhere in near real time. Connecting phones and/or tags would make it possible to send and receive electronic funds. (Angell & Kietzmann, 2006) This technology got attention in banking in 2005. VISA and Master Card started programming on this base.(http://www.usa.visa.com)

When an important document arrives in the office, a smart label can be placed on them. By checking against a document management database, it would be very simple for staff to query the location of a document (Gupta & Joseph, 2006). In this method, unlike the information bank from the physical management of the document, finding the lost document and showing the place by computer for clerk is easier and, for example, when it is time to send a document, but it is not on the desk of the clerk, this will be done automatically and the duty of the clerks will be easier and more extract. Also, the technology can be used to generate an alert when a sensitive document is removed from its designated storage space or possibly to track its movement outside the office premise. (Gupta & Joseph, 2006)

Some of applications and advantages of this technology in tracking and tracing of documents are as following: (West Industries Supplier Company, 2007; Bakhtiari, Alikhani,& Ghasemzadeh, 2008)

- Tracing files and cases
- Searching files and Documents fast and retaining them
- Controlling the expiration dare and moving of documents easily in the bank

Figure 2. A sample of RFID tag for documents

- Recording the literature of work trend of documents and operations conducted on them by the clerks
- Tracing the letters and parcels in real time
- Sorting and delivering parcels and letters automatically
- Optimizing parcel delivery and manual procedures

MONEY TRANSFERRING SYSTEM OF BRANCHES

In case the RFID tags get so cheap and small to place them inside the bills, electronic sensors can be used in banks and financial institutes to do the pre-checking and recording of the events related to delivery and transferring the money in the bank branches. This will enable the banks to do the delivery works automatically and also certify the accuracy of the work. It is just enough to put a bunch of bills under money counting machine equipped with reader technology and in this way the value of the bunch of the bills will be known for the operator.

One of the duties of treasury office of banks is conducting the money transferring system of the branches. In order that every branch of the banks can keep a special limit of money, sometimes, it is necessary to do several operation of money transferring in one day to the branch. The RFID technology can facilitate conducting the money transferring operation especially the delivery of money by branches. (Davari, Mojdehi & Jalai,

2009) By using the readers, the people responsible for money transferring can easily move in their path and in each branch of the bank touch the buttons with their own reader and prove that they were in the place at the assigned time. Then the collected information from the reader can be transferred to a reporting system to make the report ready for the being checked by the supervisor. The collected information from the reports can help to optimize the delivery ways, delivery times and delivery schedule tables. Also the RFID readers in the branches can easily show the accuracy of the sum of money. There is no need to check the bills, cheques and travel cheques in treasury offices and branches of the bank.

COUNTERING COUNTERFEITING

It is reported that the European Central Bank is investigating how RFID tags can be embedded in high-value currency notes to stem counterfeiting. (Gupta & Joseph, 2006) The bank thinks that some other features must be added to Euro to prevent cheating all over the word. This bank not only has done discussion with European countries but also contracted different countries all over the world to increase the safety of Euro. According to the opinion of banking association and chips producers, it is feasible to apply the RFID technology on the bills. (Fleur de Coin, 2005)

The idea is that the RFID tag would contain most of the data that is on the face of the note. (Gupta & Joseph, 2006) An RF-emitting tag can be small enough to fit into bank notes so as to uniquely identify each one as it passes within range of a sensor. The authorities claim its purpose is to combat counterfeiting and identify money transfers between suspicious parties. (Angell & Kietzmann, 2006) While this may not prevent counterfeiting in itself, it would certainly raise the bar for counterfeiters. (Gupta & Joseph, 2006)

One of the areas where banking fraud is widely prevalent in developing economies is in the encashing of warrants issued by corporates. The banking industry reportedly loses huge sums of money every year as a result of giving value to counterfeit dividend warrants presented to them by individuals. Again, the adoption of RFID technology would make counterfeiting more difficult and would contribute to a significant reduction in false claims. (Gupta & Joseph, 2006)

APPLICATION OF RFID IN CREDIT CARDS AND CONTACTLESS SMART CARDS

In 1970s, for the first time the idea of using Smart Card is proposed and from the late 1980s some magnetic cards containing a magnetic band with low storing capacity were practically used in the bank system of the world countries. (Dehghan& Ghaderi, 2008) At last in 2003 in most parts of the world electronic payment method overcome the paper payment. (Bakhtiari. F., & Alikhani. A., and Ghasemzadeh, 2008) MasterCard conducted a pilot study to test the acceptance of a new RFID-tagged smart card programme called Paypass. More than 5,000 customers of three different banks (Chase, Citibank and MBNA) were issued credit cards that communicated with readers by simply waving the card near the payment terminal. (Gupta &Joseph, 2006) Two years later electronic payment revolution (RFID) started so silently. (Bakhtiari. F., & Alikhani. A., and Ghasemzadeh, 2008)

A contactless smart card includes an embedded smart card secure microcontroller or equivalent intelligence, internal memory and a small antenna and communicates with a reader through a contactless radio frequency (RF) interface. Contactless smart card technology is used in applications that need to protect personal information and/or deliver fast, secure transactions, such as transit fare payment cards, government and corporate identification cards, documents such as electronic passports and visas, and financial payment cards. Contactless smart cards have the ability to securely manage, store and provide access to data on the card, perform on-card functions (e.g. encryption) and interact intelligently with a contactless smart card reader. While offering similar capabilities to contactless smart cards, contact smart cards require physical contact with the reading mechanism rather than using a contactless interface (http://www.kis-kiosk.com).

The contactless smart card with embedded RFID is conquering the market for payment transactions. Smart cards are used as an alternative, or even a substitute, for traditional cash. (Banks, Pachano, Thomas & Hanny, 2007) In this regard, contactless smart cards evolved to be a means for next-generation transaction payment with improved security, speed, and convenience. Contactless cards that are incorporated with wireless RFID technology can be directly recognized by the reader without removing the card from a user's purse or wallet. (Banks, Pachano, Thomas & Hanny, 2007)Contactless smart card could, by applying RFID without needing direct contact, do all the functions of magnetic and electronic cards and at the same time it enjoys less possibility to damage. At this time, American Express, VISA, and Master Card started developing contectless payment system in some selected retailers all over the world.

Through out the world, contactless smartcards are transforming the way people purchase commodities, pay for goods and services, and shop from home, and they are spending more, as well. (Banks, Pachano, Thomas & Hanny, 2007)

The contactless interface provides users with the convenience of allowing the contactless card to be read at short distances with fast transfer of data(www.kis-kiosk.com,(n.d.).) Evidently, the transaction payment made by these contactless smart cards provides a quick payment method for consumers when compared to a cash payment or payment made by a magnetic strip card.

(Banks, Pachano, Thomas & Hanny, 2007)In pilot programme of the Pay Pass system conducted by MasterCard, PayPass transactions were six to 10 seconds faster than other payment methods in stores and 12 to 18 seconds faster than other payment methods in drive-through. The amount spent by users of the Pay Pass devices, which included key fobs and Pay Pass-enabled cell phones, was 25% higher than the amount spent by customers using cash. Pay Pass wirelessly transmits payment details, including the account number and transaction code, between the Pay Pass device and the merchant's RFID-enabled sales terminal. (Gupta & Joseph,2007)

An RFID smart card that consists of a microchip can handle and store from 10 to more than 100 times more information than a traditional magnetic stripe card (Banks, Pachano, Thomas & Hanny, 2007). The reading of contactless cards was much faster than swiping a magnetic-strip card. (Gupta & Joseph,2007)And since these cards have no physical contacts with the card readers of ATM and other machines, they enjoy a longer durability in comparison to the magnetic cards (Schwartz, 2006). And card readers will take less expense for maintenance because of less direct contact. The cards also have little inner sensors and in case the robbers try to access the personal information of a stolen card, it will make the card unable and useless, and will keep it safe from probable misuse(Schwartz, 2006). Sometimes it is possible to leave the card in contact card reader machines like ATM which by using contacless card, this problem will be removed. Each card has a 32 bit identity code which makes it unique in the world, therefore there will be no other card with similar number in any place of the world and this will enhance the security of the card(Bakhtiari, 2008).

Contactless smart card technology is available in a variety of forms in plastic cards, watches, key fobs, documents and other handheld devices (e.g., built into mobile phones) (www.kis-kiosk.com)

Contact Smart Cards usually can be used as the following cases:

- ATM Cards
- Debt Cards
- Cost (Expense) Cards
- Credit Cards

Applying all the above mentioned cases by using contactless smart cards equipped with the radio frequency (RF) technology is possible. According to the words experts, RFID technology at last can replace the magnetic bands and in that case all of electronic payment all over the world will be contactless.(West Industries Supplier Company, 2007)

Some other advantages of using contactless smart cards of RFID can be summarized as following: (www.thebankwatch.com, (n.d.).; Dehghan & Ghaderi (2008); Bakhtiari, 2008))

- Speeding up of the affairs
- Increasing security
- Enjoying more certainty and validity for reader terminals
- Giving remarkable comfort and convenience for customers
- Increasing the operation potentially in traffic times with large volume of transactions
- Not needing to change the worn out cards
- Reducing the clerk expenses remarkably
- Reducing the maintenance costs of reader terminals

PEOPLE IDENTIFICATION SYSTEM

One of the issues on the board in banking industry is keeping the password in different method of banking. With regard to increasing importance of the information, these tools can not satisfy the mankind need in future. Now if we use the Match-on-Card technique, we can increase the security issues of the customers by putting the two categories of Biometric and RFID together in the customers' payment card; and minimize the possibility of misusing and counterfeiting of the cards to the extent of zero, and not need to memorize one's password. One of the advantages of RFID is that it can be connected to sensors. These sensors can sense the out information and respond to them (www.tagsense.com, (n.d.)). Then in addition to entering this unique information into RFID tags, it can be defined to sensors. With this description, the RFID tag is active and exchanges the radio frequency, only when the information sensed by the sensor and information from the tag is the same. In other words, The RFID is activated only when its owner has touched it and the tag can not be activated for other people and in this, the identity of the person can be known (Peyrovi & Amini, 2008).

USING RFID IN MOBILE PHONES

E-banking has developed in different forms; internet banking, web-based banking, TV-based banking, phone banking, household banking, and ATM banking can be mentioned as some examples.

It's not only that passive RFID tag technology is rapidly maturing among a passive (some might say apathetic) public. Innovators predict huge public demand for the products of the convergence of personal RFID readers and mobile telephones. The mobile telephony industry senses a killer application (Angell & Kietzmann, 2006). This idea resulted in the appearance of new kind of RFID technology called NFC (Near Field Communication) which is compatible with the cell phones. By combining this technology with the SIM card in the cell phone and by using encoding algorithms on RFID signal, high level of security levels can be achieved. The first standard in NFC was made in 2003 and in 2005 Nokia Company produced the first cell phone equipped with RFID tags by using NFC; and it was used for other purposes as its use developed and it was found to be optimal. Many countries like USA, Germany, Turkey, South Korea and others are using the advantages of NFC system (Alvandi &Mizraei, 2008).

The user can easily do the described operation only by putting his cell phone near the ATM. This has led to the increase safety in payment, and in this way, besides the encoding algorithm on the NFC cards, the SIM Card in the cell phone with the user's PIN Code are used to a certain the identity of the user and confirm the operation.

Some of the advantages of using NFC are as following (Alvandi &Mizraei, 2008):

- The possibility of contacting with other machines equipped with this technology easily
- The possibility of using the facilitation like encoding and digital signing
- The minimal possibility of misusing information or access to important information
- The capacity to transport high volume of information
- Decrease of cost and increase of income with regard to the fact that there is no need to make a separate infra structure to use NFC
- Increase of security: Since the important information about the identity of the person and bank account information are stored in the chip and cell phone, NFC system enjoy a high of security.
- Using NFC makes it possible to change using several cards of different banks to one SIM Card and password.

ESTABLISHING SECURITY

In non-service hours, the sensors sensitive to light connected to readers, in cases of noticing an anonymous person (like a person lacking the RFID equipped personnel card), inform the danger to the official and the police rapidly (Safari. H. & Koushesh. M., &Akherati, 2007). It can be used in the deposit safes of the bank as another use for RFID to increase the security. That can be done in this way that the people using these safe have cards equipped with RFID system and when the code and card code don't match with the safe, the machine siren the danger immediately to the official in charge.

The smart guard system is used in all over the world by the head guardians to check their guardian's work automatically and confirm its accuracy. This system enables the guardians to check any things easily and conveniently; and report all information to head guardian (Bakhtiari, 2008). Using this system the guardian walk in his/her district and touches the buttons in assigned places to show that those place checked at the assigned time. Then the gathered information is transported to a reporting system by guardian tag reader, so that the system can prepare the report for the head guardian. The tag reader can sense the damages caused and show the other events to inform to the head guardian, in case the guardian himself/herself wants to damage the tag reader (Bakhtiari. F., & Alikhani. A., and Ghasemzadeh, 2008)

The other uses of RFID system to establish safety are:(Bakhtiari, Alikhani & Ghasemzadeh, 2008; West Industries Supplier Company, 2007)

- Maintaining security in the thesauruses of the bank
- Supporting and guarding the machines out of bank like ATM and POS
- Preventing taking machine and equipment illegally out of bank
- Responding of the system to checking and confirming of all guards
- Checking to prevent bribery and conspiracy
- Giving extensive reports

APPLYING RFID FOR PEOPLE CHECKING PURPOSE

If the personnel cards of bank employees are equipped with RFID system and the branches or offices of the banks are equipped with the identity recognizing system, the presence/absence of the employees can be checked. A system as The Tera Tron Local Positioning System (LPS) [Terat 2005] is being used for the first time in the new Gotthard Tunnel in Switzerland. The LPS is used to determine the exact positions of tunnel workers, with the specific aim of accurately locating workers in hazard areas (Hansen & Gillert, 2008).

LPS system contain 4 parts:

(1) Position markers (2) Personal RFID cards (3) Fixed receivers (4) Workstation software

This system can also be used, in banks for controlling purposes. By using LPS, the head manager of the bank can know his/his employees' entering and leaving out and even in large branches, no time will be wasted in employees' large lines entering and leaving the branch. This system can also be used to calculate extra time work and to access the salary, to check the presence or absence of the employee in the bank, to control the place each employee goes during the day, to open automatically the door of important rooms like the room of keeping confidential documents for specific employees, to lock and unlock the system being used by the employee because of his/her presence, not to function of the branch siren in specific employee's presence in the branch and finally to open the door of the safes in the bank because of identifying the specific index code of the employee's card.

Of course the identifier itself can not show the real presence of the employees in the bank then it is necessary to take some other complementary measures into consideration, for example, the employee can be traced by using the same cards with tags. And in this way when an employee is not in his/her room, his/her place can be detected and called to his/her room (Bakhtiari. F., & Alikhani. A., & Ghasemzadeh, 2008). In another approach, connecting to the bank system and entering the user code manually by the employee can be considered as a proof for the person's presence.

This system can also prevent the take off-day of employees who want without registering in the presence and absence system to leave the bank and not to be noticed.

LIMITATION OF ACCESS TO INFORMATION

The reader determines the extent of user's access to information by using the personnel information available in the bank personnel card equipped with RFID system. And if the user wishes to enter the system in higher levels and by other names, the system prevents it (Safari. H. & Koushesh. M., & Akherati, 2007). The limitations for access are as following: (Bakhtiari, 2008)

- Controlling access to system
- Access of the employees to system by using a specific index
- Place and time registering system
- The permit to make profile for customers
- Recording the event carefully and in detail
- Counterfeiting system, encoding the information
- Access to computers, information and equipment with high security by using a specific index
- Locking and unlocking of the access to computers in the presence of a user with permit

Figure 3. A local positioning system (LPS) for persons and objects (Source: TeraTron)

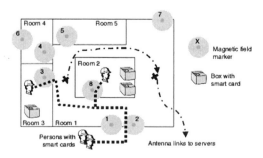

- Preventing the change of information by component people
- Increasing security

DETERMINING THE NUMBER OF CLIENT, THE CAPACITY OF BANK AND THE REQUIRED PERSONNEL

By using RFID tags in Bank documents, the proceeding of the client entering and leaving the bank can be accessed carefully and in this way a manager can know the accountability capacity and required personnel of the bank in an exact way.

THE ACCEPTANCE BARRIERS OF RFID FOR CUSTOMER

Benefits to major corporations and governments will not in and of themselves generate public acceptance of tagged cash. That acceptance is essential if the technology is to overcome privacy objections. Hence the issue of mobile RFID and tagged bank notes, while contributing to decreased anonymity, is being marketed to individuals as a self-evident personal advantage. Once people are proffered a bank note, their mobile phones read the tag, establish a connection to the authority's database, and receive confirmation of the note's authenticity and validity and of the legitimacy of the bearer. Fraud will decrease dramatically. As a byproduct of the process, the government will obtain yet more information for its database of cash transfers from private citizens, as well as from the banking, retail, and service sectors. As tagged product purchases find their way into our homes, we will be only a step away from installing indoor receivers into our shelves, floors, and doorways (Albrecht, 2002).

RFID AND DATA PROTECTION

Attention must be given to data protection and consumer protection requirements in RFID applications. The primary requirement is to ensure the right of citizens to determine how their personal data is used, which is some times called 'informational self-determination'. In order to avoid surprises, false insinuations and unjustified fears, all business processes that are associated with RFID technology should be evaluated with regard to the irrelevance to data protection. Preventive information is urgently necessary in situations where consumers come in contact with RFID. Experience shows that the impact of RFID tags on consumers must be assessed in legal as well as informatics terms. Many enterprises that pioneered the use RFID tags in the early days of technological euphoria have had painful experiences as a result of inadequate communication (Hansen & Gillert, 2008).

Consequently, groups of persons who come in to contact with RFID tags as consumers or customers must always be informed about RFID-related measures comprehensively and with an eye to future developments. Good public relations work is indispensable here. In a study by the University of St Gallen, it was found that RFID can only be successful in practice if the interests of data protection are taken in to account (Hansen & Gillert, 2008).

Among other things, the guideline can be used as an annex to general terms and conditions of business or project contracts related to the use of RFID technologies. Persons in decision-making positions can then determine which data protection criteria are applicable in a particular situation and what must be done to comply with them. The data protection requirements relevant to the use of RFID tags must generally be determined based on the specific application. For this reason, three basic RFID use scenarios are described in the guide-line: (Hansen & Gillert, 2008)

1. RFID tags that are removed when the consumer acquires the goods and are thus not linked to customer data, such as RFID tags attached to garments for theft prevention.
2. Reading product data from RFID tags, such as at a point of sale (POS) for payment purposes, with RFID tags attached to retail items. In this case the tag data can be associated with customer data via a credit card or customer card, among other possibilities.
3. Tags used to generate use profiles, such as tags in customer cards.

REFERENCES

Albrecht, K. (2002)., Supermarket cards: The tip of the retail surveillance iceberg. *Denver University Law Review,. 79*, 4, 534–539 and 558–565.

Alvandi, N., & Mirzaei, S. R. (2008). *RFID: A New Phenomenon in E-banking,* Paper presented at: 2nd International Conference on E-banking, Tehran, 9-10 August.

Angell Ian. & J. Kietzmann., (2006). RFID and the end of cash, *Communications of the ACM, 49*, (12), Available at http://portal.acm.org/citation.cfm?id=1183236.1183237

Bakhtiari, F., Alikhani, A., & Ghasemzadeh, A. (2008). *Investigating RFID Application in E-banking,* Paper presented at: 2nd International Conference on E-banking, Tehran, 9-10 August.

Bakhtiari, H. (2008)., *Application of RFID in E-banking.* Paper presented at: 2nd International Conference on E-banking, Tehran, 9-10 August.

Banks, J., Pachano, M., Thompson, L., & Hanny, D. (2007). *RFID Applied* (pp. 341–347). New York: John Wiley & Sons. doi:10.1002/9780470168226.ch18

Davari, M. R., Mojdehi, N., & Jalali, A. A. (2009). *Using RFID By Banks in E-city,* Paper presented at: 2nd International Conference on E-city, Tehran, 2-3 July.

Dehghan, A., & Ghaderi, J. (2008). *The Role of RFID in Moving Form Traditional Banking to Electronic Banking,* Paper presented at: 2nd International Conference on E-banking, Tehran, 9-10 August.

Fleur de Coin. (2005). RFID banknotes, from Euro banknotes embedded with RFID chips, Retrieved from http://www.fleur-de-coin.com/eurocoins/rfid.asp.

Gampl, B., Robeck, M., & Clasen, M. (2008). The RFID Reference Model, Retrieved from: www.gil.de/dokumente/berichte/DDD/R20_2008_012.pdf.

Hansen, W. R., & Gillert, F. (2008). *RFID for the Optimization of Business Processes.* New York: John Wiley & Sons, Ltd. doi:10.1002/9780470754160

http://thebankwatch.com/tag/smart-cards/(n.d.).

http://www.tagsense.com/index.html, (n.d.).

http://www.usa.visa.com/personal/cards/paywave/index.html?ep=a_cmp_akqa_search,(n.d.).

Management, *HSBC's Guide to Cash and Treasury Management in Asia Pacific,* (pp 191-194); Retrieved from: rfid.ctu.edu.tw/8_lab/RFID_reference/4/Infosys-RFID-in-CM.pdf?Part=NM-2005-A1-MAR-1

Peyrovi, N., & Amini, L. M. (2008). *Application of RFID in People Identification at E-banking,* Paper presented at: 2nd International Conference on E-banking, Tehran, 9-10 August.

Safari, H., Koushesh, M., & Akherati, A. (2007). Introduction to RFID and Using it in E-Banking, *Paper presented at 1nd International Conference on Management of Supply Chain and Information Systems.* Tehran, Applied Information Co.

Sanghera., Paul., et al, (2007). *How to Cheat at Deploying and Securing RFID.* Burlington, MA: Syngress Publishing, Inc.

Schwartz, J. (2006). *Researchers See Privacy Pitfalls in No-Swipe Credit Cards.*The New York Times, Retrieved from http://www.nytimes.com/2006/10/23/business/23card.html?ex=1319256000&en=76401b1601fc06e3&ei=5090

West Industries Supplier Company. (2007). *Solutions of Banking,* Paper presented at 1nd International Conference on Management of Supply Chain and Information Systems, Tehran, Applied Information Co. Article of RFID Tags, Contactless Smart Card Technology and Electronic Passports: Frequently Asked Questions.Retrieved from Available at: www.kis-kiosk.com/casestudies/assets/rfid-faq.pdf.

ADDITIONAL READING

Anderson, R. (2001). Why Information Security is Hard – An Economic Perspective In *Proceedings of the Seventeenth Computer Security Applications Conference* (pp.358-365) IEEE Computer Society.Retrieved from http://www.cl.cam.ac.uk/ftp/users/rja14/econ.pdf

Anderson, R. J. (2001). *Security Engineering – A Guide to Building Dependable Distributed Systems.* New York: Wiley.

Angeles, R. (2005). RFID technologies: supply-chain applications and implementation issues. *Information Systems Management, 22*(1), 51–65. doi:10.1201/1078/44912.22.1.20051201/85739.7

Baard, M. (2005) Will new RFID technology help or hinder security? Retreived 27 Apr 2005 from http://searchsecurity.techtarget.com/originalContent/0,289142,sid14gci1083417,00.html

Beague, L. (2007). *E-Banking service using Connected Secure Smart Cards Readers: the Covadis solution.* Geneva, Switzerland: Covaids S.A.

Boneh, D., Shacham, H., & Lynn, B. (2001). *Short signatures from the Weil pairing.* (ASIACRYPT '01),(. *LNCS, 2139,* 514–532.

Catherine, O., & Connor, M. (2005). RFID-Enabled Credit Cards Apt to Lead. RFID Journal, March 25. Retrieved from http://www.rfidjournal.com

Chuang, M., & Shaw, L. (2005). How RFID will impact supply chain networks. In *2005 IEEE International Engineering Management Conference.*

David C. (2006). RFID 101: the next big thing for management. *Management Research News, 29* (4).

Emery, G. R. (2004). IT execs prepare for an RFID revolution, Washington Technology, June 29, Retrieved from www.washingtontechnology.com/news/1_1/industry/23875-1.html

Figwer, K. (2004). RFID Technology for Distribution Operations: An RFID Primer. Retrieved from www.techlinks.com, April 05.

Holcombe, S. (2000). *Banking on Granular Information Ownership.* CEO, Pardalis.

http://www.rfidc.com/, (n.d.).

http://www.rfidjournal.com, (n.d.).

http://www.rfidnews.org/, (n.d.).

Jansen, R., & Krabs, A. (1999). Automatic identification in packing – radio frequency identification in multi-way system. *Packing Technology and Science, 12,* 229–234. doi:10.1002/(SICI)1099-1522(199909/10)12:5<229::AID-PTS479>3.0.CO;2-6

Journal, R. F. I. D. Michelin embeds RFID tags in tires. Retrieved from http://www.rfidjournal.com/article/view/269, *January2008.*

Juels, A., & Pappu, R. (2002). Squealing euros: Privacy protection in RFID-enabled banknotes. In Wright, R. N. (Ed.), *Financial Cryptography* (pp. 103–121). LNCS.

Kakkainen, M. (2003). Increasing efficiency in the supply chain for short shelf life goods using RFID tagging. *International Journal of Retail & Distribution Management, 31*(10), 529–3. doi:10.1108/09590550310497058

Li, S., Visich J.K., Khumawala, M.B., & Zhang, C., (2006). *Radio frequency identification technology: applications, technical challenges and strategies Sensor Review, 26* (3), 193–202

Porter, J. D., Billo, R. E., & Mickle, M. H. (2004). A standard test protocol for evaluation of radio frequency identification systems for supply chain applications. *Journal of Manufacturing Systems, 23*(1), 46–55. doi:10.1016/S0278-6125(04)80006-2

Rivest, R. (1997). *Electronic lottery tickets as micropayments.* In R. Hirschfeld,(Ed.) Financial Cryptography '97, (LNCS 1318, pp. 307–314). New York: Springer-Verlag. Salminen, T., Hosio, S., & Riekki, J., (2006). Enhancing Bluetooth connectivity with RFID. *Fourth Annual IEEE International Conference on Pervasive Computing And Communications.* IEEE Computer Society Press.

Sarma, R. (2001). Towards the five–cent tag. *Technical Report MIT-AUTOID-WD-006. MIT auto ID center,* Cambridge, MA, USA, November 2001.

Sarma, S., Weis. S., & Engels. D., (2003). *Radio-frequency identification: security risks and challenges.* Cryptobytes, RSA Laboratories, *6*(1), 2–9, spring2003.

Spekman, R. E., & Sweeney, P. J. (2006). RFID: from concept to implementation. *International Journal of Physical Distribution & Logistics Management, 36*(10). doi:10.1108/09600030610714571

Srivastava, B. (2004). Radio frequency ID technology: the next revolution in SCM. *Business Horizons, 47*(6), 60–80. doi:10.1016/j.bushor.2004.09.009

Suhong, L., Visich, J.K., Khumawala, B.M., & Zhang, Ch., (2006). Radio frequency identification technology: applications, technical challenges and strategies, *Sensor Review, 26,* (3).

Takaragi, K., Usami, M., Imura, R., Itsuki, R., & Satoh, T. (2001). An ultra small individual recognition security chip. *IEEE Micro, 21*(6), 43–49. doi:10.1109/40.977757

Weaver, A. C. (2004). *Electronic Commerce software laboratory.* Proceedings of the 35th SIGCSE technical symposium on Computer science education (SIGCSE 04), *36*(1), 453-356.

Yoshida, J. Euro bank notes to embed RFID chips by 2005. *EE Times.* 19 December 2001. Retrieved from http://www.eetimes.com/story/OEG20011219S0016.

KEY TERMS AND DEFINITIONS

Contactless Smart Cards: A contactless smart card includes an embedded smart card secure microcontroller or equivalent intelligence, internal memory and a small antenna and communicates with a reader through a contactless radio frequency (RF) interface. Contactless smart cards that are incorporated with wireless RFID technology can be directly recognized by the reader without removing the card from a user's purse or wallet. Contactless smart card could, by applying RFID without needing direct contact, do all the functions of magnetic and electronic cards and at the same time it enjoys less possibility to damage.

RFID: Radio-frequency identification (RFID) is the use of an object (typically referred to as a RFID tag) applied to or incorporated into a product, animal, or person for the purpose of identification and tracking using radio waves. Some tags can be read from several meters away and beyond the line of sight of the reader. Most RFID tags contain at least two parts. One is an integrated circuit for storing and processing information, modulating and demodulating a radio-frequency (RF) signal, and other specialized functions. The second is an antenna for receiving and transmitting the signal.

Tag: Refer to Personal identifiers. A small, flat, metal, electronic identification label attached to things and assigned to a piece of information; A microchip attached to an antenna that is packaged in a way that it can be applied to an object. The tag picks up signals from and sends signals to a reader. The tag contains a unique serial number, but may have other information; such as, a customer' account number. Tags come in many forms, such smart labels that can have a barcode printed on it, or the tag can simply be mounted inside a carton or embedded in plastic. RFID tags can be active, passive or semi-passive.

Tracking and Tracing: In logistics, tracking and tracing is the concept of locating property that is being forwarded from an origin to a destination through various hubs and passing along spokes, and determining the location and other status of such object. Usually this concept is supported by means of reckoning and reporting of the position of the vehicles transporting containers with the object in real-time. This approach leaves the task to compose a coherent depiction of the status reports. Another approach is to report the arrival or departure of the object and recording the identification of the object, the location where observed, the time, and the status, e.g. on damage or loading. This approach leaves the task to verify the reports regarding consistency and completeness.

Chapter 10

Improving E-Society through E-Banking

Bala Shanmugam
Monash University, Malaysia

Mahadevan Supramaniam
Taylor's University College, Malaysia

ABSTRACT

The emergence of e-banking has created a significant transformation towards the services provided by the banks. E-banking provides alternatives for faster delivery of banking services to a wider scope of customers hence creating a major impact towards e-society. Nowadays, e-banking have gained increasing popularity in delivering online services for e-society. However, prior to the implementation of e-banking, several factors and best practices must be identified to ensure a more efficient execution of e-banking services towards the development of e-society. E-banking factors are found to have a significant effect on the success of e-society.

INTRODUCTION

The banking sector has evolved from time to time. Indeed, its tradition, probity and established ways of doing business have been a source of pride to the sector. The chapter explains e-Banking, which has been characterized by its ` tried and tested" processes of service delivery as an engine of growth for e-society and vice versa. Competition is escalating, both from traditional players and new entrants, owing to deregulation. The chapter also explains about the changing consumer behavior

and needs, globalization, deregulation, disintermediation and the emergence of new financial service models which are dynamics in the financial services industry. Information technology is also having its impact (Chorafas, 1987; Scarborough & Lannon, 1988; Chen, 1999; Park, 1999).

The past few decades have witnessed a rapid technological growth within the banking industry through the introduction of electronic banking. The increase in the adoption of e-banking is a largely defensive measure against increasingly sophisticated and highly demanding consumers, escalating competition, and the necessity to control and reduce rising costs (Barra, 1990). Internet

DOI: 10.4018/978-1-61520-635-3.ch010

banking presents the industry with an electronic and remote distribution channel. It represents an electronic marketplace whereby consumers may conduct their financial transactions on a virtual level (Reiser, 1997; Daniel, 1999). The advance of this innovation has occurred worldwide with the introduction of such Internet-only banks as Smile and Egg in the UK and Security First Network Bank (SFNB) and Wingspanbank.com in the USA, to name but a few.

The spatial and temporal separation of e-commerce between customers and e- vendors as well as the unpredictability of the Internet infrastructure generate an implicit uncertainty around the initial adoption e-banking services (Pavlou, 2001). Accordingly, the initial adoption of eservice like Internet banking, basically involves the acceptance of both the Internet technology and on- line service providers.

BACKGROUND

Driven by the challenge to expand and capture a larger share of the banking market, some banks invest in more bricks and mortar to enlarge their geographical and market coverage. Others have considered a more revolutionary approach to deliver their banking services via a new medium: the Internet. Since the introduction of the Internet in 1969, it has evolved from the sole domain of the computer nerd and the academic to a mainstream channel of communication (Nehmzow, 1997). Recently, it has been rapidly gaining popularity as a potential medium for electronic commerce (Crede, 1995; Ooi, 1999; U.S. Department of Commerce, 1999). The rapid growth of the Internet has presented a new host of opportunities as well as threats to business. Today, the Internet is well on its way to become a full-fledged delivery and distribution channel and among the consumer-oriented applications riding at the forefront of this evolution is electronic financial products and services.

The Internet is now being considered as a strategic weapon and will revolutionize the way banks operate, deliver, and compete against one another, especially when competitive advantages of traditional branch networks are eroding rapidly (Nehmzow, 1997; Seitz, 1998). As *"Business Week"* noted, "Banking is essential to a modern economy, banks are not" (quoted in Financial Times, 1996). This statement is supported by a recent report from Booz Allen & Hamilton (Warner, 1996) that claims the Internet poses a very serious threat both to the customer base of the traditional banking oligopoly and to its profits. Their belief is that the Internet promises a revolution in retail banking of monumental proportions. High street or brick and mortar banks as we know them may largely disappear.

Electronic banking can be defined as the delivery of banking services through the use of electronic communication, primarily the internet. There are also other services related to e-banking such as internet banking, on-line banking, or PC banking, ATMs, wire transfers, telephone banking, electronic funds transfers, and debit cards.

The emergence of Internet banking has prompted many banks to rethink their IT strategies in order to stay competitive. Customers today are demanding much more from banking services. They want new levels of convenience and flexibility (Birch & Young, 1997; Lagoutte, 1996) on top of powerful and easy to use financial management tools and products and services that traditional retail banking could not offer. Internet banking has allowed banks and financial institutions to provide these services by exploiting an extensive public network infrastructure (Ternullo, 1997).

Claessens et al. (2000) argued that together with technological advances, the emergence of e-banking offer great benefits to consumers worldwide. This has forced the banks to review their public policy in the safety and soundness of banking, competition policy, consumer and investor protection, and global public policy towards banking. The changes can accelerate financial sector development by lowering the costs, increasing the breadth and quality, and widening access to financial services.

Claessens (2001) analyzed the impact of e-banking on the financial systems in different countries, and the leapfrogging opportunities for emerging markets. The authors addressed new policy issues and the role of government intervention in light of these developments. Special focus is given to models of financial sector development that enable and promote electronic banking in banking, capital markets, insurance, housing finance, and microfinance areas, drawing on innovative applications from the industrialized and the developing world.

Concepts of E-Banking

The concept of e-banking presents primarily about two types of e-banking which are informational e-banking and transactional e-banking. The informational e-banking has limited features of just viewing the information such as banking statements and transaction history without any transactions being done. The transactional e-banking is the latest type of e-banking which allows the users to view and initiate banking transactions to the extent of creating a virtual banking system.

E-banking or more internet banking is used to describe banking transactions via a secured internet application. E-banking was introduced in the mid 1990s especially in large banks in United States and Canada as an informational e-banking system. As the number of internet users grows internationally, the banks have taken the advantage of the internet growth by providing more e-banking services. The types of e-services include paying bills, transferring funds, viewing account statements, paying loans and mortgages.

There are three ways to initiate an e-banking service such as:

1. Using the internet: The customers can use the browser to browse through the bank's website to enable online banking services.

This kind of services requires the browser to support encryption to protect the customers from intruders. This is the most commonly used method as it is very easy to use and does not require any specific software except the browser.

2. Using personal financial management software products: The customers are allowed to use their own personal financial management application system which is connected to the bank they are registered to. The software need to be verified by the banks before being connected to their data center.

3. Using proprietary software from e-banking: The customers are provided with customized banking software by the banks which needs to be installed in the client's computer to enable the e-banking services. The software will be able to directly connect to the bank once internet connection is enabled.

E-Society and Its Components

The world is changing in a rapid pace and no sector moves as fast as banking sector. Today its impact reaches out far beyond the conventional banking customers. E-banking has given a new dimension to the people and the economy as a whole. E-banking is revolutionizing the daily life of every citizen and business. The new way of doing business using internet is fast becoming a newly established business model, forcing the banks going online to support the online industry. Today the roles of banks are not limited to the mere provision of serving the locals in a specific location but to be more integrated and diversified to serve the whole world. Through their new e-banking models and investment in tomorrow's technologies, e-banking contribute directly to the nation's sustainable growth. With the growing use of internet worldwide and globalizations, it is therefore no surprise that there has been a tremendous increase in the use of internet for financial activities in businesses, education, health industry, education and entertainment. They play a key role in creating a modern society – the e-society or borderless society – that enhances social inclusion, public services, quality banking and to be more competitive in the world. The main components of e-society can fall into five main categories such as e-commerce, e-government, e-learning, e-health and e-entertainment.

E-Commerce

E-commerce can be defined as the online transaction of business linking the buyer, vendor, banks and the host. It allows the e-society the rights to use a good or service through online banking features. Most people are familiar with business-to-consumer electronic business (B2C). Common illustrations include Amazon.com, travelocity.com, and e-bay.com.

E-commerce has a great deal of advantages to the e-society. Consumers can easily search through a large database of products and services. They can see actual prices, compare the prices, build an order and make an online payment to the selected goods.

An example of a famous e-commerce company is Amazon.com Inc which is located in Seattle, Washington USA. Amazon.com is an online bookstore with an extended variety of goods such software, video games, MPs and health products. Today customers from all over the world are buying books using Amazon.com. According to a research conducted in 2008, the company able to attract about 615 million customers per year to buy books online using their credit card, debit card or through an affiliated bank. Another company which is running an e-commerce business is Dell Inc, a US based company located in Texas, USA. Dell has made rapid progress by launching their e-commerce system which enables the people to buy computers online. In 2007, Fortune magazine ranked Dell as the most admired companies in the USA in recognition of the company's business model.

Based on the current business model, e-commerce can be divided into four main categories as below:

- E-tailing or "virtual storefronts" on Web sites with online catalogs, sometimes gathered into a "virtual mall"
- The gathering and use of demographic data through Web contacts
- Electronic Data Interchange (EDI), the business-to-business exchange of data e-mail and fax and their use as media for reaching prospects and established customers (for example, with newsletters)
- Business-to-business buying and selling (B2B)

E-commerce has gained much recognition through an improved online banking model which directly improved the e-society to a greater level. Some of the advantages of e-commerce are as follows:

1. Increased sale with a larger scale of market
2. Expand the size of the market from national to international hence creating a bigger e-society
3. Customers will be able to enjoy a competitive price as there will be a decrease in the cost of distribution, marketing and processing the goods

E-Government

Due to the rapid development in e-banking, governments has taken the initiative to use information technology to provide government services and initiating transactions between citizens and the government or companies and the government. The system allows the integration of all the government agencies thus creating a virtual organizational integration or famously known as e-government. The e-government will be linked to any affiliated banks for online payment services.

The benefits of e-government includes efficient payment services, improved services, better accessibility of public services, and more transparency and accountability.

The e-Government can be divided into four main categories as below:

- Government-to-Citizen or Government-to-Customer (G2C)
- Government-to-Business (G2B)
- Government-to-Government (G2G)
- Government-to-Employees (G2E)

The common approach used by e-government is to use an integrated electronic service delivery to interconnect the government agencies and the online banking to create a comprehensive e-government solution which will ultimately improve the e-society. The common services provided by the four main categories in affiliation with the online banks are electronic payment system to enable payment for a range of authority services via credit card, direct debit or smart card. Such a solution is increasingly perceived by early adopters, vendors and individuals as the only pragmatic route to achieve a single cohesive system.

Recently, Dubai e-government is pioneering the initiative in the region to provide online services across corporate and community life in the emirate. It also has a vision to integrate individually automated government departments under the single umbrella of the e-Government initiative, thus empowering employees across lines of businesses and levels of government, besides facilitating the lives of citizens and customers of the government. Dubai has taken a lead in the region in deploying e-Government applications and is among the first few governments in the world to provide such integrated services to its citizens. The e-Government portal (http://mobile.dubai.ae) is a single contact point masking the complexity of the bureaucratic procedures, and guiding access to all services in the easiest possible way. Dubai e-government in association with the National

Bank of Abu Dhabi has introduced an innovative Prepaid Card to enable e-payment transactions and expedite the government's online services.

E-Learning

In the area of education, new technologies bring benefits to many areas and contribute to the creation of a resource based e-society. People who were previously excluded from education due to geographical and financial factors are beginning to gain advantage of e-learning. Currently many universities and colleges have started to offer e-learning programs through online registration supported by online payment system linking to the banks.

E-learning can be CD-ROM-based, Network-based, Intranet-based or Internet-based. It can include text, video, audio, animation and virtual environments. It can be a very rich learning experience that can even surpass the level of training you might experience in a crowded classroom. It's self-paced, hands-on learning. E-learning can be divided into four different categories as follows:

Knowledge Databases

This is the most basic e-learning concept featuring a knowledge repository which can be used to look for key phrase or key word. The user will usually search the database or make selection from an alphabetical list. These are usually moderately interactive.

Online Support

Online support is also a form of e-learning and functions in a similar manner to knowledge databases. Online support comes in the form of forums, chat rooms, online bulletin boards, e-mail, or live instant-messaging support. Slightly more interactive than knowledge databases, online support offers the opportunity for more specific questions and answers, as well as more immediate answers.

Asynchronous Training

This is e-learning in the more traditional sense of the word. It involves self-paced learning, CD-ROM-based, Network-based, Intranet-based or Internet-based. It may include access to instructors through online bulletin boards, online discussion groups and e-mail. Or, it may be totally self-contained with links to reference materials in place of a live instructor.

Synchronous Training

Synchronous training is done in real-time with a live instructor facilitating the training. Everyone logs in at a set time and can communicate directly with the instructor and with each other. You can raise your cyber hand and even view the cyber whiteboard. It lasts for a set amount of time -- from a single session to several weeks, months or even years. This type of training usually takes place via Internet Web sites, audio- or video-conferencing, Internet telephony, or even two-way live broadcasts to students in a classroom.

E-Health

One patient, one file – the backbone of an e-health society supported by e-banking system. Everyone wants a world with seamless medical information flow, less waste and fewer risks of errors for both patients' safety and cost reduction. The online system allows X-rays, scans and any electronic records of patients to be digitally transmitted, stored and shared by multiple parties in a fully secured environment allows any hospitals around the world to access the patients' data. Health organizations increase work efficiency and achieve savings by rationalizing back office processes with broadband-based applications.

The e-Health approach is to move away from a system where the patient must carry parts of their medical history around a complex network of care. Through the smart use of technologies

and interconnection in between medical centre, medical records will be shared will be able to directly and securely access all medical information about a patient at their fingertips through online payment for any data access, thus enhancing their capability to deliver safe and effective care.

Most of the hospitals are implementing an Enterprise Information Repository, a centralized, state wide electronic repository of accurate and reliable patient information for care providers both within and external to the hospital. The electronic health records will be made accessible to care providers, and ultimately patients through secure Internet User Portals supported by e-banking. A number of key new information systems are used to support the electronic record and improve health care practice including medications reporting, diagnostic imaging, resource scheduling, community health, mental health and chronic disease management, and e-Prescribing and e-Ordering supported by e-banking.

E-Entertainment

The entertainment industry is fast moving into the new era of entertainment technology via e-banking. Most of the entertainment industries have realized that internet is the new source of entertainment delivery system.

For instance, 40 percent of Americans now watch television shows online, a 50 percent rise compared to the results of the first part of the Deloitte & Touche survey in an earlier survey (Helen, 2008). Most of the entertainment advertisers have also decided to advertise on the internet which includes online movies, mp3 songs, chatting session with celebrities and internet television. E-banking is used to support any online transactions that need to be done by the customers.

Current mobile phones are also being used for to purchase entertainment contents and, yet again, there has been a 50 percent rise in the number of Americans who do so to 24 percent, since the first part of the survey was carried out (Helen,

2008). Furthermore according to Helen, over half of Americans now use social networking sites, chat rooms or online messaging and 45 percent have social networking profiles, found the survey.

According to the field study of J. Eighmey, entertainment when accessing a site plays the most important role. The information offered by the site is the second most essential factor. According to a survey conducted by TGI Brasil, there were 1,089 home Internet users which are projected to 2,546,000 persons in the measured universe of 51,917,000 persons. These respondents were shown a list and asked to indicate whether they used the Internet for these reasons. Overall, 40% of the home Internet users indicated that they used the Internet for entertainment such as purchasing online songs, movies and other multimedia contents and 73% of them said that they used the Internet to obtain information. Also, 32% of the home Internet users indicated that they used the Internet for entertainment as well as information. The e-entertainment is fully supported by e-banking in order to make online purchasing.

IMPROVING THE PERFORMANCE OF E-SOCIETY THROUGH E-BANKING

As technologies have been increasingly developing, electronic products permeate into various sorts of areas and provide an opportunity for the creation of e-society. Nowadays, not electronic goods en rich people's life but also electronic services step into daily life. Banking is one of the most financial activities in this day and age. The number of financial transaction is accomplished though electronic banking which is a new type of banking has been progressing in past decades. Basically, the characteristics of electronic banking are flexible operating time and place and efficient. This has ultimately improved the performance of e-society through e-banking.

The primary advantage of electronic banking is convenience in terms of flexible operating time and place. Thus, people could simply conduct any banking transaction electronically via whatever computer access instead physically go to a branch bank. Moreover, it is always available for people in 24 hours a day, 7days a week. Hence, it is not necessary to worry about the opening time conflict with individual schedule. In short, anywhere, anytime bank is typical feature of electronic banking.

Using Online Banking Services and Products

The e-banking, both domestic and international can be broadly categorized into three categories:

- Basic information web sites, which only broadcast information on banking products and services offered to bank customers and the general public.
- Simple transactional web sites which allow bank customers to submit applications for different services make enquiries about balances and submit instructions to the bank but not permit any account transfers.
- Advanced transactional web sites that allow bank customers to electronically transfer funds to/from their accounts, pay bills and conduct other banking transactions on-line.

E-banking is the new generation tool of banks launched for maximum convenience and efficiency in generating bank transactions via the internet. It's thus called "online banking". The main e-banking services include:

- Opening a new current or saving account
- Balance inquiries
- Account statements
- Money transfers to different banks
- Paying for products or services
- Checking services

- Applying for debit card
- Applying for credit card and get prior approval
- Applying for loans and get prior approval
- Applying for E-Mobile phone banking
- Applying for E-cash card
- Applying for E-Web Shopping card

Many businesses accept various forms of electronic payments for their products and services. Financial institutions play an important role in electronic payment systems by creating and distributing a variety of electronic payment instruments, accepting a similar variety of instruments, processing those payments, and participating in clearing and settlement systems. However, increasingly, financial institutions are competing with third parties to provide support services for e-commerce payment systems. Among the electronic payments mechanisms that financial institutions provide for e-commerce are automated clearing house (ACH) debits and credits through the Internet, electronic bill payment and presentment, electronic checks, e-mail money, and electronic credit card payments.

Most financial institutions permit intrabank transfers between a customer's accounts as part of their basic transactional e-banking services. However, third-party transfers – with their heightened risk for fraud – often require additional security safeguards in the form of additional authentication and payment confirmation.

Bill payment services permit customers to electronically instruct their financial institution to transfer funds to a business's account at some future specified date. Customers can make payments on a one-time or recurring basis, with fees typically assessed as a "per item" or monthly charge. In response to the customer's electronic payment instructions, the financial institution (or its bill payment provider) generates an electronic transaction – usually an automated clearinghouse (ACH) credit – or mails a paper check to the business on the customer's behalf.

Internet-based cash management is the commercial version of retail bill payment. Business customers use the system to initiate third-party payments or to transfer money between company accounts. Cash management services also include minimum balance maintenance, recurring transfers between accounts and on-line account reconciliation. Businesses typically require stronger controls, including the ability to administer security and transaction controls among several users within the business.

E-Banking Strategies to Improve the E-Society

In order to enhance and ensure a consistent growth in e-banking, one of the first elements that need to be addressed in e-commerce transactions is to guarantee that a valid contract has been entered between the parties and it is secured. Assessing the validity of contracts is complicated in the Internet environment because the contracts are paperless. Digital signatures are therefore essential in helping to promote e-commerce because they ensure that all parties have entered in a binding contractual agreement. There are several strategies that need to be used in e-banking as below:

- Have a clear and widely disseminated strategy that is driven from the top and takes into account the effects of e-banking, together with an effective process for measuring performance against it.
- Take into account the effect that e-provision will have upon their business risk exposures and manage these accordingly.
- Undertake market research, adopt systems with adequate capacity and scalability, undertake proportional advertising campaigns and ensure that they have adequate staff coverage and a suitable business continuity plan.

- Ensure they have adequate management information in a clear and comprehensible format.
- Take a strategic and proactive approach to information security, maintaining adequate staff expertise, building in best practice controls and testing and updating these as the market develops. Make active use of system based security management and monitoring tools.
- Ensure that crisis management processes are able to cope with Internet related incidents.

In order to enhance the usage of e-banking among the e-society, the banks need to ensure it is aligned to or addressed the needs of the customers as below:

Organizational Flexibility

The first element is structural flexibility among the banks and the industry, which is about organizing different functions of an organization around business processes, rather than traditional hierarchical structures, so that a structure changes according to the changes in business environments and the needs of the customers. Having a policy of selecting best of breed products and an ability to integrate them, adds another dimension to the organization's business freedom. This enables it to choose the systems components according to the e-society's requirements, rather than building the business around its systems capabilities. Promotion of e-commerce within an organization is likely to increase an organization's ability to change itself quickly.

Fast and Responsive Products/Services

This factor mainly involve Web-specific marketing, rapid delivery of products/services, personalized marketing, fast responsive and integrated business processes, and having sufficient human/financial resources to capture the e-society market. Effective Web-specific marketing and personalizing products to individual needs, requires gathering relevant data about customers and using it to build long-term relationships. Integrated business processes and systems create opportunities to trace the trails of each transaction by a customer. If that transaction is aggregated with the customer's other transactions and analyzed, it may yield invaluable historical information about consumer preferences and how e-banking may cater for and influence those preferences. If the customer's transaction history is analyzed along with that of other customers, the bank may discover a segment preference that can be satisfied by new products and services.

Expansion of Services

In e-commerce expansion of services starts from development of an interactive and user-friendly website. The website along with associated functions or services has to be available 24 hours every day of the year. Some financial sector organizations, such as Alliance and Leicester bank are offering extra services such as car and house sales on their website, through their partner organizations. Not only does this result in extra revenues from new services, it often results in increased sales of existing products. For example, when a customer buys a car through the Alliance and Leicester website, their first choice for finance is likely to be same bank which is advertised on the same website. This process can be taken further by offering discounts on packages of different products. This, combined with other factors discussed in this section, should increase the ability to grow the e-society.

Enhanced Customer Service

This factor is mainly concerned with improving customer service to accommodate ever rising expectation and addressing their fears about the security of their personal data and transactions. The often cited time squeeze from long commutes, heavy workload, family obligations, and household management problems for consumers, are pushing them towards integrated services that can speed up financial procedures. Once they become aware of the integrated and secure services available somewhere,

Factors Influencing the Development of E-Banking in E-Society

The diffusion of innovative technology such as e-banking is highly related to communication channels, individuals, organizational members and efficiency. Accordingly there are eight important factors which influence the use of e-banking in e-society as below.

Shared Value

E-society may refuse any new technologies that fail to provide value to them. Customer trust can be affected by shared value such as ethics, security and privacy which are the main components of shared values. Shared value has a significant positive impact and is the most important determinant of trust. Shared value directly and positively affects e-trust among internet banking users.

Security Issues

If a person has a disposition to trust, he/she is less likely to see the potential for risk, and implicit trust between people can lead to long-term personal relationships, but if the relationship is broken, this will affect the organization in which the individual has placed trust. Security was found to be the most important determinant of consumer trust in the online retailer context. Security systems have a significant impact on internet banking adoption in the e-society.

Reputation

Banks' negative reputation can be negatively correlated with customer trust. In order to be trusted, supplier firms have to have a good reputation, which means that they have to be honest and concerned about their customers.

Customers' Experiences

Customers' experience may affect trust when it comes to purchasing products or services online. Trust may be built incrementally following experience online, and customers may build trust by starting with small purchases and building up to bigger ones.

Communication

Communication has a significant positive role on trust and speed of response is the most critical to communication. It is considered that quality of response is a significant component of communication between customers and online retailers. Personalized and customized customers dialogues that are helpful, positive, timely, useful, easy and pleasant can strengthen a trust-based customer relationship.

Perceived Usefulness

It is believed that perceived usefulness and perceived easy of use is fundamental determinants of use acceptance. Perceived usefulness is usually affected by the level of customer trust found that perceived usefulness of online banking were the most influential factors in explaining the use of online banking.

Perceived Ease of Use

The appearance of a web site, ease of navigation and customer-oriented interface attract a positive customer response, but difficulties with navigation and links can deter online customers. Ease of use seems to be one of important to use internet banking, which may be related to customer apprehension about the efforts required to learn to use internet banking and customer interest in new services provided by internet banking.

Customers' Attitudes toward Using Internet Banking

Customers' attitudes are a significant factor affecting customer behaviors in accepting or rejecting technology. It was found that the relationship between attitude towards using and usage is very significant. Attitude towards using systems was significantly affected by perceived usefulness and ease of use, but usefulness was stronger in its relation with attitude to use.

Internet Banking Usage

Perceived usefulness and ease of use are the most critical variables in predicting whether a technology tends to be used or not. Usefulness had a significantly strong relation with usage, greater than that between perceived ease of use and usage.

Risks Management and Challenges in E-Banking

A number of specific risk management principles need to be adhered by the banking institutions to extend and develop their risk management oversight of e-banking business. The risk management can be divided into three broad categories.

Board and Management Oversight

These focus on the responsibility of the Directors and Senior Management for development of the institution's business strategy and management oversight of risks.

They are obliged to document and explain the strategic decisions of how the bank will develop their e-banking services. This process encapsulates accountabilities, policies and controls to address risks. Management supervision should include approval and review of the bank's security control process, development and maintenance of security control infrastructure, safeguard of e-banking systems and data from internal and external threats.

Equally critical is establishing the process for management of the risks arising from the increased complexity of reliance on outsourcing and third party arrangements for operation and performance of the e-banking services.

Legal and Reputational Risk Management

Banks open themselves to legal and reputational risks if they are unable in practice to provide a consistent, timely, high standard service in accordance with the expectations they have set for the customer base.

E-banking services must have the capability to deliver e-banking services to all users, maintaining the utmost levels of availability. To support this they must have in place response mechanisms which reduce to an absolute minimum operational, legal and reputational risks arising from events and incidents both internal and external. Response mechanisms cover business continuity and contingency planning and their attendant communications strategies.

Security Controls

The security challenges to e-banking services are greater than those of conventional banking services. They require more specific attention by bank management. As part of their responsibility for ensuring appropriate levels of security control, a number of detailed measures must be addressed:

- establishment of relevant authorization privileges and authentication measures
- logical and physical accesses and controls
- sufficient infrastructure security for maintenance of appropriate boundaries and restrictions on internal and external user activity
- data integrity for transactions, records and information
- clear audit trails for e-banking transactions
- measures to preserve confidentiality of e-banking information

The dimensions of e-banking risk management differ and extend when a cross-border dimension is added encapsulating enhanced strategic, reputational, operational risk as well as country risk. Consider some of the detailed issues:

- Non compliance with different national laws, including applicable consumer protection laws, advertising and disclosure laws, record keeping and reporting requirements, privacy and money laundering laws.
- The legal uncertainties over which countries laws apply to cross-border e-commerce activities.
- The respective roles and responsibilities of home country and local authorities for internet based transactions with local residents.

There is a greater requirement for the home country supervisor to ensure that its regulatory regime extends to adequate supervision of its banks' e-banking cross-border activities:

- "Prior to engagement in cross-border e-banking activities, a banking institution should conduct appropriate risk assessment and due diligence. It needs to establish an effective risk management program for these activities."

- "A banking institution intending to engage in cross-border e-banking activities should provide sufficient disclosure on its Web site to allow potential customers to determine the bank's identity, home country and regulatory license."

SUCCESSFUL IMPLEMENTATION OF E-BANKING

Implementation Structure

Electronic banking capabilities have changed the framework of payment systems, but banks will continue to participate in a number of dynamic roles, ranging from issuer to transaction authorizer and processor. E-banking systems can vary significantly in their configuration depending on a number of factors. Financial institutions should choose their e-banking system configuration, including outsourcing relationships, based on four factors:

a. Strategic objectives for e-banking
b. Scope, scale and complexity of equipment, systems and activities
c. Technology expertise
d. Security and internal control requirements

The implementation of e-banking can be structured into three main components as shown in Table 1.

Payment systems can be broadly categorized according to process methodology, in addition to system components and structure. The combination of such attributes will determine - to a large degree - the systems' inherent risk. Importantly, risk will vary significantly depending on system implementation, administration, and the controls employed. In 1999, the Office of the Comptroller of the Currency (OCC) highlighted a number of characteristics consistent with an electronic payment system, many of which are currently relevant as shown in Table 1.

Table 1 also highlights the primary decision areas in developing a payment system. Software is not specifically included, since it serves principally to convert the decisions regarding components, methodology and structure into an operative system.

Financial institutions may choose to support their e-banking services internally or can outsource any aspect of their e-banking systems to third parties. The following entities could provide or host (i.e., allow applications to reside on their servers) e-banking-related services for financial institutions:

a. Another financial institution
b. Internet banking software vendor
c. Internet Service provider
d. Bill payment provider
e. Credit Bureau
f. Security Service provider

The components of e-banking as shown in Table 1 rely on a good administration system such as:

a. Website design and hosting
b. Firewall configuration and management
c. Network administration
d. Security management
e. Internet banking server
f. E-commerce applications
g. Automated decision support systems
h. Intrusion detection system

These administration system works together to deliver e-banking services. Each component represents a control point to consider. Through a combination of internal and outsourced solutions, management has many alternatives when determining the overall system configuration for the various components of an e-banking system. First,

Table 1. Components of e-banking

Component Groups	Details
System Components	1. System Hardware
	2. Chip versus magnetic strip technology
	3. Card versus computer-based systems
Process Methodology	1. Batch versus real-time processing
	2. Online versus offline access
System Structure	1. Legal currency versus branded (proprietary) value
	2. Single versus multiple currency
	3. Debit versus stored value based systems
	4. Open versus closed systems
	5. Reloadable versus single use systems
	6. Controlled versus secured access
	7. Single versus multiple purpose
	8. Integrated versus stand alone systems
	9. User anonymity
	10. Payment mechanics (buyer and seller interaction)
	11. Payment system settlement (processing)
	12. Transaction size (micro or large-dollar payments)
	13. Geographic reach

one or more technology service providers can host the e-banking application and numerous network components. The institution's service provider hosts the institution's website, Internet banking server, firewall, and intrusion detection system. While the institution does not have to manage the daily administration of these component systems, its management and board remain responsible for the content, performance, and security of the e-banking system.

In all cases, there must be trust in the participants that issue, process, and settle payments. This level of confidence in the process is crucial to a payment system's acceptance, and these factors have historically maintained the banking industry's central position within the payment system. Payment systems are evaluated on a number of criteria, including:

- User privacy;
- Transaction legitimacy, security, and non-repudiation;
- System dependability, efficiency, and cost
- Merchant acceptance and convenience

Apart from that, the front-end controls related to the initiation, storage, and transmission of bill payment transactions prior to their entry into the industry's retail payment systems need to be looked into as well. The extent of front-end operating controls directly under the financial institution's control varies with the system configuration.

Best Practices

E-banking can improve a bank's efficiency and competitiveness, so that existing and potential customers can benefit from a greater degree of convenience in effecting transactions. This increased level of convenience offered by the bank, when combined with new services, can expand the bank's target customers beyond those in traditional markets. Consequently, financial institutions are therefore becoming more aggres-

sive in adopting electronic banking capabilities that include sophisticated marketing systems, remote-banking capabilities, and stored value programs. Internationally, familiar examples include telephone banking, automated teller networks, and automated clearinghouse systems. Such technological advances have brought greater sophistication to all users, commercial and "the man in the street".

A bank may be faced with different levels of risks and expectations arising from electronic banking as opposed to traditional banking. Furthermore, customers who rely on e-banking services may have greater intolerance for a system that is unreliable or one that does not provide accurate and current information. Clearly, the longevity of e-banking depends on its accuracy, reliability and accountability. The challenge for many banks is to ensure that savings from the electronic banking technology more than offset the costs and risks involved in such changes to their systems.

According to best practices in e-banking, electronic capabilities can be segregated into three (3) categories by degree of functionality. These levels range from Level I to Level III systems

Level 1: Information Only Systems

Banks should ensure that consumers are alerted to the potential risks associated with unencrypted electronic mail sent over such a medium. Information-only systems are defined as those that allow access to general-purpose marketing and other publicly available information, or the transmission of non-sensitive electronic email.

Level 2: Electronic Information Transfer Systems

Since communication and system security risks include data privacy and confidentiality, data integrity, authentication, non-repudiation, and access system design, some risk mitigation methods are therefore necessary. Electronic information transfer systems are interactive in that they provide the ability to transmit sensitive messages, documents, or files among a group of users, for example, a bank's web site that allows a customer to submit online loan or deposit account applications.

Level 3: Fully Transactional Information Transfer Systems

Fully Transactional Information Transfer Systems represent the highest degree of functionality and also involve high levels of potential risks. These systems provide the capabilities for information-only applications, electronic information transfer systems, as well as online, transactional banking services. These capabilities are provided by interactive connectivity between a customer's device and the bank's internal systems. Many systems will however involve a combination of these capabilities

Each bank must evaluate the risk it faces and its readiness to react to those risks. Electronic banking relies on a networked environment, such as the Internet. Importantly, not all networks carry the same degree of risk, and so not all networks are equally vulnerable or sensitive. Although the current dollar volume of e-banking activity is small relative to the overall financial activity, the associated risks can be significant. Electronic banking can substantially increase access to a bank's internal systems via public networks, and expose those systems to hackers, viruses and other forms of risk.

Any reliance on service providers and software vendors for e-banking will require sound risk management practices. Typically, e-banking can increase a bank's reliance on service providers and software vendors who design, implement, or even manage these electronic systems. The degree to which banks choose to operate their systems through service providers and software vendors will affect the extent of the bank's involvement in actual systems design, planning, and other day-to-day operational and monitoring

issues. Essentially, banks that outsource all of these functions will initially have less "hands on" involvement in detecting unauthorized intrusions into a bank's e-banking system, compared with banks that perform some or all of their security and operational functions in-house.

Risk identification and analysis should direct the bank to adopt appropriate oversight and review guidelines, operating policies and procedures, audit requirements, and contingency plans. These risks can be mitigated by adopting a comprehensive risk management program that incorporates a sound strategic plan. Importantly, the extent of a financial institution's risk management program should be commensurate with the complexity and sophistication of the activities in which it engages. Essentially, a bank which offers a simple information-only site is generally not expected to have undertaken the same level of planning and risk management as Institutions that engage in more complex activities.

Each financial institution should apply guidelines based on its scope and level of sophistication. Typically, electronic banking amplifies the scale of exposure of banks to traditional risks, such as transaction, strategic, reputational, and compliance risk, among others. Many of these risk categories have been identified in the Basel Committee's *Core Principles for Effective Banking Supervision*, published in September 1997. As information systems become more connected and interdependent, the risk of computer intrusion will increase. Arguably, this is the single most important aspect of the 'new' electronic delivery system. Banks with weak physical security and systems substantially increase their exposure to a plethora of risks, many of which could lead to collapse. Potential consequences include direct dollar loss, damaged reputation, improper disclosure, and lawsuits or regulatory sanction

E-banking should be consistent with the bank's overall strategic and business plans, and adequate expertise should be employed to operate and maintain such systems. It is therefore imperative that e-banking risks be managed as part of a bank's overall risk management process. The levels of risk assumed need to be consistent with the bank's overall risk tolerance, and not exceed its ability to manage and control risks.

Banks' management should establish an effective planning process to implement and monitor systems. Overall, through the various controls, programs and policies, banks should seek to:

- Adopt effective and reliable security controls for electronic banking, that integrate into the bank's overall security program, including system-wide access controls, user authentication, encryption, transaction verification, and virus protection controls;
- Update "know-your-customer" and suspicious activity reporting (SAR) considerations consistent with appropriate identification, authentication and transaction verification methods
- Implement policies and controls according to the sensitivity and importance of data
- Update plans, policies and systems regularly, removing key elements of sensitivity risk assessments
- Establish effective risk monitoring processes, with specific emphasis on security and performance monitoring, as well as audit/quality assurance reviews
- Develop e-banking systems in tandem with regularly tested bank contingency, business continuity and customer service plans
- Identify expertise, as well as address staffing needs, and training requirements
- Monitor developments and changes in relevant consumer and banking laws, rules and regulations, and take adequate measures to ensure compliance
- Ensure that customer/depositor education is sufficient for the optimal use of the authentication and transactional functions of e-banking

- Assess whether e-banking products offered may be subjected to unexpected assertions of jurisdiction by courts, agencies and taxing authorities in new geographic, product, or service markets
- Assess the legality of customer transfers and ensure that all relevant information has been included

FUTURE RESEARCH DIRECTION

This chapter has focused on factors which could determine the development of e-society through e-banking. As such there is still room for further research into improving the performance of e-society through e-banking.

Most of the factors are highly related to the user acceptance towards the development of banking technology via e-banking. However it is suggested that a research on the determinants of behavioral intention and attitude towards e-banking to be conducted to further understand the acceptance of e-banking among e-society based on users' level of experience. The future studies should also be carried out on non-internet users to investigate their adoption intentions of such services.

The study on adoption intentions of Internet banking services should also be extended to corporate customers. Comparison can then be made between individual customers and corporate customers in terms of the factors influencing their adoption decisions, the criteria for selecting an online banking service, and the types of products and services perceived to be useful. This could further enhance the performance of e-society in adopting e-banking. Additional research, both longitudinal and cross-sectional, is needed to examine the differences of this framework as users evolving from being aware of the e-service (internet banking), to having experience with the e-service (internet banking), to being continued use of the e-service (internet banking).

CONCLUSION

The evolution and growth of e-banking has been phenomenal during the last decade. The adoption of internet technologies around the world and the implementation of key regulatory measures, such as electronic signatures and cross-border contacts should spur further growth in e-commerce and e-society as a whole. Financial services industry was among the earliest adaptors of information technology. E-business in the financial services industry has been slow to evolve because of complexity of inter-organizational relationships, regulations, security concerns, lack of standards, and conservative principles.

E-banking builds on new business models and processes and demands new paradigm and software to clearly position finance as a service center within e-society. The benefits of e-banking towards e-society are many and include: reducing the cost of transaction processing, expanding the information scope of accounting and finance's systems, extending the information reach of the finance department, and improving the quality of financial information. However, to realize these gains, finance professionals must embrace and leverage new technology, realign the traditional accounting mind-set and skill set, engage in process transformation initiatives, and focus on delivering value-added information services to the organization. Furthermore, they must have a solid understanding and implementation of the technology platform.

The impact of the e-banking on e-society is clear. However, certain trends are emerging: expansion of B2B e-finance, automation of customer services, consolidation in local and regional financial operations, growth in global services, migration towards 24/7 global trading, blurring of business and product lines, disintermediation of traditional products and services, creation of alternative partnerships and alliances, and consolidation of portals, storefronts, exchanges, and marketplaces. This study has extended the e-banking

by considering the characteristics of e-banking and factors that influence the development of e-banking. This study shows that recognizing both technological and trust-based issues are important in increasing customer's behavioral intention to use e-banking. The results of this study provide valuable insights into the online banking products and services, challenges in e-banking and best practices approach for e-banking adoption.

REFERENCES

Barra, R. (1990). Interactive innovation in financial and business services: the vanguard of the service revolution. *Research Policy, 19*, 215–237. doi:10.1016/0048-7333(90)90037-7

Birch, D., & Young, M. A. (1997). Financial Services and the Internet: What Does Cyberspace Mean for the Financial Services Industry. *Internet Research, 7*(2), 120–128. doi:10.1108/10662249710165262

Chen, T. (1999). Critical success factors for various strategies in the banking industry. *International Journal of Bank Marketing, 17*(12), 83–92. doi:10.1108/02652329910258943

Chorafas, D. N. (1987). *Strategic Planning for Electronic Banking, Butterworths, London. CSFI (Centre for the Study of Financial Innovation) (2000), Banana Skins 2000*. London: CSFI.

Claessens, S. (2001).*E-finance in emerging markets: is leapfrogging possible?* Financial Sector Discussion Paper, No. 7, World Bank, June.

Claessens, S., Glaessner, T., & Klingebiel, D. (2000), *Electronic finance: reshaping financial-landscapes around the world.*Financial Sector Discussion Paper, No. 4, World Bank, September, available at: www.worldbank.org

Crede, A. (1995). Electronic Commerce and the Banking Industry: The Requirement and Opportunities for New Payment Systems Using the Internet. *Journal of Computer-Mediated Communication, 1*(3).

Daniel, E. (1999). Provision of electronic banking in the UK and Republic of Ireland. *International Journal of Bank Marketing, 17*(2), 72–83. doi:10.1108/02652329910258934

Eighmey, J. (1997). Profiling User Responses to Commercial Web Sites. *Journal of Advertising Research, 37,* 59–66.

Lagoutte, V. (1996). *The Direct Banking Challenge.* Unpublished Honours Thesis, Middlesex University

Leggat, H. (2008). *Americans turn to Internet for entertainment.* BizReport Research. http://www.bizreport.com/2008/01/americans_turn_to_internet_for_entertainment.html

Nehmzow, C. (1997). The Internet will Shake Banking Medieval Foundations. *Journal of Internet Banking and Commerce, 2*(2).

Ooi, S. (1999) *Surge in E-commerce Transactions* (p. 6). SME IT Guid.

Paper, D. No. 7, World Bank, June. Claessens, S., Glaessner, T. and Klingebiel, D. (2000), *Electronic finance: reshaping financial landscapes around the world.* Financial Sector Discussion Paper, No. 4, World Bank, September, available at: www.worldbank.org

Park, R. (1999). The global transformation of financial services. *European Business Journal, 11*(1), 7–16.

Pavlou, P. A. (2001). *Consumer Intentions to adopt Electronic Commerce – Incorporating Trust and Risk in the Technology Acceptance Model.*(pp.1-28) DIGIT Workshop, New Orleans, Louisiana, 16 December 2001, Available, www.mis.temp.edu/digit/digit2001/files/consumerIntentionsToAdopt_Digit2001.

Reiser, S. J. (1997), The information highway and electronic commerce: what does it mean for you? *Current Issues,* March, pp. 12-15.

Scarborough, H., & Lannon, R. (1988). The successful exploitation of new technology in banking. *Journal of General Management, 13*(3), 38–51.

Seitz, J., & Stickel, E. (1998). Internet Banking: An Overview. *Journal of Internet Banking and Commerce, 3*(1).

Ternullo, G. (1997)Banking on the Internet: New Technologies, New Opportunities and New Risks. Boston Regional Outlook, Second Quarter (http://www.fdic.gov/index.html).

Warner, J. (1996)Internet Waits in Wings for Banking Dinosaurs. The *Independent, August 17,* pp.17

ADDITIONAL READING

Allen, F., McAndrews, J., & Stratran, P. (2002). E-finance: an introduction. *Journal of Financial Services Research, 22*(1-2), 5–27. doi:10.1023/A:1016007126394

Barnes, S.J. & R, T. (2003). Measuring web site quality improvements: a case study of the forum on strategic management knowledge exchange. *Industrial Management & Data Systems, 103*(5), 297–309. doi:10.1108/02635570310477352

Beckett, A., Hewer, P., & Howcroft, B. (2000). An exposition of consumer behavior in the financial services industry. *International Journal of Bank Marketing, 18*(1), 15–26. doi:10.1108/02652320010315325

Birch, D., & Young, M. A. (1997). Financial Services and the Internet: What Does Cyberspace Mean for the Financial Services Industry. *Internet Research, 7*(2), 120–128. doi:10.1108/10662249710165262

Bohle, K. (2002), Integration of Electronic Payment Systems into B2C Internet Commerce – Problems and Perspectives. *Background Paper No. 8*; Electronic Payment Systems Observatory (ePSO)

Chou, D., & Chou, A. Y. (2000). A guide to the internet revolution in banking. *Information Systems Management, 17*(2), 51–57. doi:10.1201/1 078/43191.17.2.20000301/31227.6

Claessens, S., Glaessner, T., & Klingebiel, D. (2000).Electronic finance: reshaping financial landscapes around the world. *Financial Sector Discussion Paper*, No. 4, World Bank, September, available at: www.worldbank.org

Crede, A. (1995). Electronic Commerce and the Banking Industry: The Requirement and Opportunities for New Payment Systems Using the Internet. *Journal of Computer-Mediated Communication, 1*(3).

Dandapani, K., Alfried Lassar, S., & Sharon, L. (2004). Success and failure in web-based financial services. *Communications of the ACM, 47*(5). doi:10.1145/986213.986233

Daniel, E. (1999). Provision of electronic banking in the UK and Republic of Ireland. *International Journal of Bank Marketing, 17*(2), 72–83. doi:10.1108/02652329910258934

Eighmey. (1997)Profiling User Responses to Commercial Web Sites. *Journal of Advertising Research*, 37, 59-66.

Gournaris, S. P., Stathakopoulos, V., & Athanassopoulos, A. D. (2003). Antecedents to perceived service quality: an exploratory study in the banking industry. *International Journal of Bank Marketing, 21*(4), 168–190. doi:10.1108/02652320310479178

Jayawardhena, C. (2004). Measurement of service quality in internet banking: the development of an Instrument. *Journal of Marketing Management, 20*, 185–207. doi:10.1362/026725704773041177

Kolodinsky, J. M., Hogarth, J. M., & Hilgert, M. A. (2004). The adoption of electronic banking technologies by US Consumers. *International Journal of Bank Marketing, 22*(4), 238–259. doi:10.1108/02652320410542536

Kontogeorgou, P., & Alexiou, M. G. (2002), *Enhancing consumer confidence in electronic commerce: consumer protection in electronic payments*. 17th Annual BILETA Conference, Free University, Amsterdam, April.

Leggat, H. (2008). Americans turn to Internet for entertainment. *BizReport Research*, Retrieved from http://www.bizreport.com/2008/01/americans_turn_to_internet_for_entertainment.html

Malhotra, R., & Malhotra, D. K. (2006).The impact of internet and e-commerce on the evolving business models in the financial services industry. *International Journal of Electronic Business*, available at: www.inderscience.com/storage/f896101112715243.pdf

Mersha, T., & Adlakha, V. (1992). Attributes of service quality: the consumers' perspective. *International Journal of Service Industry Management, 3*(3), 34–45. doi:10.1108/09564239210015157

Nehmzow, C. (1997). The Internet will Shake Banking Medieval Foundations. *Journal of Internet Banking and Commerce, 2*(2).

Ooi, S. (1999). *Surge in E-commerce Transactions* (p. 6). SME IT Guid.

Park, R. (1999). The global transformation of financial services. *European Business Journal, 11*(1), 7–16.

Scarborough, H., & Lannon, R. (1988). The successful exploitation of new technology in banking. *Journal of General Management, 13*(3), 38–51.

Seitz, J., & Stickel, E. (1998). Internet Banking: An Overview. *Journal of Internet Banking and Commerce, 3*(1).

Shanmugam, Bala, K.G. (2003). *Electronic Banking in Malaysia.* IBBM Press

Shanmugam, Suganthi, Balachander (2001). I-banking in Malaysia. *Banking in the New Millenium.* ICFAI Publishing

Shanmugam & Sohail. (2002, March). *Electronic Banking & Customer Preferences in Malaysia: An Empirical Investigation.* Paper presented at the The Fourth Workshop on Information and Computer Science, King Fahd University of Petroleum and Minerals

Shanmugam (2001). Finance in Knowledge-based Economy. In Abdullai (Ed), *Malaysia and the Knowledge-based Economy: Prospects, Challenges and the Road Ahead.* Singapore: Pelanduk Press.

Stoneman, B. (2003). Banking Strategies; *BAI*-http://www.bai.org/bankingstrategies/2000-july-aug/ChoicesChoices/

Trocchia, P. J., & Janda, S. (2000). A phenomenological investigation of Internet usage among older individuals. *Journal of Consumer Marketing, 17*(7), 605–616. doi:10.1108/07363760010357804

Yuntsai, C., Chiwei, L., & Jianru, C. (2004). Understanding m-commerce payment systems through the analytic hierarchy process. *Journal of Business Research, 57*(12), 1423–1430. doi:10.1016/S0148-2963(02)00432-0

KEY TERMS AND DEFINITIONS

Business-to-Consumer Electronic Business: It describes activities of businesses serving end consumers with products or services. An example of a business-to-consumer transaction would be a person buying a book and initiating a purchase and payment transactions.

Digital Signature: A digital signature is a mathematical scheme for demonstrating the authenticity of a digital message or document.

Electronic Banking: Electronic banking is an online banking which allows the customers to perform financial transactions through internet.

Electronic Data Interchange (EDI): EDI is a structured transmission of data between organizations by transferring electronic documents from one computer system to another.

Globalization: in broad terms " 'globalisation' is a short form for a cluster of related changes. (1) Economic changes that include the internationalisation of production, the harmonisation of tastes and standards and the greatly increased mobility of capital and of transnational corporations. (2) Ideological changes that emphasise investment and trade liberalisation, deregulation and private enterprise. (3) New information and communication technologies that shrink the globe and signal a shift from goods to services.

Intranet: Intranet can be defined as a private network that is contained within an organization to share information among the employees in the enterprise.

Virtual-Mall: A virtual mall is defined as an internet website offering products or services.

Compilation of References

Aarma, A., & Vensel, V. (2001). Banks' retail customer satisfaction and development of bank-customer relationships. In Vensel, V., & Wihlborg, C. (Eds.), Estonia on the Threshold of the European Union: Financial Sector and Enterprise Restructuring in the Changing Economic Environment. Tallinn Technical University.

Abdul-Gader, A. H. (1997). Information system strategic for multinational companies in Persian Gulf Countries. International Journal of Information Management, 17(1), 3–12. doi:10.1016/S0268-4012(96)00038-2

Abe, M., & Fujisaki, E. (1996). How to Date Blind Signatures. Advances in Cryptology (pp.244-251), (ASIACRYPT '96. Binh D. Vo, (2007), A Fair Payment Scheme with On-line Anonymous Transfer (pp.3-27) MS.c Thesis, MIT.

Abou-Zeid, E. S. (2003). Developing business aligned knowledge management strategy. In E Coakes, Knowledge management current issues and challenges (pp. 156–172). Hershey, PA: IRM Press.

Abu-Nimeh, S., Nappa, D., Wang, X., & Nair, S. (2007). A Comparison of Machine Learning Techniques for Phishing Detection (pp.60-69). APWG eCrime Researchers Summit, Pittsburgh, PA, USA.

Afuah, A., & Tucci, C. (2003). Internet Business Models and Strategies. New York: McGraw-Hill.

Aidemark, J., & Sterner, H. (2003), A framework for strategic balancing of knowledge management initiatives. In Proceeding of the 36th Hawaii International Conference on System Sciences (HICSS'O3), 6-9 Jan. 2003, Hawaii, USA

Ajayi, O. (1991). The Regulation of banks and financial institutions. Lagos, Nigeria: Greyhouse African Resources Development Project.

Aladwani, A. (2001). Online banking: A field study of drivers, development challenges, and expectations. International Journal of Information Management, 21, 213–225. doi:10.1016/S0268-4012(01)00011-1

Al-Ammary, J., & Fung, C. C. (2007). Knowledge Management in the Gulf Cooperation Council (GCC) Countries: a Study on the Alignment between KM and Business Strategy. In Cader, Y. (Ed.), Knowledge Management Integrated – Concepts and Practice (pp. 187–211). Australia: Heidelberg Press.

Al-Ammary. Jaflah Hassan (2008). Knowledge Management Strategic Alignment in the Banking Sector at the Gulf Cooperation Council (GCC) Countries, PhD. Dissertation, University of Murdoch, Perth, Australia

Al-Ashban, A. A., & Burney, M. A. (2001). Customer adoption of tele-banking technology: the case of Saudi Arabia. International Journal of Bank Marketing, 19(5), 191–200. doi:10.1108/02652320110399683

Alavi, M & Leidner DE (1999). Knowledge Management systems: Issues, challenges, and benefits, Communication of the Association of Information Systems, 1, Article 7, Feb 1999.

Alexander von Graevenitz, G. (2007). Biometric Authentication In Relation To Payment Systems And Atms. Datenschutz und Datensicherheit, 31(X), 1–3.

Albrecht, K. (2002)., Supermarket cards: The tip of the retail surveillance iceberg. Denver University Law Review,. 79, 4, 534–539 and 558–565.

Al-Hajri, S. (2008). The Adoption of e-Banking: The Case of Omani Banks. International Review of Business Research Papers, 4(5), 20–128.

Al-Shammari, M. (2008). Toward a Knowledge Management Strategic Framework in Arab Region. International Journal of Knowledge Management, 4(3).

Alvandi, N., & Mirzaei, S. R. (2008). RFID: A New Phenomenon in E-banking, Paper presented at: 2nd International Conference on E-banking, Tehran, 9-10 August.

American Productivity & Quality Center (APQC) (1997) Knowledge Management: Consortium Benchmarking Study Final Report. Retrieved from. [online: http://www.store.apqc.org/reports/summary/know-mng.pdf]

Amini, A. (2006). Investigating Barriers And Challenges of E-banking Development and Improvement in Parsian Bank of Iran, M.Sc dissertation, Shahid Beheshti University, Iran.

Amoda, J. M. (2008, October 7). Transparency international's annual corruption perception index. Vanguard Newspaper (Lagos, Nigeria).

Angell Ian. & J. Kietzmann., (2006). RFID and the end of cash, Communications of the ACM, 49, (12), Available at http://portal.acm.org/citation.cfm?id=1183236.1183237

Applegate, L. M. (2000). Emerging e-Business Models: Lessons from the Field. Boston: Harvard Business School Press.

Arab Human Development Report AHDR. (2003). Building a knowledge society. Retrieved from. [online: http://www.undp.org/rbar/ahdr/english2003]

Asoh, D., Belardo, S., & Neilson, R. (2002). Knowledge Management: Issues, Challenges and Opportunities for Governments in the New Economy. In Proceeding of the 35th Hawaii International Conference on System Sciences (HICSS'O2), 5, Hawaii, USA pp. 129.2.

Avoine, G. (2004). Privacy Issues in RFID Banknote Protection Schemes, In Proceedings of The 6th International Conference on Smart Card Research and Advanced Applications - CARDIS, Toulouse, France, (pp.33-48).

Awamleh, R., Evans, J., & Mahate, A. (2003). Internet Banking in Emergency Markets. Journal of Internet Banking and Commerce, 8(1). Retrieved from www.arraydev.com/commerce.

Azar, A., & Momeni, M. (2001). Statistics and its Application in Management. Tehran, Iran: SMT Publication.

Bahramian, Y. (2003). A Short Perusal for E-Banking Birth in Iran. Journal of Bank Va Eghtesad, N. 50, 52-53.

Bakhtiari, F., Alikhani, A., & Ghasemzadeh, A. (2008). Investigating RFID Application in E-banking, Paper presented at: 2nd International Conference on E-banking, Tehran, 9-10 August.

Bakhtiari, H. (2008)., Application of RFID in E-banking. Paper presented at: 2nd International Conference on E-banking, Tehran, 9-10 August.

Bamber, R., Falkena, H., Llewellyn, D., & Store, T. (2001). Financial Regulation in South Africa. Revonia. South African Financial Sector Forum.

Banks, J., Pachano, M., Thompson, L., & Hanny, D. (2007). RFID Applied (pp. 341–347). New York: John Wiley & Sons. doi:10.1002/9780470168226.ch18

Bareki, A. (2004). The cost and quality of banking services and their impact on performance of the banking industry in Botswana using Standard charter Bank as a Case Study, Unpublished MBA dissertation, Faculty of Business Law, De Montfort University, UK

Barra, R. (1990). Interactive innovation in financial and business services: the vanguard of the service revolution. Research Policy, 19, 215–237. doi:10.1016/0048-7333(90)90037-7

Barrett, M. (1997). Playing the Right Paradigm. Bank Marketing, 29(9), 32–39.

Barto, G. L. (1999). E-Banking 1999: New Model of Banking Emerges. Stamford, CT: Gartner Group.

Bawany, S. (2001). Developing a Knowledge strategy: Aligning knowledge management programs to business strategy. Retrieved from. [online: http://www.bawany.com.sg]

Bayat, Gh.R. (2002). Electronic Banking, Choice or Committal! Elm Va Ayandeh, 1(2), 52–58.

Beatty, A. (1998). Online Business: Internet and Electronic Payments. Mallesons Stephen Jaques Solicitors, Sydney, Retrieved from www.ecomlaw.com/articles

Berg, T., Janowski, W., & Sarner, A. (2001). Personalization: Customer Value Beyond the Web. Stamford, CT: Gartner.

Berger, A. N., Demsetz, R. S., & Strahan, P. E. (1999). The consolidation of the financial services industry: Causes, consequences, and implications for the future. Journal of Banking & Finance, 23(2-4), 135–194. doi:10.1016/S0378-4266(98)00125-3

Bernstein, M., & Claps, C. (1999). Web Personalization- Possibilities, Problems, and Pitfalls. Stamford, CT: Gartner Group.

Bhargava, V. (2006). Curing the cancer of corruption. V. Bhargava (Ed), Global issues for global citizens: an introduction of key development challenges (pp.341-369). Washington DC: The World Bank.

Birch, D., & Young, M. A. (1997). Financial Services and the Internet: What Does Cyberspace Mean for the Financial Services Industry. Internet Research, 7(2), 120–128. doi:10.1108/10662249710165262

Bloodgood, J. M., & Morrow, J. L. (2003). Strategic organizational change: Exploring the roles of environmental structure, Internal conscious awareness and knowledge. Journal of Management Studies, 40(7), 1761–1782. doi:10.1111/1467-6486.00399

Bons, A. (1999). Internet Banking: Early Stage Experiences. Kingston, RI, USA: University of Rhode Island.

Bons, A. (1999). Internet Banking: Early Stage Experiences. Kingston, RI, USA: University of Rhode Island.

Bose, I., & Leung, A. C. M. (2007). A Comparative Study of Anti-Phishing Preparedness of Hong Kong and Singa-pore Banks. In Proceedings of the IEEE Conference on Industrial Engineering and Engineering Management, (pp. 1893-1897).

Boudreau, M.-C., & Robey, D. (2005). Enacting integrated information technology: A human agency perspective. Organization Science, 16(1), 3–19. doi:10.1287/orsc.1040.0103

Brickell, E., Gemmell, P., & Kravitz, D. (1995). Trustee-based Tracing Extensions to Anonymous Cash and the Making of Anonymous Exchange. In Proceeding of 6th International Conference of ACM-SIAM SODA (pp. 457-466).

Buchanan, J. and & Grant, A. J. (2001, November). Investigating and prosecuting Nigerian fraud. United States Attorneys' Bulletin, (pp. 39-47).

Bughin, J. (2003). The Diffusion of Internet Banking in Western Europe. Electronic Markets, 13(3), 251–258. doi:10.1080/1019678032000108329

Burr, W. (1996). Wir informationstechnik die bankorganisation verandern konnte. Bank und Markt, 11, 28–31.

Business Continuity Planning for Banking and Finance. retrieved on February 7, 2007 from http://www3.ca.com/technologies/subsolution.aspx?id=3936

C.S.I. 2002, Cyber Crime Bleeds U.S Corporations, Survey Shows, Financial Losses from Attacks Climb for Third Year in row, www.gocsi.com.

Camenisch, M., & Stadler, M. (1996). Digital Payment Systems with Passive anonymity-revoking trustees. Computer Security-ESORICS 96, (Lecture Notes in Computer Security 1146 pp.33-34). New York: Springer-Verlag.

Carlson, J., Furst, K., Lang, W. W., & Nolle, D. E. (2001). Internet Banking: Market Developments and Regulatory Issues. Paper Presented at the Society of Government Economists Conference 2000, Washington D C.

Carlson, J., Furst, K., Lang, W., & Nolle, D. (2000) Internet Banking: Markets Developments and Regulatory Issues. Office of the Comptroller of the Currency, Economic and Policy Analysis Working Papers 2000-9.

Carrillo, P. M., Robinson, H. S., Anumba, C. J., & Al-Ghassani, A. M. (2003). IMPaKT: a framework for linking Knowledge Management to business performance. Electronic Journal of Knowledge Management, 1(1), 1–12.

Cedar, (2003), How Knowledge Management, Drives Competitive Advantage. Cedar white paper, released December, Maryland, USA

Centeno, C. (2004). Adoption of Internet Services in the Acceding and Candidate Countries, Lessons from the Internet Banking Case. Telematics and Informatics, 21(4), 293–315. doi:10.1016/j.tele.2004.02.001

Central Bank of Nigeria (Various Dates). Annual reports and statement of accounts, Lagos.

Central Bank of Nigeria. (2001a). The effects of economic crimes in the financial industry (pp. 55–63). Central Bank of Nigeria Banking Supervision Annual Report.

Central Bank of Nigeria. (2001b). Bank licensing (pp. 27–29). Central Bank of Nigeria Banking Supervision Annual Report.

Central Bank of Nigeria. (2002). Banking supervision annual report. Lagos. Central Bank of Nigeria Research and Publication Department.

Central Bank of Nigeria. (2003, August), Guidelines on electronic banking in Nigeria. Retrieved February 27 2009 from http://www.cenbank.org/OUT/PUBLICA-TIONS/BSD/2003/E-BANKING.PDF

Chaum, D. (1983). Blind Signature for untraceable payments. Advances in Cryptology, Crypto'82 (pp. 199–203). New York: Plenum Press.

Chaum, D., Amost, F, & Moni, N. Untraceable Electronic Cash, Advances in Cryptology - CRYPTO '88, (LNCS 403, pp. 318-327).

Chen, T. (1999). Critical success factors for various strategies in the banking industry. International Journal of Bank Marketing, 17(12), 83–92. doi:10.1108/02652329910258943

Chiemeke, S. C., Evwiekpaefe, A. E., & Chete, F. O. (2006). The adoption of internet banking in Nigeria: an empirical investigation. Journal of Internet Banking and Commerce, 11(3). Retrieved 8 February 2009 from http://www.arraydev.com/commerce/jibc/

Choi, Y. S. (2003). Reality of Knowledge Management Success. Journal of Academy of Business and Economics, 11(1), 184–188.

Chorafas, D. N. (1987). Strategic Planning for Electronic Banking, Butterworths, London. CSFI (Centre for the Study of Financial Innovation) (2000), Banana Skins 2000. London: CSFI.

Chou, D., & Chow, A. Y. (2000). A guide to the internet revolution in banking. Information Systems Management, 17(2), 51–57. doi:10.1201/1078/43191.17.2.20000301/31227.6

Chuhan, P. (2006). Poverty and inequality. In Bhargava, V. (Ed.), Global issues for global citizens: an introduction of key development challenges (pp. 31–50). Washington, DC: The World Bank.

Chung, W., & Paynter, J. (2001). An Evaluation of Internet Banking in New Zealand. Department of Management Science and Information Systems. Auckland, New Zealand: The University of Auckland.

Claessens, S. (2001).E-finance in emerging markets: is leapfrogging possible? Financial Sector Discussion Paper, No. 7,World Bank, June.

Claessens, S., Glaessner, T, & Klingbiel, D. (2001). Electronic finance: A new approach to financial sector development. World Bank Discussion Paper No.431.

Claessens, S., Glaessner, T., & Klingebiel, D. (2000), Electronic finance: reshaping financial landscapes around the world. Financial Sector Discussion Paper, No. 4, World Bank, September, available at: www.worldbank.org

Claver-Cortes, E., Zaragoza-Saez, P., & Pertusa-Ortega, E. (2007). Organizational structure features supporting knowledge management processes. Journal of Knowledge Management, 11(4), 45–57. doi:10.1108/13673270710762701

Comptroller's Handbook. (1999, October). Internet banking. comptroller of the currency. Administrator of

National Banks. Retrieved February 8 2009 from http://www.occ.treas.gov/handbook/intbank.pdf

Constantine, G. (2000). Banks provide internet on ramp. Hoosier Banker, Indianapolis, March, USA.

Cooper, V., Lichtenstein, Sh., & Smith, R. (2009). Successful Web-based IT Support Services: Service Provider Perceptions of Stakeholder-oriented Challenges. International Journal of E-Services and Mobile Applications. Hershey, PA: Idea Group Publishing, 1 (1): 1-20.

Coventry, L., De Angeli, A., & Johnson, G. (2003). Usability and Biometric Verification at the ATM Interface. Conference on Computer-Human Interaction, 5 (1), 153-160.

Crede, A. (1995). Electronic Commerce and the Banking Industry: The Requirement and Opportunities for New Payment Systems Using the Internet. Journal of Computer-Mediated Communication, 1(3).

Crede, A. (1999). Electronic Commerce and Banking Industry: the requirement and opportunities for new payment system using The Internet. Science policy research unit university p 27. Retrieved January 5, 2009, from http://jcmc.indiana.edu/vol1/issue3/crede.html

Cruz, M. G. (2002). Modeling, measuring and hedging operational risk. London: John Wiley & Sons.

Cyree, K.B., Delcoure, N., & Dickens, R. (2008).An examination of the performance and prospects for the future of internet-primary banks.Journal of Economics and Finance, June.

Damanpour, F. (1987). The adoption of technological, administrative, and ancillary innovations: Impact of organizational factors. Journal of Management, 13(4), 675–678. doi:10.1177/014920638701300408

Daniel, E. (1999). Provision of electronic banking in the UK and the Republic of Ireland. International Journal of Bank Marketing, 17(2), 72–82. doi:10.1108/02652329910258934

Daniel, E. (1999). Provision of electronic banking in the UK and Republic of Ireland. International Journal of Bank Marketing, 17(2), 72–83. doi:10.1108/02652329910258934

Daniel. E. & Story, Ch. (1997). Online Banking: Strategic and Management challenges. Long rang planning. 30 (6), 890-898.

Darch, H. & Lucas, T. (2002). Training as an E-Commerce Enabler. Journal of Workplace Learning, 14 (4), 148-155. Dejpasand. F., (2006). Cash Electronic Transmission and E-banking. Tehran, Commerce Ministry Publication, 178-209.

Datamonitor, (2003), European Retail banks 2003. Retrieved February 14th 2008, from www.datamonitor.com/industries/research

Davari, M. R., Mojdehi, N., & Jalali, A. A. (2009). Using RFID By Banks in E-city, Paper presented at: 2nd International Conference on E-city, Tehran, 2-3 July.

Davenport, T. H. (1999). Knowledge management and the broader firm: Strategy, advantage, and performance. In J Liebowitz (Ed.), Knowledge Management Handbook: 2.1—2.11, Boca Raton, FL:CRC Press.

Davenport, T. H., & Prusak, L. (2000). Working Knowledge, how organizations manage what they know. Boston: Harvard Business School Press.

De Young, R., & Rice, T. (2004). How do Banks make Money? A Variety of Business Strategies. Federal Reserve Bank of Chicago Economic Perspectives, 28, 52–68.

Dehghan, A., & Ghaderi, J. (2008). The Role of RFID in Moving Form Traditional Banking to Electronic Banking, Paper presented at: 2nd International Conference on E-banking, Tehran, 9-10 August.

Delgado, J., Hernando, I., & Nieto, M. J. (2007). Do European Primarily Internet Banks Show Scale and Experience Efficiencies? European Financial Management, 13(4), 643–671. doi:10.1111/j.1468-036X.2007.00377.x

Demil, B., Lecoq, X., & Warnier, V. (2004).Le business model: l'oublié de la stratégie? 13th AIMS Conference, Normandie, 2-4 June.

Demirguc-Kunt, A., & Huizinga, H. (2000), Financial structure and bank profitability. World Bank, Policy Research Working Paper Series 2430.

Department of Commerce. National Institute of Standards and Technology, (1994). Digital Signature Standard. Federal Information Processing Standard Publication 186, USA.

Devlin, J. F. (1995). Technology and Innovation in Retail Business Distribution. International Journal of Bank Marketing, 13(4), 19–25. doi:10.1108/02652329510082915

DeYoung R. (2001), The financial progress of pure-play internet banks Bank for International Settlements, Monetary and Economic Department, BIS Papers n°7, 80-86.

DeYoung, R. (2005). The Performance of Internet-Based Business Models: Evidence from the Banking Industry. The Journal of Business, 78(3), 893–947. doi:10.1086/429648

Dignum, F. P. M., & Eijk, R. M. (2007). Agent communication and social concept. New York: Springer. [online: eijk_07_agentcommunication.pdf]

Diniz, E. (1998). Web Banking in the USA. Journal of Internet Banking and Commerce, from www.arraydev.com/commerce

Doh, J. P., Rodriguez, P., Uhlembruck, K., Collins, J., & Eden, L. (2003). Coping with corruption in foreign markets. The Academy of Management Executive, 17(3), 114–127.

Douglas, R. Stinson, (2006). Cryptography and Practice (pp.232-254). Hartford, CT: CRT Press

Dourish, P., & Redmiles, D. (2002). An approach to usable security based on event monitoring and visualization. Paper presented at proceedings of the 2002 workshop on new security paradigms (pp.75-81), New York.

Drucker, P. F. (2002). Managing in the Next Society. New York: St Martin's Press.

Dunnick, R (1996), Strategy as if knowledge mattered. Fast company, Issue 2, [online: www.fastcompany.com/online/02/stratsec.html].

Durkin, M. (2004). In Search of the Internet Banking Customer, Exploring the Use of Decision Styles. International Journal of Bank Marketing, 22(7), 484–523. doi:10.1108/02652320410567917

EFMA (2007). Online consumer behaviour in retail financial services, with Novametrie, Capgemini and Microsoft, EFMA Studies, December

Egbu, C. O., & Botterill, K. (2002). Information Technologies for Knowledge Management: Their Usage and Effectiveness. ITcon, 7, 125.

Egland, K. L., Robertson, D., Furst, K., Nolle, D. E., & Robertson, D. (1998). Banking over the Internet. Office of the Comptroller of the Currency. Currency Quarterly, 17, 25–30.

Eid, R., Truman, M., & Ahmed, A. M. (2002). A Cross Industry Review of B2B Critical Success Factors. Internet Research, 12(2), 110–123. doi:10.1108/10662240210422495

Eighmey, J. (1997). Profiling User Responses to Commercial Web Sites. Journal of Advertising Research, 37, 59–66.

El Sawy, O. A., Malhotra, A., Gosain, S., & Young, K. M. (1999). IT-Intensive Value Innovation in the Electronic Economy: Insights from Marshall Industries. Management Information Systems Quarterly, 23(3), 305–335. doi:10.2307/249466

El-Kharouf, Farouk (2000), Strategy corporate governance and the future of the Arab banking industry. The Arab bank review, 2, (2), 30-39.

eMarketer, (2004). Can Online Banking Reach Widespread US Adoption. Retrieved 12th March 2007, from www.emarketer.com

Engler, H., & Essinger, J. (2000). The Future of Banking, Reuters. London: Pearson Education, UK.

Ennew, C., & Watkins, T. (1992). Marketing Strategy and the Marketing Mix in Financial Services. In Baker, M. (Ed.), Perspectives on Marketing Management, 2. Chichester, UK: John Wiley & Sons.

Essayan, M., Rutstein, C., & Wetenhall, P. (2002). Activate and Integrate: Optimizing the Value of Online Banking. Boston: Boston Consulting Group.

Essinger, J. (1992). Electronic Payment System: Winning New Customer. UK: Chapman and Hall. Imprint by Thompson Corporation.

Evans, C. (2003). Managing for knowledge HR's strategic role. Oxford, UK: Butterworth Heinemann.

Ezeduiji, F. U. (1997). Bank failures in Nigeria: causes and dimensions. Central Bank of Nigeria Bullion, 21, 17–22.

Ezeoha, A. E. (2005a). Regulating internet banking in Nigeria: part 1 – problems and phallenges. Journal of Internet Banking and Commerce, 10(3). Retrieved February 23 from http://www.arraydev.com/commerce/JIBC/2006-02/abel.asp

Ezeoha, A. E. (2005b). Increasing incidence of poverty in Nigeria: an impact assessment of the government's economic reform programme. Journal of Social Development in Africa, 22(2), 112–131.

Ezeoha, A. E. (2006). Regulating internet banking in Nigeria: part 2 – some success prescriptions. Journal of Internet Banking and Commerce, 11(1). Retrieved February 23 2009 from http://www.arraydev.com/commerce/JIBC/2006-04/Nigeria-2_F.asp

Ezeoha, A. E. (2007). Structural effect of banking industry consolidation in Nigeria: a review. Journal of Banking Regulation, 8(2), 159–176. doi:10.1057/palgrave.jbr.2350044

Ezeoha, A. E., & Chibuike, U. C. (2006). Rethinking monetary and fiscal policies in Nigeria. Journal of Sustainable Development in Africa, 8(2), 93–105.

Fanawopo, S. (2004, August 2). Federal government moves to enforce cyber crimes laws. The Sun Newspaper, (Lagos, Nigeria).

Federal Government of Nigeria. (1990). Criminal code act. Laws of the Federation of Nigeria.

Federal Government of Nigeria. (1991). Banks and other financial institutions decree No 25. Lagos, Laws of the Federation of Nigeria.

Federal Government of Nigeria. (1995). Advance fee fraud and other fraud related offences decree No. 13 of 1995. Lagos, Laws of the Federation of Nigeria.

Federal Government of Nigeria. (1995). Money laundering (prohibition) decree No. 3 of 1995. Lagos, Laws of the Federation of Nigeria.

Federal Government of Nigeria. (2004). Money laundering (prohibition) act of 2004. Abuja: Laws of the Federation of Nigeria.

Federal Government of Nigeria. (2006). Advance fee fraud and other fraud related offences act of 2006. Abuja: Laws of the Federation of Nigeria.

Feller, W., & Petit, C. (2008). Harnessing the power of Web 2.0 to rebuild trust in banking. IBM Institute for Business Value, Retrieved from http://www-935.ibm.com/services/us/gbs/bus/pdf/gbe03117-usen-bank2.pdf

Ferguson. R. W., (2000, October). Information Technology in Banking and Supervision, At the Financial Services Conference, Online Banking Report, Piper Jaffray Equity Research, Available at: www.pjc.com/ec-ie01.asp?team=2 [Accessed 15 September 2008]

Filotto, U., Tanzi, P. M., & Saita, F. (1997). Customer Needs and Front Office Technology Adoption. International Journal of Bank Marketing, 15(1), 13. doi:10.1108/02652329710155679

Finextra, (2005b). Online Banking Services Key to Bank Selection. Retrieved 20th January 2008, from www.finextra.com

Finextra, (2005c). Web Banking Growth Stalls in Canada. Retrieved 20th January 2008, from www.finextra.com

Fleur de Coin. (2005). RFID banknotes, from Euro banknotes embedded with RFID chips, Retrieved from http://www.fleur-de-coin.com/eurocoins/rfid.asp.

Fonseca, I., Hickman, M., & Marenzi, O. (2001). The Future of Wholesale Banking: The Portal. Commercial Lending Review. Boston, summer.

Fox, S. (2002). Online Banking. Retrieved 22nd April 2008, from www.pewinternet.com

Fruin, J. (2001). What is CRM? InfoTech Update, 2, 5–6.

Furst, K., Lang, W. W., & Nolle, D. E. (2002). Internet banking. Journal of Financial Services Research, 22, 95–117. doi:10.1023/A:1016012703620

Furst, K., Lang, W. W., & Nolle, D. E. (2002). Internet Banking. Journal of Financial Services Research, 22(1/2), 95–117. doi:10.1023/A:1016012703620

Gampl, B., Robeck, M., & Clasen, M. (2008). The RFID Reference Model, Retrieved from: www.gil.de/dokumente/berichte/DDD/R20_2008_012.pdf.

Gerrard, P., & Cunningham, J., B. (2003). The diffusion of Internet banking among Singapore consumers. International Journal of Bank Marketing, 21, 16–28. doi:10.1108/02652320310457776

Ghose, T. K. (1987). The Banking System of Hong Kong. Singapore: Butterworths.

Gkoutzinis, A. A. (2006). Internet banking and the law in euro – regulation, financial integration and electronic commerce. Cambridge, UK: Cambridge University Press. doi:10.1017/CBO9780511494703

Graham, B. (2003). The Evolution of Electronic Payments. BE Thesis, Division of Electrical and Electronics Engineering, School of Information Technology and Electrical Engineering, The University of Queensland, Australia. (http://innovexpo.itee.uq.edu.au/2003/exhibits/s334853/thesis.pdf)

Gurau, C. (2002). E-banking in transistion economies: The case of Romania. Journal of Financial Services Marketing, 6(4), 362–379. doi:10.1057/palgrave.fsm.4770065

Gurteen, D. (1999), Greeting a knowledge sharing culture. Knowledge Management Magazine, 2, (5).

Guru, B., Shanmugam, B., Alam, N., & Perera, C. J. (2003). An Evaluation of Internet Banking Sites in Islamic Countries. Journal of Internet Banking and Commerce, 8(2), from www.arraydev.com/commerce

Gwebu, K. L., & Wang, J. (2007). The Role of Organizational, Environmental and Human Factors in E-learning Diffusion, International Journal of Web-Based Learning and Teaching Technologies, 2 (2), 59-78., Hershey, PA: Idea Group Publishing, Information and Communication Technology News Agency, (2008). Investigating The Rate of E-banking Usability in Iran, Retrieved March 23, 2009, from http://www.ictna.ir/report/archives/016012.html [Accessed 23 March 2009]

Hamid, J. A. (2003). Understanding Knowledge Management. Malaysia: University of Putra Malaysia Press.

Hansen, MT, & Nohria, N & Tierney, Thomas. (1999). What's your strategy for managing knowledge? Harvard Business Review, 77(2), 106–116.

Hansen, W. R., & Gillert, F. (2008). RFID for the Optimization of Business Processes. New York: John Wiley & Sons, Ltd.doi:10.1002/9780470754160

Hasan, H., & Handzic, M. (2003). Australian Studies in Knowledge Management. Wollongong: UOW Press.

Hasan, I., Zazzara, C., & Ciciretti, R. (2005). Internet, Innovation and Performance of Banks: Italian Experience. unpublished manuscript.

Hassanali, F. (2002), Critical Success Factor Of Knowledge Management.Retrieved from [online: www.providersedge.com/docs/km-articles/critical_success_factor_of_KM.pdf

Heng, S. (2007). Implications of Web 2.0 for financial institutions: Be a Driver, Not a Passenger. Deutsche Bank Research, E-conomics, 63, 1–11.

Hensman, M., Van den Bosch, F. A., & Volberda, H. (2001). Clicks vs. Bricks in the Emerging Online Financial Services Industry. Long Range Planning Journal, 34, 33–235.

Hernando, I., & Nieto, M. J. (2007). Is the Internet delivery channel changing banks' performance? The case of Spanish banks. Journal of Banking & Finance, 31(4), 1083–1099. doi:10.1016/j.jbankfin.2006.10.011

Hertzum, M., Juul, N. C., Jorgensen, N., & Norgaard, M. (2004). Usable security and ebanking: Ease of use vis-a-vis security. Technical Report, from www.ruc.dk

Hofmann, F., Baesens, B., Martens, J., Put, F., & Vanthienen, J. (2002). Comparing a genetic fuzzy and neurofuzy classifier for credit scoring. International Journal of Intelligent Systems, 17(11), 1067–1083. doi:10.1002/int.10052

Hohenberger, S. (2006), Advances in Signatures Encryption and E-Cash from Bilinear Group (pp.95-142), PhD Thesis, MIT.

Holsapple, C. W., & Joshi, K. D. (2000). An investigation of factors that influence the management of knowledge in organizations. The Journal of Strategic Information Systems, 9(2/3), 235–261. doi:10.1016/S0963-8687(00)00046-9

Horsti, A., Tuunainen, V. K., & Tolonen, J. (2005). Evaluation of Electronic Business Model Success: Survey among Leading Finnish Companies. Proceedings of the 38th Annual Hawaii International Conference on System Sciences, Volume 7.

Howcroft, B., Hamilton, R., & Hewer, P. (2002). Consumer Attitude and the Usage and Adoption of Home Banking in the United Kingdom. International Journal of Bank Marketing, 20(3), 111–121. doi:10.1108/02652320210424205

Hsieh, N. C. (2005). Hybrid mining approach in the design of credit scoring models. Expert Systems with Applications, 28(4), 655–665. doi:10.1016/j.eswa.2004.12.022

http://thebankwatch.comtag/smart-cards/(n.d.).

http://www.tagsense.com/index.html, (n.d.).

http://www.usa.visa.com/personal/cards/paywave/index.html?ep=a_cmp_akqa_search, (n.d.).

Huang, J.-J., Tzeng, G.-H., & Ong, C.-S. (2006). Two-stage genetic programming (2SGP) for the credit scoring model. Applied Mathematics and Computation, 174(2), 1039–1053. doi:10.1016/j.amc.2005.05.027

Hwang, H.-G., Ku, C.-Y., Yen, D. C., & Cheng, C.-C. (2004). Critical factors influencing the adoption of data warehouse technology: a study of the banking industry in Taiwan. Decision Support Systems, 37, 1–21. doi:10.1016/S0167-9236(02)00191-4

Hwang, M. S., & Sung, P. C. (2006). A study of micropayment based on one-way hash chain. International Journal of Network Security, 2(2), 81–90.

Ibbotson, P., & Moran, L. (2003). E-banking and the SME/ bank relationship in Northern Ireland. International Journal of Bank Marketing, 21, 94–103. doi:10.1108/02652320310461474

Infoline, I. (2000). Electronic Fund Transfer and Clearing System. Retrieved 25th February 2008, from www.indiainfoline.com

Islam, Mazhar M. (2003), Development and performance of domestic and foreign banks in GCC countries. Managerial finance, 29, (2-3), 42.

Jacobson & Markus Wetzel. (2003). Security Weaknesses in Bluetooth, Retrieved from www.bell.labs.com.

Jacobson, M., & Youg, M. (1997), Applying Anti-Trust Policies to Increase Trust in a Versatile E-Money System. In Proceeding of International Workshop on Financial Cryptography, (21 pages).

Jain, A., Hong, L., & Pankanti, S. (2000). Biometric Identification. Communications of the ACM, 43(2), 91–98. doi:10.1145/328236.328110

Jashapara, A. (2004). Knowledge management an integrated approach. Upper Saddle River, NJ: Prentice Hall. Essex, UK: Pearson Educaion Ltd.

Jayawardhena, C., & Foley, P. (2000). Changes in the Banking Sector – the Case of Internet Banking in the UK. Internet Research: Electronic Networking Applications and Policy, 10(1), 19–30. doi:10.1108/10662240010312048

Jeevan, M. T. (2000). Only banks – No bricks. Voice and Data.

Jesse, H. (1996). The Impact of Technology and Changing Distribution Strategies on Workforce Planning within Australian Financial Industry over the Next Decade. Melbourne: Australian Institute of Banking and Finance.

Johannessen, J. A., Olaisen, J., & Olsen, B. (2000). Mismanagement of tacit knowledge: knowledge management, the danger of information technology, and what to do about it. SKIKT. Retrieved from. [online: www.program.forskningsradet.no/skikt/johannessen.php3]

Jones, PH (2000), Knowledge strategy: Aligning knowledge programs to business strategy. Knowledge Management World 2000, Santa Clara, CA, September 12-15.

Joseph, M., & Stone, G. (2003). An empirical evaluation of US bank customer perceptions of the impact of technology on service delivery in the banking sector. Journal of Retail and Distribution Management, 31, 190–202. doi:10.1108/09590550310469185

Junnarkar, B., & Brown, C. (1997). Re-assessing the enabling role of information technology in KM. Journal of Knowledge Management, 1(2), 142–148. doi:10.1108/EUM0000000004589

Kalakota, R., & Frei, F. (1998). Frontiers of online financial services. In Cronin, M. J. (Ed.), Banking and Finance on the Internet. New York: John Wiley and Sons Inc.

Kambil, A., & Nunes, P. F. (2001). Personalization? No Thanks. Harvard Business Review, 79(4), 32–34.

Kamel, Sh., & Hassan, A. (2003). Assessing The Introduction of Electronic Banking in Egypt Using the Technology Acceptance Model, In: M. Kosrpw-Pour (Ed), Annals of Case on Information Technology, 5, 1-25, Hershey,PA: Idea Group Publishing.

Kankanhalli, A., Tanudidjaja, F., Sutanto, J., & Tan, B. C. Y. (2003). The role of IT in successful knowledge management initiatives. Communications of the ACM, 46(9), 487–505. doi:10.1145/903893.903896

Kannabiran, G., & Narayan, P. C. (2005). Deploying internet banking and e-commerce - case study of a private - sector bank in India. Information Technology for Development, 11(4), 363–379. doi:10.1002/itdj.20025

Kanniainen, L., (2001). The Perfect Payment Architecture. Technical Document Mobey Forum,Retrieved from www.mobeyforum.

Kapulos, A., Ellis, N., & Murphy, W. (2004). The Voice of the Customer in E-banking Relationships. Journal of Customer Behaviour, 3, 27–51. doi:10.1362/147539204323074592

Karakostas, B., Kardaras, D., & Papathanassiou, E. (2005). The state of CRM adoption by the financial services in the UK: an empirical investigation. Information & Management, 42, 853–863. doi:10.1016/j.im.2004.08.006

Kass, R. (1994). Looking for the link to customers. Bank Systems and Technology, 31(2), 64.

Kassem, M., & Habib, G. (1989). Strategic Management of Services in the Persian Gulf States. Berlin, New York, NY: Company and Industry Cases, Walter de Gruyter.

Kehzadi, N. (2002). E-Banking: Prerequisites, Limitations and its Implementing Methods in Iran, Paper presented at 11th Annual Conference of Monetary and Financial Policies, Tehran.

Kerem, K., Lustsik, O., Sorg, M., & Vensel, V. (2003). The development of e-banking in a EU candidate country: An Estonian case. Proceedings of International Atlantic Economic Society Conference, Vienna, March 11-17.

Khalfan, A. M. S. AIRRefaei, Y.S.Y,& Al-Hajery M.,(2006). 'Factors influencing the adoption of internet banking in Oman: a descriptive case study analysis', InInternational Journal Financial Services Management, 1 (2/3), 155-163.

King, S. F., & Liou, J. (2004). A Framework for Internet Channel Evaluation. International Journal of Information Management, 24(6), 473–488. doi:10.1016/j.ijinfomgt.2004.08.006

Koblitz, N. (1987). Elliptic Curve Cryptosystems. Mathematics of Computation, 48, 203–209.

Kolodinsky, J. M., Hogarth, J. M., & Hilgert, M. A. (2004). The adoption of electronic banking technologies by US consumers. International Journal of Bank Marketing, 22(4), 238–259. doi:10.1108/02652320410542536

Kungpisdan, S., Srivnivasan, B., & Le, P. D. (2004), A Secure Account-Based Mobile Payment Protocol.In Proceedings of the International Conference on Information Technology: Coding and Computing, (ITCC'04).

Kuzic, J., Fisher, J., & Scollary, A. (2002, June). Electronic Commerce Benefits, Challenges and Success Factors in the Australian Banking and Finance Industry. In S. Wrycza (Ed.), Tenth European Conference on Information Systems, (pp. 1607-1616). Gdansk, Poland.

Ladd, A. & Ward, Mark (2002). An investigation of Environment factors influencing Knowledge transfer. Journal of Knowledge Management Practice, vol. 3

Ladd, D. A., & Heminger, A. R. (2003). An investigation of organizational culture factors that may influence knowledge transfer. in Proceedings of the 36th Hawaii International Conference on System Sciences

Lagoutte, V. (1996). The Direct Banking Challenge. Unpublished Honours Thesis, Middlesex University

Lee, T.-S., & Chen, I.-F. (2005). A two-stage hybrid credit scoring model using artificial neural networks and multivariate adaptive regression splines. Expert Systems with Applications, 28(4), 743–752. doi:10.1016/j.eswa.2004.12.031

Leggat, H. (2008). Americans turn to Internet for entertainment. BizReport Research. http://www.bizreport.com/2008/01/americans_turn_to_internet_for_entertainment.html

Legris, P., Ingham, J., & Collerette, P. (2003). Why people use information technology? A critical review of the technology acceptance model. Information & Management, 40, 191–204. doi:10.1016/S0378-7206(01)00143-4

Leibowitz, J. (2002). The role of the chief knowledge officer in organizations. Research and Practice in Human Resource Management, 10(2), 2–15.

Leitch, J. M., & Rosen, P. W. (2001). Knowledge Management, CKO, and CKM: The Keys to Competitive Advantage. The Manchester Review, 6(2&3), 9–13.

Li, C., Xu, Y., & Li, H. (2005). An empirical study of Dynamic Customer Relationship Management. Journal of Retailing and Consumer Services, 12(6), 431–441. doi:10.1016/j.jretconser.2005.01.003

Li, X., Ying, Y., Tuo, J., Li, B., & Liu, W. (2004). Applications of classification trees to consumer credit scoring methods in commercial banks. Proceedings of IEEE International Conference on Systems, Man and Cybernetics, October, 5, 4112-4117.

Li, Y., & Li, J. (2006). Application Study on Public Key Cryptography in Mobile Payment.In Proceeding of the 5th WSEAS International Conference on Information Security and Privacy, Venice, Italy, November 20-22.

Liao, S., Shao, Y. P., Wang, H., & Chen, A. (1999). The adoption of virtual banking: An empirical study. International Journal of Information Management, 19, 63–74. doi:10.1016/S0268-4012(98)00047-4

Liao, Z., & Choeung, M. T. (2002). Internet based E-banking and Consumer altitudes: an empirical study. Information & Management, 39(4), 283–295. doi:10.1016/S0378-7206(01)00097-0

Library of Congress. (2008, July). Federal research division country profile: Nigeria. Retrieved February 8 2009 from http://lcweb2.loc.gov/frd/cs/profiles/Nigeria.pdf.

Limam, I. (2001), A comparative study of GCC banks technical efficiency. Economic Research Forum ERF working paper, No. 200119, Retrieved from [online: http://www.erf.org.eg].

Linder, J., & Cantrell, S. (2000). Changing Business Models: Surveying the Landscape. Accenture Institute for Strategic Change.

Liu, J. K., Wei, V. K., & Wong, S. H. (2001). Recoverable and Untraceable E-Cash, EUROCON' 2001. Trends in Communications, International Conference on Information Technology, 1, 342-349.

Loilier, T., & Tellier, A. (2001). Nouvelle Economie, Net organisations. Paris: EMS Eds.

Luarn, P., & Lin, L. H. (2004). Towards an understanding of the behavioural intention to use mobile banking. Computers in Human Behaviour, 1-19.

Luftman, J., Papp, R., & Brier, T. (1999). Enablers and inhibitors of business-IT alignment. Communications of the association for information system, 1, (3es), Article No. 1.

Lustsik, O. (2004). Can E- Banking Services be Profitable? University of Tartu - Faculty of Economics & Business Administration Working Paper Series; Issue 30, p3-38. Retrieved January 24, 2009, from http://connection.ebscohost.com/content/article/1037621009.html;jsessionid=B45ED229D0A55C9679323C87043C07A7.ehctcl

Lymperopoulos, C., & Chaniotakis, I. E. (2004). Branch employees' perceptions towards implications of e-banking in Greece. Journal of Retail and Distribution Management, 32, 302–311. doi:10.1108/09590550410538006

M'Raihi, D. (1996). Cost Effective Payment Schemes with Privacy Regulation: Advances in Cryptology. ASIACRYPT 96, ([).New York: Springer-Verlag.]. Lecture Notes in Computer Science, 1163, 266–275. doi:10.1007/BFb0034853

Magretta, J. (2002). Why Business Models Matter? Harvard Business Review, (May): 90–91.

Mahadevan, B. (2000). Business Models for Internet-based e-Commerce: An anatomy. California Management Review, 42(4), 55–69.

Maier, R., & Remus, U. (2002). Defining process-oriented knowledge management strategies. Knowledge and Process Management, 9(2), 103–118. doi:10.1002/kpm.136

Management, HSBC's Guide to Cash and Treasury Management in Asia Pacific, (pp 191-194); Retrieved from: rfid.ctu.edu.tw/8_labRFID_reference/4/InfosysRFID-in-CM.pdf?Part=NM-2005-A1-MAR-1

Manasco, B. (1996). Leading firms develop knowledge strategies. Knowledge Inc, 1(6), 26–29.

Marina, B. (2008). Improved conditional e-payment. Department of Computer Science and Engineering (pp. 18–19). University of Notre Dame.

Marshall, J. J., & Heslop, L. A. (1988). Technology Acceptance in Canadian Retail Banking: A Study of Consumer Motivation and Use of ATMs. International Journal of Bank Marketing, 6(4), 31–41. doi:10.1108/eb010836

Mattila, M., Karjaluoto, H., & Pento, T. (2003). Internet Banking adoption among mature customers: early majority or laggards? Journal of Services Marketing, 17, 514–528. doi:10.1108/08876040310486294

Menezes, P. Van. Oorschot, & Vanstone S, (1997). Handbook of Applied Cryptography (pp.321-358), Hartford, CT: CRT Press.

Mentzas, G. N. (1997). Re-engineering Banking with Object-Oriented Models: Towards Customer information Systems. International Journal of Information Management, 17(3), 179–197. doi:10.1016/S0268-4012(96)00060-6

Mertins, K; Heising, P & Alwert, K (2003). Process-oriented knowledge structuring. Journal Of universal computer science, 9, (6), 542-550.

Mia, M. A. H., Rahman, M. A., & Uddin, M. M. (2007). E-Banking evolution, status and prospects. Coastal Management, 35(1), 36–48.

Micali, S. (2003), Simple and Fast Optimistic Protocols for fair e-exchange.In proceeding in International Conference of 22nd Annual ACM Symposia. On Principles of Distributed Computing (PODC'03)(pp. 12-19).New York: ACM Press

Miller, K. R. (1978). Structural organization in the photosynthetic membrane. In Akoyunoglou, G. (Ed.), Chloroplast Development (pp. 17–30). Amsterdam: Elsevier Press.

Milligan, J. W. (1997). What do Customers want from you? Everything. US Bankers Magazine, 107(12), 38–45.

Mirzaei, H. (1998, May). Toward a conceptual scheme for verification and Analisys of effective effective factors in "Work ethics" and social dicipline in organization. In Proceedings of the 2th Conference on Investigating Methods of Conscience and Social Discipline Implementation, Tehran, Islamic Azad University, 305-329.

Mirzaei, H., & Amiri, M. (2002). Developing a Three Dimensional Model for Analysis of Philosophical Bases and Fundamental Substructures of Management Theories. Management Knowledge, 15(56), 3–21.

Mishra, R. (2001). Internet Banking in India. Retrieved 10th June 2008, from www.banknetindia.com/banking/ibkg.htm

Mols, N. (1998). The behavioural consequences of PC banking. International Journal of Bank Marketing, 16(5), 195–201. doi:10.1108/02652329810228190

Morgan, R. E., & Strong, C. A. (2003). Business performance and dimensions of strategic orientation. Journal of Business Research, 56(3), 163–176. doi:10.1016/S0148-2963(01)00218-1

Mu, Y., Nguyen, K. Q., & Varadharajan, V. (2001). A fair electronic cash scheme. In Proc. of the International Symposium in Electronic Commerce,(LNCS 2040, pp. 20-32.) New York: Springer- Verlag, NCSC-TG-017. (2000). A Guide to understanding Identification and Authentication in Trusted Systems, U.S National Computer Center.

Muijen, van; Koopmam, Pul; Witte, Karel De; Cock, Gaston; Lemoine, Calaude;& Bourantas, Dimitri (1999). organizational culture: the FOCUS Questionnaire. European Journal of Work and Organizational Psychology, 8.

Murray, P. (2000). Designing business from knowledge management. In C Despres, D Chauvel,(eds.) The present and the promise of knowledge management.(pp. 171-194). Boston: Butterworth-Heinemann, Boston, MA.

Muylle, S. (2001).e-Business in Financial Services", KPMG,Retrieved from http://www.e-investments.be/KPMG.pdf.

Nathan, L. (1999). Community banks are going online. Community and Banking. Federal Reserve Bank of Boston.

National Consumers League. (2002). Internet fraud statistics. Retrieved February 27 2009 from (www.nclnet.org/shoppingonline)

Nehmzow, C. (1997). The Internet will Shake Banking Medieval Foundations. Journal of Internet Banking and Commerce, 2(2).

Neuman, W. L. (1997). Social Research Methods: Qualitative and Quantitative Approaches. Boston: Allyn and Bacon.

Nigerian Deposit Insurance Corporation (for Various Years). Annual reports and statements of account.

Norgren, C. (2001, June). Impact of the internet in the functioning and regulation of markets. Paper presented at Public Documents of the XXVIth Annual Conference of the International Organization of Securities Commissions (IOSCO), Stockholm, Sweden.

Novak, T.P., & Hoffman, D.L. (2001). Profitability on the Web: Business Models and Revenue Streams. eLab Position Paper, Owen Graduate School of Management, Vanderbilt University, January: 9-18.

O'Brien, A. J. (2002). Management informational system – managing information technology in the e-business enterprises (5th ed.). Boston: McGraw-Hill Irwin.

O'Hanlon, J., & Rocha, M. (1993). Electronic Banking for Retail Customers. London: Banking Technology Ltd.

O'Mahony, D., Peirce, H., & Tewari, H. (1997). Electronic Payment System. Artech House Computer Science Library.

Ogunleye, E. (1999). A review of banking activities and its regulatory framework in Nigeria. Nigerian Deposit Insurance Quarterly, 9(4), 35–36.

Ojo, M. O. (1991). Deregulation in the Nigerian banking industry: a review of appraisal. Central Bank Nigeria Economic and Financial review, 29(1), pp.1-6.

Oke, B. A. (1994). Regulations of bank and other financial institutions with special reference to the regulation of discount houses in Nigeria. Central Bank Nigeria Economic and Financial Review, 3(1), 3–15.

Okunoye, A. (2003). Large-scale Sustainable Information Systems Development in Developing Country: The Making of an Islamic Banking Package. [ACIT]. Annals of Cases on Information Technology, V, 168–183.

Ooi, S. (1999). Surge in E-commerce Transactions (p. 6). SME IT Guid.

Orr, B. (2004). E-Banking job one: Give customers a good ride. American Bankers Association Banking Journal, 96(5), 56–57.

Oyesanya, Y. (2004a, August 4). Nigeria: heaven for terrorist Internet communication? The Nigerian Village Square. Retrieved February 15 2006 from http://www.nigeriavillagesquare.com

Oyesanya, Y. (2004b, July 13). Review of central bank guidelines for electronic banking. The Nigerian Village Square. Retrieved February 27 2009 from http://www.nigeriavillagesquare.com

Padova, A. (2009). Concerns of CKO. Inside-knowledge. Retrieved from. [online: www.ikmagazine.com]

Paper, D. No. 7,World Bank, June. Claessens, S., Glaessner, T. and Klingebiel, D. (2000), Electronic finance: reshaping financial landscapes around the world. Financial Sector Discussion Paper, No. 4, World Bank, September, available at: www.worldbank.org

Park, R. (1999). The global transformation of financial services. European Business Journal, 11(1), 7–16.

Patel, D., & Luo, X. (2007). Take a Close Look at Phishing. Information security curriculum development. Proceedings of the 4th annual conference on Information security curriculum development, ACM, Kennesaw, Georgia, USA, 1-4.

Pavlou, P. A. (2001). Consumer Intentions to adopt Electronic Commerce – Incorporating Trust and Risk in the Technology Acceptance Model.(pp.1-28) DIGIT Workshop, New Orleans, Louisiana, 16 December 2001, Available, www.mis.temp.edu/digit/digit2001/files/consumerIntentionsToAdopt_Digit2001.

Peyrovi, N., & Amini, L. M. (2008). Application of RFID in People Identification at E-banking, Paper presented at: 2nd International Conference on E-banking, Tehran, 9-10 August.

Pohjola, M. (2002). The new economy: Facts, impacts and policies. Information Economics and Policy, 14, 133–144. doi:10.1016/S0167-6245(01)00063-4

Porter, D. (2003). BASEL II: Heralding the rise of operational risk. Computer Fraud & Security, 7, 9–12.

Porter, M.E. (2001).Strategy and the Interne.Boston: Harvard Business Review, June.

Prahalad, C. K., & Hamel, G. K. (1990). The core competence of the corporation.In MH Zack (Ed.), Knowledge and Strategy (pp.41-62).Boston: Harvard business review, May-June, Butterworth-Heinemann.

Pyun, C. S., Scruggs, L., & Nam, K. (2002). Internet Banking in the U.S., Japan and Europe. Multinational Business Review, 10(2), 73–81.

Rao, G. R., & Prathima, K. (2003). Internet Banking in India. Retrieved 15th February 2008, from www.mondaq.com

Rao, S. S., Metts, G., & Monge, C. A. (2003). Electronic Commerce Development in Small and Medium Sized Enterprise: A Stage Model and its Implications. Business Process Management Journal, 9(1), 11–32. doi:10.1108/14637150310461378

Rappa, M. (2001)Business models on the Web. Retrieved from http://digitalenterprise.org/models/models.html.

Regan, K., & Macaluso, N. (2000. October). Report: Consumers Cool to Net Banking. e-Commerce Times, Retrieved November 18, 2008, from http://www.linux-insider.com/story/4449.html?wlc=1249845342

Reiser, S. J. (1997), The information highway and electronic commerce: what does it mean for you? Current Issues, March, pp. 12-15.

Rempel, J. K., Holmes, J. G., & Zanna, M. (1985). Trust in close relationships. Journal of Personality and Social Psychology, 49, 95–112. doi:10.1037/0022-3514.49.1.95

Renzt, B. (2006). Trust in management and knowledge sharing: the mediating effects of fear and knowledge documentation. Special Issue on Knowledge Management and Organizational Learning, 36(2), 206–220.

Research Markets Brochure. (2009), Nigerian internet user survey. Retrieved February 8 2009 from http://www.researchandmarkets.com/reports310872

Ribadu, N. (2006, May 18). Nigeria's struggle with corruption. Paper presented to US Congressional House Committee on International Development, Washington DC.

Ribadu, N. (2007, July). Cybercrime and commercial fraud: a Nigerian perspective, Modern Law for Global Commerce. Paper presented to a Congress to celebrate the Fortieth Annual Session of UNCITRAL, Vienna.

Riggins, F. J. (1999). A Framework for Identifying Web-based Electronic Commerce Opportunities. Journal of Organizational Computing and Electronic Commerce, 9(4), 297–310. doi:10.1207/S153277440904_4

Rivest, R., Shmir, A., & Adlman, L. (1978). A Method for Obtaining Digital Signatures and Public Key Cryptosystems. Communications of the ACM, 21, 294–299. doi:10.1145/359340.359342

Rollyson, C. S. (2007). Enterprise 2.0: Game-Changer for Investment Banks. Retrieved from http://rollyson.net/download/GHCJ/Adv_Ent20_i-banking.pdf

Rotchanakitumnuai, S., & Speece, M. (2003). Barriers to Internet banking adoption: a qualitative study among corporate customers in Thailand. International Journal of Bank Marketing, 21, 312–323. doi:10.1108/02652320310498465

Roth, A. (2001). Middle East Web could draw US Bankers. Retrieved 8th February 2008, from www.itp.net/features

Rowe, F. (1994). Des Banques et des Réseaux: Productivité et Avantages Concurrentiels. ENSPTT-Economica, janvier: 246-247

Rygielski, C., Wang, J.-C., & Yen, D. C. (2002). Data mining techniques for customer relationship management. Technology in Society, 24(4), 483–502. doi:10.1016/S0160-791X(02)00038-6

Saatcioglu, K., Stallaert, J., & Whinston, A. B. (2001). Design of a Financial Portal. [June.]. Communications of the ACM, 44, 6. doi:10.1145/376134.376151

Sabherwal, R., & Sabherwal, S. (2003). How do knowledge announcement affect firm value? A study of firm pursuing different business strategies. Working paper University of Missouri, [online: http://misrc.umn.edu/workshops/2003/fall/Sabherwal_100303.pdf].

Sachs. J. D. (2000). Readiness for the Networked world: A Guide for Developing Countries, Center for International Development at Harvard University, (pp. 62-85). Retrieved January 7, 2099, from http://ictlogy.net/bibciter/reports/projects.php?idp=206

Safari, H., Koushesh, M., & Akherati, A. (2007). Introduction to RFID and Using it in E-Banking, Paper presented at 1nd International Conference on Management of Supply Chain and Information Systems. Tehran, Applied Information Co.

Sahut, J. M. (2004). Why does SSL dominate the e-payment market? Journal of Internet Banking and Commerce, 9(1).

Sahut, J.M. (2000), L'impact de l'Internet sur les métiers de la banque. Les Cahiers du Numérique, septembre: 158-162.

Sahut, J.M. (2001).Vers une révolution du secteur bancaire ? La Revue du Financier n°131, 34-38.

Sampson, S. E. (1998). Gathering Customers Feedback via the internet: Instruments and Prospects. Industrial Management & Data Systems, 98(2), 71–82. doi:10.1108/02635579810205511

Sanghera., Paul., et al, (2007). How to Cheat at Deploying and Securing RFID. Burlington, MA: Syngress Publishing, Inc.

Sargazi, K. Z. (2007). Investigating Deterrent Factors of E-banking Fixing and Development in Sistan Baluchestan State, M.Sc dissertation, Sistan and Baluchestan University, Iran.

Sarlak, M.A., & Abolhasani, H., A., Forozandeh. D., L., & Ghorbani, A. (2009). Investigating on E-commerce Acceptance Barriers in Dried Fruits Producing- Exporting Companies of Iran. World Applied Sciences Journal, 6(6), 818–824.

Sarlak, M.A., Mirzaei, A., H. (2005). A Review of Organizational Epistemology: Evolution Process, Schools and Management Applications, Peyke Noor Journal (Quarterly), Special issue on management, 3 (3), 21-35.

Sarlija, N., Bensic, M., & Zekic-Susac, M. (2006). A neural network classification of credit applicants in consumer credit scoring. Proceeding of the Conference on Artificial Intelligence and Applications, Innsbruck, Austria, 205-210.

Sarrafizadeh. A. (2005). IT in Organization, Tehran, Mir Publication.

Sathye, M. (1999). Adoption of internet banking by Australian consumers: An empirical investigation. International Journal of Bank Marketing, 17(7), 324–334. doi:10.1108/02652329910305689

Scandizzo, S. (2003). Connectivity and measurement of operational risk: An input-output approach. Soft Computing, 7, 516–525. doi:10.1007/s00500-002-0236-0

Scarborough, H., & Lannon, R. (1988). The successful exploitation of new technology in banking. Journal of General Management, 13(3), 38–51.

Schneider, I. (2001). Getting to Know You. Bank Systems & Technology, 38(10), 20–24.

Schwartz, J. (2006). Researchers See Privacy Pitfalls in No-Swipe Credit Cards.The New York Times, Retrieved from http://www.nytimes.com/2006/10/23/business/23card.html?ex=1319256000&en=76401b1601fc06e3&ei=5090

Scratchier, A. (2002). Issues in electronic banking: an overview. International Monetary Funds, 2(6), 1 26.

Seeley, C. P. (2002). Establishing a business-driven strategy igniting knowledge in your business processes. Knowledge Management Review, 5(4), 12–15.

Seitz, J., & Stickel, E. (1998). Internet Banking: An Overview. Journal of Internet Banking and Commerce, 3(1).

Sergent, C. (2000), Impact of E-banking on Traditional services.Retrieved from www.encylopedia.com/doc/1027-sergent.html.

Shah, M. H., Ahmed, W., Meckel, M., & Shah, M. A. (2008). Organisational Barriers in e-Banking: A Case from UK Banking Industry, In Proceedings of the 7th Annual ISOnEworld Conference, June 2-4, Las Vegas, NV.

Shah, M. H., Khan, S., & Xu, M. (2006). A Survey of Critical Success Factors in e-Banking. European Journal of Information Systems, Retrieved Desember 5, 2008, from http://www.csgstrategies.com/download.php?id=302

Shao, G. (2007). The Diffusion of Online Banking: Research Trends from 1998 to 2006. Journal of Internet Banking and Commerce, 12(2), from www.arraydev.com/commerce

Shao, J., Ivanov, P. C., Podobnik, B., & Stanley, H. E. (2007). Quantitative relationships between corruption and economic factors. The European Physical Journal B – Condensed Matter and Complex System, 56(2), pp.1434-6028

Shapiro, C., & Varian, H. R. (2003). Information rule. Ethics and Information Technology, 5(1).

Sheng, S., Magnien, B., Kumaraguru, P., Acquisti, A., Cranor, L. F., Hong, J., & Nunge, E. (2007). Anti-Phishing Phil: The Design and Evaluation of a Game That Teaches People Not to Fall for Phish. Symposium on Usable Privacy and Security (SOUPS), Pittsburgh, USA, pp.88-99.

Shih, H. A., & Chiang, Y. H. (2005). Strategic alignment between HRM, KM, and corporate development. International Journal of Manpower, 26(6), 582–605. doi:10.1108/01437720510625476

Shih, Y., & Fang, K. (2004). The use of decomposed theory of planned behaviour to study internet banking in Taiean. Internet Research, 14(3), 213–223. doi:10.1108/10662240410542643

Sin, L. Y. M., Tse, A. C. B., Chan, H., Heung, V. C. S., & Yim, F. H. K. (2006). The effects of relationship marketing orientation on business performance in the Hotel Industry. Journal of Hospitality & Tourism Research (Washington, D.C.), 30, 407–426. doi:10.1177/1096348006287863

Singer, D. D., Ross, D., & Avery, A. (2005). The evolution of online banking. Journal of Internet Banking Business, 2(Spring).

Singh, A. M. (2002). Internet Banking: To Bank or Not To Bank. Where is the Question?Durban: University of Durban Westville.

Singh, S., & Chhatwal, S. S., Yahyabhoy, T., M., & Heng, Y., C., (2000). Dynamics of Innovation in E-banking. Retrieved February 15, 2007, from School of Computing, National University of Singapore in the website http://csrc.lse.ac.uk/asp/aspecis/20020136.pdf

Sivakumaran, M. V. (2005). Banking Technology Course material, for M.Tech (IT) with Specialization in Banking Technology and Information Security. IDRBT.

Slywotzky, A. J. (2001), Revving the Engines of Online Finance. Cambridge, MA: MIT Sloan Management Review, Cambridge, Summer.

Smith, R.G., Holmes, M. N., & Kaufmann, P (1999, July). Nigerian advance fee fraud, trends and issues in crime and criminal justice, Australian Institute of Criminology, Canberra, No. 121.

Snyman, R., & Kruger, C. J. (2004). The interdependency between strategic management and strategic knowledge management. Journal of Knowledge Management, 8(1), 5–19. doi:10.1108/13673270410523871

Sohail, M., & Shanmugham, B. (2003). E-Banking and Customer Preferences in Malaysia: An Empirical Investigation. Information Sciences, 150(4), 207–217. doi:10.1016/S0020-0255(02)00378-X

Solms, V., & Naccache, D. (1992). Blind Signatures and Perfect Crimes. Computers & Security, 11, 581–583. doi:10.1016/0167-4048(92)90193-U

Solms, V., & Naccache, D. (1992). Blind Signatures and Perfect Crimes. Intl. J. Computers & Security, 11, 581–583. doi:10.1016/0167-4048(92)90193-U

Solomon, E. H. (1997). Virtual Money. New York: Oxford University Press.

Soludo, C.C. (2004, August 6). Guidelines and incentives on consolidation in the Nigerian banking industry. Thisday Newspaper (Lagos, Nigeria)

Song. R., & Larry Korba, (2004). How to Make E-cash with Non-Repudiation and Anonymity, In Proceedings of the International Conference on Information Technology: Coding and Computing, (ITCC'04, 167-172).

Sotudeh, S. M. (2003). E-banking: Success Ways, Challenges and Threats. Bank Magazine, 14, 27–31.

Spong, K. (2000). Banking regulation: its purposes, implementation and effects (5th ed.). Division of Supervision and Risk Management, Federal Reserve Bank of Kansas City.

Stadler, M., Piveteau, J. M., & Camenisch, J. (1995). Fair blind signature. In Proc. EUROCRYPT 95,(LNCS,Vol 921, pp. 209–219). New York: Springer-Verlag

Stamoulis, D. S. (2000). How banks fit in an internet commerce business activities model. Journal of Internet Banking and Commerce, 5 (1), from www.arraydev.com/commerce

Stamoulis, D. S. (2000). How Banks fit in an Internet Commerce Business Activities Model, Journal of Internet Banking and Commerce, No. 1, Retrieved December 11, 2009, from http://www.arraydev.com/commerce/jibc/0001-03.htm

Stewart, K. A., Baskerville, R., Storey, V. C., Senn, J. A., Raven, A., & Long, C. (2000). Confronting the assumptions underlying the management of knowledge: an agenda for understanding and investigating knowledge management. ACM SIGMIS Database, 31(4), 41–53. doi:10.1145/506760.506764

Steyen, P., & Chan, E. (2003). Over Half a Million Hong Kong People Visited an Internet Banking Site in January 2003. Retrieved 10th February 2008, from www.neilson-netratings.com

Stoddart, L. (2001). Managing internets to encourage knowledge sharing opportunities and constraints. Online Information Review, 25(1), 19–28. doi:10.1108/14684520110366661

Storey, A., & Thompson, J. B. Bokma, & Bradnum, A. J. (2000, August). An Evaluation of UK and USA Online Banking and WebSites, Paper was presented at the Association for Information Systems 2000 Americas Conference on Information Systems, Long Beach, California. Vol. 2: 723-728.

Straeel, H. (1995). Virtual banking: gearing up to play the no-fee retail game. Bank Systems and Technology, 32(7), 20–22.

Straub, D. W., Loch, K. D., & Hill, C. E. (2001). Transfer of Information Technology to Arab world: A test of cultural influence modeling. Journal of Global Information Management, 9(4), 6–28.

Suarez, Luis (2006), Enabling Knowledge sharing- a matter of cultural and organizational changes?- The role of communities. Social computing evangelist

Suganthi, B., & Balachandran, G. (2001). Internet Banking Patronage: An Investigation of Malaysia. [from www.

arraydev.com/commerce]. Journal of Internet Banking and Commerce, 6(1), 23–32.

Suh, B., & Han, I. (2000). Effect of trust on customer acceptance of Internet banking. Retrieved February 15, 2007, from Graduate School of Management, Korea Advanced Institute of Science and Technology in the website http://afis.kaist.ac.kr/download/inter_jnl031.pdf

Sullivan, RJ (2000), How has the adoption of internet banking affected performance and risk in banks? Federal Reserve Bank of Kansas City, Financial Perspectives, December: 1-16.

Sunassee, N., & Sewry, D. A. (2002), A theoretical framework for knowledge management implementation", In Proceeding of 2002 annual research conference of the South African insiture of computer scientists and information technologists on Enablement through technology, (SAICSIT), Port Elizabeth, South Africa, (pp. 235-245).

Swiss Federal Department of Foreign Affairs. (2008). Economic report on business and economy in Nigeria. Retrieved February 8 2009 from http://www.eda.admin.ch/eda/en/home/reps/afri/vnga/ref_bufor/busnga.html

Syed-Ikhsan, Syed Omar S.& Rowland, Fytton. (2004). Knowledge management in a public organization: a study on the relationship between organizational element and the performance of knowledge transfer. Journal of Knowledge Management, 8(2), 95–111. doi:10.1108/13673270410529145

Talmor, S. (1995). New Life for Dinosaurs. The Banker, 145, 75–78.

Tanna, G. B. (2002). SAN and information security in banking. Buffalo, New York, USA: School of Management, University of Buffalo.

Tedeschi, B. (2005). Banks see Online Gain via Updated Cash Sites. International Herald Tribune, 1-2.

Teece, D. (2000). Managing intellectual capital: organizational, strategic and policy dimensions. Oxford, UK: Oxford University Press.

Ternullo, G. (1997)Banking on the Internet: New Technologies, New Opportunities and New Risks. Boston

Regional Outlook, Second Quarter (http://www.fdic.gov/index.html).

Timmers, P. (1998). Business models for electronic markets. Electronic Markets, 8(2), 2–8. doi:10.1080/10196789800000016

Tiwana, A. (2002). The Knowledge Management Toolkit: Orchestrating IT, Strategy, and Knowledge Platforms (2nd ed.). Upper Saddle River, NJ: Prentice Hall.

Today, C. R. M. (2003a). New eMarketer Interactive Banking Report Released. Retrieved January 12th, 2008, from www.crm2day.com

Today, M. (1998). Service Excellence Company of the Year – Winner Financial Services Category: First Direct. Management Today, 10, 55–56.

Toufaily, E., Daghfous, N., & Toffoli, R. (2009). the Adoption of "E-banking" by lebanese banks: Success and Critical factors. International Journal of E-Services and Mobile Applications, 1(1), 67-93. Hershey, PA: Idea Group Publishing, Enos, L. (2001). Report: Critical Errors in Online Banking. E-Commerce Times, April 11, Retrieved December 6, 2008, from http://www.ecommercetimes.com/perl/story/8867.html

Transparency International, National Integrity System, Country Study Reports [For Various Years] Retrieved from http://www.transparency.org/publications/publications

Trappe W., & Lawrence Washington, (2006). Introduction to Cryptography with Coding Theory, 2nd Edition,(pp.287-295), Upper Saddle River, NJ: Prentice Hall.

Turban, E., Lee, J., King, D., & Chung, H. M. (2008). Electronic Commerce: a Managerial Prspective, 5re Edn. London: Prentice Hall.

Uche, C. U. (2000). Banking regulation in an era of structural adjustment: the case of Nigeria. Journal of Financial Regulation and Compliance, 1(2), 157–169. doi:10.1108/eb025040

Uche, C. U. (2001). The adoption of universal banking in Nigeria. Butterworths Journal of International Banking and Financial Law, 16(9), 421–428.

Uche, U. C. (1998). The adoption of money laundering law in Nigeria. Journal of Money Laundering Control, (pp. 220-228).

Uit Beijerse, R. P. (2000). Knowledge management in small and medium-sized companies: knowledge management for entrepreneurs. Journal of Knowledge Management, 4(2), 162–179. doi:10.1108/13673270010372297

United Nations Conference on Trade and Development, (2000). E-commerce and development report 2000, United Nations, New York & Geneva.

United Nations. (2005, April 19). Eleventh UN congress on crime prevention and criminal justice. (BKK/CP/08). Bangkok Thailand, Committee 1, 2nd and 3rd Meetings.

Usoro, A. (2006). An investigation into trust as an antecedent to knowledge sharing in virtual communities of practice. Computing and Information System.

Van Someren, N. (2001). The practical problems of implementing Micromint. In Proc. of the International Conference of Financial Cryptography,(LNCS 2339,pp.41-50). New York: Springer-Verlag.

Van Someren, N., Odlyzko, A., Rivest, R., Jones, T., & Scot, D. G. (2003). Does anyone really need micropayments? Proceeding of the International Conference of Financial Cryptography, (LNCS 2742,pp.69-76). New York: Springer-Verlag.

Varma, Y. (2001). Banking: The network is the bank, Public Sector: why the lag? Dataquest, January 29th. www.dqindia.com/content/top_stories/301012904.asp

Vartak, N., Patwardhan, A., Joshi, A., Finin, T., & Nagy, P. Protecting the privacy of passive RFID tags. Technical Report, TR-CS—6-10, Department of Computer Science and Electrical Engineering, University of Maryland, Baltimore County, USA.

Victor, Cascella (2002).Efective Strategic Planning. Quality Progress, 35, (11).

Victor, D. (2008). The New Technologies Extension in Banking: The Case of E-Banking in the Romanian Practice. Academy of Economic Studies, Bucharest Romania, 723-727. Retrieved May 14, 2009, from http://steconomice.uoradea.ro/anale/volume/2008/v3-finances-banks-accountancy/130.pdf

Vinnem, J. E., & Liyanage, J. P. (2008). Human-Technical Interface of Collision Risk Under Dynamic Conditions: An Exploratory learning Case from the north sea, edited by Bernd Carsten Stahl, International Journal of Technology and Human Interaction, Idea Group Publishing, 4 (1), 35-47.

Violano, M., & Van Collie, S. (1992). Retail Banking Technology: Strategies and Resources that Seize the Competitive Advantage. New York: John Wiley and Sons, Inc.

Wallman, S. (1999). The Information Technology Revolution and its Impact of Regulation and Regulatiory structure (1st ed.). Booking - Wharton Papers on Financial Services.

Wallsten, S. (2003). Regulation and internet use in developing countries (No. 2979). World Bank Policy Research Paper, The World bank Development Research Group.

Wang, C., Chang, C., & Lin, C. (2002). A new micropayment system using general payword chain. Electronic Commerce Research Journal, 2(1-2), 159–168. doi:10.1023/A:1013360606669

Wang, Y., & Vassileva, J. (2003)Bayesian Network Trust Model in Peer-to-Peer Networks. In Proceedings of Second International Workshop Peers and Peer-to-Peer Computing, July 14, Melbourne, Australia.

Wang, Y., Lin, H., & Tang, T. (2003). Determinants of users acceptance of Internet Banking an Empirical study. International Journal of Service Industry Management, 14(5), 501–519. doi:10.1108/09564230310500192

Wang, Y., Wang, S., & Lai, K. K. (2005). A new fuzzy support vector machine to evaluate credit risk. IEEE Transactions on Fuzzy Systems, 13(6), 820–831. doi:10.1109/TFUZZ.2005.859320

Warner, J. (1996)Internet Waits in Wings for Banking Dinosaurs. The Independent, August 17, pp.17

Warwick, D. R. (1998). Ending Cash: The Public benefits of federal Electronic Currency. Westport, Conn.: Quorum Books.

West Industries Supplier Company. (2007). Solutions of Banking, Paper presented at 1nd International Conference on Management of Supply Chain and Information Systems, Tehran, Applied Information Co. Article of RFID Tags, Contactless Smart Card Technology and Electronic Passports: Frequently Asked Questions.Retrieved from Available at: www.kis-kiosk.com/casestudies/assets/rfid-faq.pdf.

Wiig, K. M. (1997). Knowledge Management: where did it come from and where will it go? Expert Systems with Applications, 13(1), 1–14. doi:10.1016/S0957-4174(97)00018-3

Williams, P. (2002). Organized crime and cyber-crime: implications for business. CERT Coordination Center.

Williams, Randy (2008). Critical success factors when building knowledge management system.Share Point Magazine, December

Wright, J. D. (2002, May). Electronic banking. new developments and regulatory risks. Paper present at the International Monetary Fund (IMF) Conference – Washington D.C.

Xu, Y., Yen, D. C., Lin, B., & Chou, D. C. (2002). Adopting Customer Relationship Management Technology. Industrial Management & Data Systems, 102(8), 442–452. doi:10.1108/02635570210445871

Yen, S., Ho, L., & Huang, C. (1999). Internet micro-payment based on unbalanced one-way binary tree. In Proc. of the International Conference of Cryptec'99, 155-162.

Yiu, C. S., Grant, K., & Edgar, D. (2007). Factors affecting the adoption of Internet Banking in Hong Kong - implications for the banking sector. International Journal of Information Management, 27(5), 336–351. doi:10.1016/j.ijinfomgt.2007.03.002

Yousafzai, S. Y., Pallister, J. G., & Foxall, G. R. (2005). Strategies for building and communicating trust in electronic banking: A field experiment. Psychology and Marketing, 22(2), 181–202. doi:10.1002/mar.20054

Zack, M. H. (1999). Developing a knowledge strategy. California Management Review, 41(3), 125–145.

Zack, M. H. (2002a), A strategic pretext for knowledge management. Proceeding of the Third European Conference on Organizational Knowledge, Learning and Capabilities, Athens, Greece, April 5.

Zack, M. H. (2002b). Developing a Knowledge strategy. In Choo, C. W., & Bontis, N. (Eds.), The strategic management of intellectual capital and organizational knowledge (pp. 255–267). Oxford, UK: Oxford University press.

Zdanowicz, J. S. (2004). Detecting money laundering and terrorist financing via data mining. Communications of the ACM, 47(5), 53–55. doi:10.1145/986213.986239

Zhang, Z., Salerno, J. J., & Yu, P. S. (2003). Applying data mining in investigating money laundering crimes, SIGKDD'03, Washington DC, USA.

Zheng, X., & Chen, D. (2003). Study of Mobile Payments System. Proceedings of the IEEE International Conference on E-Commerce, (CEC'03).

About the Contributors

Mohammad Ali Sarlak is an associate professor of public administration at the Payam Noor University (PNU). He is currently serving as the president at the doctoral education and research center in same university. PNU is a distance education university and mega university in Iran with more than 900,000 students. He holds a PhD in OB management and an MBA and a bachelor degree in business administration from the University of Tehran .In addition to his research in e- entrepreneurship, students trust in virtual universities, e-business, e-commerce, and e-government, he has published several articles and presented several papers on the IT applications in organizations. He has won numerous research, teaching, and administrative awards. Sarlak has written several text books related to IT applications in organizations for master's students. In addition to serving as the editor-in-chief of the International Journal of E-Entrepreneurship and Innovation, he is a member of editorial review board of the Journal of Electronic Commerce in Organizations and the Journal of Information Technology Research.

* * *

Sattar J. Aboud is a Professor and advisor for Science and Technology at Iraqi Council of Representatives. He received his education from United Kingdom. Dr. Aboud has served his profession in many universities and he awarded the Quality Assurance Certificate of education at Philadelphia University, Faculty of Information Technology in 2002. Also, he awarded the Medal of Iraqi Council of Representatives for his leading the first international conference of Iraqi Experts in 2008. His research interests include the areas of both symmetric and asymmetric cryptography, area of verification and validation, performance evaluation and e-payment schemes.

Sujana Adapa is a doctoral candidate in the School of Business, Economics and Public Policy at the University of New England, Australia. She received her MBA and Masters in Agriculture from Madras University and Dr. Panjabrao Deshmukh Krishi Vidyapeet, India. She is a unit coordinator for the unit International Marketing oriented to the students of Graduate School of Business at University of New England. She conducts tutorials for the units Consumer Behaviour, Marketing Communications and Introduction to Marketing. She worked as a teaching assistant in India and was involved in effective coordination of the units International Marketing and Marketing Management. Her industry experience covers research related to the Indian banking sector. Her research interests include services marketing, international business environment and cross-cultural studies.

Jaflah Hassan Al-Ammary is an assistance professor in the Information System Department of the college of the IT at the University of Bahrain. She holds a B.S in computer science from the University of Bahrain, MS.c. from the Arabian Gulf University, and PhD from the University of Murdoch. Al-Ammary's research interest focuses on Strategic alignment, Knowledge Management, and E-learning. Currently Al-Ammary is conducting three researches; one research is aim at investigating the current situation regarding the knowledge strategies and KM-strategic alignment at the organizations of the kingdom of Bahrain. The second one is conducted to investigate the knowledge sharing and its effect on the professional communities. The third research is conducted to find out the effect of the relationship between the CIO and CKO and how this relationship contributes to the organization performance.

Alireza Aliahmadi an Associate Professor at at University of Science and Technology (IUST). He holds a PhD in production management from Instructors' Training University. He currently is serving as head of management and planning Faculty at IUST. Aliahmadi Published nine books and more than 90 papers in national and international journals such as Business Process Management Journal.

Abel Ezeoha is a lecturer in the Department of Banking and Finance, Ebonyi State University Nigeria and a fellow of the African Institute for Applied Economics. He has a PhD in Finance from the University of Nigeria. Abel's main areas of research interest include: banking development (with a niche in Internet banking regulation and minority lending), corporate governance and micro-impact of economic reforms. Abel is one of the pioneers of Internet banking research in the Sub-Saharan African region. His lead-article in this area is titled Internet Banking Regulation in Nigeria – Problems and Challenges and was published in 2005 by the Journal of Internet Banking and Commerce.

Lotfollah Forozandeh Dehkordi is an assistant professor and chairman of business administration department at Payame Noor University. PNU is a distance education university and mega university in Iran with more than 1,000,000 students. He holds a PhD in strategic management from the University of Tehran. Fotoozandeh published four books entitled "Strategic Management, Strategic Thinking and creativity, Islamic Management", and etc. Also he has almost twenty manuscripts in national and international journals.

Ali Ghorbani is a PhD candidate of Business Administration at Payame Noor University (PNU), Tehran, Iran. PNU is a distance education university and mega university in Iran with more than 1,000,000 students. He holds M.Sc and B.Sc degrees in business administration from Payame Noor University. Ghorbani has published several articles and presented several papers in international and national journals and conference about e-commerce, e-business, e-banking, IT application in organizations and marketing strategies. He has won third rank award in 6th Scientific Congress of Payame Noor University Students.

Mirza Hassan Hosseini is an assistant Professor and chairman of the MBA Department at Payame Noor University. PNU is a distance education university and mega university in Iran with more than 1,000,000 students. He holds PhD degree in business administration from Bradford University, UK. Hosseini published three books in the "Marketing, Importing and Exporting" area. Also he has more than thirty articles in national and international journals.

Asma Mobarek is an assistant professor at Stockholm Business School, Sweden. She did her PhD from the University of Leeds, UK. Her research interest includes market efficiency, asset pricing, market microstructure, micro health insurance, e-banking, and dividend policy. She has produced a number of papers in refereed journals. Currently, she is a member of the editorial board of the journal of Managerial System.

Vadlamani Ravi is an Assistant Professor in IDRBT, Hyderabad since April 2005. He holds a Ph.D. in Soft Computing from Osmania University, Hyderabad & RWTH Aachen, Germany. Earlier, he was a Faculty at NUS, Singapore for three years. He published 74 papers in refereed Journals / Conferences and invited book chapters. He edited "Advances in Banking Technology and Management: Impacts of ICT and CRM" published by IGI Global, USA, 2007. He is a referee for several international journals and on the Editorial board of IJIDS, IJDATS, IJISSS, IJITPM & IJSDS. He is listed in Marquis Who's Who in the World 2009, 2010. He is an Invited Member of "Top 100 Educators in 2009" published by International Biographical Centre, UK and an Invited Member in "2000 Outstanding Intellectuals of the 21st Century 2009/2010" published by International Biographical Centre, UK.

Jean-Michel Sahut is a Professor and Director of the Research Center at Amiens School of Management (France). He is also an associate researcher at CEREGE EA 1722 – University of Poitiers. He teaches Financial Market, Financial Analysis and ICT for Finance (e-banking, electronic payments.) for engineering and management students. Previously he was professor of Finance at Telecom & Management Paris Sud and director of the RESFIN Laboratory (studying impacts of New Technologies on Finance). He has a wide international experience of executive education, in France and abroad, especially in Eastern European Countries. He is co-author of the Mobilix simulation game for the mobile market. He is also an expert for the 7th EU Framework Program. He has published more than twenty articles about Electronic Finance in peer review journals: International Journal of Business, Journal of Internet Banking and Commerce, La Revue du Financier, Finance & Technologies, Bankers Markets & Investors.

Bala Shanmugam, FCPA, obtained his PhD in Banking and Finance from Australia. An author of more 100 papers and more than 30 books he received many prestigious awards for his research and scholarship. He is currently attached to the School of Business at Monash University Malaysia, where he is the Chair of Accounting and Finance and also Director of Banking and Finance. Professor Shanmugam has extensive industry experience and has served as consultant and Board Director to a number of financial institutions. He is also on the editorial boards of a number of reputed journals in the areas of banking and finance. Professor Shanmugam was also admitted as an Independent Consultant for UNDP under the Asian Poverty Reduction Programme. He is also a Consultant to the World Bank on the Retail Finance Programme.

Mahadevan Supramaniam is a SAP Certified Solution Consultant as well as an Oracle Certified expertise. He is currently attached to the School of Computing at Taylor's University College Malaysia. Prior to joining Taylor's University College, he was an R&D Engineer (Software) in Motorola Malaysia and Xyratex, United Kingdom. Mahadevan has extensive industrial experience and participated in many projects such as Intelligent Bank Management Simulation system, virtual reality simulation systems, Online Web Database Application and Product Management Test Systems. As the foremost exponent in Enterprise Research Planning in Taylor's, his expertise and research interest lie in the optimization of ERP and database technologies for the banking industry and SMEs.

Index

Symbols

21st Century 64
419 Fraud 74

A

accessibility 2, 4, 9
achievement 53
Advanced Fee Fraud (419) Act of 2006 65, 74, 79, 82, 83, 84, 88
affiliation 53
anonymity 18, 21, 22, 30, 31
anonymous payment scheme 18
Arab countries 53, 57
Arab Gulf region 39
ATM networks 134
authoritarian-paternalistic 50
automated clearing house (ACH) 171
Automatic Teller Machines (ATMs) 3, 4, 5, 6, 7, 8, 10, 16, 36, 37, 40, 72, 98, 115, 129, 135, 143, 98, 99

B

bank 17, 18, 19, 20, 21, 22, 23, 24, 25, 26, 27, 28, 31
banking legislation 69
banking regulation 94, 98
banking transactions 2, 6, 8, 10, 11, 16
Bank Performance 113
Banks and Other Financial Institutions (BOFI) 70
Basle Committee on Banking Supervision (BCBS) 58
Bayesian Additive Regression Trees (BART) 144

beating competitors 54
blindfolded protocols 18
blinding signature scheme 21, 22
blogs 145
BOFI Decree No. 25 of 1991 70
business continuity plans (BCP) 142, 148
business environment 46, 49
business model (BM) 102, 103, 104, 105, 106, 108, 110, 113
business-to-business buying and selling (B2B) 167, 180
business-to-consumer electronic business (B2C) 167
business-to-consumer transaction 183

C

capabilities 46, 47, 48, 49, 50, 52, 53, 54
cardholder pricing and profitability 139
card marketing 139
Central Bank of Nigeria (CBN) 65, 70, 84, 85, 86, 87
Centralized Banking Solution (CBS) 136
Challenges of E-Banking 45
channeling financial resources 2, 4
Chaum 18, 19, 21, 29
Chi-Squire Test 117, 120
Classification and Regression Trees (CART) 144
Click-and-Mortar Banks 113
combat money laundering 38, 40
commercial payment processing 4
competitive advantage 102, 106, 109
compliance/legal 41
conditional e-payment 23, 29
consumer credit 101

9 781615 206353

	DATE DUE		